AF496602

UNDERSTANDING EUROPEAN SOCIAL POLICY

Edited by
PETER ABRAHAMSON
& CHRISTIAN ASPALTER

CASA VERDE PUBLISHING

FOR THE ASIAN ASSOCIATION FOR SOCIAL WELFARE

Hong Kong Taipei Seoul New Dehli Manchester

Contents

List of Tables and Figures

Foreword

March 7th 2008 the European Commission's Representation in Copenhagen invited interested citizens in Denmark to a seminar concerning "social reality stocktaking." Local experts and interested parties debated for a full day various aspects of "Social Europe." This was part of a Europe wide self-reflective process concerning social well being currently under way. It was initiated by the European Commission under the heading of "the new social reality of Europe," and it was quickly endorsed by the European Council in June 2006. A year later, the Commission quickly launched a public consultation to take stock of present social realities and trends in European societies, with an emphasis on *access* and *opportunity*.

This consultation and stocktaking process is explained by two factors. Firstly, main social indicators demonstrate that despite considerable welfare state interventions social problems are on the increase in Europe, and, generally, central elements of social protection policies are challenged by expected future demographic and economic developments.

Secondly, from the very start of the European Communities in 1958, there has been, at least in rhetoric, a commitment to considering economic and social development to go hand in hand, hence emphasizing the social dimension as part and parcel of the cooperation. In the preamble to the Treaty of Rome it was stated that signatories "resolved to ensure the economic and social progress of their countries …affirming as the essential objective of their efforts the constant improvements of the living and working conditions of their peoples." Such formulations are to be found in all treaties since then and especially with the preparation of the single market (up to 1993) there was an enhanced focus on the so-called social dimension of European cooperation. With the Lisbon strategy and the implementation of the *Open Method of Coordination* from 2000 the European Council has set some very tangible goals for social development. However, they have, far from, been met, and the European institutions have had to reformulate and moderate these objectives.

So, in its self-understanding Europe has developed a particular social model based on a number of shared values. These include democracy and individual rights, free collective bargaining, the market economy, equality of opportunity for all, and *"social welfare and solidarity."* It is precisely the commitment to social welfare and solidarity that sets Europe apart from any other region in the world it is argued. Yet, it is increasingly difficult for the Member States to deliver on these issues.

Inequality calculated as the ratio of total income received by the 20 percent of the population with the highest income—top quintile—to that received by the 20 percent of the population with the lowest income—lowest quintile—moved from 4.5 in 2000 to 4.9 in 2005 for EU25. With a very few exceptions (Belgium, Bulgaria, and Estonia) this increase is a general trend in most Member States. The dispersion is considerable, however, with the Baltic and the Latin Rim countries having the highest inequality of 6.7 to 6.9, and the former state socialist Central European and the Scandinavian countries with the lowest rates of around 3.5. Hence, there is a factor two difference in the distribution of income inequality between the most and the least unequal societies. The increase in inequality is reflected in a (small) increase in poverty, or, as the European institutions prefer to name it: the *at-risk-of-poverty* rate calculated as those whose equivalized income after transfers is less than

60 percent of the median. Measured as such the risk of poverty has increased from 15 percent in 1998 to 16 percent in 2006. For 10 of the new Member States the poverty risk increased from 14 percent in 2001 to 17 percent in 2006. Again, differences among the European countries are considerable with risk of poverty rates in 2006 being around 10 percent in Scandinavia and the Netherlands, while the rates in the Baltics and the Latin Rim countries—including Romania—stood around 20 percent (Eurostat).

In international comparison these levels of inequality and poverty are very low, but that is irrelevant to those within European societies that experience a relative deprivation vis-à-vis the majority of the population. It is not so that social protection interventions do not work overall; rather, those Member States that spend the highest share of their gross domestic product on welfare provisions—Scandinavia and North-Western Continental Europe—are the ones that manage to reduce the *at-risk-of poverty* after transfers the most, from around 30 percent to 10 percent, while e.g. in Ireland and the UK the same or higher before transfers rates are only reduced to 19 percent. Ireland only spent 18 percent of GDP on social protection in 2004 while Sweden spent 33 percent. Admittedly, these values are, of course, influenced by changes in the remunerator (social spending) as well as the denominator (overall economic performance), hence countries with a very high GDP can deliver substantial transfers and services without it showing up in high levels of the share of GDP. Luxembourg is an example of this; it "only" spent 22 percent of GDP on social protection in 2004, but it had the highest per capita spending in all of Europe—12,180 €PPP –; the double compared to the average for EU25 of 6,188 €PPP. However, in general those countries with the highest shares of GDP are also the ones with the highest absolute spending. The small spenders are to be found in Southern Europe and the Baltics with Romania and Lithuania spending the least—1,089 and 1,220 €PPP per capita. Hence there is a factor 10 difference between the highest and the lowest spender within the European Union (Eurostat).

These huge differences reflect the increasing diversity within the EU following each consecutive expansion of the union. In the early beginnings when Germany, France, Italy and the Benelux countries created the Coal and Steel Community in 1955 and the European Economic Community in 1958 it was cooperation among countries with roughly the same degree of development and very similar systems of social protection. With the inclusion of Denmark, Ireland and the UK in 1973, countries with a very different social protection system entered including a relatively poor country at the time—Ireland. The next expansion in 1985, awaiting the fall of military dictatorship in Southern Europe brought in the considerably less developed countries of Greece, Portugal and Spain. The inclusion in 1993 of the neutral or non-NATO members of Austria, Finland and Sweden had to await the fall of the Berlin wall and the end of the cold war, but did not add to the already considerable diversity of the Union. However, with the inclusion of the Central, Southeastern and Baltic countries from 2004 (Czech Republic, Cyprus, Estonia, Hungary, Latvia, Lithuania, Malta, Poland, Slovakia, Slovenia) and 2007 (Bulgaria and Romania) the diversity both with respect to economic development and social protection organization increased tremendously: "Enlargement is adding a whole new dimension to regional disparities. Two thirds of the EU 10 lives in regions where GDP per head is half or less the EU 15 average. Furthermore, the fact that the Union went from 15 to 27 Member States created the necessity for changing the internal governing structures of the Union; a process not yet completed.

One of the more obvious problems with respect to poverty and marginalization is that even among the "big" spenders or "generous" welfare states, transfers to the poor are so low that they cannot lift them over the poverty line. This is illustrated with an example from one of the "best" performers, Denmark. In 1995 the compensation rate for a couple receiving old-age pension was 45 and 47 percent for a single social assistance recipient. It is calculated as the net transfer set against an average net income of a production worker. If it is assumed that the average production worker makes close to the median income then the pensioner couple and the social assistance recipient have less than half the median income to their disposal, and are, thus, per definition income poor and way below the threshold for being at risk of poverty (60 percent cut-off line). To aggravate the situation the compensation rates have continuously fallen to 40 and 41 percent respectively in 2004.

More generally, dramatic changes are underway in European societies: in the nature of work; modern family life; the position of women in society; and social mobility. Values are changing. Societies are becoming increasingly multicultural. New patterns of inequality and poverty are emerging. New problems such as the rise in obesity and an increasing number of factors impinging on mental health are affecting the health of Europeans.

Some of these changes offer opportunities for European citizens, but they, unfortunately, also pose problems for a considerable number of them. When the nature of work changes from an industrial to a postindustrial structure it threatens low skilled people. It has been calculated that at least half of existing jobs demand a high level of cognitive and/or personal skills, and a quarter of the jobs demand advanced qualifications in IT. At the same time one third of the present workforce have very few skills and one in six young people are still leaving school without quailfications. More and more women are joining the formal labor market; but they disproportionately do so as part-timers, which add strongly to an increasing gender pay gap, and furthermore pose problems for reconciliation of work and family life. Family life itself is changing with many more single person households and decreasing total fertility rates. Values are becoming more individualized, which challenges traditional forms of social solidarity, and the multicultural nature of European societies has generated xenophobic extreme right-wing political mobilezation in many places.

A Eurobarometer survey conducted in late 2006 tried to grasp how European citizens perceives a number of dimensions of social life in the European Union. It starts out by asking people if they, everything taken into consideration, consider themselves happy; and in average 87 percent find that to be the case. It varies from 97 percent of Danes to 39 percent of Bulgarians; but with this exception the majority does find itself to be happy, although the tendency is that people in the former EU15 tend to feel happier than people in the new Member States. The same rank order is identified concerning questions on standard of living and quality of life. A particular question concerning confidence about the future of one's pension draws very different responses, ranging from 74 percent of Danes to 25 percent of Germans (and Bulgarians); but also the French, the Portuguese, Hungarians and Czechs show low degrees (around 33 percent) of confidence in this respect.

Asked about what they consider important, Europeans give top priority to the issues of health (99 percent), family (97 percent), friends and acquaintances (95 percent), and they rank leisure time (90 percent) over work (84 percent). Perhaps surprisingly, they also rank religion (52 percent) over politics (43 percent). In average only slightly more than half of European citizens with young children are satisfied with child-care facilities—55 percent—and the variation is considerable ranging from 78 percent in Cyprus to only 28 percent in Malta. Satisfaction with the local school is higher, in average 71 percent and with a smaller variation from 90 percent in Cyprus to 51 percent in Bulgaria. Trust in political institutions appears to be rather low in Europe, and the less so the longer the distance to the institutions. Hence, people tend to trust the local council more than the national parliament, and political parties are only trusted by 20 percent of Europeans on average. Trust levels are higher in Northern and Western countries and lower in the Eastern and Southern parts of Europe.

More than six out of 10 Europeans believe that anyone is at risk of poverty at some time in their lives, and again the average masks profound differences among the 27 countries; 86 percent of Frenchmen think so, while that is only the case for 43 percent of Swedes. To a question of whether they could perceive of themselves falling into poverty in average one in four thinks so, ranging from nearly half in Hungary and Latvia (45 percent) to only six and seven percent in Luxembourg and Malta. Half of Europeans (51 percent) hold the view that their social welfare system provides wide enough coverage and roughly the same share considers it too expensive (53 percent). Satisfaction is the highest in Luxembourg and France (75 and 74 percent) and the least in Portugal and Bulgaria (10 and 8 percent) (Eurobarometer).

This is the complex reality that exists in Europe, and that is the topic which is being discussed in this book.

Peter Abrahamson
University of Copenhagen, Denmark
Co-Founder of the European Foundation on Social Quality

1

European Social Policy:
An Introduction

CHRISTIAN ASPALTER AND PETER ABRAHAMSON

European social policy requires a renewed commitment to the welfare state at both the national government level and the EU central government level. The Lisbon goals have been developed by the European Council in the year 2000. The new set of policies proposed envisioned a new balance between social cohesion and economic competitiveness. However, a shift in the balance of interpretation of this two-fold goal has occurred. The goal of reviving the welfare state has subsequently in many small steps been making place for the goal of reviving the economy. Every balancing policy goal has the problem that the balance can be shifted to embody a very different interpretation of policy strategies for policy implementation on the ground. The Lisbon strategy, as it is also frequently called, suffers from this phenomenon. Some observers note that is has become today a somewhat infamous wide-ranging economic and social policy strategy (cf e.g. Mudge, 2005).

Without a new commitment to a strong—that is, effective and efficient—welfare state, the extension of social rights to all citizens of the European Union cannot be guaranteed.

After all the discourse of welfare retrenchment of the past two to three decades, there is still strong public support within the EU member states for the welfare state systems they have established and learned to support and rely on over the past good half a century. Even though most national and invernational government agencies are not fond of admitting it, the resources available to alleviate poverty are sufficient. The problem only is that most national poverty standards are set at a too low level, so that poverty continues to plague those who are dependent on the government's aid and support (cf Abrahamson, 1997). People are trapped in poverty by the low level of support given by the government.

Along with the spread of neoliberal discourse, we have come to blame the victims of poverty, and to avoid blame of govermnent's actions and policies altogether. The idea and philosophy of social investment is needed to revise our day-to-day thinking of how poverty is created and recreated in a person's life, and how poverty is reproducing itself over a person's lifetime and spreading out through families and neighborhoods. A strong commitment to wholesome, effective and efficient, social investment is required. Social investment in children, families, education, health prevention and cure, and social services are vital for the survial of a fit economy and society, as a result of post-modernization and globalization of threats, risks, and adverseries that surpass those known to us during the period of industrialization. The welfare state today needs to cater to many more needs, threats and risks, as that it was designed for from the very outset of its development in the 1880s and during the boom of the postwar period (Esping-Andersen, 2002; Taylor-Gooby, 2005).

In this book, a number of key experts have gathered an essential compilation of articles that investigate the workings of European Social Policy, from a wholesome, as well as issue-based perspective. In the first part of the book, authors put forward studies that focus on international developments, written from a European-wide and/or comparative perspective. The second part of this book is devoted to the important study of issues, policies and fields of study within the academic discipline of soical policy, as articles focus on social rights, moral values, gender and poverty, gender and carework, childcare policy, family policy, and policies related to social security reform and development.

Chapter 2, by Josef Weidenholzer and Christian Aspalter, sets out to unravel the overall picture of the two dominant social models in the Western world, that of the European Union and that of the United States. The American model, or "American (social) dream," is put into direct comparison with the European counterpart, the "European social dream" using the method of juxtaposition to analyze, in a strictly normative (i.e. evaluative) manner, the current status, trends, and future applicability of each model under scrutiny. Weidenholzer and Aspalter conclude in their analysis that the costs for "*non-social policy*" are staggering. They note that the implementation of a comprehensive and, more important, effective welfare state system is essential for the survival of societies and the continuation of their particular path of social development. The absence thereof leads to a great deal of costly side-effects. The juxtaposition of the American and the European model leads to the conclusion that the American welfare state model is built on unsustainable notions of *penal policy*, while the European welfare state model offers a real win-win solution, in terms of investment in sustainable, and hence efficient and effective, social welfare systems.

In Chapter 3, we see that the European Union has undergone manifold changes in the last decade. Peter Abrahamson's study highlights the implementation and extension of the social dimension of the European Union, in particular the new method of coordination of social policy across the 27 member countries of the European Union, the Open Method of Coordination (OMC). In depicting the most recent developments and trends of social citizenship in the European Union, this chapter emphasizes the role of "hard" and "soft" law in the development of the European welfare state, which is often referred to as the *European social dimension*. In doing so, this study takes a closer look at the role of social citizenship by investigating the new Open Method of Coordination and contemporary changes in social and labor law. Peter Abrahamson arrives at the conclusion that, for the time being, social citizenship rights are being both *Europeanized* (i.e., equalized throughout the European Union) and *localized* (i.e. differentiated according to the local context and policies) at the same time. This increasingly challenges the embeddedness of social rights at the level of nation-state based social policies, i.e. national welfare states.

Gillian Pascall researches the relationship of gender and the welfare state in Europe, in both the western and the eastern part of the European Union (Chapter 4). In the western part of the European Union, observers noted an increase in female labor force participation rate. Conversely, in the eastern part, post-state socialist countries have been seen to "re-traditionalize" towards a male breadwinner model, as there was a reduction in the support for mothers participating in the labor market. This chapter will argue that unpacking the male breadwinner model into component parts—that is, paid work, care work, income, time, and power—allows us to understand the recent history and current developments of gender inequality in male breadwinner systems throughout the European Union. In the past, social democratic welfare regimes supported gender equality much more than other welfare state regimes. In Scandinavia, a more collective approach in social policy making has been applied to ensure greater degree of gender policy, including direct state support for children and childcare. In Eastern-Central Europe, governments have by and large retained social welfare systems which support gender equality. At the end of this chapter, Gillian Pascall arrives at the conclusion that systems of state support for gender equality—in particular, by supporting the social costs of children and care—are at the heart of the success of the Scandinavian social democratic states, as well as in most other more gender-equal welfare states in the European Union and, to a lesser extent, in some parts of Eastern-Central Europe.

In Chapter 5, Jason Powell and Azrini Wahidin explore in greater depth the concept of risk and its relationship to the study of old age and social policy in Europe. Ever since the 1980s/1990s, European governments have set out on a journey of introducing market dynamics into the delivery of services by e.g. creating *quasi*-markets that are based on the mechanism of separation of providers from suppliers and the establishment of a complex contracting system. In addition it is said that the onset of aged and super-aged societies brings about structural welfare state retrenchment, as well as the introduction of a greater degree of reliance on personal financial provision and privately provided care arrangements. These proposals are linked to ideological shifts in the 1980s/1990s towards pure neoliberalism and/or mixed ideologies that are based on or contain core principles thereof. This chapter depicts the transformation of European societies and their welfare state systems, from a state of "trust" during the golden period of welfare state extension in the period from the 1960s to the 1980s to the current state of "distrust" and "risk" in social welfare policy. Powell and Wahidin demonstrate that the cure for the mounting social problems for the elderly population (especially the problem of income maintenance and poverty of the aging society, and mounting needs for health care and long-term care services) is to rebuild "trust" by strengthening old and building up new systems of social protection that minimize and avoid old and new adversities and risks. In addition to the onset of aged and super-aged societies, societies and their welfare states, Powell and Wahidin argue, need to take into consideration and prepare for additional new risks of the post-modern era: such as e.g. new forms of crime, new threats to national and personal security, risks of unhealthy foods and lifestyles, food and water insecurity, global unemployment, environmental pollution, global warming, and depletion of natural resources.

Chapter 6, written by Christian Aspalter, sheds light onto the changed nature of European welfare states, the new reality of welfare state systems. It applies a comparative, historical a case-study approach (cf e.g. Esping-Andersen and Hicks, 2006). In this chapter, Aspalter investigates Europe's most-studied welfare state systems: the United Kingdom, France, Germany, Italy, and Sweden. Each country case study gives a historical account of welfare state development and change, with a special focus on the last two to three decades. The concluding part of the chapter debates the performance of European welfare state systems in international comparison. Across the board, a new trend of convergence in European spending on tax-financed social benefits can be observed, due to a long-term shift towards a greater reliance on regulatory measures, in an age of increased fiscal constraints in the global social policy arena. The study also highlights the ongoing systematic shift from tax-financed to contribution-financed social security provision in European social policy. This paradigm shift in the financing of welfare state regimes first occurred in the Continental European countries like the Netherlands, Germany, and Austria, starting as early as in the 1980s. In the Nordic countries, the reforms took effect (in terms of a reduction of overall social spending), by and large, only in the 1990s. When applying a global perspective in the comparative study of real-typical welfare state regimes, Aspalter concludes that there are *four general dimensions of welfare state reform*: (a) parametric changes inside the old system, (b) privatization of the old system, (c) individualization of the old system, and (d) implementation of a new logic within the welfare state system, or its key elements, altogether.

Kim Jinsoo and Park Sojeung, in Chapter 7, investigate the experience of welfare state systems in three Eastern Central European countries, Poland, the Czech Republic and Hungary. Compared to the changes undergone by its counterparts in the Western part of Europe, these three welfare states systems have lived through "shocking"—rather abrupt and major parametric and systemic—changes. The greatest system changes are to be found in old-age pension systems, while novel cash benefits with regard to unemployment and health care insurance have also been introduced. By and large, the developmental trajectory of welfare state systems over the last two decades had to deal with financial difficulties as well as administrative difficulties. As a result of East European governments trying to stabilize their finances of their social security systems, even greater shocks and long-term difficulties for the people of these countries occurred. The "security" function of welfare state systems have been lacking completely, or largely deficient at best. Kim and Park note that East European countries are unlikely to go through the same appaling difficulties and confusion as experienced in most of Latin American countries as they conducted their major systemic social security reforms, as lessons from close-by countries are directly available, and since being member states of the European Union, these countries are now part of the EU's social security network, which leads to greater degrees of convergence among different welfare state systems in place (cf Aspalter, 2008; Aspalter *et al.*, 2008; Ferrera and Gualmini, 2004).

At a time of rapid change in European welfare states, the Danish welfare state has also experienced a great deal of changes in all major social policy fields. In Chapter 8, Peter Abrahamson investigates the role of social citizenship rights in the welfare state and, in view of that, analyses the development of the welfare state in Denmark. Three models of citizenship rights are identified in the theoretical part of the study: (a) a *universal type* of social rights, (b) a *performative type* of social rights, and (c) a *clientelistic type* of social rights. The theoretical approach set forth by Abrahamson echoes the famous tripartite classifications of Titmuss (1974) and Esping-Andersen (1990, 1998), but it fully departs from the macro approaches of Titmuss and Esping-Andersen. Peter Abrahamson looks at the meso and micro levels of social rights in one particular country first, and only then he goes on to classify the very same welfare state system. The issue at hand is the social rights perspective applied in each field of policy (the meso level) and the policy/program level (the micro level of social policy analysis). Abrahamson focuses on the method of "theoretical *induction*," whereas Titmuss and Esping-Andersen before him emphasized the method of "theoretical *deduction*." Hence, each policy field, rather than welfare state system, may now be classified accordingly. This new approach allows for greater sharpness in welfare state analysis, be it welfare state analysis across time or across international borders. In the case of Denmark, Abrahamson concludes that the Danish welfare state, all in all, moves in the direction of more performative social rights, particularly with regard to health care and pension rights. Both the methods of deduction and induction need to be applied by welfare research over time, in order to double check earlier findings and to develop a greater sharpness in the theoretical understanding of welfare state in Europe, and worldwide.

Arthur Gould, a renowned expert on Swedish social policy, offers an in-depth analysis of social policy formulation, and contradiction, in one of the most studied welfare states on earth, Sweden (Chapter 9). In doing so, Gould reveals a new, mostly unstudied and hence unknown, important, part of the Swedish welfare state. In studying the "side issues" of the welfare state in Sweden, Arthur Gould unveils the nature of the Swedish welfare state system as a whole. In this way, Gould is stepping in the footsteps of Richard Titmuss who pioneered this particular approach of studying welfare state systems by studying the system of blood donations to analyze the core logic of the UK welfare state earlier on (Titmuss, 1971). Though being renowned as a very progressive country in terms of social welfare policy in general, Sweden has chosen in the past to be rather restrictive and conservative when it comes to the issues of prostitution and drugs. In this chapter, Gould advances a thorough explanation of this seeming contradiction, as he puts forward the conclusion that the postmodern Swedish mind is caught between its own orderly past and the onset of the disorderly postmodern, globalized world. The Swedish welfare state, in other words, is caught between "order, rationality, and morality" (Apollonian values) on the one side and "disorder, irrationality, excess, and spontaneity" (Dionysian values) on the other. The contradiction between these two value systems and the resulting paradoxes of social policies lay at the heart of the Swedish welfare state.

Chapter 10, by Dominique Wang and Christian Aspalter, takes on the interesting case of Switzerland (which besides Greece and Portugal) has experienced a golden phase in the development of its welfare state system in the last two decades, despite, or because, of the recent societal and global changes—that spurred social spending across the board, rather than curb social spending, in some countries. Switzerland is not part of the European Union. The EU membership of Greece, Portugal and Italy was accounted for either the increase or the defense of the welfare state in the respective countries (cf Ferrera and Gualmini, 2004). In the case of Switzerland, system-immanent features, of e.g. the private quasi-market based health care system, the rather generous universal pension system, as well as generous regulations for early retirement and invalidity pensions, have triggered an astounding increase of social spending in Switzerland, marking its breathtaking transition from one of Europe's welfare laggards to a leader in welfare state provision in Europe. The model of Switzerland gives twofold lessons, so Wang and Aspalter. On the one hand, it exemplifies the problem of quasi-market solutions (its inefficiencies, i.e. its inability of providing high quality health care provision with relatively less money). But, also in addition, the Swiss old-age security system offers a good record of preventing poverty during old-age by avoiding contribution caps in its basic old-age pension system—hence, allowing for greater redistribution from high-income to low-income segments of the salaried classes.

In the following chapter, Enkeleida Tahiraj examines the problem of increased feminization of poverty in one of the poorest countries in the world, namely Albania (Chapter 11). This study constitutes a genuine attempt to suggest a broader consideration of the way poverty can be perceived, measured, and reflected in the policy agenda of any government, not just the Albanian government. In the local Albanian context, there is a huge gap between *what official data shows* and *what the reality is* pertaining to the feminization of poverty. Enkeleida Tahiraj stresses the fact that *"poverty means a failure of our welfare state."* She states that until official data matches the reality women face in their everyday lives, social policies are not likely to increase the welfare or avert, reduce diswelfare—that is, the suffering of the most vulnerable population groups and above all women. Enkeleida Tahiraj arrives at the conclusion that the status differentials, as well as lack of experiences and visibility of women in relation to poverty is as a matter of fact inadequately researched, little acknowledged, and poorly understood. It is for this reason that the consequences of women in dire poverty will continue to include, for many years and decades to come, problems like bad health and prostitution, as well as lack of education.

In Chapter 12, Michael Opielka takes on the case of the German welfare state, and the recent attempts of gendering the German welfare model by introducing generous carework salaries. The German social policy arena has undergone fundamental changes by which new options that only seemed out of reach a few years earlier have become a vital cornerstone of current and possible future social policy paradigms, as well as welfare state models. This chapter concentrates on the issue of introducing universal carework salaries. Opielka demonstrates the fundamental changes caused by this new issue, as it has fully penetrated the heartland of German party politics and the overall governmental strategy for welfare state development. This study presented applies a historical case study approach, depicting and explaining the historical development and the current role of carework salaries in German social welfare policy. Michael Opielka concludes that the current reorientation of German social welfare policy points toward the direction of the State taking on a new role as a "guarantor" of people's well-being and livelihood.

Jim Goddard, in Chapter 13, investigates the concept of parenting as used by local and central authorities in the United Kingdom, the expansion of the state's direct parenting responsibilities over time, the institutional conflict between central government power and local government responsibilities, as well as the impact of recent policy reforms. The study furthermore examines the strong relationship between care leavers, most of them at age 18, and a high incidence of social exclusion. The study suggests that for children leaving public care services (service centers) to be the same successful in education and their subsequent professional lives as their non-care peers, they would have to rely on continued support throughout their young adulthood, well beyond age 18. It also concludes that the lack of trust between central and local authorities in this regard makes a successful implementation of child-care policy reforms difficult to accomplish in the case of the United Kingdom. This study hence sheds light on the importance of key concepts in policy formation, planning, development and execution. The concept of governmental/corporate parenting exemplifies the role current policy paradigms play in the formulation of general social policies and the provision of particular social services. This chapter supports the need for "a new welfare state" as put forward by Esping-Andersen (2002), by looking at the present state of social service provision in a neoliberal welfare state, that of the UK.

In Chapter 14, Jason Powell investigates the particular relationship between old age and family life by means of studying the role of grand-parenting and the way it is perceived by the elderly, the family, and the public at large. The study applies a narrative approach, which has been gaining a great deal in significance in present-day social policy studies internationally. Powell's study focuses on the meaning of the family and grandparenting, which is being told, constructed and reconstructed, continuously in form of personal stories and public discourse. The theoretical approach applied by Powell is based on theories of Michel Foucault. The findings in the concluding part of the chapter suggest that identities of family and grandparenting are built on multiple grounds, and that for this reason theory should be sensitized accordingly, as identities are managed at different levels, for different audiences, and at different levels of awareness.

Jason Powell and Azrini Wahidin, in Chapter 15, look at the problems of introducing and the relying on private pension plans instead of public social security provision, taking the example of the United Kingdom. Powell and Wahidin provide a critical analysis of the lack of regulation and safety of private pension plans and the consequent surfacing of a number of corporate scandals involving illegalities and the mis-selling of pensions. The ideology of neoliberalism does not account for real-life problems of power and information imbalance between private pension providers (mostly billion dollar strong pension coroporations) and the individual, especially the ordinary citizens who are member of the working classes. As exemplified in the case of the United Kingdom, private pension companies provide, more often than not, false, misleading and insufficient information to its customers, incurring great losses with regard to their pension entitlements. Successive UK governments that have underscored the hypothetical necessity to change from a public to a private system based their claims on overrated projections of a demographic time-bomb in the United Kingdom. The UK, in fact, does not suffer from a demographic time-bomb, but—due to the privatization policies of the last decades—from a severe poverty time bomb (Walker and Aspalter, 2008). This chapter reveals how both Conservative and Labour governments have endorsed the replacement of public with private pension plans, and subsequently failed to prevent or adequately punish corporate crime associated with ill-fated pension provision by the private market economy.

The future of European social policy is not one that is marked by welfare retrenchment, nor will it be one that is immune to the neoliberal offensive that has taken position in the echelons of power and the minds of many, as the discourse war machinery of neoliberalism keeps on rolling out one attack after the other at the believe system and moral convictions of the welfare state, and modern civilizations alike. These often silent and continuous attacks rattle the confidence of many professionals, government administrators and policymakers, who can proudly look at a successful record of policymaking in the fields of both economic and social policy, throughout all of the "golden" postwar period in most developed countries in the world today.

Today, Europeans wake up into a new reality: (a) a harsher attitude towards the individual as a result of ideological shifts and mind-boggling neoliberal propaganda, and (b) the new reality of post-modern risk society, where each individual is exposed to ever-more risky life-time choices, to which we formerly did not (and did not need to) pay much attention. These include the choice of the right amount and content of education and the right entry into the labor market, the choice of healthy foods versus hamburgers and French fries, the choice between family responsibilities and the development of career prospects and life-time savings/investments, the choice between different sexual partners, the choice between traveling to a high-risk travel destination (where one may encounter a tsunami, terrorist attack, etc.) or to stay at home or travel elsewhere, the choice to take on overseas employment, and the choice between gene-manipulated and chemically treated supermarket foods and planting vegetables in one's own garden.

The fields where Social Policy is actively engaged in or expected to do so by the new *risk citizens* have expanded and multiplied—from maternity leave to radioactive salad and mass obesity, from poverty to broken life-time careers and broken families, and from work accidents to investment in health promotion and cultural capital. Post-industrial Social Policy is a reality—but Europe still has to catch up to it, by means of e.g. social investment in: (a) political capital of particulary women, youth, children, the weak and socially excluded parts of society, (b) health capital (healthy minds and bodies), (c) healthy food and sports culture, (d) health- and family-based urban social planning (especially housing, transportation/vicinity to jobs, shopping, as well as recreational and cultural facilities), (e) environmental social policy, such as e.g. planting of trees and flowers, playgrounds, recreational areas, family and health-friendly environment (this policy idea has been already partially implemented in parts of China), (f) conducting social work and psychological counselling while e.g. hiking through a national park (using the natural environment and fauna in the process of healing, as applied in e.g. Krueger National Park in South Africa), and (g) using public/private media to promote happiness and friendliness, to enhance public safety, as well as to teach people how to support family and community and how to smile again and how to see life from a more positive angle (as applied in e.g. Hong Kong through APIs, "advertisement in the public interest" which is mandatory for TV stations).

REFERENCES

Abrahamson, Peter (1997), Combating Poverty and Social Exclusion, in W. Beck, L.v.d. Measen, and A. Walker (eds.), *The Social Quality of Europe*, Kluwer Law: London.

Aspalter, Christian (2008), Strategies of Pension and Health Care Reform in the United Kingdom, Sweden, Germany, Italy, and Slovenia, in A. Walker and C. Aspalter (eds.), *Securing the Future for Old Age in Europe*, Casa Verde: Hong Kong.

Aspalter, Christian; Uchida, Yasuo, and Gauld, Robin (eds.) (2008), *Health Care Systems in Europe and Asia*, Casa Verde: Hong Kong.

Esping-Andersen, Gøsta (1990), *The Three Worlds of Welfare Capitalism*, Polity: Cambridge, UK.

Esping-Andersen, Gøsta (1998), The Three Political Economies of the Welfare State, in J. O'Connor and G.M. Olsen (eds.), *Power Resources Theory and the Welfare State: A Critical Approach*, University of Toronto Press: Toronto, Canada.

Esping-Andersen, Gøsta (2002), *Why We Need a New Welfare State*, Oxford University Press: Oxford, UK.

Esping-Andersen, Gøsta and Hicks, Alexander (2006), Comparative and Historical Studies of Public Policy and the Welfare State, in T. Janoski, R.R. Alford, A.M. Hicks, and M.A. Schwartz (eds.), *The Handbook of Political Sociology: States, Civil Societies, and Globalization*, Cambridge University Press: Cambridge, UK.

Ferrera, Maurizio and Gualmini, Elisabetta (2004), *Rescued by Europe?: Social and Labour Market Reforms in Italy from Maastricht to Berlusconi*, University of Chicago Press: Chicago, IL.

Mudge, Stephanie L. (2005), Regime Shift of the European Social Model in European Union Policymaking: 2000 to 2004, paper presented at the *Annual Meeting of the American Sociological Association*, Philadelphia, August 13-16.

Taylor-Gooby, Peter (ed.) (2005), *New Risks, New Welfare: The Transformation of the European Welfare State*, Oxford University Press: Oxford, UK.

Titmuss, Richard M. (1971), *The Gift Relationship: From Human Blood to Social Policy*, Pantheon: New York.

Titmuss, Richard M. (1974), *Social Policy—An Introduction*, Allen & Unwin: London.

Walker, Alan and Aspalter, Christian (eds.) (2008), *Securing the Future for Old Age in Europe*, Casa Verde: Hong Kong.

2

The Contrast of Welfare Regimes: American Penal Policy Versus European Social Policy

JOSEF WEIDENHOLZER AND CHRISTIAN ASPALTER

In Social Policy, the public discourse has centered in the last two decades on micro issues like that of workfare or welfare-to-work programs, reciprocal/mutual obligations and duties of welfare recipients, the strengthening and reinvention of the "patronizing/parental" role of the state in welfare and social service provision. This chapter, instead, focuses the macro issue of what model, dream or philosophy of social policies are applied, using the comparative method, while also addressing and integrating the issue of welfare regime theory as developed and extended over the years by Esping-Andersen (1987, 1990, 1998), Esping-Andersen and Hicks (2006), and Aspalter (2001a,b, 2005, 2006). This study sets out with a critical examination of the American social model, clarifying the meaning of social policy as penal policy in the context of American social policy, while also discussing the consequences thereof. Next, the authors examine the European social model, that in actual fact represents an amalgamation of three ideal-typical social models, that of Scandinavia, Continental Europe, and that of the United Kingdom. The authors, in their normative attempt to evaluate social models of each sides of the Atlantic, conclude that the European model cannot follow the American model, as it would be too costly, and counterproductive in terms of social and economic development of countries within the European Union. The Continental model *as a whole* is also out of the question, as it failed to solve the problem of chronically high unemployment rates in much of the countries involved. Hence the authors suggest that a new, perhaps revised, model based on Scandinavian, social democratic welfare regime model is more apt to solve the big social questions of our time, while also contributing a great deal to economic efficiency through the development of human and societal resources and capabilities (human and societal capital), as well as social integration and social harmony.

The American Welfare Model

Ayn Rand (2000) a prominent trailblazer of neoliberalism once wrote that "America is not based on selfless service to one's fellow-men, nor on self-sacrifice, self-denial or any kind of altruism. In fact, the basis of this country is the right of every man to bring about happiness. His own happiness. Not other people's happiness." Results of empirical opinion research show how differently the role of the individual and his responsibility is seen on both sides of the Atlantic.

In the United States, poverty is deemed to be self-inflicted in the first instance, and this is why it is not primarily subject of state action. The disparity of opinions may become even more obvious from the answer to the question whether poor people are lazy: 60 percent of the Americans answer in the affirmative, as opposed to 26 percent of the Europeans (Alesina, 2004).

The apologists of neoliberalism take pleasure in holding America up as a unique example, praising their citizens' unconditional will to perform and giving the Europeans a dressing-down for being unwilling to perform and idle for being far too secured.

But is America really the shining example? There are many ways of assessing the success of an economy. In the United States, the average per capita GDP amounts to approx. US$ 39,700, in Austria approx. US$ 35,800 and in France a little less than US$ 32,900. It takes Americans 1,822 hours per year, Austrians 1,550 and French 1,431 hours per year to reach this figure (OECD, 2005a,b).

Europeans, lost in morbid self-underestimation, should be careful to declare the US their super-paragon. The much-vaunted productive capacity of American economy does not exist as it is presented to be, it is financed on the nod with high public debts and a tremendous current account deficit. In addition, America's success is not ascribable merely to a superiority of the market as a management tool, but it can be attributed to the fact that the military-industrial complex is a major economic factor. Nowhere does the economy depend so directly and causally on state capital spending decisions.

America's prosperity has a high price to pay: the country is divided into the poor and the rich. Nowhere else in an industrialized society are the social differences so great. As a result, poverty is not hidden, it is visible for everyone. In the United States, the share of the poor in the population is three times higher than in Austria and totals more than 12 percent (Rifkin, 2004). If one considers that the US, which is praised for its employment policy by the leading neoliberal economists in Europe, has an unemployment rate of about 6 percent it is easy to conceive that even employment is no safeguard against poverty due to the widespread phenomenon of the working poor. In the US, the gap between the rich and the poor widens every year, for social policies fail to succeed with many voters. Gradually, the *war on poverty* has become a *war on welfare*. Backed by think tanks like the Cato Institute or the Heritage Foundation, the apologists and propagandists of neoliberalism, also known as neo-conservativism, thunder against any form of social insurance and any kind of social programs. The vast majority of social programs in place, as a matter of fact, are represented to be inefficient, expensive, opposed to performance, patronizing, even largely restraining individuals' liberty (cf Kingfisher, 1996, 2002; Goodin, 2003).

When in 1994/1995 a Republican majority in Parliament headed by Newt Gingrich blocked Bill Clinton with an ultraconservative program *Contract on America* and demanded departure from New Deal, President Bill Clinton made himself the executor of the demands in an opportunistic strong-man act, not least to make sure he was going to be re-elected. Along with numerous aggravations, the welfare reform of 1996 brought about abolishment of individually enforceable legal claims and linking of welfare benefits to the duty to work and constituted a radical departure from New Deal. These measures entail an increase of risks, a limitation of chances, and a heavy loss of social rights. Introduction of coercive measures *(workfare)* into the repertoire of social policy is remarkable (Gilbert, 2004).

But most of all, it is the limitation of all benefits to a maximum of five years during the life-time of a person irrespective of whether there is neediness or not that signifies a turning point whose consequences have not really been perceived yet. Thus for the first time in a Western democracy, groups of persons are ostentatiously excluded from the opportunity to receive welfare benefits and left to their fate beyond the social state. Often this ends in criminalization of socially susceptible persons. Since the beginning of the 1980s, there has been a noticeable trend in America to stop solving social problems in a „soft" way, shifting to „tough" ways. This change may be explained by the necessities of a *symbolic policy* (Weidenholzer, 2001a), whose significance is increasing, not only in America.

The call for decisive measures, even if they may fail to solve the problem, certainly attracts more votes than a more distinguishing course of action. As a consequence of these continuous cuts in social welfare, the number of imprisoned persons in the United States increased from 380,000 in 1975 to 1,600,000 in 1995, male blacks constituting the biggest share. Now more than 2,200,000 persons have been imprisoned already (cf Wacquant, 1998; 2004, Garland, 2002). Since 1995, more money has been spent on building prisons than on building schools.

The significance attached to the prison sector, which, by the way, is increasingly transferred into private hands, is shown in an analysis, according to which the high percentage of imprisonment has reduced the unemployment rate in the United States by 2 percent. This is also a way to make employment policy. Penalty is one of the basic elements of the American social model to guarantee social bonds.

Low spending on social matters requires high spending on the prison system. A society preventing violence must be preferred to a society needing to stage violence in order not to fall apart. But the American way is inefficient, too. Social inequality is not only inhumane, it is also costly. It causes not only an increase in delinquency, but also means destruction of social capital and destroys chances in life. Today the imprisonment rate (rate of population constantly in prison) is about six times higher than in China. The United States and any other society that builds on this American model of "penal policy and practice," is far from the original American Dream of the 1950s, where employment was plenty, and the middle and working classes enjoyed higher purchase power for their monthly/weekly salaries than they do today.

The European Welfare Model

Europe does not only mean competition, but also care for others. Europe does not exhaust itself in appealing to the self-responsibility of the individuals. Conversely, Europe encourages a social sense of responsibility. Its citizens are not only driven to compete with others unswervingly, they also know the importance of respect and consideration. On the one hand, we know exactly what constitutes or could constitute the value of Europe when we compare ourselves with other continents, but on the other hand the outlines of what we want to talk about are unclear. When we travel all over the world, we consider ourselves Europeans, but when we are back in Europe we become Austrians, Belgians, French, Poles, Portuguese, etc. again.

Yes, there is the oft-quoted European social model, but only when we look at our continent from the outside. It is the social dimension which (still) makes Europe discernible irrespective of egalitarian tendencies of the globalization process. But as soon as we look at the European social model from the inside, clearness fades away quickly (Weidenholzer, 2001b).

In the meantime, there is a host of learned articles distinguishing between various types of European welfare states. Usually, they enumerate three, often four, sometimes five and seldom seven types. It is appropriate to speak of three ideal types, which are never met in their pure form, though (Esping-Andersen, 1990, 1998; cf Aspalter, 2006). The residual welfare state is an Anglo-Saxon phenomenon and may also be termed liberal. The corporatist welfare state can be found in continental Europe and is termed the corporatist/Christian Democratic model. The universalistic welfare state is a prominent feature of the North European states and a result of the decades of predominance of social democracy. Southern Europe has not managed to form a specific type of welfare state because industrialization came late there, and Eastern Europe is still fundamentally characterized by the problems of a transition to market economy without ever being able to really get rid of its remembrance of its communist past.

The relevance of European social policy will increase in the years to come (cf Ferrera and Gualmini, 2004; Ferrera, 2005). A social vision is needed to make Europe more visible and to restore the faith of its citizens. It is for this reason that it is important that there is a European social policy, but even more important is what it consists of. In theory there are four ideal-typical models altogether that could led the way for the European social model: first, the Nordic solution, the Continental European solution, the Anglo-Saxon solution, and last but not least the East Asian solution (cf Aspalter, 2006). But in the case of Europe, it is most likely that policymakers are either reorienting themselves towards two models, either the Nordic model of a full-fledged welfare state, or the neoliberal variant, the Anglo-Saxon model. The Continental European welfare model is out of the question, as high rates of unemployment and low rates of labor force participation rates are squeezing the room for maneuver for policymakers. The East Asian variant is simply not known in the European policy arena, low overall rates of social spending in East Asia are paired with relatively high levels of social regulation and, also increasingly now, social provision by the public hand (Aspalter, 2007a,b).

The Lisbon Summit of the European Union in spring 2000 led to the establishment of the Lisbon Goals, which constitute a good framework for the alliance of social and economic policies. In 2000, governments of the European Union intended to sustain Europe as the most competitive and dynamic knowledge-based economy in the world, capable of sustainable economic growth "with more and better jobs and greater social cohesion."

Over the last years, it seemed that the Lisbon process has reached a deadlock, first of all because it has not been taken seriously by the governments and has been conducted only half-heartedly. It failed to capture the imagination and support of the wider public over a longer period of time. Hence, as a consequence, politics has already nearly surrendered to the marketization of all spheres of life as pushed by the neoliberal *zeitgeist*.

It needs the European civil society, all of us, to prevent such unconditional surrender. The message is clear: The European social model guarantees prosperity and competitiveness, it prevents splitting society by securing social fundamental rights and it contributes to rigidifying the European idea with the citizens of Europe.

What the vision of a peaceful Europe without war and frontiers meant for the end of the 20th century (Judt, 2005) might become the vision of a European social model for the beginning of the 21st century: to give the citizens of Europe a perspective how to cope with the risks of life in a world getting more complex and insecure without having to abandon themselves in complete competition.

Comparing Ideal-Typical Welfare Regimes

In identifying different families of welfare state regimes, Gøsta Esping-Andersen (1987, 1990, 1998) has arrived at a tripartite typology, distinguishing between a social democratic, a liberal and a corporatist welfare regime—which has created its own legacy and path dependency in the comparative study welfare state systems.

In 1990, Esping-Andersen argued that the history of class coalitions is the most distinctive cause of welfare state variations. He advanced the idea that once the interests of political actors are articulated, class alliances formed, and welfare ideologies of majoritarian groups develop, each welfare regime follows its own path of development (Esping-Andersen, 1990, 1998).

Esping-Andersen's comparative analysis that mainly centered on European countries and the Anglo-Saxon world found that there are three such distinct welfare "trajectories," hence welfare state regimes. Esping-Andersen understood them as being *"ideal-typical"*—that is to say, *smaller and larger variations from the norm may occur, but still the greater picture would remain intact and valid.*

Table 2.1: Overview of Four Ideal-Typical Welfare Regimes

	Social Democratic Welfare Regime	Christian Democratic Welfare Regime	Liberal Welfare Regime	Conservative Welfare Regime
The underlying logic of welfare provision— social welfare is understood as representing:	• social rights based on citizenship (including, social insurance, social services, and public employment)	• a right to social insurance, plus charity welfare provision	• a limited right to charity welfare provision and social insurance provision	• a right to public investment in social development, plus a moderate right to social security and/or public charity welfare provision
Leading instruments in social welfare policy	• universal social security systems • public social services • public employment • social transfers	• occupational social security systems • preferential treatment of special interest groups • corporatism in social service provision (NGOs, Church) • social transfers	• means-tested welfare benefits • private savings and insurance	• occupational social security systems • preferential treatment of special interest groups • employment-based welfare and social security programs (including mandatory savings)
Social policy focuses on: • the Individual • the Family • the Market • the State	• strong • weak • weak • strong	• weak • strong • weak • strong	• strong • weak • strong • weak	• weak • strong • strong • weak
Countries that belong the this *ideal-typical* regime type are for example:	Sweden, Norway, Finland, Denmark, Iceland	Germany, Austria, France, Belgium, The Netherlands, Luxembourg, Italy, Spain, Slovenia, Czech Republic, etc.	US, Canada, Australia, New Zealand, UK	Japan, South Korea, China, Hong Kong, Taiwan, Malaysia, and Singapore

Sources: based on Aspalter (2005, 2006) and Esping-Andersen (1990, 1998).

In 1998, Esping-Andersen reclassified the one or other case, particularly worth mentioning here is the United Kingdom, which from then on he only partially, i.e. only to a limited extent, treated as being a member of the liberal family of nations. Aspalter (2005, 2006) discovered a fourth type of ideal-typical welfare regime in East Asia (cf Table 2.1). Hence it may be worth reexamining his new theoretical analyses anew, while laying particular emphasis on each welfare regime's specific development trajectory.

The Social Democratic Regime. According to Esping-Andersen, a social democratic trajectory in welfare state development leads, in the ideal-typical case, to the establishment of a comprehensive welfare state, with universal social security provision, comprehensive full-employment policies (e.g., public employment particularly aimed at women), and a strong network of social service provision by the state—as the majority of people support public provision of social security and social welfare services, even at the cost of high taxation. The government assumes a commanding role in welfare provision, resulting in the erection of a comprehensive, redistribution-heavy welfare state system.

The government takes care of the individual, so to speak, from the cradle to the grave. Individuals stay at the heart of public welfare provision; eligibility is typically tight to social citizenship—not to work records, or family status. Welfare provision by the family or the private market economy is not emphasized in social security and social service provision. Countries that belong to this regime type are Sweden and Norway, and to some extent also Finland and Denmark (Esping-Andersen, 1998: 142).

A typically social democratic welfare state would reduce status differentials and, thus, the class-divide—leading to low levels of stratification. The second major yardstick aiming at conceptualizing welfare outcomes is the degree of decommodification that refers to the extent to which citizens may rely on the social safety net without considering their work status and past work record. The level of decommodification in a typically social democratic welfare regime, so Esping-Andersen, is very high—thus, pushing back the boundaries of the market economy even further.

Furthermore, social democratic welfare state systems focus on the provision of employment in the public sector, up to 90 percent of which is taken up by women—what Esping-Andersen has called soft-economy jobs.

The Christian Democratic Welfare Regime. The ideal-typical corporatist/Christian Democratic model—which can be found in e.g. Germany, Austria, the Netherlands, Belgium, France, Switzerland, and Italy—rests on the idea of preserving status differentials (cf Esping-Andersen, 1998). Without a doubt, so Kersbergen (1995), occupationally divided social insurance systems form a basic element of Christian Democratic social welfare policy.

A further key element of the corporatist—Christian Democratic— welfare regime is the corporatist system of social service provision that gives high priority to welfare provision by NGOs and especially Church organizations (cf Bode, 2003).

Both the *principle of subsidiarity* and the *principle of solidarity*, as laid down and amplified in a great number of social encyclicals (e.g., *Rerum Novarum* and *Quadragesimo Anno*), form the base of Christian social teachings, and, hence, also the key features of the "Christian Democratic" welfare state (cf Kersbergen, 1995; Aspalter, 2001a; Huber and Stephens, 2001). The strong emphasis on the *principle of solidarity*—which emphasizes the duty of the state to help those in need— explains high levels of social expenditure and the comprehensiveness of government welfare provision in Continental European welfare states.

Both social democrats and Christian democrats fully subscribe to this core principle. Esping-Andersen (1990, 1998) stated that in the corporatist welfare regime "the liberal obsession with market efficiency and commodification was never pre-eminent and, as such, the granting of social rights was hardly ever a seriously contested issue." With regard to both the induced degree of stratification and decommodification, the corporatist welfare regime ranks amid the social democratic and liberal regimes.

The Liberal Welfare Regime. In a liberal, Anglo-Saxon welfare state regime, the majority stance of middle-class voters is to reject a comprehensive welfare state, as they throw in their support for keeping personal income and consumer taxes low. As a result, the government's role in providing and regulating welfare is kept to a minimum. The individual is expected to care for him- or herself. Lower taxes lead to higher average wages, and thus greater capacities of the working and middle classes to provide for themselves. The state's engagement in public housing, education, and health care is either non-existent, or plays a marginal role.

The workings of an "undistorted" market economy and individual actors themselves are expected to meet and prevent welfare needs. Social assistance programs are highly targeted—for the most part applying asset and means tests in allocating the generally meager resources to those most in need. There is room, though, for the implementation of modest universal transfers and modest social insurance plans.

The state encourages the market by providing only a minimum safety net, or actively by subsidizing private welfare schemes. Liberal welfare regimes reveal, typically, high levels of stratification and social exclusion, as well as a low degree of decommodification, and hence a large dependency of the population on income generated directly from wages, or private capital assets, such as savings.

Countries that are considered to belong to the Liberal type of welfare regime are the United States, Canada, Australia, and New Zealand; while the United Kingdom approximates this model only to some extent (Esping-Andersen, 1998) (cf Table 2.2).

Understanding European Social Policy / edited by Peter Abrahamson and Christian Aspalter.
Includes bibliographical references and index.
ISBN 978-986-80414-8-6
1. Europe 2. Europe Union 3. Social Policy 4. European Social Model
5. Ideal-Typical Welfare Regime Theory 6. Open Method of Coordination
7. Risk Society 8. Aging Society 9. Social Rights 10. Gender Policy
11. Family Policy 12. Child and Youth Welfare Policy 13. Social Security
14. Pensions 15. Health Care 16. Drugs and Prostitution.

First Published in 2008.

For all international orders,
subscriptions and
submissions contact:
Casa Verde Publishing
Jennifer@cv-pub.com
http://www.cv-pub.com

Casa Verde Publishing
International Distribution Center
187 Da Xing Rd.,
334 Bade City,
Taoyuan, Taiwan.

Casa Verde Publishing
UK Distribution & Support Office
36 Chretien Road,
Manchester, M22 4FS
United Kingdom

British Library Cataloguing in Publication Data.
A catalogue record for this book is available from the British Library.

Casa Verde Publishing
visit our online store
http://www.cv-pub.com

10   9   8   7   6   5   4   3   2   1
09 08 07 06 05 04 03 02 01 00

Printed in Taiwan

Table 2.2: Main Regime Characteristics of Four Ideal-Typical Welfare Regimes

The Social Democratic Welfare Regime	*The Christian Democratic Welfare Regime*
1. Principle of universal benefits 2. Principle of social rights 3. Many columns and systems of welfare provision (all sorts of social policies are implemented) 4. High benefits (high replacement ratios, long duration of benefits, high level of benefits) 5. Dominance of public social service Provision 6. Dominance of public employment (especially in the local government sector, and especially for women) 7. Focus on active labor market policies, ALMPs (besides unemployment benefits, also schooling and retraining, subsidies for companies not to lay off employees, regulations of reducing/delaying/ smoothening layoffs, etc.) 8. Focus on large-scale and long-term social investment in education, housing, and health care.	1. Principle of benefits based on performance and achievements 2. Insurance principle (Bismarckian-type insurance systems dominate 3. Strong emphasis on asset- and means-tested social assistance benefits 4. Many columns and systems of welfare provision (all sorts of social policies are implemented) 5. High benefits (high replacement ratios, long duration of benefits, high level of benefits) 6. Dominance of social service provision by NGOs 7. Focus on active labor market policies, ALMPs (besides unemployment benefits, also schooling and retraining, subsidies for companies not to lay off employees, regulations of reducing/delaying/ smoothening layoffs, etc.) 8. Focus on large-scale and long-term social investment in education, housing, and health care.

Table 2.2: Main Regime Characteristics of Four Ideal-Typical Welfare Regimes (continued)

The Conservative Welfare Regime	*The Liberal Welfare Regime*
1. In general, the principle of universal benefits is applied coexists with the principle of benefits based on performance and achievements, in different program and policy areas. 2. Principle of social investment (especially in education, health care, and sometimes also public housing) 4. The variety of columns and systems of welfare provision is being extended (new systems and policies are being erected) 3. In general, medium benefits (replacement ratios, medium duration of benefits, mediocre level of benefits) 4. Dominance of employment-based social security and welfare benefits. 5. A growing emphasis on fully-funded provident fund systems in social security provision (mandatory individual savings accounts with no inter-personal redistribution) 6. Dominance of social service provision by NGOs and the family. 7. In general a growing focus on active labor market policies, ALMPs	1. The principle of asset- and means-testing dominates welfare philosophy, as well as policies and programs of the government (with leads to a growing number in poor people and a shrinking support for the welfare state) 2. Public interference in social affairs is limited, and as a rule concentrated on education and/or health care 3. Strong emphasis on asset- and means-tested social assistance benefits 4. Many columns and systems of welfare provision are missing (there are large holes in the spectrum of social policies applied) 5. In general, very low benefits (replacement ratios, short duration of benefits, extreme low level of benefits) 6. Dominance of social service provision by companies, NGOs, and the individuals. 7. Focus on passive labor market policies 8. Focus on *penal policies* (a overloaded criminal justice system, punitive social welfare regulations and programs, paternal welfare agencies, close supervision and strong control by social service administrators, and stigmatizing role of social welfare benefits)

The Contrasting Experience of Welfare Regimes:
By Way of Conclusion

It is often argued that the welfare state damages a great deal the economic competitiveness of the nation-states. High social insurance contributions, as dominant in the Social Democratic and the Christian Democratic welfare regime are *said* to force undertakings to relocate production facilities to cheaper countries. Politicians hence *think* they are compelled to reform their welfare state systems in order to prevent such developments and to remain competitive.

Of course, such arguments cannot be dismissed entirely. Pay differentials play an important part in global investment decision-making, but so do social peace and harmony, social investments made by governments, and the overall productivity, that is, ability and motivation of the workforce.

Relocation of production facilities is a significant aspect of globalization, it is a major lever for reducing the costs of the labor factor. However, this can be achieved only to a certain limit. It is not possible to relocate all sorts of production, and too high unemployment rates and too low wages harm mass' purchasing power and deteriorate growth prospects.

But is this really the true story. If the theory of a deterioration of the competitive position by high social spending is to be true, states with high social spending would have experience difficulties with their competitive position.

In point of fact, no matter what ranking you use, be it a list of the richest countries of the world compiled by the World Bank or the competitiveness index made up by the World Economic Forum, the top positions are always taken by European states which mostly hold the highest social spending, by it welfare states in Northern and Continental Europe.

With the exception of the United States, the classical competitors of Europe on the world market, e.g. Taiwan, South Korea and Japan have also increased the proportion of their social spending lately, partly even quite remarkably—cf the Conservative welfare regime in Table 2.2.

In view of that the connection between economic performance and social security is complex and cannot be explained by simplifying acclamations like that who spends less on social services is in a better competitive position a priori. For instance, the *Growth Competitiveness Index* of the World Economic Forum lists eight states with a social spending proportion of more than 25 percent of the GDP among the *top ten*. Scandinavian states hold the top positions.

In 2006/2007, Switzerland, Finland and Sweden are the world's most competitive economies according to *The Global Competitiveness Report,* based on extensive data compiled by the World Economic Forum (WEF, 2007). Denmark, Singapore, the United States, Japan, Germany, the Netherlands, and the United Kingdom completed the top-ten list. It needs to note that the United States had shown the most pronounced drop, falling from first to sixth place. Switzerland which came in first place has extended is base of social spending, having become the top four social spender in Western Europe, tightly behind Sweden and other Nordic countries (Wang and Aspalter, 2006).

European social policy has begun to see the merits of the Social Democratic welfare regime for some time now. As a matter of fact, the Social Democratic welfare regime may become a paragon for a future European social policy, as Europe is marked by a steady but constant progress in terms of universalization or quasi-universalization of welfare benefits and services (cf Deacon, 2005)—take e.g. the example of universalistic benefits of long-term care services or high level benefits in the area of family/child allowance in Austria, France, and Germany, or e.g. the universalistic features of health care systems in Italy, Spain, France, and Slovenia.

Welfare states in the Social Democratic welfare regime, according to empirical outcomes and facts, are "the most efficient and effective" welfare state system, which are able to fully support both economic development *and* social development. And this is the case because they invest in a smart, healthy, and active workforce and population, and especially its increasing aged population (cf Walker, 2002, Walker and Aspalter, 2008). On the other hand, there are still doubts about the possibility of the Social Democratic model really becoming the new paragon for European social policy as a whole (cf WEF, 2006).

Not too long time ago, the European Commission Directorate-General for Employment and Social Affairs commissioned a study on costs of non-social policy, which emphasizes these connections decidedly and makes clear that social policy as a whole constitutes an important productive factor. It proves meticulously that a flourishing economy wants public efforts in the field of social protection, and even constitutes a vital precondition for high economic growth.

It is for this reason that those who put the case for cuts in social services also put economic prosperity on the stake(cf Fourage, 2003). Perhaps we find it (still) difficult to propagate this. In a nutshell, we would like to conclude that *the social costs of non-social policy are high and the consequences of non-social policy are dramatic.*

REFERENCES

Alesina, Alberto and Glaeser, Edward L. (2004), *Fighting Poverty in the US and Europe: A World of Difference*, Oxford University Press: Oxford, UK.

Aspalter, Christian (2001a), *Importance of Christian and Social Democratic Movements in Welfare Politics: With Special Reference to Germany, Austria and Sweden*, Nova Science: New York.

Aspalter, Christian (2001b), *Conservative Welfare State Systems in East Asia*, Praeger: Westport, CT.

Aspalter, Christian (2005), East Asian Welfare Regime, in N.T. Tan (ed.), *The Challenge of Social Care in Asia*, Marshall Cavendish: New York.

Aspalter, Christian (2006), The East Asian Welfare Model, *International Journal of Social Welfare*, Vol. 15, pp. 290-301.

Aspalter, Christian (2007a), *From Neoliberal Discourse to the Real-Politik of Increased Social Intervention: A Worldwide Comparison*, paper presented at the conference on Reasserting the Public Hand, Lee Kwan Yew School of Government, National University of Singapore, Singapore, September 29-30.

Aspalter, Christian (2007b), The Asian Cure for Health Care, *Far Eastern Economic Review*, Vol. 170, No. 9, pp. 56-59.

Bode, Ingo (2003), The Welfare State in Germany: Corporatism and the German Welfare Model, in C. Aspalter (ed.), *Welfare Capitalism Around the World*, Casa Verde: Hong Kong.

Deacon, Bob (2005), From Safety Nets Back to Universal Social Provision: Is the Global Tide Turning?, *Global Social Policy*, Vol. 5, No. 1, pp. 19-28.

Esping-Andersen, Gøsta (1987), The Comparison of Policy Regimes, in M. Rein and G. Esping-Andersen (eds), *Stagnation and Renewal in Social Policy*, M.E. Sharpe: New York.

Esping-Andersen, Gøsta (1990), *The Three Worlds of Welfare Capitalism*, Polity: Cambridge, MA.

Esping-Andersen, Gøsta (1998), The Three Political Economies of the Welfare State, in J. O'Connor and G.M. Olsen (eds.), *Power Resources Theory and the Welfare State: A Critical Approach*, University of Toronto Press: Toronto, Canada.

Esping-Andersen, Gøsta and Hicks, Alexander (2006), Comparative and Historical Studies of Public Policy and the Welfare State, in T. Janoski, R.R. Alford, A.M. Hicks, and M.A. Schwartz (eds.), *The Handbook of Political Sociology: States, Civil Societies, and Globalization*, Cambridge University Press: Cambridge, UK.

Ferrera, Maurizio (2005), *The Boundaries of Welfare: European Integration and the New Spatial Politics of Social Solidarity*, Oxford University Press: Oxford, UK.

Ferrera, Maurizio and Gualmini, Elisabetta (2004), *Rescued by Europe?: Social and Labour Market Reforms in Italy from Maastricht to Berlusconi*, Amsterdam University Press: Amsterdam, The Netherlands.

Fourage, Didier (2003), Costs of Non-Social Policy: Towards an Economic Framework of Quality Social Policies—and the Costs of Not Having Them, Report for the Employment and Social Affairs DG, European Commission, Brussels, *europa.eu.int*.

Garland, David (2002), The Culture of Control: Crime and Social Order in Contemporary Society, Oxford University Press: Oxford, UK.

Gilbert, Neil (2004), Transformation of the Welfare State, The Silent Surrender of Public Responsibility, Oxford University Press: Oxford, UK.

Goodin, Robert E. (2003), Perverse Principles of Welfare Reform, in D. Pieters (ed.), *European Social Security and Global Politics*, Kluwer Law International: London.

Huber, Evelyne and Stephens, John D. (2001), *Development and Crisis of the Welfare State: Parties and Policies in Global Markets*, University of Chicago Press: Chicago, IL.

Judt, Tony (2005), *Postwar: A History of Europe*, Penguin: London.

Kersbergen, Kees v. (1995), *Social Capitalism, A Study of Christian Democracy and the Welfare State*, Routledge: London.

Kingfisher, Catherine (1996), *Women in the American Welfare Trap*, University of Pennsylvania Press: Philadelphia, PA.

Kingfisher, Catherine (ed.) (2002), *Western Welfare in Decline, Globalization and Women's Poverty*, University of Pennsylvania Press: Philadelphia, PA.

OECD (2005a), *OECD in Figures*, Statistics on the Member Countries, OECD: Paris.

OECD (2005b) OECD Employment Outlook, *www.oecd.org*.

Rand, Ayn (2000, 1943), *Der Ursprung*, Gewis: Augsburg, Germany.

Rifkin, Jeremy (2004), *Der Europäische Traum: Die Vision einer leisen Supermacht*, Fischer: Frankfurt am Main, Germany.

Wacquant, Loïc (1998), In den USA wird Armut bekämpft, indem man sie kriminalisiert, *Le Monde diplomatique*, German edition, July 10.

Wacquant, Loïc (2004), The Penalization of Poverty and the Rise of Neoliberalism, in T. Freytag and M. Hawel (eds.), *Arbeit und Utopie*, Humanities: Frankfurt am Main, Germany.

Walker, Alan (2002), A Strategy for Active Ageing, *International Social Security Review*, Vol. 55, No. 1, pp. 121-39.

Walker, Alan and Aspalter, Christian (eds.) (2008), *Securing the Future for Old Age in Europe*, Casa Verde: Hong Kong.

Wang, Dominique and Aspalter, Christian (2006), The Austrian and the Swiss Welfare State System in International Comparison, *Journal of Societal and Social Policy*, Vol. 5, No. 2, pp. 25-45.

WEF, World Economic Forum (2006), *The Global Competitiveness Report 2005-2006*, World Economic Forum: London.

WEF, World Economic Forum (2007), *The Global Competitiveness Report 2006-2007*, World Economic Forum: London.

Weidenholzer, Josef (2001a), Muss der Wohlfahrtstaat neu konzipiert werden?, in C. Stelzer-Orthofer *et al.* (eds.), *Zwischen Welfare und Workfare: Soziale Leistungen in der Diskussion*, Sozialwissenschaftliche Vereinigung: Linz, Austria.

Weidenholzer, Josef (2001b), A European Social Model?, in C. Aspalter and J. Weidenholzer (eds.), *Welfare State Development in East Asia*, Sozialwissenschaftliche Vereinigung: Linz, Austria.

3

The Social Dimension of the European Union

PETER ABRAHAMSON

Since the formation of the Coal and Steel Union in 1955 and the European Communities in 1958 the European cooperation has both widened and deepened. The original six countries (France, Germany, Italy, the Netherlands, Belgium and Luxembourg) have gradually been joined with many other countries. The European Union now comprise of 27 member states. Bulgaria and Romania have joined the EU in January, 2007. The areas of common policy has also expanded since the early beginnings, but with regard to social policies developments have been cautious; yet extended economic integration has meant an extension of social rights defined at a European level through the so-called social dimension. This article is about the most recent developments of social citizenship within the European Union. It will be demonstrated how the boundaries and content of the European social space are expanding and developing through the interactions between national and European regulation and intervention.

To begin with European regulation of social citizenship was confined to the question of equal treatment (of men and women) and social protecttion of migrant workers; later, issues of work environment was incorporated; but it was not until the introduction of the European Single Market, which was to be completed immediately after 1992, that the social dimension gained momentum. The reasons were the combined fear of social dumping and social tourism voiced most strongly by the Commission.

The central idea with the Single Market was the introduction of the four freedoms: free passage across the borders of capital, commodities, services and labor power in order to increase and improve competition conditions. By social dumping is understood a situation where the individual Member States in order to facilitate their national enterprises under these conditions of increased competition is holding back on, or even cutting back, social protection. By doing that companies would have to pay there employers less or the same in wages because taxes would not increase and the same goes for employers and workers contributions it was speculated.

Another anticipated aspect of social dumping was investments disproportionately going to the areas of Europe where social and environmental protection was the least developed. Social dumping is a scenario of a race to the bottom regarding social protection. By social tourism is understood a situation where marginalized segments of the various populations migrate to the areas within Europe where social protection is most generous. The consequence would be a movement of poor people from the South to the North, simultaneously with investments moving from North to South. Such movements were considered inappropriate by the Commission and an expansion of the Social Dimension should be the answer to these stipulated problems (Abrahamson, 2004a).

On the other hand, the European cooperation has always been cautious when the question of a European social citizenship came up. Welfare systems are differently structured across Europe, and Member States have been rather protective of their own particular setup. Hence, harmonization of social protection systems, initially suggested by the Commission in the 1960s has been rejected, and since then discussions have instead been about coordination of the different systems. This coordination has since the 1980s taken place within the tension between on the one hand wanting to prevent social dumping and social tourism, and on the other hand preserving the autonomy of the various welfare regimes. The result has been a situation where decisions on social protection have to be unanimous, i.e. any Member States can veto a suggestion it does not approve of.

More and more the welfare state debate is borrowing its metaphors from sciences focusing on space and place like architecture, geography and planning (cf e.g. Offe, 2003; Esping-Andersen *et al.*, 2002; Ferrera, 2003, 2005; Castel, 2000; Jenson, 2004; MacKinnon, 2004). This indicates that contemporary changes in welfare state provision are dealing with new locations and new borders. Control over and administration of social and other welfare policies are simultaneously gravitating towards the local level and the supra national level in Europe and as a tendency also elsewhere.[1] The borders of jurisdiction concerning social rights and obligations are changing and new spaces for implementation of welfare provision are created.

These changes in place and space of welfare are triggered by an increase in *mobility* across the globe of both information, people, capital, goods and services. These processes are usually named globalization. The aim of this chapter is to consider consequences for the well being of citizens when the foundation of social rights and obligations are being globalized. The European Union is taken as the case.

Two Different Modes of Regulation: Hard and Soft Law

Formally speaking interventions from the EU institutions into the Member States can take two forms: hard and soft law. Hard law is stipulations that has to be followed and if not, can be sanctioned; it comes in the form of:

(a) regulations, which have direct judicial effect in all Member States,
(b) directives which must be implemented in national legislation,
(c) the rulings of the European Court of Justice (ECJ), and
(d) the formulations of the Treaties.

Soft law is a label for stipulations formulated as recommendations, solemn declarations, resolutions and action programs. These cannot be sanctioned if not followed in other ways than "shaming and blaming." Hitherto, the vast majority of interventions in the area of social protection have come in the form of various soft law initiatives; exceptions are the Recommendation 1408/71 which coordinates social protection for migrant workers (but only EU citizens, hence—so far—excluding third country nationals), the directive on child care, which nevertheless is very vague in its stipulations, and a few court rulings (especially the Kohll and Dekker rulings from 1998 and 1999) that some observers have characterized as potentially path breaking. Instead quite a number of soft law initiatives have been taken especially during the last 20 years, starting with the solemn declaration on rights of workers from 1987, the resolution on combating social exclusion from 1989, the action program to combat social exclusion of the least privileged from 1990 to 1994, the Commission White Paper on the Future of Social Protection in Europe also from 1994, and last, but perhaps not least, the adoption of the Open Method of Coordination in 1997, which was first applied to the area of employment, then extended in 2000 to the areas of social inclusion, and now also involving pensions and health and long-term care (Abrahamson, 2004a).

The Theoretical Perspective: De- and Re-Territorialization

There are very important theoretical reasons for considering space when post-industrial or post-modern welfare provision is under investigation. As Krishan Kumar sums it up:

> "With the devaluation of time comes the elevation of space. The plane of the timeless present is the spatial. If things do not get their significance from their place in history they can receive it only from their distribution in space. Post-modernity traffics in the contemporaneous and the simultaneous, in synchronic rather than diachronic time. Relations of nearness and distance in space, rather than in time, become the measure of significance" (Kumar, 1995: 146).

The future of European welfare is caught in the tension between the local and the global.[2] The condition of post-modernity is one that emphasizes the locality and views the nation state as of declining importance in general. This goes for the area of politics where (not so new) social movements, rather than traditional nation-wide political parties and trade unions, carry the potential for changes, and they are very often concerned about issues confined to localities. On the other hand, the importance of place is also expressed through the processes which are now being named globalization as already pointed to by David Harvey:

"the more unified the space, the more important the qualities of the fragmentations become for social identity and action. The free flow of capital across the surface of the globe ... places strong emphasis on the particular quality of the spaces to which that capital might be attracted. The shrinkage of space that brings diverse communities across the globe into competition with each other implies localized competitive strategies and a heightened sense of awareness of what makes a place special and gives it a competitive advantage. This kind of reaction looks much more strongly to the identification of place, the building and signaling of its unique qualities in an increasingly homogeneous but fragmented world" (Harvey, 1998: 271).

Zygmunt Bauman (2000) has coined the concept of *liquid modernity* to describe contemporary society. It is hence indicated that our time is indeed modern, but as already Karl Marx foresaw in 1848: "everything solid melts into air" (Marx and Engels, 1970: 17).[3] What distinguishes liquid modernity from early modernity is the lack of stable institutions. There is no condition; everything is process. With liquid or fluid modernity the relationship between time and space has been altered. Modernity started by the separation of time and space from living practice and from one another as opposed to pre-modern time when they were inseparable.

In early modernity space was the dominant category. Citizenship, e.g., was (and is) bound to space. However, now "power can move with the speed of the electronic signal—and so the time required for the movement of its essential ingredients has been reduced to instantaneity.

For all practical purposes, power has become truly *exterritorial*" (Bauman, 2000: 10-11). Bauman talks about the "revenge of nomadism over the principle of territoriality and settlement. In the fluid stage of modernity, the settled majority is ruled by the nomadic and exterritorial elite" (Bauman, 2000: 13). While *trust* and *confidence* were constitutive of early modernity, *risk* and *uncertainty* is now the hallmark of liquid modernity. He finds that "the present-day uncertainty is a powerful individualizing force. It divides instead of uniting" (Bauman, 2001a: 24).

The spatial consequences of current developments is summarized as follows: "the new fragmentation of the city space, shrinkage and disappearance of public spaces, falling apart of urban community, separation and segregation—and above the exteritorriality of the new elite and the forced territoriality of the rest" (Bauman, 1998: 23). So, spatial differentiation in a globalizing world works very differently for the affluent majority and the deprived minority. The former transgresses space while the latter is confined to the ghettos. In *Wasted Lives* (Bauman, 2004: 41) the reference is to (economic) immigrants and asylum seekers who are considered superfluous, hence connecting to those characterized as vagabonds in some of his other writings. Furthermore, the criminalization of these poor people on the move is done through associating them with the great new fear of our time: terrorism (Bauman, 2004: 54). According to Bauman we have moved away from the social state which was committed to inclusion to an exclusionary state, committed to criminal justice and penal or crime control following the considerations of criminalizing the poor (Bauman, 2004: 67; for a more comprehensive discussion of Bauman and current welfare state issues, cf Abrahamson, 2004b).

The paradox is that the more modernity turns liquid the more significance is attached to space and place: "A bizarre adventure happened to space on the road to globalization: it lost its importance while gaining in significance" (Bauman, 2001b: 110). In the following two spatial takes on contemporary welfare state developments are presented as new welfare state architecture and new welfare state geography.

A New Welfare State Architecture

Recently, some scholars have started applying architectural metaphors when discussing welfare state structures and developments (cf e.g. Castles, 2004). The most common metaphor is, of course, the house. The welfare state can be portrayed as a building with various floors, rooms, a foundation and a roof.[4] Thus, e.g. Claus Offe (2003: 450-51) stated:

The welfare state is an accumulation of status rights that must not be earned, but come as an original endowment of "social" citizenship. It can be visualized as an edifice that was erected over a period of more than one and a half centuries in what is now the OECD world. Very schematically speaking, this structure of security has three floors and a roof. Each of the floors is—and has always been since its inception— the scene of a dynamic process of ongoing remodeling, expansion, partial demolition, reconstruction, and innovation.

Actually, according to Offe (2003: 451) the house also has a *basement*: here "the non-working poor are dealt with trough programs of welfare and poverty relief"—but otherwise the house is composed in the following way:

1. *The ground floor* contains provisions regulating access to labor markets and to jobs and issues of health and safety *at work*.

2. *The second floor* is the scene of provisions pertaining to the ("social") security of the wage worker *outside* of work.

3. On *the third floor*, the institutional devices are located which are intended to deal with the decline of workers' capacity to defend their income. The institutional pattern that serve this purpose is trade unionism and the making of collective wage arrangements, including its ultimate weapon of strike action.

4. Finally, *the roof* of the building, it protects the integrity of the entire building and prevents its lower parts from being damaged. It includes labor market and employment policies, together with the monetary, fiscal, trade, and economic policies which are designed

to promote and maintain "full" employment on which the security of the three security arrangements critically depends (Offe, 2003: 451-53.)

The building is under change, or even threatened—some would argue—because of globalization. Offe distinguishes three social forces with each their solution to the challenges of globalization: reluctant social democrats, aggressive market liberals, and more or less militant rightist populists: the former advocate restoring full employment and a maintenance of welfare state institutions; the liberals, on the contrary see welfare institutions as an impediment for high employment, and, therefore want to reduce their scope and generosity; finally the latter argue that the only way to maintain social protection of national workers and citizens is to seal off national borders to "foreign people, foreign workers, foreign goods, and those praying to 'foreign' gods" (Offe, 2003: 454). So, consequences for the (in this case "European") welfare state are different according to the power and combination of the three different ideological dynamics or discourses. In the liberal case, the "architecture of security [sic!] is gradually demolished giving way to an impoverished version of the liberal equality of rights ... or ... a populist backlash will be triggered by the repercussions of internationalization, resulting in potentially most illiberal forms of paternalistic protectionism ... [or] some functional equivalent of security-enhancing status rights will be transferred from the nation-state to the supranational forms of organization" (Offe, 2003: 456).

In the first case the house is changing shape from a three storey building with an effective roof and basement to a suburban single storey house with no basement and a flat roof, that—which is well known by home owners during the 1970s—do not offer the same protection against rain as the former tilted roofs. This is every-one for himself and protection through insurance; the poor have been chased out of the basement and into the ghettos, and the other floors have been abandoned.

The second scenario is "Fortress Europe," in the housing allegory it is castles surrounded by ramparts and moats; virtually inaccessible unless invited with no-man's-lands in between where immigrants and refugees are trying to make a living as out-laws (i.e., *sans papiers*).

Finally, a stronger "Social Europe" is the last scenario where maintenance of the roof and some of the floors are transferred away from the nation state and on to the European institutions.

An equally illustrative metaphor can be applied to descriptions of pension systems which often, albeit maybe unconsciously, borrow from the architecture of All India Railways' sleeper wagons which are composed of first, second and third tier bunks plus a smaller secluded "women's" compartment at one end of the car. Transferred to pension systems, the first tier is the bottom public state (often) universal provision; the second tier consists of negotiated/contractually defined occupational pensions organized corporately with employers; and the third tier refers to various private pension savings individual citizens may have arranged via financial institutions or investment in home ownership.

Historically privileged groups such as civil servants and military personnel have their separate systems. Most citizens (in the developed world) have access to a first tier bunk in their old age train travel; those in steady organized employment will, furthermore, have a second and much more comfortable second tier bunk at their disposal (allowing for servants or family members to occupy the bottom bunk); and, finally, those who have been able (and willing) to put away private savings will have earned the right to a third tier bunk (so that their luggage can be stowed there and travel safely). At the bottom of the wagon in their segregated compartment we find the retired civil and military officers of the state where the placement, size and comfortability of the bunks are arranged according to prior status of the civil servant occupying it.

Current discussions over pension systems in Europe are all about the availability, accessibility, comfortability, size, and, of course, price and financing of the various pension tiers. Tendencies are that the bottom tier bunks on the old age trains are getting harder and narrower, while the second tier bolstered ones are getting more expensive, and since they are wider, there are fewer of them, yet more are put in since more citizens have entered occupational pension schemes. More and more, if one wants to travel in style in old age command over a third tier bunk is, if not absolutely essential, at least highly desirable. The separated women's compartments are getting smaller and smaller while waiting to be phased out.

These changes are gradually applied when the old age trains make their stops at the time stations. Hence, changes in pension policies alter the layout of pension systems. Metaphorically speaking, the rooms sheltering pensioners are decomposed or restructured. The architecture of old-age risk management changes. (For a more conventional and referenced discussion of pension systems in Europe, cf e.g. Abrahamson *et al.*, forthcoming.)

A New Welfare State Geography

Geography is the study of places and spaces.[5] Spaces are defined by their borders or boundaries. They decide who is inside and who is outside. So, when the talk is about geography of welfare, it is about its borders, and when it comes to a changing geography of welfare, what is meant is that its borders are changing. Yet, we have learned from Stein Rokkan (1987, 1999a,b) that space has two dimensions: a territorial one and a membership one (cf also Flora, 1999).

During the golden years of the welfare state, or the *trente glorieuse*, the two dimensions were identical in the sense that the welfare state viewed as the sum of social rights enjoyed by its citizens and the boundaries of the welfare state coincided. Citizens were in this connection defined as those residing legally within the territory of the nation-state. This affinity has been challenged by the development of the last 30 years: authority is being transferred from the national level to both the local/regional level and to the supra-national level. In what follows the focus is on the supra-nationalization of the welfare state.

According to Maurizio Ferrera (2003: 632) expansion of EU regulations—and especially court rulings—has gradually eroded the following:

1. *National Control Over Beneficiaries*. In compliance with freedom of movement, Member States can no longer restrict welfare state access to their on citizens only.

2. *Spatial Control Over Consumption*. Benefits paid by each member state (e.g. a pension) have become portable across the whole internal market, and the insured of a given national system can increasingly shop around and consume services of the other EU systems (e.g. in the field of health care).

3. *Exclusivity of Coverage in Their Own Territory*. Member States are increasingly obliged to accept the "infiltration" within their territory of other countries' regimes e.g. posted workers remaining under the jurisdiction of the country of employment.

4. *Control Over Access to the Status of the Benefit Producer*. In compliance with the active freedom of service, states must grant access to foreign providers into their national welfare systems (e.g. in the case of supplementary, second-tier insurance).

5. *Control Over Administrative Case Adjudication*. The member state must in fact accept that the determination of beneficiary status (e.g., of being "sick" or "disabled") be carried out by the bureaucratic agencies of other Member States.

As a consequence of these processes, European welfare states have witnessed increasing erosion of their external boundaries and of their capacity to control them. This, in turn has meant a "significant redrawing of social citizenship boundaries" both with respect to the territorial dimension—a new European (i.e., EU) space has been created—and with respect to the membership dimension. Here, "the main novelty is the cap posed on statutory, first-pillar schemes and the emergence of an increasingly salient space occupied by supplementary (second-pillar) and private (third-pillar) schemes: a space that extends beyond the reach of obligatory affiliation and public monopoly on provision" (Ferrera, 2003: 640).

Following the same line of thought and also applying the framework developed by Rokkan,[6] Luis Moreno and Bruno Palier confront the obvious convergence of economic policies within the European Union with the much more complicated trends regarding the governance of social policies. They identify a quest for decentralization which they view as a response to a demand for territorial subsidiarity:

> In a European and global perspective ... the harmonization of economic development has gone hand in hand with the decentralization of political institutions and the regionalization of welfare development. Sub-state layers of government have found in the principle of European subsidiarity a renewed impulse for the running of public affairs, and new opportunities for policy experimentation (Moreno and Palier, 2004: 10).

They conclude with regard to functional developments that "welfare policies have faced a progressive adaptation to the demands of deregulation and flexibility." They find that all EU countries are facing the same new social risks of increased female labor market participation, the "graying" of society, the increase in social exclusion among low skilled people, and privatization and deregulation of public benefits and services. They claim that "recipes to meet new risk challenges are analogous in the four European welfare regimes" (Moreno and Palier, 2004: 19). Taken together this must add up to a convergence of welfare regimes in Europe. Regarding changes in the territorial dimension they claim:

> The polycentric nature of Europeanization and the multi-tier structuring of European institutions do not lead to the constitution of the United States of Europe along the lines of the American experience. Rather, it confronts a gradual and necessarily "slow" process of accommodating cultural, historical and political diversity within the Old Continent while respecting the principles of democratic accountability and territorial subsidiarity (Moreno and Palier, 2004: 19-20).

Concerning the new form of governance applied to the European Union, the Open method of Coordination (OMC) it is considered in congruence with what has happened to economic policies, i.e. a Europeanization in this case safeguarding coherence and coordination.

Rulings of the European Court of Justice: An Example of Hard Law

Both in the territorial sense and in the membership sense the European Court of Justice (ECJ) is changing the European social space. Three court decisions seem to be path breaking in this respect. The first two are the "twin" cases of Kohll and Dekker. They are both concerning citizens from Luxembourg. The first case is about purchasing a pair of glasses in Belgium; the second about dental surgery in Germany (for the daughter). After returning home they both claim the expenditure from their health insurance, and are both denied reimbursement. The court ruled that the services were covered by the right to move freely among the Member States and they should be reimbursed. After the Kohll and Dekker rulings the internal borders regarding health care have potentially been erased by the ECJ. As Ferrera (2003: 635) sums it up: "The Kohll (1998) and Dekker (1999) cases are unquestionably of great importance for the neutralization of territoriality conditions in EU health care systems."

The third case is Martinez Sala which is about a Spanish woman which had been residing in Germany since she was 12 years old and who applied for child benefits in 1993 in connection with her pregnancy. Since she was not active in the labor market at the time of application the authorities denied her benefits; but the court ruled that all citizens have the right to free movement, not only economically active citizens, and she should be granted child benefits (Wind, 2000).

Furthermore, the ECJ has, successively, interpreted the concept of worker wider and wider so that it now includes spouse and children; and also students and pensioners are now regarded either potential or previous workers and are enjoying the right of free movement and the social rights of workers at the place of residence. Also the amount of hours needed to be worked weekly has been reduced by the court, so that part-time employed are now enjoying social protection on par with full time employees. By these rulings the ECJ has changed the citizenship dimension of the European social space. It has decided that many more categories of people are to be considered inside than was hitherto the understanding.

This development can be understood within the perspective of an increasing awareness of recognition and a decreasing awareness of inequality in welfare state discussions. As Axel Honneth (2004: 351) wrote:

> "Through to the 1980s ... there could be no doubt as to the guiding principle of a normative theory of a political order ... there was agreement in calling for the elimination of all such inequalities as could not be justified with reasonable arguments. For some time now, this influential idea of justice, which can be comprehended politically as an expression of a social democratic epoch, seems to have been replaced by a new idea ... Here it is no longer the elimination of inequality which appears to represent the normative aim, but the avoidance of humiliation or disrespect; 'equal distribution' or 'equality of goods' no longer forms its central categories, but 'dignity' or 'respect ... [or in the words of] Nancy Fraser ... a transition from the idea of 'redistribution' to the notion of 'recognition.'"

Social policy court rulings are not about changing distribution of resources, but abut who can be recognized as citizens eligible for certain welfare rights.

The Open Method of Coordination: An Example of Soft Law

Since the Amsterdam Treaty effective from 1997 the European Union has implemented a new form of governance now known as the Open Method of Coordination (OMC). It is a soft law instrument where the European Council, i.e. the intergovernmental bi-annually meeting of the heads of states or governments, decide on a number of objectives and bench marks on a certain policy area. It is then left to the Member States themselves to choose the means they see fit to reach the goals. The means shall be written into a national action plan, and later the achieved results must be reported to the European Commission which then evaluates to what extent the previously set goals have actually been achieved. If performance proved to be unsatisfactory the sanctions are soft, in the realm of "shaming" and "blaming." In the White Book on European Governance from 2001 the European commission defined the OMC thus:

The open method of coordination is used on a case by case basis. It is a way of encouraging co-operation, the exchange of best practice and agreeing common targets and guidelines for Member States, sometimes backed up by national action plans as in the case of employment and social exclusion. It relies on regular monitoring of progress to meet those targets, allowing Member States to compare their efforts and learn from the experience of others. In some areas, such as employment and social policy or immigration policy, it sits alongside the program-based and legislative approach; in others, it adds value at a European level where there is little scope for legislative solutions (EC, 2001: 21).

The OMC was first applied to the area of employment and resulted in drafting of the so-called National Action Plans (NAPs) in which the Member States should explain how they expected to improve national employment conditions.

With the Lisbon summit in 2000 the method was expanded to the area of social exclusion, and here the heads of states adopted some very specific benchmarks to be met: From 2000 to 2010 overall employment should be increased from 61 to 65 percent; unemployment should be reduced to four pct; female employment should be up from 51 to more than 60 percent; poverty should be reduced from 18 to 15 percent, and child poverty should be halved. Furthermore, by 2001 all schools should be connected to the internet and all teachers should be "computer literate" by 2002, and there should be a 50 percent reduction in 18 to 24 year-olds with neither tenth grade nor education. These goals have, however not been met, and the commission and the council have had to develop a "revised Lisbon agenda" which fits better to the realities in Europe (EC, 2006: 5; Council of Ministers, 2006).

Nevertheless, the OMC are been extended to more and more policy areas. In 2003 pensions were included with the following three major objectives: adequate, sustainable and future prove. By adequate is meant that pensioners in the future can expect a reasonable level of living enabling them to participate in the public, cultural and social life of their communities, and this should happen with due respect to solidarity within as well as between generations. By sustainability is meant that there must exist a high level of employment in the Member States; that there are incentives to stay in the labor market, and that both public finances as well as private pension funds are economically "sound."

This again implies a balance between labor market flexibility and mobility; no gender discrimination; that pension systems is transparent, predictable and adjustable. The indicators to demonstrate goal achievement were the following: disposable income of those 65 and older should be around 90 percent of the younger cohorts; the risk of poverty should not greatly exceed that of the rest of the population, even it is expected to increase with age. Furthermore, the employment goals already defined in Lisbon are repeated, and the average retirement age should be increased by five years (Glynos, 2003).

Most recently, the areas of elderly care and health care have come under the OMC with some very broad objectives: easy access for everyone; quality and financial sustainability. Ferrera (2005) cites Zeitlin for judging that the OMC has had the following effects:

1. Both the employment and social exclusion processes have contributed to substantive changes within Member States which have led to broad shifts in policy orientation.

2. Participation to the OMC has induced procedural shifts in social policy governance, e.g. through administrative reorganizations and institutional capacity building for overall policy steering.

3. A growing mobilization of sub-national and non-state actors are clearly visible around both processes: regions, municipalities, the social partners and various advocacy networks from civil society, representing the views of stakeholder groups, are increasingly directing their attention and efforts towards both processes.

4. Through the OMC some (admittedly still limited) mutual learning dynamics have taken place.

A more pessimistic evaluation was given by Bea Cantillon (2004: 15) when she wrote: "It should be noted that the OMCs that are already in place have not been very successful. In the case of the OMC on social exclusion, this is primarily due to the fact that the output indicators—however important they may be—are not really operational for policy-makers." She does, however, suggest how they could become more potent: "If the OMC on inclusion could be coupled with an OMC on social protection, i.e. if a political link could be made at the European level between such output indicators such as poverty, income inequality and unemployment on the one hand and social protection on the other, then the political impact of European peer review might be much greater than it is at present" (Cantillon, 2004: 16).

An interesting interpretation of the OMC is given by Annikke Savio and Elina Palola (2004). Rather than getting the inspiration from Rok-kan, the spirit of Foucault is felt in their writing. They see the OMC as a sign which shows that the "EU social policy has left its customary place and has become a project to invent the social[7] within the confines of the European Union" (Savio and Palola, 2004: 2). They give an historical outline of the development of "Social Europe," and, interestingly, they trace the term to its Francophone original as "*l'espace sociale*," i.e. the social space or domain; a spatial term! They argue that this space is being transformed by the implementation of the OMC. Earlier the con-flicts and debates revolved around whether to try and harmonize or, at least aim at conversion of national social policies by giving more com-petences to the European institutions, or leave all developments to the individual Member States. However, after Lisbon, it has no longer been relevant to make a distinction between EU-level and national level in the area of social policy. Based on the new definition of competences in the area of social policy, it is now recognized to achieve a common modernization of social protection systems in EU member countries by way of applying the OMC:

By this method the Member States have committed themselves to translating the EU's social aspirations to their national practices. This means that with the Lisbon strategy, the Union turned its attention away from the differences of national welfare state arrangements and gave up the attempts to create convergence between the Anglo-Saxon and Central, Northern and Southern European models (Savio and Palola, 2004: 4).

If we force upon Savio and Palola the Rokkan scheme they argue with respect to the functional division that a change has taken place from passive income support to an active welfare state based on incentives to work. They apply, true to their methodology, a governmentality approach to the analyses of the various technologies that the European institutions, first and foremost the European Council, since this is the institution that endorsed and contextualized the OMC, are implementing. They write: "It is perhaps in the case of poverty and social exclusion that shaping subjects is most obvious in the OMC: you must (by work incentives) liberate and capitalize yourself and make full use of your resources" (Savio and Palola, 2004: 8-9). It can be summed up as promoting a do-it-yourself society and can be conceptualized as "responsibilization."

Regarding what Rokkan would label the territorial dimension Savio and Palola claimed that "post Lisbon social policy no longer recognizes *boundaries* between the Union and the Member State. It makes all actors in society capable of participating in the exercise of political power within the Union" (Savio and Palola, 2004: 13). Via the OMC the European Council and Commission can, so to say, by-pass the nation states and address and involve the various actors directly.

Conclusion

From Bauman we learned that in liquid modernity space has become more significant, but that space means very different things to middle class citizens and to marginalized segments of the population. The mobile elites can transport their entitlements across space, while the poor are more and more confined to their ghettos and to an increased monitoring and control. He pinpointed the development as one away from the social state toward the exclusionary state. This dystopia is an extrapolation of the liberal turn in welfare state development and the particular European Union development can, to some extent, be seen as a counter movement to tendencies toward individualization, segregation and criminalization of the poor.

With reference to the metaphor of a new welfare state architecture the vision of a "Fortress Europe" was unfolded where the poorest are either kept out or not formally recognized, resulting in a situation where they have no rights because they have no papers. This is a political perspective currently gaining ground in many European nation states, but it is strongly condemned within the European Union institutions. By a new welfare state geography for Europe was indicated a change of borders and membership definitions. Increasingly the nation states are experiencing an erosion of their boundaries and membership is increasingly dependent upon contributory systems and less so on residency. This has come about as gradual adaptations to demands for deregulation and flexibility. Both the new welfare architecture and geography point toward liberal leanings with a stronger emphasis on individualization, marketization and differentiation.

Considering the development of rulings from the European Court of Justice it was shown that the concept of who is regarded a worker and, hence entitled to various benefits has been expanded considerably over time. It was also demonstrated that the court basically has dealt with who can be recognized as having social rights and it has not been concerned with the generosity of degree of compensation. Recognition and not redistribution has been the main consequence of court rulings with respect to social citizenship in Europe. The Open Method of Coordination is now the preferred soft law instrument applied within the European Union. It was interpreted that by this application the European Commission is able to by-pass national governments and deal directly with a multitude of actors on the sub-national level.

To cut a long story short, the overall tendency is that social citizenship rights are simultaneously being Europeanized and localized thus increasingly challenging the embeddedness of social rights at the nation state level.

Notes

1. The proliferation of free trade agreements and establishment of single markets across the globe are indication of the potential supra-nationalization of welfare provision. With the establishment of the free movement of capital, goods, services and workers, the so-called four freedoms, the call for coordination and harmonization of welfare policies were increasing as we have seen it within the European Union. In a document from the World Trade Organization (WTO) it was stated that: "The total number of RTAs [Regional Trade Agreements] identified in this study is 240, of which 172, or roughly 70 percent, were in force as of July 2000" (2000: 3). Very few of them are as encompassing as the European Union, yet the trend is clear. "Over half of them were concluded since 1990" Yeates (2005: 6) stated.

2. The interesting case of sub-state nationnalism and social policy is analyzed in Béland and Lecours (2005).

3. Concerning this point Bauman is very close to Karl Marx, as is evident from the following quotation: "All modernity means incessant, obsessive modernization (there is no modern *state* of modernity, only a *process*; modernity would cease being modernity the moment that the process ground to a halt); and *all* modernization consists in "disembedding," "disencumbering," "melting the solids," etc.; in other words in dismantling the received structures or at least weakening their grip" (Bauman, 2002: 4). Yet, he argues that the "melting the solids" which Marx referred to was only a means to an end: the establishment of new solids (Bauman, 2000: 3).

4. This metaphor was first brought to my attention by Nordic sociologist Olli Kangas during one of his presentations at the European Conference of Sociology in Amsterdam, the Netherlands 1999.

5. Except for the space which is left to astronomers.

6. "In order to identify reforms and paradigm changes in EU countries, our following analyses single out key developments in the two main dimensions of political life: the functional and the territorial, following Stein Rokkan's 'model of Europe'" (Moreno and Palier, 2004: 7).

7. Foucaultian sociologist Jacques Donzelot publicized the term the invention of the social when publishing his book *L'Invention du social: Essai sur le décline des passions politiques* in 1984; English translation of the central chapter in Donzelot (1988).

REFERENCES

Abrahamson, P. (2004a), Den sociale dimension i EU, in J.E. Larsen and I.H. Møller (eds.), *Socialpolitik*, Hans Reitzels: Copenhagen.

Abrahamson, P. (2004b), Liquid Modernity: Bauman on Contemporary Welfare Society, *Acta Sociologica*, Vol. 47, No. 2, pp. 171-79.

Abrahamson, P. *et al.* (forthcoming), The Role of the Different Actors in the Development of Social Policy, in Y. Jorens (ed.), *Social Protection of Migrant Workers in the New Europe*, forthcoming.

Bauman, Z. (1998), *Globalization: The Human Consequences*, Polity Press: Cambridge, UK.

Bauman, Z. (2000), *Liquid Modernity*, Polity Press: Cambridge, UK.

Bauman, Z. (2001a), *The Individualized Society*, Polity Press: Cambridge, UK.

Bauman, Z. (2001b), *Community: Seeking Safety in an Insecure World*, Polity Press: Cambridge, UK.

Bauman, Z. (2002), A Postmodern Grid of the Worldmap?, *Critique and Humanism*, www.eurozine.com.

Bauman, Z. (2004), *Wasted Lives: Modernity and Its Outcasts*, Polity: Cambridge, UK.

Béland, D. and Lecours, A. (2005), The Politics of Territorial Solidarity: Nationalism and Social Policy Reform in Canada, the United Kingdom, and Belgium, *Comparative Political Studies*, Vol. 38, No. 6: 676-703.

Cantillon, B. (2004), European Subsidiarity Versus American Social Federalism: Is Europe in Need of a Common Social Policy?, paper presented at the *ESPA-net Conference*, Oxford, UK, September

Castel, R. (2000), The Road to Disaffiliation, *International Journal of Urban and Regional Research*, Vol. 24, No. 3.

Castles, F. (2004), *The Future of the Welfare State: Crisis Myths and Crisis Realities*, Oxford University Press: Oxford, UK.

CM, Council of Ministers (2006), *Working Together, Working Better: A New Framework for the Open Coordination of Social Protection and Inclusion Policies in the European Union*, COM(2005)706.

Donzelot, J. (1988), The Promotion of the Social, *Economy and Society*, Vol. 17, No. 3, pp. 395-426.

Esping-Andersen, G.; Gallie; D. Hemerijck, A., and Myles, J. (2002), *Why We Need a New Welfare State*, Oxford University Press: Oxford, UK.

EC, European Commission (2001), *European Governance: A White Paper*, COM (2001) 428.

EC, European Commission (2006), *Implementation and Update Reports on 2003-2005 NAPs-Inclusion*, COM(2006) 62.

Ferrera, M. (2003), European Integration and National Social Citizenship: Changing Boundaries, New Structuring?, *Comparative Political Studies*, Vol. 36, No. 6, pp. 611-52.

Ferrera, M. (2005), *The Boundaries of Welfare: European Integration and the New Spatial Politics of Solidarity*, Oxford University Press: Oxford, UK.

Flora, P. (1999), Introduction and Interpretation, in P. Flora, S. Kuhnle, and D. Urwin (eds.), *State Formation, Nationbuilding, and Mass Politics in Europe: The Theory of Stein Rokkan*, Oxford University Press: Oxford, UK.

Glynos, G. (2003), The European Union and Pension Reform: Eurozone Membership and the Open Method of Coordination, paper presented the *Pension Reform Conference*, London School of Economics and Political Science, London, December.

Harvey, D. (1989), *The Condition of Post-Modernity*, Basil Blackwell: Oxford, UK.

Honneth, A. (2004), Recognition and Justice: Outline of a Plural Theory of Justice, *Acta Sociologica*, Vol. 47, No. 4, pp. 351-64.

Jenson, J. (2004), *Canada's New Social Risks: Directions for a New Social Architecture*, Canadian Policy Research Networks: Ottawa.

Kumar, K. (1995), *From Post-Industrial to Post-Modern Society: New Theories of the Contemporary World*, Blackwell: Oxford, UK.

MacKinnon, M.P. (2004), *Citizens' Values and the Canadian Social Architecture*, Canadian Policy Research Networks: Ottawa.

Marx, K. and Engels, F. (1970, 1848), *Det kommunistiske Manifest*, Tiden: Copenhagen.

Moreno, L. and Palier, B. (2004), The Europeanization of Welfare: Paradigm Shifts and Social Policy Reforms, paper presented at *ESPA-net Conference*, Oxford, UK, September.

Offe, C. (2003), The European Model of "Social" Capitalism: Can It Survive European Integration?, *Journal of Political Philosophy*, Vol. 11, No. 4, pp. 437-69.

Rokkan, S. (1987), *Stat, Nasjon, Klasse: Essays i politisk sosiologi*, Universitetsforlaget: Oslo.

Rokkan, S. (1999a), *State Formation and Nation Building*, in P. Flora; S. Kuhnle, and D. Urwin (eds.), *State Formation, Nation Building, and Mass Politics in Europe: The Theory of Stein Rokkan*, Oxford University Press: Oxford, UK.

Rokkan, S. (1999b), *Mass Politics*, in P. Flora; S. Kuhnle; D. Urwin (eds.) *State Formation, Nation Building, and Mass Politics in Europe: The Theory of Stein Rokkan*, Oxford University Press: Oxford, UK.

Savio, A. and Palola, E. (2004), Post-Lisbon Social Policy—Inventing the Social in the Confines of the European Union, paper presented at *ESPA-net Conference*, Oxford, UK, September.

Wind, M. (2000), Det post-nationale medborgerskab: EU som rettighedsgenerator [Post-National Citizenship: EU as a Rights Generator], *Politologiske Studier*, Vol. 3, No. 4, pp. 19-27.

WTO, World Trade Organization (2000), *Mapping of Regional Trade Agreements: Note by the Secretariat*, World Trade Organization: Geneva, Switzerland.

Yeates, N. (2005), Globalization and Social Policy in a Development Context, United Nations Research Institute for Social Development (UNRISD), Programme on Social Policy and Development, *paper*, No. 18. Geneva.

4

Gender Models and European Social Policy

GILLIAN PASCALL

How can we understand the varied ways in which gender assumptions underpin welfare states across Europe, how they are changing and the implications for gender equality? Gender equality is an important goal at the EU level, and member states (and other European nations) are committed to it. But the 27 states of the current European Union have contrasting histories and contemporary gender systems: in particular, gender models in former state socialist countries, where women's employment was strongly socially and economically supported, contrast with many Western European countries, where women's dependence on a male breadwinner has been a norm of gender inequality entrenched in social assumptions and social legislation. Are European welfare states becoming more gender equal or less? And which welfare states offer the best model for gender equality?

Across Europe, gender regimes—seen as the key policy logics of welfare states in relation to gender—have been challenged by transformations in families, in economies and polities. The male breadwinner model, which was a core underpinning principle of most Western European welfare states in the postwar era, has been undermined by women's increasing labor market participation: in the EU 15 countries together the employment rate (albeit measuring a very low level of one hour per week) rose over the decade from 1995 to 2005 from 49.7 to 57.4 percent, a trend which was shared by all the EU 15 members (Eurostat structural indicators). Women have joined the labor market, whether or not supported by government policies. In those countries with a stronger male breadwinner tradition, such as the UK, women's joining the labor market has taken place with little social support and fragmented childcare services (Lewis, 2003; Land, 2004). But even in the social democratic countries of Scandinavia, policies for support have often lagged behind women's needs and demands for childcare, resulting in a deeply divided labor market: this disadvantages women in paid work and pensions, and discourages men's participation in childcare (Leira, 2006).

Most of all, the decline of marriage, and increase in births outside marriage undermine a male breadwinner system, which depended on low rates of divorce and illegitimacy (Creighton, 1999). While these trends show changes in the social constitution of families in practice, the male breadwinner ideal has also declined (Lewis, 2001a,b, 2002). Changes in families—increases in cohabitation and divorce, decreases in marriage and fertility—are also trends in common, though they started earlier in Scandinavian countries and have reached different points in different places. In post-state socialist countries, these trends are strongest in the Baltic States, and weakest in Poland (Pascall and Kwak, 2005).

The dual earner model in those major parts of Europe which were dominated by state socialism has been challenged by the transformation. Under state socialism, women's labor was supported by government, through education, workplace nurseries, parental leave and benefits and kindergartens. Women's employment was effectively supported, producing very high levels of participation (around 80 percent in some countries at the point of transition) and low gender pay gaps (UNICEF, 1999). While legislation about marriage appeared to make women equal individuals, the lack of freedom in civil society inhibited the development of a women's movement and protected a gendered domestic division of labor. State socialist regimes therefore enhanced gender equality in employment and public life, while inhibiting it at home (Ferge, 1998).

The transformation brought democratic freedom to the former state socialist regimes, but it also brought insecurity, inequality, and immediate losses of GDP and employment for both men and women. Gender regimes in the soviet era were built on very high levels of public expenditure around 55 percent in the Central European countries, reducing now to around 45 percent (UNICEF, 2001). This brings reduced public spending on most social systems, including childcare, and more varied welfare instruments (Ferge and Tausz, 2002). It has also brought changes in ideology, with room for doubt about the appropriate role of the state, reducing the legitimacy of the collective spending which supported women's employment and childcare.

Commentators have feared "re-traditionalization" in post-state socialist countries, with male breadwinning prioritized over women's, and over gender equality. Transition may bring both continuity and change in gender relations (Einhorn, 2006: 95). Four decades of state socialist government might be expected to leave some residue in gender assumptions, even after transformation, while democratization has also brought divergence. Poland and Slovenia could be seen as the most extreme, with Catholic influence in Poland, bringing limits to abortion and some government pressures towards traditional motherhood, whereas Slovenia's 90 days' paternity leave and several indicators suggest a more gender equal tendency. The argument here is that post-state socialist countries—even Poland—are not going back to the past, but developing something new.

Gender in EU Social Policy

Should we expect to see increasing gender equality as a result EU policy and widening membership? Gender equality has been widely acknowledged as an important EU goal. The early commitment to equal pay for men and women, built into the Treaty of Rome in 1957, has developed into an employment strategy concerned with increasing women's participation. Directives on part-time work, working time and parental leave, and more recently work-life balance policies and childcare targets show a concern with the domestic gender inequalities that underpin employment inequalities. At the Millenium, the Council and Ministers for Employment and Social Policy gave support to a "new social contract on gender" which supported development of policies for "equality of men and women in the public and private domains" (CEU, 2000).

All these may suggest a widening and deepening of EU concern with gender inequalities, bringing concern with gender equality at home as well as in employment. But the meaning of gender policy developments for member states, and for women in member states, is a matter for serious debate. Some see the Open Method of Coordination as bringing a new development of the social in Europe, bringing shared social objectives (Atkinson, 2003), while others ask whether the Open Method of Coordination, which has replaced the legally binding directives, means that EU social objectives are becoming softer (Rubery, 2005). While work/family reconciliation policies may be seen as deepening gender policy, they may also be interpreted as serving an economic agenda, with increasing women's employment prioritized over gender equality at home or in employment. And while a narrow focus on equal opportunities, or work/family reconciliation may lead to a positive assessment of EU policy for women and for gender equality, a wider lens may interpret these policies as serving a market agenda rather than a social justice one (Lewis, 2006).

The weaker economic situation of transition countries, the socio-economic situation of women, its degradation in transformation, and declining fertility are common features of former soviet countries (European Commission, 2004: 108), as is the freedom now to develop civil society. We may ask whether EU membership will protect policies which have supported women's position in the labor market, while widening concerns with gender equality in family, civil society and polity, too?

In the Tables below, EU 27 data are given, where available, to cover the 27 EU countries, including very recent accessions, Bulgaria and Romania. The Scandinavian, or Nordic countries are represented by Sweden and Denmark, the post-state socialist countries by Slovenia, Hungary and Poland, the Western European continental countries by France and Germany, and countries with a strong male breadwinner tradition by Ireland, the UK and Malta. Among European countries which are not EU members, EFTA countries are included in the published indicators: Norway and Iceland share much with those Social Democratic countries which are EU members, while Switzerland is more similar to its continental neighbors.

Gender in Comparative Frameworks

The characterization of gender regimes based on the male breadwinner/dual earner spectrum (Lewis, 1992) puts gender at the centre of comparative analysis and is a starting point here. Gender regimes are understood as systems of gender equality or inequality through which paid work is connected to unpaid, state services and benefits are delivered to individuals or households, costs are allocated, and time is shared between men and women in households as well as between households and employment. The decline of the male breadwinner model has widespread implications (Creighton, 1999; Lewis 2001a,b). The decline of state support for dual earner arrangements in the new CEE member states is also momentous (Pascall and Lewis, 2004; Pascall and Kwak, 2005; Einhorn, 2006). European welfare states are analyzed here in component parts of the male breadwinner/dual earner spectrum: paid work, care work, income, time and power, asking to what extent they can be seen as systems of gender equality or as systems of traditional gender roles in each of these parts.

But we also need to ask about the level and nature of policy intervention. The *Three Worlds of Welfare Capitalism* (Esping-Andersen, 1990) are relevant to gender, because the Social Democratic countries have had gender equality as well as social equality at their heart (Ellingsaeter and Leira, 2006). Social democratic regimes have also underpinned gender equality with social policies, social spending and social commitment to parents and children. Elsewhere, commitment to traditional gender difference or free markets may play a greater role than gender equality.

The welfare modeling business has been very fruitful in comparative debate and understanding (Abrahamson, 1999). But models are simplifications. The UK has moved from male breadwinner assumptions, and from free market ones, in support for "universal childcare" under the Labor governments of the period from 1997. Germany's "red-green" coalition also changed traditional assumptions about gender roles and families. And beliefs—especially among younger people—about gender equality in work and care, are often not consonant with their governments' policies.

Are there alternative scenarios for a more gender equal future in Europe? The Dutch Combination Scenario (see below) offers a new vision, in which work is redistributed at the household level, with men as well as women envisaged as part-time workers and carers. The idea of making men's lives more like women's is also at the heart of Fraser's *universal caregiver model*, in which all employees would be assumed to have care responsibilities, while developments in civil society would enable care to be shared (Fraser, 1997). But it is argued here that gender equality needs more systematic support, beyond the capacity of civil society. The French working time model also has something to contribute to thinking about how to turn the one and a half earner model into a two x three-quarter one in which men and women have time to care as well as to work and to earn. Government commitments to gender equality need underpinning with regulation of time and with social investment. Comparative data clearly show that Scandinavian social democratic countries are the most gender equal: but they have still prioritized women's employment over men's care. In a model of Universal Citizenship gender equality would go beyond paid employment—important as that has been—and attend to gender inequalities in care, time, income and power: men's and women's obligations to paid work and care as citizens would be underpinned by regulation of working time and electoral systems and by social investment in citizenship rights.

Gender in Paid Work

Policies for equal opportunities in employment have been part of the EU agenda since the Treaty of Rome in 1957 brought a commitment to equal pay for men and women. More recently an employment strategy has focused on women's employment, with participation targets agreed at the Lisbon summit in 2000, including increasing childcare provision. At the EU level, increasing women's employment is widely seen as a key policy (Rubery *et al.*, 2001; Threlfall, 2007), albeit also criticized as market and economic growth oriented rather than women and gender-equality oriented (Lewis, 2006).

At the nation-state level, policies of member states are constrained by EU directives, and by commitments to meet agreed Lisbon targets through the Open Method of Coordination. For new member states, joining the EU has meant accepting these agreements. European countries are therefore widely committed to increasing women's employment. While EU policy has been to draw women into the labor market, which brings some convergence over time towards a dual worker model, there remain great differences between men and women, particularly in the quality of their employment, as well as between welfare states in the extent and nature of support for women's labor market participation.

The literature suggests several ways to make cross-national comparisons in gender differences in employment to illuminate differences in welfare regimes (cf especially Korpi, 2000; Van der Lippe and Van Dijk, 2002; Daly and Rake, 2003). Eurostat structural indicators allow comparison of gender gaps in employment and unemployment, and gender pay gaps across EU member states. Does women's increasing employment participation in Western countries bring equality in security, in women's ability to support themselves in the context of family change? And do changes in former state socialist countries represent generally increasing insecurity, or re-traditionalization, with women's employment marginalized in favor of men's?

In Western Europe, women's increasing employment has been closing the gap, but was still 15.5 percent below the male employment rate of 72.9 percent. Those countries with strong and long-established support for a dual earner model have the highest women's employment rates, with Sweden, Norway, Denmark and Iceland all over 70 percent, while Sweden has the lowest gender employment gap at 4 percent. At the other extreme, Malta's employment rate for women of 33.7 percent and gender employment gap of 40.1 percent shows a persistent male breadwinner system in a relatively small and new member state (Camilleri-Cassar, 2005).

 Understanding European Social Policy

In other countries with historically strong male breadwinner traditions, women may appear to be closing the gap, as, for example in the UK, women's employment has reached 65.9 percent and is 11.7 percent behind men's. But these figures include paid employment from one hour per week, and we have to look in more detail at working hours and pay to see how far women's ability to sustain themselves through employment remains below men's (Table 4.1).

Table 4.1: Female and Male Employment Rates, as Percentage of the Labor Force, and Difference Between Male and Female, 2005[1]

	Employment rate: female	Employment rate: male	Employment rate male-female
Sweden	70.4	74.4	4.0
Denmark	71.9	79.8	7.9
Slovenia	61.3	70.4	9.1
Hungary	51.0	63.1	12.1
Poland	46.8	58.9	12.1
France	57.6	68.8	11.2
Germany	59.6	71.2	11.6
UK	65.9	77.6	11.7
Ireland	58.3	76.9	18.6
Malta	33.7	73.8	40.1
EU 27	56.0	70.8	14.8

Source: based on Eurostat structural indicators and Europa New Cronos website (2007).

In the very large part of Europe dominated during the postwar period by state socialism, patterns of women's employment have been quite different. Gender equality under state socialism—even more than in other regimes—was about women's place in the labor market, with social investment in childcare and other services. Women's labor market participation was high by international standards, supported by occupational welfare: at the point of transition from state socialism in 1989, it was over 80 percent in the Baltic States, and Czechoslovakia, somewhat lower in Hungary and Poland, but everywhere well above France or the UK. At the point of political and economic transformation dual earner households were well established: women were in full time employment, with earnings not far below men's (UNICEF, 1999). Has economic restructuring dominated, with markets putting gender politics in a back seat (Einhorn, 2006)? In so far as policies supporting women's employment survive the transition from state socialism—how well do state socialist practices work in a capitalist market place?

Among post-state socialist countries, the highest level of women's employment is currently in Estonia, with 62.1 percent, with Slovenia close behind, while women's employment is particularly low in Poland, at 46.8 percent. These figures show an enormous change in women's employment compared with the soviet era. But the transformation period reduced employment for men and women. Most post-state socialist countries have gender employment gaps below the EU average: even Poland, where women's employment is at its lowest, has a gap between women and men of 12.1 percent. This is well above Sweden's (4 percent), but below the gender employment gap in Ireland (18.6 percent) or Malta (40.1 percent). In this respect the dual earner model appears alive and well in CEE countries, with more equal participation in employment between men and women than in the EU 15, and a much lower gap than in countries with a male breadwinner tradition, such as e.g. Ireland and Malta.

Across the EU 27, greater insecurity of paid work for women is indicated by an unemployment rate for women of 8.8 percent, while men's is 7.1 percent. It had been particularly feared that the changing economic landscape in post-state socialist regimes would see women's jobs marginalized in favor of men's. But men have also been vulnerable to losing jobs in the transformation process, and gender gaps in unemployment are not in practice higher in post-state socialist countries than elsewhere. Poland's experience is the worst in Europe, with women's unemployment at 15.1 percent, but men's also very high at 13.1 percent (Table 4.2).

Table 4.2: Female and Male Unemployment Rates, as Percentage of the Labor Force, and Difference Between Male and Female, 2006[2]

	Unemployment rate: female	Unemployment rate: male	Unemployment rate female-male
Sweden	7.3	6.9	0.4
Denmark	4.5	3.3	1.2
Slovenia	7.2	5.0	2.2
Hungary	7.8	7.2	0.6
Poland	15.1	13.1	2.0
France	10.0	8.2	1.8
Germany	9.1	7.7	1.4
UK	4.3	5.1	-0.8
Ireland	4.1	4.6	-0.5
Malta	9.2	6.5	2.7
EU 27	8.8	7.1	1.7

Source: based on Eurostat structural indicators and Europa New Cronos website (2007).

Gender pay gaps in hourly earnings show women across EU countries women earning on average 15 percent less per hour than men (Figure 4.1). Germany's pay gap is among the highest, at 22 percent, which might be expected from a country with conservative gender traditions; the UK's pay gap (20 percent) is above the EU average, reflecting its male breadwinner traditions and its preference for free markets. But Sweden and Denmark also show above average pay gaps, resulting from their segregated labor markets. Somewhat lower pay gaps appear in former state socialist countries, with Slovenia's at 8 percent, again suggesting that, while levels of employment are much lower than before the transformation, women's employment is closer to men's than it is in Western countries.

Figure 4.1: Gender Pay Gap in Unadjusted Form, 2005*[3]

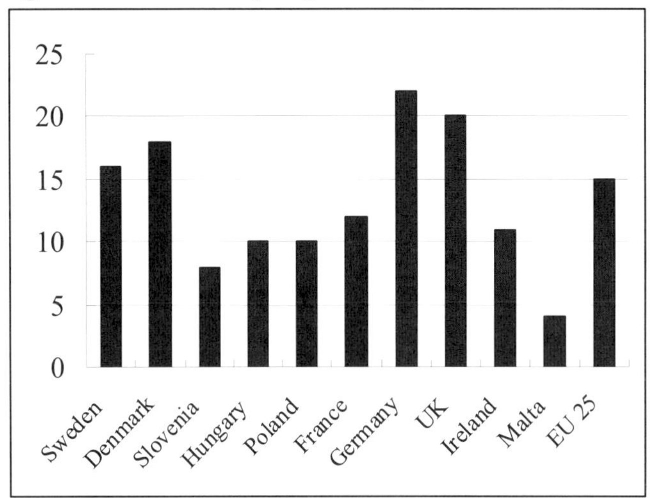

Note: Difference between men's and women's average gross hourly earnings
as a percentage of men's average gross hourly earnings.
Source: based on Eurostat structural indicators and Europa New Cronos website (2007).

On a number of measures of job quality, women in Europe have a worse
experience of work than men. The share of European women in low
paying occupations is nearly twice that of men (Weiler, 2005). Occupational segregation did not disappear under state socialism, but the
labor market is less segregated in the east than the west, with more
women in higher-level categories, as managers, and in technical occupations and skilled workers, and fewer in service and sales. There is also
a higher proportion of women in higher paid jobs: 41 percent of women
full time workers in the (then) acceding and candidate countries,
compared with 20 percent of full timers in the EU 15 (Paoli and Parent-
Thirion, 2003: 73-74). We ask below about part-time work (under time)
to help us to unravel the extent to which women are able to support themselves and about work-family reconciliation policies (under care) such
as parental leave.

Women's participation in employment has been growing in Western Europe, but it is still below men's; in former state socialist countries, the transformation has indeed damaged women's employment possibilities, but they have held on more tenaciously to full time employment than had once been feared (Fodor, 2005) and are a little more equal with men on most measures of work quality than their Western peers. But across Europe, the quality of women's jobs is below men's with a pay gap in hourly earnings averaging 15 percent, segregated labor markets and under-representation in higher-level positions. While EU nations are all committed to increasing women's employment, and to equal pay, there are great variations between nation states in the effectiveness with which they are achieving these. Social democratic countries sustain women's employment more systematically and effectively than elsewhere, though with deeply segregated labor markets, and lower pay for women, while former state socialist countries also have somewhat more equal employment than countries with a rooted male breadwinner tradition.

Incomes

Women are clearly seeking a more equal opportunity to earn, as they have increased their labor market participation, with or without support from governments. In individualizing societies, with increasing insecurity of relationships, and risk of divorce, earning is crucial to security. Equal pay, a fairer share of quality work, decent minimum wage levels, and sufficiency of work for self-support have been sought by women's movements in Western Europe, and are increasingly necessary everywhere. While governments have promised these, the reality is that women's earnings are below men's, even on an hourly basis, and on a lifetime basis, in some countries they may be much below men's. For example, in the UK, despite increasing employment, and changing government assumptions about gender, women's lifetime earnings are around half men's (Rake, 2000). Social supports for families, against risk of unemployment, and for pensions in old age, are crucial to women's security, as well as to gender equality.

The European Union regulates but does not play a direct role in designing and implementing the redistributive systems of member states, and has relatively small social budgets. But there are shared social objectives, with a social cohesion agenda established at the Lisbon summit in 2000, to be achieved through the Open Method of Coordination. While many critics see the Open Method as too open, these developments can be seen as a positive commitment to social policy and redistribution. National governments are "not free to determine the objectives of *redistributive* policy ... their freedom lies solely in the choice of means towards commonly agreed ends" (Atkinson, 2003). Social ideals have been turned into social indicators, with structural indicators on social inclusion, including poverty and income inequality with all indicators available by gender. While we may debate how effectively this social agenda will be implemented, we can use the indicators to understand how different now are European member states achievements in reducing poverty and inequality.

Exploring how regimes deal with poverty among men and women enables understanding of differences between them. Structural indicators allow us (in Table 3) to compare poverty, before and after transfers, for representative regimes. These set the threshold at 60 percent of national equivalized median disposable income showing relative poverty: it is important to note that absolute standards of living in former state socialist countries are well below the EU average. We might expect that countries with social security systems designed on the male breadwinner model, as the UK Beveridge system was, would be less successful in dealing with poverty among women than countries where women's employment is more established and supported by tax and benefit structures.

A high risk of poverty among women and men appears as common in countries as different as Sweden, Denmark, the UK and Ireland, all with over 30 percent of women at risk of poverty. The risk of poverty before transfers is just greater on average in the EU 25 for women than for men. Overall, the impact of social transfers was to reduce poverty from 27 percent of women to 17 percent, and from 25 percent of men to 15 percent. While welfare states reduced the risk of poverty, they did not—overall—reduce the gender gap. The main differences in welfare states are the extent to which they reduce the risks of poverty rather than the extent to which they reduce the gender gap in poverty risk. Sweden's very active welfare state reduces poverty risk among women from 30 to 10 percent, the lowest among the EU countries, though Iceland (not an EU member) had a post-transfer figure of 9 percent. Slovenia and Hungary, among the post-state socialist country examples, reduce women's risk of poverty to levels similar to these Social Democratic countries, at 11 and 13 percent respectively, while Poland leaves 20 percent of women at risk of poverty after transfers, figures comparable to the male breadwinner examples the UK (19 percent) and Ireland (21 percent) (Table 4.3).

Table 4.3: Risk of Poverty, Before and After Transfers, Male and Female, 2005*[4]

	Before transfers female	After transfers female	Before transfers male	After transfers male	Before transfers female - male	After transfers female - male
Sweden	30	10	27	9	3	1
Denmark	32	12	29	12	3	0
Slovenia	18	11	15	9	3	2
Hungary	29	13	30	14	-1	-1
Poland	29	20	31	21	-2	-1
France	27	14	25	12	2	2
Germany	25	14	22	12	5	2
UK	30	19	28	18	2	1
Ireland	34	21	30	19	4	2
Malta	22	15	20	14	2	1
EU 25	27	17	25	15	2	2

Note: * or most recent figures.
Source: based on Eurostat structural indicators and Europa New Cronos website (2007).

These data show the great importance of welfare states' role in reducing the risk of poverty. Social support for families is also crucial for women, who are still likely to assume responsibility for care, despite changing ideals. Family allowances are particularly important to women in protecting family living standards with or without a male breadwinner. The state-socialist tradition, in which family benefits have formed a high proportion of family incomes and of GDP, has been a crucial support to motherhood, as well as keeping children out of poverty. Pressures on government spending, from international agencies and inflation, brought lower values and more targeting after the transformation. By the end of the 1990s, the typical pattern in Central Europe was for high coverage, but much lower value in relation to household income and GDP than had been usual under communism. In Hungary, family allowances were 8.1 percent of household income in 1991 and 3.8 percent in 1999, while in Poland they fell from 4.2 to 1.2 percent (UNICEF, 2001: 42-44). Means-testing of family allowances in the Czech Republic, Poland and Slovenia, brings a more stringent and contingent system of support, with means-testing of childcare benefits also in Poland (Förster and Tóth, 2001; MISSOC, 2004).

But protection for children and their parents remains strong by western standards, with the Czech Republic, Hungary and Poland more successful than the UK and USA in using taxes and transfers to keep children out of poverty, as evidenced in various ways by the succession of Innocenti Research Centre Report Cards on child poverty and well-being in richer countries. Scandinavian countries fill most of the top places in the last of these reports (UNICEF, 2001, 2005, 2007).

Pension reform—East and West—has brought trends towards individualization (against rights through partners), towards equalization of pension ages, towards closer connection between contribution and benefits, for privatization and against redistribution. Equalizing pension ages, and making benefits depend more closely on individual contributions, rather than on entitlements through partners may appear to offer gender equality: but these will only bring gender equality in old age if there is gender equality in working life and caring life. There are many threats to older women's security in these changes: the gender pay gap, giving time to motherhood, increasing divorce, and women's tendency to live longer—all this reduces women's protection and pensions.

Women are increasingly being assumed to be able to earn their own pensions, but without sufficient attention to the processes that bring lower pay and capacity to contribute. These trends towards individuallizing risk and away from more socially oriented pooling of risk "threaten to magnify gender inequality in later life income" (Ginn *et al.*, 2001: 230).

The great diversity of European systems of social support is reflected in measures of how successfully they are meeting needs in the context of family change and increasing insecurity, both in Western countries as well as in the post-state socialist societies. Across the EU 25 women were somewhat more exposed to poverty than men. But the Scandinavian countries, are achieving most in reducing these risks. Women in the post-state socialist countries have high risks of poverty, but state structures to reduce these have been better sustained through the transformation period than many feared.

Care Work

Women's employment in paid work has been shaped and constrained by their unpaid care work as mothers and carers. Everywhere in Europe women are more likely to be mothers, with primary responsibility for care, while men are more likely to be paid workers, with primary responsibility for employment. These patterns have been challenged and changed, and there is some convergence between men's and women's work (Gershuny, 2000). But gender inequalities in care responsibilities and time are persistent and important factors underlying women's unequal position in labor markets of European countries. Here we ask about social policy support for care in and outside the family and for changing the gender relations of care in the family. Even in social democratic countries, policies for enabling women to do more paid work have been more extensive than policies for encouraging men to do more unpaid care work. In state socialist countries, women were conceived as workers and brought into the labor force. But this was done by state support for women's care work, and not by transforming the domestic division of labor, which remained unchallenged in soviet times by government or by feminist influences.

European childcare policy has been less developed than employment policy, but childcare is increasingly being seen in the EU as a prerequisite for increasing employment, which is itself a strong priority. Current EU targets are for one third of under-threes and 90 percent of children from three to mandatory school age to have access to childcare by 2010, but only the Scandinavian countries are thought likely to meet these targets (Ellingsaeter and Leira, 2006). National systems are varied. The most universal, supply-side childcare systems of the Scandinavian countries, particularly Sweden and Denmark stand out in quality measures for childcare, especially for younger children: Sweden has University educated staff, high staffing ratios, with public funding at 100 percent for pre-school and 75 percent for younger children. Public childcare covers 87 to 96 percent of 2-, 3-, 4- and 5-year-olds (Gornick and Meyers, 2003; Nyberg, 2004, 2006; Plantenga and Siegel, 2005). Post-socialist countries have lost state and employer support for nursery-age children, but provision and support for pre-school children remain strong. Hungary's provision is strongest among these, with kindergarten enrolments sustained at 85 to 88 percent of 3-6 year-olds throughout the transition period (UNICEF TransMONEE database). Hungary's family support system—including family allowances and kindergartens—is close to the Nordic model, with extensive public responsibility, and has remained comparatively stable through political changes because people see children's care as a social responsibility (Szikra, 2005: 12, 2006: 16).

Elsewhere in Western Europe public support for childcarc and coverage are more limited. While in Sweden and Denmark, coverage for 0-3-year-olds is already twice the EU target (each with around two-thirds children), France is just short of the one-third target, and the UK and Germany have places for around 10 percent of the population or below. Coverage for pre-school children is higher, but often part-time (Plantenga and Siegel, 2005: 14). The assumption of maternal care and responsibility may be strong, whether because family care is assumed to be better for children, or because parents are thought best able to make market choices. In the UK, until the end of the twentieth century mothers were assumed to be responsible for children: most fitted employment around children's needs. Current policy is for a mixed economy, which makes access and quality uncertain. Problems of trustworthiness, supply and affordability of childcare places still encourage discontinuous and part-time employment, especially among less qualified mothers (Lewis, 2003). And for pre-school children the UK's 2.5-hour day is among Europe's lowest provision, contrasting with France, which has allowed mothers to choose employment more easily, partly through stronger public educational provision, with a pre-school day from 8.30 to 4.30. The UK's provision shows its male breadwinner history, despite ten years of government support for childcare and public funding through tax credits.

Childcare leave to enable parents to care for nursery-age children has been a strong feature of former state socialist countries. In 2002, the Czech Republic had the longest parental leave in Europe, until the child is four years old. At transition, as workplace nurseries closed, childcare leave schemes were made more attractive. Parents in the Czech Republic may have rights to four years' leave, but they also suffer "a gradual erosion in the value of their qualifications and previous work experience, and find it more difficult to return to their jobs after such a long break," while childcare benefit is set at one fifth of average incomes and brings the risk of poverty (Kocourkova, 2002). Shorter leaves may offer a better fit between the needs of children for parental care, the needs of parents to earn, and the requirements of gender equality (Gornick and Meyers, 2003).

The Swedish system has been based on shorter periods of leave, which are strongly supported, with 80 percent income replacement: now 480 days of parental leave, which can be used flexibly on a full-time or part-time basis. This allows parents to care for their children at home for 16 months on average, before using other forms of childcare (Duvander et al., 2005: 13). After this public support for childcare is extensive, as we have seen. Sweden's leave system has been rated as highest in Europe if measuring "effective parental leave," to take account of payment levels, with Hungary close behind, Finland and the Czech Republic following. By this measure, Germany and France are middle range countries, with the UK just above Ireland and the Netherlands, which have the shortest periods of effectively supported leave. Sweden also has one of the shortest gaps between the end of effective parental leave and pre-primary admission age (Plantenga and Siegel, 2005: 9-11).

Parents in Sweden also have a right to work reduced hours—30 hours per week—until their children are twelve. Thus, Sweden's flexible system allows parents to stay at home during the first year and more, on high levels of replacement income. Along with other Scandinavian countries, these systems sustain women's labor market participation in a more continuous manner, and with stronger levels of social support, than other European countries.

So far, most parental leave policies have been designed to protect mothers and children through childbirth, and enable mothers to balance childcare with employment. While these arrangements have brought important benefits to mothers and children, they have also put mothers into a more vulnerable position in the labor market. Can parental leaves can be designed to support gender equality in employment, underpinned by increasing gender equality in care, rather than just supporting maternal employment?

Commitments to men's participation in care work are much weaker than European and nation states' commitments to increasing women's participation in paid employment. But since the 1996 European Parental Leave Directive, member states have been obliged to provide fathers' entitlement to care time (three months but unpaid) after the birth of a child, as well as mothers'. Scandinavian countries, beginning with Norway, had been developing stronger entitlements, to a paid, non-transferable Daddy month to give fathers an incentive to take parental leave. Sweden borrowed this policy in 1995, increasing the month to two in 2002. Currently, Iceland has the most developed policy, with a 3x3 system: three months for the mother, three for the father, and three for sharing between them. These policies are also the most effective in Scandinavia. They have encouraged a rapid increase in fathers' taking a share of parental leave, with three-quarters taking their three-month quota. Scandinavian parents are subject to contradictory pressures too, to work long hours, and fathers still take only a small proportion of parental leaves in Nordic countries, (Nyberg, 2004, 2006; Ellingsaeter and Leira, 2006; Lammi-Taskula, 2006). However modest in effect, these are important changes, bringing new assumptions about men as fathers, in households as well as among policymakers. European policy for work-family balance has put gender at home on the agenda as well as gender at work, but it has been a new year/new millenium resolution (CEU, 2000) rather than a comprehensive commitment.

Beliefs about gender equality in care show widespread agreement that childcare should belong equally to men and women. Respondents across 28 countries (including Turkey, a candidate country) were asked about: playing, taking children to activities, dealing with nappies dressing, taking to the doctor, helping with schoolwork, reading, buying toys, publishing, putting to bed, answering important questions. The resulting index (from zero, wholly unshared) to 100 (fully shared) suggests that beliefs in gender equality in care are widespread in Western, Central and Eastern Europe, with an overall index of 81.8 in the EU 15 and of 76.6 in the new member countries: "most people of Europe believe that childcare is basically a non-specific task: both mother and father are expected to carry out childrearing" (Fahey and Spéder, 2004: 60). Beliefs and practice may of course be very different, and some degree of disjuncture is to be expected between what people say they think should happen in childcare, and what actually does.

Fathers themselves have been spending more time on parenting, with paternal time now between a quarter and a third of maternal time (Eurostat, 2004). However, this varies widely across countries, with very low levels of paternal time in Greece and Portugal. There is some evidence of greater gender equality in post-socialist households, with 31 percent of men involved in raising and caring for children, in the (then) Acceding and Candidate Countries, compared with 24 percent in the EU 15 (Paoli and Parent-Thirion, 2003: 78). In social democratic countries there is some evidence of fathers influenced by father-friendly legislation, with parental leave rights for fathers (not just to their families) and government encouragement to use them. But in liberal, free-market countries fathers may also contribute more time to their children, in response to an absence of social support (Smith, 2004; Smith and Williams, 2007).

European systems of support for childcare show great variety. In most countries mothers are still primary carers, and fathers are primary breadwinners, even where governments have established social rights for children's care. Scandinavian countries are clear leaders in parental rights and childcare services. But the systems of post-state socialist countries are less damaged than commentators have feared: nurseries have closed, but parents have rights to leave for nursery-age children and pre-school provision remains strong. The European Union's emphasis on increasing women's employment has supported childcare development, mainly through encouragement and targets, which are establishing new norms. Policies to encourage fathers to play a stronger role in childcare are beginning, but for the most part policymakers follow the widespread belief in gender equality in this respect rather than leading it.

Time

Time is integral to gender systems: traditional male breadwinner regimes depended on men's full-time and lifetime paid employment. Britain's postwar social security system was devised by Beveridge on this model of a male working life, while allowing for married women to be full-time carers, dependent on their husbands for income and pension contributions. The working time models that have emerged from the ashes of the male breadwinner model—most often one and a half earner, with mothers in part-time work—have rarely brought gender equality in time (Lewis, 2001a). Even in the weakest male breadwinner states, women do shorter hours of paid work than men, and longer hours of unpaid. In contrast, state socialist working time regimes meant full-time work for men and women: parental leaves and non-competitive conditions, allowed mothers to exit and re-enter work to meet their children's needs. Both time systems now bring risks to parents, as mothers can no longer rely on marriage and male breadwinners to bring security, income or pensions, while post-state socialist countries bring competitive conditions in which women cannot safely use their rights. Increasingly, policy strategies include time regulation.

Hours for full-time employees are nearly gender equal, with a 41-hour week for men and 39-hour week for women in the EU 25: gender differences are greatest in the UK, where men' working week is 44 hours, four hours longer than women's, while Sweden, Bulgaria and Luxembourg record equal full-time working hours (Eurostat, 2007). The major gender differences in Western European countries are in part-time work, which is the way that women in countries with a male breadwinner tradition have joined the labor market, fitting paid work around unpaid care responsibilities. In the (mainly western) countries covered by Eurostat (2004) women aged 20 to 74 spent more time on domestic work than on paid work, while the opposite was the case for men.

Working time arrangements in former state socialist countries are distinctive. First, working hours are longer than in the EU15, averaging 44 hours rather than 38. Second, very long working weeks are commoner, 38 percent working more than 45 hours a week, against 21 percent in the EU15. Thirdly, fewer people work short hours, fewer work part-time, and part-time hours are long, at 32 hours on average (Paoli and Parent-Thirion, 2003: 45). There is more gender equality in working time in these new member states than in Malta, but this kind of gender equality makes reconciling work and family a challenge, especially for mothers. There is little debate about working time in the new CEE member states, or making space for women or men to engage in care: employees need full-time incomes for living standards and future pensions. Working time is also less flexible than the EU15 (Weiler, 2005). These countries appear to follow their state socialist predecessors: men and women are expected to be in the labor market, equally in full time jobs with long full time hours. But the conditions under which they do this have become more challenging, with inflexibility and competition for jobs. Now mothers find difficulty using parental leaves, or re-entering after childbirth. While men appear to be playing a more serious role in these obligations, they are still primarily mothers' obligations, bringing serious difficulties in keeping jobs and caring for children (Pascall and Kwak, 2005).

Women's part-time work is a crucial way in which they may be marginalized and disadvantaged by caring responsibilities (Rubery *et al.*, 1998, 1999) (Table 4.4). Very high levels of insecure, low paid work, with short hours and limited rights: these were one of Jane Lewis' key reasons for describing the UK as a strong male breadwinner model, while Swedish women were likely to do part-time work, but with longer hours and conditions equivalent to full-time work (Lewis, 1992). The EU Part-Time Work Directive has improved rights, but part-time work remains one way UK women bend their employment to their family, and suffer the consequences in terms of life-time earnings half men's (Rake, 2000). In Western Europe, 33.5 percent of total employment is women's part-time, over five times men's. Table 4.4 shows how much part-time work is women's work. The ratios of women's part-time employment to men's show women in Western Europe with around five times the rate for men, and even Sweden around three times. Distinctive differences between East and West also persist here. Poland's women part-timers contribute the highest rate to total employment among post-state socialist countries at 13.4 percent, but this is much below western countries, and further below traditionally male breadwinner countries, the UK and Ireland.

Table 4.4: Part-Time Workers as Percentage of Total Employment, in 2005

	Part-time rate: female	Part-time rate: male	Part-time rate female-male
Sweden	39.6	11.5	3.4: 1
Denmark	43.8	7.8	5.6: 1
Slovenia	11.1	7.2	1.5: 1
Hungary	5.8	2.7	2.1: 1
Poland	14.3	8.0	1.8: 1
Netherlands	75.1	22.6	3.3: 1
France	30.7	5.7	5.4: 1
Germany	43.8	7.8	5.6 :1
UK	42.7	10.4	4.1: 1
Ireland (2002)	30.4	6.5	4.7: 1
Malta	21.1	4.5	4.7: 1
Euro area	34.8	6.9	5.0: 1
EU 25	32.4	7.4	4.4: 1

Source: based on European Commission/Eurostat (2007).

What routes are there to more equal working time? The Swedish route has been to support full-time employment—or nearly full-time employment—for women and men within a dual earner model, through high public spending on childcare and parental rights and leaves. These include the right to a six-hour working day for parents of young children, introduced in Sweden in 1979. One consequence of parental rights introduced in the 1970s has been a deeply divided labor market, in which women are more likely to use parental leave and to work shorter hours, and to have lower paid public sector jobs. More recent policy developing strategies—including dedicated "Daddy leave" in the 1990s—to encourage men to use parental leave has been one response, with the assumption that both paid and care work should be shared. Among Nordic countries Sweden is seen as coming the nearest now to a model which facilitates "the dual-darner, care-sharing family, in which both mothers and fathers are economic providers and carers for children" (Leira, 2006: 44).

A part-time route to more equal working time has been pursued by the Netherlands. The "Polder model" adopted part-time work for economic goals, to share employment, and enabled the absorption of women into the economy, but was not specifically a model for gender equality. However, the "Combination Scenario"—adopted as a guideline for work and family policies in 1995—brought an ideological commitment to gender equality in care work as well as paid employment, challenging "not only women's gender position but also men's" (Knijn, 2001: 170; Knijn and Selten, 2002). Part-time work was integral to the "Combination Scenario" whose core concepts are the equal valuation of unpaid care work with paid employment, a balanced combination of care and paid work, and gender equality in both care and paid employment. In the Netherlands, women's move into part-time work has been rapid. Men's part-time work has increased, but as younger and older workers rather than as parents (Plantenga, 2002). Both men and women in the the Netherlands have the highest part-time rates in Europe, but women's at 75.1 percent is over three times men's at 22.6 percent. The official ideal is still far from reality, and the Netherlands is a distinctive version of the Western European norm of a one and a half work pattern, with women as the half, rather than transforming the gender division of time.

A shorter working week, making more room for care, is an alternative strategy for gender equality, with policies in several Western European countries. France has national legislation for a maximum 35-hour working week, beginning in larger firms in 2000 and in smaller firms in 2002. As in the Netherlands, this started as a policy to share employment, at a time of high unemployment, but more equal sharing of paid and unpaid work in families was also an objective (Fagnani and Letablier, 2004, 2006). Despite significant difficulties, especially for low earners, early research suggests that the 35-hour week enables work-family reconciliation. Among parents with at least one child under six, 59.5 percent of women and 55.2 percent of men replied that the 35-hour week law had made reconciling their working life and family life easier (Fagnani and Letablier, 2006: 86).

Parents were more positive when working within a family-friendly working climate, reducing hours on a weekly basis (71 percent positive), and—in the context of legislation not fully implemented at the time of this research—actually working near to the 35-hour norm (65 percent positive). Negative responses were associated with employers not being perceived as family-friendly, reduced working time not arranged to produce a 35-hour week (instead being annualised and giving longer holidays), or working hours above the 35-hour norm (Fagnani and Letablier, 2004: 560-66).

In another study, public sector employees with children under 12 are reported as spending more time with their children: 90 percent of fathers and 87 percent of mothers (Fagnani and Letablier, 2006). There is also evidence of preferences for more equal working time, with the current French model not far from widespread preferences in Europe (Fagan and Warren, 2001).

These three routes could be characterized as Sweden making women's working lives as far as possible like men's, the Netherlands making men's working lives more like women's, while France offers a mid-point between men's lives and women's. In Western countries some residue of the male breadwinner model remains, as men are more tied to their jobs and women more tied to childcare, but this varies a great deal. Sweden is clearly the leading country, in Scandinavia and in Europe: here gender equality policy is the most deep-rooted, with rights for parents developing since the 1970s, and a strong women's movement. Incentives for men to care since the 1990s mean that Sweden now offers official and financial support for men to care as well as for women's employment.

Gender and Power

Gender systems are also systems of power: welfare states affect gender relations, women's autonomy as individuals, their ability to support themselves and their place in public politics. Equality legislation has brought women important rights, but inequalities in paid work, care, income and time bring unequal voice in households, civil society, local politics, state and European governments.

In households the continuing gender division of labor suggests that women's voice is weaker, and their lower incomes may give them less say in major decisions than men. Women's political representation in national parliaments has been shown to relate positively to their level of employment, education compared with men, length of time since enfranchisement, secularization, social democratic political parties and electoral systems based on proportional representation. But even where women's employment, education and mobilization have brought steady improvements in representation, these have not brought parity with men. Increasingly women's low level of political representation is being targeted by quotas (Dahlerup, 2006, 2007).

Women's representation in European parliaments (EU 25) is now 23 percent on average, despite commitments to international conventions such as CEDAW, and EU persuasion to member states to increase representation of women in decision-making positions. Countries vary widely, from Sweden's 45 to Malta's 9 percent (Table 4.5).

On this measure, Germany is somewhat above average, and the UK and France somewhat below. Malta shares its low position in women's representation with Ireland, another traditionally male breadwinner state, and with former state socialist countries, Hungary and Romania, which also have around 10 percent women in their parliaments.

Table 4.5: Women in Decision-Making

	Percentage of women Senior Ministers in national government	Percentage of women members of single/lower house Parliaments	Percentage of women at one level below the minister	Percentage of women at two levels below the minister
Sweden	52	45	40	45
Slovenia	7	15	41	67
Hungary	12	9	3	23
Poland	6	22	29	31
France	18	13	0	18
Germany	33	33	11	9
UK	27	18	21	18
Ireland	14	13	11	11
Malta	15	9	7	12
Average EU 25	23	23	16	24

Source: EC Database on Women and Men in Decision-Making (2005).

Restriction of social, civil and political action under state socialism limited women's politics, and challenges to patriarchal families from within (Molyneux, 1990: 44-48). But the democratization that came with the end of soviet authority has been a gendered process and has not opened space for women's participation to the same extent as men's. Amid all the priorities of economic upheavals and the development of class differences, gender and women's political action may have taken a back seat (Ferge, 1997a,b, 1998; Watson, 1997, 2000a,b). Women tend to be doing better in civil service positions, with several countries above the EU average, and Slovenia exceeding Sweden's representation. Women's position in employment, perhaps the legacy of state socialism, appears to give them better access to decision-making within government departments than in many western countries, while access to formal political positions is more restricted. Accession to the EU has put gender equality on the political agenda of post-state socialist countries, and is enabling civil action. But gender equality as a political norm, and the civil action to achieve it in post-socialist countries have still a distance to travel.

Accumulated evidence points to discriminatory processes as the key to women's continued under-representation, rather than women's choices or poorer qualification for election (Phillips, 1991). In this case solutions may be found through changing political processes. Proponents of the parity principle argue democratic representation is not democratic unless both men and women are equally represented. Proposals for gender quotas come in many forms, and are designed to ensure a minimum proportion of women are elected, or to give parity between men and women. A "parity law" has been used in France to regulate the proportion of women candidates in local regional and European elections, though not in national parliamentary ones: it increased women's representation from 22 to 47.5 percent in the cities in March 2001 (Squires and Wickham-Jones, 2001).

Nordic countries are used to being at the top of gender leagues. They have adopted strategies to foster more equal representation of women in parliaments. The long, unbroken women's movement has worked to increase acceptability of stronger women's participation and the unacceptability of men's over-representation. Women's stronger position in employment, proportional representation, social democratic party dominance and party quotas—though not compulsory legal quotas—have increased women's representation in parliamentary politics. This has been gradual process built on consensual politics over decades. Sweden is still at the top of European countries, with its 45 percent of women parliamentarians. But Nordic feminists are now surprised to find their position at the top of the international league taken by Rwanda, bringing debates in Scandinavia about whether the consensual process has been too gradual (Dahlerup, 2006, 2007; Freidenvall *et al.*, 2006). New parliaments in Scotland and Wales have also offered opportunities to build systems in which women can win seats in Europe too (albeit at a devolved rather than UK level) and have reached 50 percent in Wales. Quotas are rapidly growing as a means to avoid a hundred-year wait for women to be fully represented, though they face barriers in some developed democracies, particularly those without proportional representation, with entrenched male MPs and party selection processes, and where the dominant ideology is based on liberal ideals emphasizing equal opportunity rather than equality of result.

Women's political representation in formal politics is clearly below men's. But there are great differences. Scandinavian countries remain the leaders in Europe from women's point of view, with women in Sweden challenging men in parliamentary representation, while Malta and Ireland have the fewest women in parliamentary politics. Women in former state socialist countries have had a disappointing transition to democracy, in their relatively low position in parliamentary politics. However, the tradition of women's employment does allow women in post-state socialist countries to achieve influential civil service positions, while the EU is enabling the development of women's organizations (and others) in civil society. The EU has offered advice to member states over increasing women's representation, but no binding directive: quota debates suggest a practical means to increasing women's representation at EU and national levels, to which in theory governments are committed.

Conclusion

The gender models underpinning state socialist societies in Eastern Europe, and the male breadwinner model in Western Europe have been challenged by social and economic transformation in the east, and by family change and individualization across Europe. The soviet tradition was one of relative gender equality, particularly in employment, underpinned by social spending on children and families. Transformation has brought markets, and has reduced, but not destroyed the social systems that supported women's employment. In Western Europe, women have challenged the male breadwinner model by entering the labor market. But they have done so with very varied levels of state support, which has brought very different levels of gender equality and the ability of women to support themselves and their children through sustained high-quality employment. It has also brought very different power in national—and probably domestic—decision-making.

Analyzing the male breadwinner model into its component parts—paid word, care work, income, time and power—allows us to compare countries with very different histories, to understand social policies across different elements. In any likely future scenario, European women are likely to want and need a stronger and more equal position in paid employment. But work is not the whole. Greater equality in paid employment will not bring gender equality unless greater attention is paid to gender differences in care, income, time and power.

We also need to consider the different qualities of regimes in terms of their commitments to intervention at different levels: to influencing the household division of labor, as well as to social spending and to equality. While European countries are all committed in principle to gender equality, their achievements are very different. This may be partly understood in terms of competing commitments to markets and to traditional families. The UK may be seen as a liberal example (though not an entirely consistent one) of commitments to markets often winning over commitments to gender equality, which has made gender equality a privilege for better-off and better educated women who can afford to pay for care. Germany's conservative tradition may be seen as limiting its commitment to changing gender roles in families and outside them (again not entirely consistently). Among post-state socialist countries, Poland's commitment to traditional families has also brought more inequality, while Slovenia is more like the social democratic countries. Only the Scandinavian social democratic countries have made an ideological commitment to gender equality, supported by social spending, which puts them at the forefront in Europe for social policies designed to produce gender equality in employment, care, income, time and power, and in measures of these in practice. Even here there are costs to women in segregated employment, with lower pay than men's.

It will not be news to anyone interested in gender and welfare states that, while all European governments are committed to gender equality, the Nordic countries achieve it more consistently than elsewhere. But the evidence of the superiority of the Scandinavian model is now clarified by the structural indicators, which allow comparison across the wider Europe. Evidence also accumulates of the superiority of Scandinavian model in broader economic and social measures, as well as the child poverty data already mentioned (UNICEF, 2007). In *Choosing to Grow*, reporting on the Lisbon Strategy, the Commission points to

Swede, Denmark and Finland as consistently best performers, in terms of general economic performance, employment, research and innovation, economic reform, social cohesion and the environment (EC, 2003b: 29). Similar conclusions are drawn by Goodin (1999) and by Panić (2007), who compares seven contrasting regimes using a wide range of measures: The best performing industrial economies at the beginning of the 21st century are those that have least in common with the neoliberal model: the Scandinavian social democracies in particular (Panić, 2007).

The European Union is committed to gender equality in Europe, and may bring convergence between its different member states. Gender equality in employment has been part of the EU since the Treaty of Rome in 1957. Debates about gender equality in Europe have been lively and effective in developing wider commitments by member states. But the European Union is not a consistent supporter of social Europe, often emphasizing markets, economic growth and employment rather than social objectives. And while member states are committed to increasing women's labor market participation, childcare and so on, many fear that current commitments may not be relied upon.

As the structures which underpinned state socialist and male breadwinner models have both transformed, new structures are needed in Europe. In Nordic countries as in the rest of Europe, gender equality policies have tended to start with women's employment, and have been much more active in supporting women's work than in supporting men's care. Scandinavian countries are now developing policies to encourage gender equality in care as well as in employment, and give the best lead towards a more gender-equal future in Europe.

A Universal Citizenship model—in which men's and women's rights and obligations to care were recognized and supported—would emphasize the need to change men's employment as well as women's, to give men and women time to earn to support themselves. The research and policy agenda begins to include men as fathers and carers, with models such as the Netherlands' Combination Scenario and Scandinavian Daddy leave. But policies for gender equality are hindered by gender inequality in decision-making, especially in politics, which could be transformed by quotas. The evidence about European people's desire for more equal working time, and belief in more equal obligations, is that Europeans are ahead of their policymakers in support for gender equality as more equal obligation and time to care and not just as increasing women's participation in employment

Notes

1. The employment rates are calculated by dividing the number of women aged 15 to 64 in employment by the total female population of the same age group. The indicator is based on the EU Labor Force Survey. The survey covers the entire population living I private households and excludes those in collective households such as boarding houses, halls of residence and hospitals. Employed population consists of those persons who during the reference week did any work for pay or profit for at lease one hour, or were not working but had jobs from which they were temporarily absent.

2. Unemployment rates represent unemployed persons as a percentage of the labor force = active population. The labor force is the total number of people employed and unemployed. Unemployed persons comprise persons aged 15 to 74 who were: (a) without work during the reference week, (b) currently available for work, i.e. were available for paid employment or self-employment before the end of the two weeks following the reference week, (c) actively seeing work, i.e. had taken specific steps in the four weeks period ending with the reference week to seek paid employment or self-employment or who found a job to start later, i.e. within a period of, at most, three months.

3. Gender pay gap is given as the difference between average gross hourly earnings of male paid employees and of female paid employees as a percentage of average gross hourly earnings of male paid employees. The population consists of all paid employees aged 16-64 that are 'at work 15+ hours per week'.

4. The share of women and men with an equivalized disposable income below the risk-of-poverty threshold, which is set at 60 percent of the national median equivalized disposable income.

REFERENCES

Abrahamson, P. (1999), The Welfare Modelling Business, *Social Policy and Administration*, Vol. 33, No. 4, pp. 394-415.

Atkinson, A. (2003), Social Europe and Social Science, *Social Policy and Society*, Vol. 2, No. 4, pp. 261-72.

Camilleri-Cassar, F. (2005), *Gender Equality in Maltese Social Policy? Graduate Women and the Male Breadwinner Model,* Agenda: Malta.

CEU, Council of the European Union (2000), Resolution of the Council and of the Ministers for Employment and Social Policy on the Balanced Participation of Women and Men in Family and Working Life, *Official Journal*, 2000C 218/02.

Creighton, C. (1999), The Rise and Decline of the Male Breadwinner Family in Britain, *Cambridge Journal of Economics,* Vol. 23, pp. 519-41.

Dahlerup, Drude (ed.) (2006), *Women, Quotas and Politics*, Routledge: London.

Dahlerup, Drude (2007), Electoral Gender Quotas—Between Equality of Opportunity and Equality of Result, *Representation, the Journal of Representative Democracy*, Vol. 24, No. 2.

Daly, M. and Rake, K. (2003), *Gender and the Welfare State: Care, Work and Welfare in Europe and the USA*, Polity: Cambridge, UK.

Duvander, A.Z., Ferranini, T., and Thalberg, S. (2005), *Swedish Parental Leave and Gender Equality: Achievements and Reform Challenges in a European perspective*, Swedish Institute for Futures Studies: Stockholm.

EC, European Commission (2003), *Choosing to Grow: Knowledge, Innovation and Jobs in a Cohesive Society*, Report to the Spring European Council on the Lisbon Strategy of Economic and Social and Environmental Renewal, Office for Official Publications of the European Commission: Luxembourg.

EC, European Commission (2004), *The Social Situation in the European Union*, Office for Official Publications of the European Commission: Luxembourg.

Einhorn, B. (2006), *Citizenship in an Enlarging Europe: From Dream to Awakening*, Macmillan: London.

Ellingsaeter, A.E. and Leira, A. (eds.) (2006), *Politicisng Parenthood in Scandinavia*, Bristol: Policy Press.

Esping-Andersen, G. (1990), *The Three Worlds of Welfare Capitalism*, Polity: Cambridge, UK.

Eurostat (2004), *How Europeans Spend Their Time: Everyday Life of Women and Men*, Office for Official Publications of the European Commission: Luxembourg.

Eurostat (2007), *Living Conditions in Europe Data 2002-2005*, Office for Official Publications of the European Commission: Luxembourg.

Fagan, C. and Warren, T. (2001), *Gender, Employment and Working-Time Preferences in Europe: report for the European Foundation on Living and Working Conditions*, Office of Official Publications of the European Communities: Luxembourg.

Fagnani, J. and Letablier, M.T. (2004), Work and Family-Life Balance: The Impact of the 35-Hour Laws in France, *Work, Employment and Society*, Vol. 18, No. 3, pp. 551-72.

Fagnani, J. and Letablier, M.T. (2006), The French 35-Hour Working Law and the Work-Life Balance of Parents: Friend or Foe?, in D. Perrons *et al.* (eds.), *Gender Divisions and Working Time in the New Economy*, Edward Elgar: Cheltenham, UK.

Fahey, T. and Spéder, S. (2004), *Fertility and Family Issues in an Enlarged Europe*, Office for Official Publications of the European Communities: Luxembourg.

Ferge, Z. (1997a), The Changed Welfare Paradigm: The Individualization of the Social, *Social Policy and Administration*, Vol. 31, No. 1, pp. 20-44.

Ferge, Z. (1997b), A Central European Perspective on the Social Quality of Europe, in W. Beck, L. Maesen and A.Walker (eds.), *The Social Quality of Europe*, Kluwer Law International: The Hague.

Ferge, Z. (1998), Women and Social Transformation in Central-Eastern Europe: The Old Left and the New Right, *Social Policy Review,* Vol. 10, pp. 217-36.

Ferge, Z. and Tausz, K. (2002), Social Security in Hungary, *Social Policy and Administration*, Vol. 36, No. 2, pp. 176-99.

Fodor, E. (2005), *Women at Work: The Status of Women in the Labor Markets of the Czech Republic, Hungary and Poland*, Occasional Paper, No. 3, United Nations Research Institute for Social Development: Geneva.

Förster, M.F. and Tóth, I.J. (2001), Child Poverty and Family Transfers in the Czech Republic, Hungary and Poland, *Journal of European Social Policy*, Vol. 11, No. 4, pp. 324-41.

Fraser, N. (1997), *Justice Interruptus: Critical Reflections on the Postsocialist Condition*, Routledge: London.

Freidenvall *et al.* (2006), The Nordic Countries: An Incremental Model, in D. Dahlerup (ed.), *Women, Quotas and Politics*, Routledge: London.

Gershuny, J. (2000), *Changing Times: Work and Leisure in Post-Industrial Society*, Oxford University Press, Oxford, UK.

Ginn, J.; Street, D., and Arber, S. (2001), *Women, Work and Pensions: International Issues and Prospects*, Open University Press: Buckingham, UK

Goodin, R.E. *et al.* (1999), *The Real Worlds of Welfare Capitalism*, Cambridge University Press: Cambridge, UK.

Gornick, J.C. and Meyers, M.K. (2003), *Families that Work: Policies for Reconciling Parenthood and Employment* Russell Sage Foundation, New York.

Knijn, T. (2001), Care Work: Innovations in the Netherlands, in M. Daly (ed.), *Care Work: The Quest for Security*, ILO: Geneva.

Knijn, T. and Selten, P. (2002), Transformations of Fatherhood, in B. Hobson (ed.), *Making Men Into Fathers: Men, Masculinities and the Social Politics of Fatherhood*, Cambridge University Press: Cambridge, UK.

Kocourkova, J. (2002), Leave Arrangements and Childcare Services in Central Europe: Policies and Practices Before and After the Transition, *Community, Work and Family*, Vol. 5, No. 3, pp. 301-18.

Korpi, W. (2000), Faces of Inequality: Gender, Class, and Patterns of Inequalities in Different Types of Welfare States, *Social Politics*, Vol. 7, pp. 127-91.

Lammi-Taskula (2006), Nordic Men on Parental Leave: Can the Welfare State Change Gender Relations?, in A.E. Ellingsaeter and A. Leira (eds.), *Politicising Parenthood in Scandinavia*, Policy: Bristol, UK.

Land, H. (2004), *Women, Child Poverty and Childcare: Making the Link*, Daycare Trust: London.

Leira, A. (2006), Parenthood Change and Policy Reform in Scandinavia, in A.E. Ellingsaeter and A. Leira (eds.), *Politicising Parenthood in Scandinavia*, Policy: Bristol, UK.

Lewis, J. (1992), Gender and the Development of Welfare Regimes, *Journal of European Social Policy*, Vol. 2, No. 3, pp. 159-73.

Lewis, J. (2001a), The Decline of the Male Breadwinner Model: The Implications for Work and Care, *Social Politics*, Vol. 8, No. 2, pp. 152-70.

Lewis, J. (2001b), *The End of Marriage: Individualism and Intimate Relations?*, Edward Elgar: Cheltenham, UK.

Lewis, J. (2002), Gender and Welfare State Change, *European Societies*, Vol. 4, No. 4, pp. 331-57.

Lewis, J. (2003), Developing Early Years Childcare 1997-2002: The Choices for Mothers, *Social Policy and Administration*, Vol. 37, No. 3, pp. 219-38.

Lewis, J. (2006), Work/Family Reconciliation, Equal Opportunities and Social Policies: The Interpretation of Policy Trajectories at the EU Level and the Meaning of Gender Equality, *Journal of European Public Policy*, Vol. 13, pp. 420-37.

MISSOC (2004), Social Protection in the 10 New Member States, *ec.europa.eu*.

Molyneux, M. (1990), The Woman Question in the Age of Perestroika, *New Left Review*, Vol. 183, pp. 23-59.

Nyberg, A. (2004), Parental Leave, Public Childcare and the Dual Earner/Dual Carer-Model in Sweden, *discussion paper*, Swedish National Institute for Working Life: Stockholm.

Nyberg, A. (2006), Economic Crisis and the Sustainability of the Dual-Earner, Dual Carer Model, in D. Perrons *et al.* (eds.), *Gender Divisions and Working Time in the New Economy*, Edward Elgar, Cheltenham, UK.

Panić, M. (2007), Does Europe Need Neoliberal Reforms?, *Cambridge Journal of Economics*, Vol. 31, No. 1, pp. 145-69.

Paoli, P. and Parent-Thirion, A. (2003), *Working Conditions in the Acceding and Candidate Countries*, European Foundation for the Improvement of Living and Working Conditions: Dublin.

Pascall, G. and Kwak, A. (2005), Gender Regimes in Transition in Central and Eastern Europe, Policy, Bristol, UK.

Pascall, G. and Lewis, J. (2004), Emerging Gender Regimes and Policies for Gender Equality in a Wider Europe, *Journal of Social Policy*, Vol. 33, No. 3, pp. 373-94.

Phillips, A. 1991 *Engendering Democracy*, Polity: Cambridge, UK.

Plantenga, J. (2002), Combining Work and Care in the Polder Model: An Assessment of the Dutch Part-Time Strategy, *Critical Social Policy*, Vol. 22, No. 1, pp. 53-71.

Plantenga, J. and Siegel, M. (2005), Position Paper: Childcare in a Changing World, *www.childcareinachangingworld.nl*.

Rake, K. (2000), *Women's Incomes over the Lifetime*, The Stationery Office: London.

Rubery, J. (2005), Gender Mainstreaming and the Open Method of Coordination: Is the Open Method Too Open for Gender Equality Policy?, in J. Zeitlin and P. Pochet (eds.), *The Open Method of Coordination in Action: The European Social Inclusion and Employment Strategies in Action*, European Union Center: Madison, WI.

Rubery, J. *et al.* (2001), The Future European Labor Supply: The Critical Role of the Family, *Feminist Economics*, Vol. 7, No. 3, pp. 33-69.

Rubery, J.; Smith, M., and Fagan, C. (1999), *Women's Employment in Europe: Trends and Prospects*, Routledge: London.

Rubery, J.; Smith, M.; Fagan, C., and Grimshaw, D. (1998), *Women and European Employment*, Routledge: London.

Smith, Alison J. (2004), Who Cares? Fathers and the Time They Spend Looking After Children, *working paper*, Department of Sociology, University of Oxford, Oxford, UK.

Smith, A. and Williams, D. (2007), Father-Friendly Legislation and Paternal Time Across Europe, *Journal of Comparative Policy Analysis*, Vol. 9, No. 2, pp. 175-92.

Squires, J. and Wickham-Jones, M. (2001), *Women in Parliament: A Comparative Analysis*, Equal Opportunities Commission: Manchester, UK.

Szikra, D. (2005), Family and Child Support in a Post-Communist Society: Origins of the Mixed Hungarian Welfare Capitalism, paper presented at *ESPAnet Annual Conference*, University of Fribourg, Switzerland.

Szikra, D. (2006), Schools as Agents of Social Policy: Childcare in the Hungarian Education System in a Comparative and Historical Perspective, paper presented at *ESPAnet Annual Conference*, University of Bremen, Germany.

Threlfall, M. (2007), The Social Dimension of the European Union: Innovative Methods for Advancing Integration, *Global Social Policy*, Vol. 7, No. 3, pp. 271-93.

UNICEF (1999), *Women in Transition*, UNICEF Innocenti Research Centre: Florence, Italy.

UNICEF (2001), *A Decade of Transition*, UNICEF Innocenti Research Centre: Florence, Italy.

UNICEF (2005), *Child Poverty in Rich Countries*, UNICEF Innocenti Research Centre: Florence, Italy.

UNICEF (2007), *An Overview of Child Well-Being in Rich Countries*, UNICEF Innocenti Research Centre: Florence, Italy.

Van der Lippe and Van Dijk (2002), Comparative Research on Women's Employment, *Annual Review of Sociology*, Vol. 28, pp. 221-41.

Watson, P. (1997), Civil Society and the Politics of Difference in Eastern Europe, in J.W. Scott, C. Kaplan, and D. Keates (eds.), *Transitions, Environments, Translations: Feminisms in International Politics*, Routledge: London.

Watson, P. (2000a), Politics, Policy and Identity: EU Eastern Enlargement and East-West Differences, *Journal of European Public Policy, Special Issue*, Vol. 7, No. 3, pp. 369-84.

Watson, P. (2000b), Rethinking Transition: Globalism, Gender and Class, *International Feminist Journal of Politics*, Vol. 2, No. 2, pp. 185-213.

Weiler, A. (2005), *Quality in Work and Employment*, European Foundation for the Improvement of Living and Working Conditions: Dublin.

5

Aging, Risk, and Welfare
in Europe

JASON POWELL AND AZRINI WAHIDIN

This chapter explores the concept of "risk" in relation to the theoretical study of old age and welfare in Europe. Ideas related with what has been conceptualized as the "risk society" (Beck, 1986, 1992) have, it might be argued, become part of the organizing ground of how we define and position the "personal" and "social spaces" in which to grow old. This has startling continuities across Europe. These spaces have served to place the definition of what it means to be an older person—shifts from state care to individualized care (Phillipson and Powell, 2004). As Ulrich Beck (1992) claims, in the conditions of advanced modernity, growing old moves from being a collective to an individual experience and responsibility. Further, Anthony Giddens (1998) suggests that old age is a social constructed category shaped in "late modernity" by its politically pioneered definition in terms of retirement:

> "Old age at sixty-five is a creation, pure and simple, of the welfare state. It is a form of welfare dependency much more widespread than

> any of the dependencies noted by the rightist interpreters of the under-
> class [and] ... A society that separates older people from the majority
> in a retirement ghetto cannot be called inclusive" (Giddens, 1998: 120).

However, Giddens claims that risk is an important factor in the reflexive shaping of old age. First, it is claimed that traditional responses to risk are no longer appropriate. Second, and a key factor highlighting the point above, European societies are themselves less predictable. Faith in the ability of the State or scientific experts to manage risk on our behalf has therefore diminished. Third, people must anticipate and address risk. Whether this is best achieved by collectively sharing the responsibilities that may lead to individualization. Four, traditional definitions of risk, premised on technical measures, neglect the social construction of these and of the risks themselves. This in turn poses fundamental questions about the way we define old age. By representing risk as a centrally defining discourse of "late modernity" offers a new perspective: it allows the interrogation of how older people are made subjects in Europe (Phillipson and Powell, 2004).

Foremost in European societies with little developed welfare systems the concerns regarding the side effects of a society governed by the concepts of risk and individualization are widely disseminated (Giddens, 1991). Linked to this, neoliberalism gives the impression that older people have the capacity to generate their own autonomy and responsibility as indicative of "consumer culture" irrespective of structural constraints. Similarly, theorists advocating positive aging pontificate from a cultural approach by focusing on the benefits of neoliberalism. This is particularly apparent in a move toward neoliberal discourses of consumerism which artificially appears to indicate a reallocation of attention from responding to problems such as "poverty" for example to an attempt to define what it is to allegedly "age positively" in an neoliberal era were older people "have never had it so good" (Gilleard and Higgs, 2000).

For Gilleard and Higgs (2000) this trend is happening in western culture and greatly reconstructs both the formal expectations and personal experiences of later life. Interestingly, Gilleard and Higgs do not see the relevance of risk to the uncertain postmodern times through which older people express their performativity. Whilst such account is highly idealistic it does not highlight the dystopian features of everyday life of older people and the impingement on risk (cf Tullock and Lupton, 2003; Lupton, 1999). Such an account represents an ideological distortion by not focusing on the uneven distributions of power across Europe for older people—such neoconservative writers overlook the risk of hardship and poverty in old age (cf Townsend and Wedderburn, 1965; Townsend, 1981).

Indeed, Alan Walker and Gerhard Naegele (1999) convey the critical message that there is a pressing need for governments and other agencies to respond to changing circumstances of an aging European population. European political processes have become preoccupied with the fiscal support of the delivery of social services to an aging population as this demographic shift alters the balance between those in work and paying taxes, and those in retirement receiving benefits and consuming health care and other social services. Consumption theorists such as Gilleard and Higgs (2000) overlook and underemphasize the risks attached the structural positioning of old age in Europe. The historical lesson is this.

Throughout the 1980s and 1990s European governments uniformly sought to introduce market dynamics into the delivery of services by creating quasi-markets that rely on internal commissioning and purchasing by providers. In the United Kingdom for example, legislation required that local authorities embark upon a phased program, directed by central government, of compulsory competitive tendering, with the strategy of decreasing the role of local authorities and stimulating greater provision of services by the private sector. This program, like its cousins elsewhere on the continent such as France and Germany, rested on the belief that a competitive market and a mixed economy of welfare inevitably provides services that are better and cheaper than those available through the public sector, the reasoning being that a protected public bureaucracy is capable only of furnishing services that are limited, inflexible, and indeterminate and many users are unable to obtain the services they require.

European governments assume that they can put in place a mixed economy of welfare to meet the needs of their populations and to facilitate consumer choice among the various services. However, the introduction of "choice" may in fact reduce the number of options available because a reduction in public sector provision may not be matched by the development of a diverse range of service options in the voluntary and private sector (Phillipson and Powell, 2004). Planning is necessary, particularly in light of the demographic changes. The statistical reality that Europe's population must inevitably age because the fertility boom in the late 1950s and early 1960s and the increasing expected average lifespan will greatly increase the number of older persons across the European Union from about 2020 forward. The specter of an aging population is said to necessitate the dismantling of the welfare state and the introduction of a greater degree of reliance on personal financial provision and privately provided care arrangements. These proposals are linked to ideological shifts during the latter part of the 20th century, and the concomitant reassessment of the social contract between the state and its population.

As a result, "cradle-to-grave" principles of postwar social planning have been replaced by policies which encourage those with resources to make provision for themselves, with the less well off depending on minimal state support. This exclusion has serious implications for the workings of EU states, for over time the issues raised will test the stability and security of health and political structures in all European countries. In order to preserve the basic tenets of intergenerational solidarity and to develop a more inclusive society, it will be necessary to find ways in which the views of older people can be appropriately represented (Phillipson and Powell, 2004).

Older citizens must have a greater "voice" in the decision-making process of welfare services provision. The point made by Walker and Naegele (1999) is a bold one that a new political economy of aging is needed to engender social policy that rests on a broader view of what older persons need and the manner in which they can contribute to and make a different society, rather than the current policies that focus alone on pension arrangements and the provision of social welfare. New policies are needed to meet the requirements of the risk society. The politics of old age is not just about learning to live with an older population and how to arrange the provision of services, but is more about rethinking the nature of European society itself (cf Stearns, 1977; Vincent, 1995, 1999; Thane, 2000; Walker and Aspalter, 2008).

Indeed, in contemporary European society, risk is a broad concept that extends over a broad range of social practices that impinge on the experiences of older people. Current debates about older people and relationship to sexuality, crime, national security, food safety, employment and welfare are all underscored by risk (Phillipson, 1998).

Moreover, there is growing recognition that potential risks of the future that transcends EU States—"global warming," "genetic cloning," "GM foods" and "bio-terrorism"—shatter the rigid boundaries of nations and demand global co-operation and control. Awareness of the trans-national nature of risk has led the United Nations to form its own Commission on Human Security. A recent report by the UN Commission suggests ways in which the security of older people, for example, might be advanced—from humanitarian and military strategies through to economic, health and educational strategies. Whilst "freedom from want" continues to be the most pressing global imperative, in recent years "freedom from fear" has risen up the global political agenda (Commission on Human Security, 2003: 4). Coupled with this, the US Central Intelligence Agency's (2004) *World Fact Book* suggests that an "aging population" is a risk to the financial safety of western nation states in US and Europe.

In science, risk has traditionally been approached as an objective material entity, to be mastered by processes of calculation, assessment and probability. In the 21st century, "advances" in science and medicine led to the eradication of many infectious diseases, raised life expectancy in old age and improved quality of life across Europe. The nature of scientific knowledge about risk and impact on aging has articulated the perspective that as a person goes through aging process there are heightened risks to the human body—in the mind and internal organs of the body. It has gradually become clear that the very institutions entrusted with regulating risks have themselves transmuted into risk producers. In recent times, multinational corporate business, science, medicine and government have all been accused of generating various dangers to public health which impinges on the safety of older people (cf e.g. Reddy, 1996).

In response to public concerns about unbounded techno-scientific development and the apparent inefficacy of expert systems, interest in risk has gathered momentum within social science disciplines in recent years (cf Giddens, 1991; Castel, 1991). However, whilst the language of risk has become prolific, the concept itself remains cloaked in ambiguity and its relationship to aging scantily researched; making risk and aging an important and significant issue for social policy. Yet, it is under theorized and reified in its conceptualization.

Such an approach seeks to capture the dimensions of subjectivity within the social-political constraints that shape individual lives. This allows reconstructions of logics of action or structuration behind current neoliberal self-representations of aging identity. It could be supposed that such constructions enable us to reconstruct the complexity of aging in social contexts and the influence of, for example, social welfare on these experiences as a ground for risk perception. Importantly, the notion of an aging society becomes secondary to the emphasis on the way in which families and individuals handle the demands associated with an aging population. Phillipson and Powell (2004: 33) suggest that there are three factors that make risk important to understanding old age:

"First, the globalisation of aging is increasingly recognised. All societies (poor as well as rich) are undergoing similar population transformations (albeit with notable exceptions such as those in countries devastated by the AIDS virus). Aging thus becomes simultaneously both a biographical event and one shared with different cultures and societies across the globe. Second, aging experiences are themselves hugely (and increasingly) diverse. Under the guise of the welfare state, growing old was compressed into a fairly limited range of institutions and identities (notably in respect of income and life-styles). Aging in the post-welfare society, however, has substantially expanded in respect of social opportunities as well as economic inequalities. Third, old age is also being changed by what Beck (1992) describes as the era of reflexive modernization. This may be conceived in terms of how individuals and the lay public exert control and influence on the shape and character of modernity."

The more European societies are modernized, the more older people acquire the ability to reflect upon the social forces of their existence within the conditions of risk constraints. Hence, we need to understand the major *social forces* which impinge on aging itself. Such social forces that create risk associated with aging implies a breakdown in *trust* as a key modernist principle in contemporary society. Hence, the rest of the chapter is in three parts: we introduce the relevance and breakdown in trust relations; map out the key assumptions of risk society in Europe; and critically engage with old age and examples drawn from social welfarism to consolidate an understanding of the constructedness of old age in Europe.

From Trust to Risk

There are increasing attempts to conceptualize the notion of "trust" in social theory as a pivotal dimension of European society (Giddens, 1991). However, the early statement that "social science research on trust has produced a good deal of conceptual confusion regarding the meaning of trust and its place in social life" (Lewis and Weigert, 1985; quoted in Powell, 2005: 104) seems to be still valid especially as applied to aging studies. Trust is on the one hand incompatible with complete ignorance of the possibility and probability of future events, and on the other hand with emphatic belief when the anticipation of disappointment is excluded. Someone who trusts has an expectation directed to an event. The expectations are based on the ground of incomplete knowledge about the probability and incomplete control about the occurrence of the event. Trust is of relevance for action and has consequences for the trusting agent if trust is confirmed or disappointed. Thus, trust is connected with risk (Giddens, 1991).

Up to now there have been few attempts to work out a systematic scheme of different forms of trust in between older people and individuals, institutions or policies that impinge on their identity performance. Social trust tends to be high among older people who believe that their public safety is high (Walker and Naegele, 1999). Since the erosion of public trust in institutions such as, for example, the Brown government in UK with it losing 25 million people's bank details and identity or the £25 billion financial loss of UK bank Northern Rock in late 2007, "trust" has attracted more and more attention.

There are differences between trust in contracts between people and State (such as pension provision), trust in friendships across intergenerational lines, trust in love and relationships and trust in foreign issues (associated with national identity across the EU) (cf Mölling, 2001). However, sociological theories which suppose a general change in modernity (e.g. Beck, 1992) assume that with the erosion of traditional institutions and scientific knowledge trust becomes an issue more often produced actively by individuals than institutionally guaranteed.

There are a number of implications of risk perception and risk taking that indicates: trust is much easier to destroy than to built; if trust is once undermined it is more difficult to restore it; familiarity with a place, a situation or a person produces trust; persons will develop trust if a person or situation has ascriptive characteristics positively valued. Trust seems to be something that is produced individually by experience and over time and cannot be immediately and with purpose be produced by European governments without dialogical interaction with older people on issues affecting their lifestyles and life-chances such as care, pensions, employment and political representation in the EU (Walker and Naegele, 2000). Though as Giddens (1991) stresses risk is the feature of a society shifting its emphasis away from trust on traditional ties and social values. How risks are perceived and formulated as a breakdown in trust reflects the essentially discursive practices of politics and power in European society. The ability to control and manage perceptions about moral intentions of a pervasive governmental rationality may be part of an understanding of risk.

Beck and "Risk Society" Theory

The concept of risk has come to assume accelerating prominence in sociological writings of Ulrich Beck. Beck (1992) claims that modernization helps the self become an agent via processes of individualization which they both see as indicative of neoliberalism; they advocate that the self become less constrained by traditional group identities and institutions but more constraint by the dynamics of markets (labor markets, consumer-markets) and secondary institutions, and becomes therefore a project to be reflexively worked on in the context of a globalized world. As we see the development of this the new global order, some risks such as those caused by hazardous industries, are transferred away from the developed countries to the Third world. Thus while Beck sees risk society as a catastrophic society, what we are seeing is the transference of certain risks through aversion and management which in turn include a *reorganization of power and authority* (Beck, 1992: 4; Beck, 1994, 2001).

Beck acknowledges that some social groups are more affected than others by the distribution and growth of risks, and these differences may be structured through inequalities of class and social position. The disadvantaged have fewer opportunities to avoid risk because of their lack of resources compared with the advantaged. By contrast, the wealthy to a degree (income, power or education), can purchase safety and freedom from risk (Beck, 1992: 33). However, it is the gestation and the constellations of the risks, which are unknown, and thus risk affects those who have produced or profited from them, breaking down the previous social and geographic boundaries evident in modern societies.

Beck (1992), argues that the "former colonies" of the western world are soon becoming the waste dumps of the world for toxic and nuclear wastes produced by more privileged countries. Risks have become more and more difficult to calculate and control. Hence it can be argued that Risks often affect both the wealthy and poor alike: "poverty is hierarchic and smog is democratic" (Beck, 1992: 36). At the same time, because of the degree of interdependence of the highly specialized agents of modernization in business, agriculture, the law and politics, there is no single agent responsible for any risk: "there is a general complicity, and the complicity is matched by a general lack of responsibility. Everyone is cause *and* effect" (Beck, 1992: 33) and so "perpetrator and victim become identical" (Beck, 1992: 38) in a consuming society. It is this immateriality and invisibility of the threats that saturate the "risk society" making it harder to identify the offender of global risk.

Beck (1992), argues that this fundamentally poses the second challenge for analyses of these socially constituted industrial phenomena: interpretation becomes inherently a matter of perspective and hence political. Politicians constantly invoke science in their attempts to pesuade the public that their policies and products are safe. The inescapability of interpretation makes risks infinitely malleable and, as Beck (1992: 23) insists, "open to social definition and construction," This in turn put those in a position to define (and/or legitimate) risks—the mass media, scientists, politicians and the legal profession—in key social positions (Phillipson and Powell, 2004).

Ulrich Beck (1996) makes the point that risk "is not an option which could be chosen or rejected in the course of political debate" (1996: 28). Instead this is an inescapable product and structural condition of advance industrialization of where we produce the hazards of that system, in Beck's words (1996: 31) "undermine and/or cancel the established safety systems of the provident state's existing risk calculation." Beck (1996) further exemplifies this point by examining contemporary hazards associated with nuclear power, chemical pollution and genetic engineering and bio technology that cannot be limited or contained to particular spaces, and that which cannot be grasped through the rules of causality, and cannot be safeguarded, compensated or insured against (cf Krohn and Krücken, 1993; Latour and Woolgar, 1986). They are therefore "glocal"—both local and global. Risk society is thus "European risk society" and risks affect a European citizenship. The questioning of the outcomes of modernity in terms of their production of risks is an outcome of reflexive modernization. An awareness of risk, therefore, is heightened at the level of the everyday.

In Europe, risk, in its purely technical meaning, came to rely upon conditions in which the probability estimates of an event are able to be known or knowable. This has the effect of paralyzing action and bringing insurance systems that promised to cover eventualities into chaos. In Great Britain for example, the welfare state, an insurance system that promised to cater for people from cradle to the grave, is unable to sustain that promise for future generations. The welfare system as a system of social insurance is beginning to lose its legitimacy with the rise of private health insurance. In the United States, 70 percent of its population do not have private health insurance (cf Macnicol, 1998; Powell and Wahidin, 2004; Phillipson and Powell, 2004).

Scientists have lost their authority in relation to risk assessments most evidently seen in the collapse of endowment and certain pension funds. Scientific calculations are challenged more and more by political groups and activists (Beck, 1995: 125-26). The nature of such hazards, therefore, returns the concept of risk to the pre-modern notion of "incalculable insecurities." In common with such hazards, they "undercut the social logic of risk calculation and provision" (Beck, 1995: 77). For Beck, then, risk may be defined as "systematic way of dealing with hazards and insecurities induced and introduced by modernization itself" (Beck, 1992: 21).

If this *might* be happening to older people, what are the implications? Two developments seem to be responsible for the growing risk awareness in modern industrialized societies in Europe, even though their respective contribution is contested. The new awareness of the limits of the technical and the mathematical/statistical calculation of risk would cause an increase of concerns regarding the rational controllability of an uncertain future (Beck, 1992; Bonß, 1995, 1997; Bonß and Zinn, 2005). Furthermore, the sustained endeavor to apply a new liberal style of governing modern societies would increasingly shift the responsibility of the management of risks and uncertainties from the state to the individual. Socio-demographic changes as well as shifts in governance contribute to the perception of risk and uncertainty regarding old age in two ways: First, they promote the understanding of risk and uncertainty *in* old age and second, they suggest to perceive age *as* risky and uncertain.

In order to approach the concept of risk and old age it is suggested that by conceptualizing risk in a broader framework of (un-)certainty (Zinn, 2005) where risk is seen as a specific strategy to produce certainty in order to enable to act. Risk appears then as a certainty construction—a specific way to produce the necessary certainty as a prerequisite for action (Zinn, 2004). Thereby the future becomes accessible for planning and action. In order to work on itself, the "self" or at least according to Beck (1992: 181) relates to self-political rationalities and risk: "risks become the motor of *self-politicization* of modernity in industrial society."

One element of the "motor" of self-politicization is how successful neoliberalism has been in fashioning *common sense* discourses around its political rhetoric. Jürgen Habermas (1986: 13-14) claims what we are witnessing is a "completely altered relationship between autonomous and self-organized public spheres on the one hand, and subsystems steered by money and administrative power on the other." *Self-autonomization* coupled with *administrative power* is indicative of neoliberal features of social policy for older people. Older people living in neo-liberal EU societies have therefore moved towards a greater awareness of risk and are forced to deal with risks on an everyday basis: "Everyone is caught up in defensive battles of various types anticipating the hostile substances in one's manner of living and eating" (Beck, 1994: 45). The media for their part have taken up warnings of experts about risk and communicate them to their mass publics in the EU.

There is ambivalence at the heart of Europe: on the one hand, older people are to be "managed" by other administrative powers such as professional experts in modernity (Phillipson and Powell, 2004); on the other hand, older people are left to govern themselves. This moral idea of freedom and responsibility is involved in the modern notion to govern European societies (Foucault, 1991) but is determined by the limits of everyday life in socio-culturally different circumstances (Bourdieu, 1979) within a "risk society" (Beck, 1992). The tension between ideal and socio-cultural structured life constitutes the battleground of the disputes on the governance of old age. These, along with ties between generations, created a social, economic and moral space within which growing numbers of older people could be channeled and contained. For example, for a period of 20 years or more, moving older people into the zone of retirement and the welfare state, held at bay the underlying issue of securing a place and identity for aging within the framework of an advanced capitalist society. The meaning of later life was, temporarily at least, constructed out of a modernist vision where retirement and welfare were viewed as natural end-points to the human life cycle.

The Governance of Uncertainty in Welfare and Old Age

The governance of old age originally developed and was closely linked to the creation of a social security system and the welfare state. The idea of prudence and self-responsibility among the working class was expressed through such institutions as the friendly society and the revolving building society and promoted both political quiescence and the stability needed to ensure steady growth in the later half of the 19th century (Dean, 1999). This system was supplanted by the development of insurance in the 20th century leading to the modern welfare state (Ewald, 1986). The provision for old age was originally not central, because at the end of the 19th century most people did not reach the age of 70 to claim a pension and live through this last phase of their life without having to work. The original concept was to save the worker and its family in case of death or disablement of the breadwinner.

The strategies of risk-management by means of insurance were understood as sharing them between all insured people, which should be in principle as much as possible. But this fundamental concept has changed recently as part of a general change in the idea of insurance as well as the government of citizens. The responsibility of the state and thereby the risks are given back to the public. As Baker and Simon (2002: 4) recently pointed out, "private pensions, annuities, and life insurance are engaged in an historic shift of investment risk from broad pools (the classic structure of risk spreading through insurance) to individual (middle-class) consumers and employees in return for the possibility of greater return."

The understanding of the individual as a self-responsible actor as given for granted underestimates the various resources and life experiences different people possess. The strategies to cope with risk and uncertainty in the life course are rather oriented on the circumstances of everyday life, personal values and life experiences that relate to self-responsibility. Governmental programs are mainly developed against the background of the model of a self-responsible actor, and increasingly address people with significant lack of cultural and economic resources as self-reflexive and rational actors. Although this concept might be generally helpful in order to formulate political programs they regularly fail because of this assumption.

The governmental constructions of risks and old age converge in the notion of rational acting old people. It does conceptually ignore that the ability to be autonomous and rational is not a question of context-independent (free) will or something what is just given, but it is provided by context factors as well as biographical experiences which shape expectations regarding the future. Thereby accumulated "local knowledge" (Wynne, 1996) produces logics of how to act best in an uncertain context (e.g. Zinn, 2005), which include the policy of the government as well. This is not only important when people are old, but in earlier life phases when they have to deal with their expectations regarding old age and have to take precautionary measures. The unequal resources available, the unreflected routines and the needs and execution of everyday life shape what is the basis to act in "old age" (Phillipson and Powell, 2004).

The extrication of these actions can be traced to at least three types of crisis affecting the management of aging populations in the last quarter of the twentieth century: economic, social and cultural. The economic dimension has been well-rehearsed, with successive crises from the mid-1970s onwards undermining, first, the goal of full employment (and hence destabilizing retirement), and, second, the fiscal basis of the welfare state (accelerated with the onset of a privatization from the 1980s onwards) (Estes *et al.*, 2001).

However we are neither a *provident state* and or a *providing state.* The dialectic of risk and social insurance systems of calculation have failed to address or predict the increase in longevity, the blurring of the life-course and the growing trend for smaller families. What we are beginning to see occur with entry and immersion in to a risk society is the fracturing of insurance social systems that have failed to make accurate predictions in the EU (Phillipson and Powell, 2004). This has led for those who can afford to invest in various insurance policies ways of minimizing risk that may befall them in times, when illness occurs, unemployment (i.e., mortgage protection), death, which are all sold on the basis of what may happen in the future. The short fall of this is that elders from lower socio-economic groups who without insurance will be caught within the widening fractures appearing in the welfare state. Old age is also being changed by what Beck (1992) describes as the era of reflexive modernization. This may be conceived in terms of how in-dividuals and the lay public exert control and influence on the shape and character of Europe.

Conclusion

How do we define "old age"? Is it a stage in life defined by a particular age or event such as retirement, is it determined by physical character-istics and the loss of independence, or is it an artifact of social structures? Indeed, is it helpful to categorize people as being "old" at all, as op-posed to being "disadvantaged" or "dependent"? It may be inaccurate to expect older people to see themselves as a category with particular health needs and wants. Hence, the key task is to analyze the interplay between social policy and the lives of individuals, families or groups and communities. The expectation of negative events in the future and the different ways of how to respond to such expectations is central for the sociological approach to risk and uncertainty (Zinn, 2004; cf Luh-mann, 1993).

Part of this reflexive response is the importance of recognizing self-subjective dimensions of emotions, trust, biographical knowledge and resources that impinge on the existential shaping old age (Zinn, 2005; cf Slovic, 1999; Loewenstein *et al.*, 2001; Slovic *et al.*, 2002). Hence, our discussion provides a critical narrative to the importance to the study of old age and welfarism in Europe. It has become commonplace for academics and practitioners to explore, develop and apply an assortment of social science perspectives on risk. In a post 9/11 world, questions around risk and risk management have become ever more pertinent (cf Zinn and Taylor-Gooby, 2006), leading to reflections on a number of different levels about "ontological security." We are left with two questions: how do older people manage their sense of well being in a world in which less and less can be taken for granted? To what extent does the specter of global risks interplay with more routine insecurities which reach to the capillary texture of day-to-day life of older people? There is an urgency to reflect on these questions to understand the subject positioning of older people in a European society that is charac-terized by increasing uncertainty.

REFERENCES

Baker, T. and Simon, J. (2002), Embracing Risk, in T. Baker and J. Simon (eds.), *Embracing Risk: The Changing Culture of Insurance and Responsibility*, University of Chicago Press: Chicago, IL.

Beck, U. (1986), *Riskogesellschaft: Auf dem Weg in eine andere Moderne*, Suhrkamp: Frankfurt a.M., Germany.

Beck, U. (1992), *Risk Society: Towards a New Modernity*, Sage: London.

Beck, U. (1994), The Reinvention of Politics: Towards a Theory of Reflexive Modernization, in U. Beck, A. Giddens and S. Lash (eds.), *Reflexive Modernisation: Politics, Tradition and Aesthetics in the Modern Social Order*, Polity: Cambridge, UK.

Beck, U. (1995), *Ecological Politics in the Age of Risk*, Polity: Cambridge, UK.

Beck, U. (1996), Risk Society and the Provident State, in S. Lash, B. Szerzynski, and B. Wynne (eds.), *Risk Environment and Modernity: Towards a New Ecology*, Sage: London.

Beck, U. (2001), *World Risk Society*, Polity: Cambridge, UK.

Bonß, W. (1995), *Vom Risiko: Unsicherheit und Ungewissheit in der Moderne*, Hamburger Edition: Hamburg, Germany.

Bonß, W. (1997), Die gesellschaftliche Konstruktion von Sicherheit, in E. Lippert, A. Prüfert, and G. Wachtler (eds.), *Sicherheit in der unsicheren Gesellschaft*, Westdeutscher Verlag: Opladen, Germany.

Bonß, W. and Zinn, T. (2005), Erwartbarkeit, Glück und Vertrauen: Zum Wandel biographischer Sicherheitskonstruktionen in der Moderne, *Soziale Welt*, Vol. 56, No. 2/3, pp. 79-98.

Castel, R. (1991), From Dangerousness to Risk, in G. Burchell, C. Gordon, and P. Miller (eds.), *The Foucault Effect: Studies in Governmentality*, Harvester Wheatsheaf: London.

Dean, M. (1999), *Governmentality,* Open University Press: Milton Keynes, UK.

Estes, C. *et al.* (2001), *Social Policy and Aging*, Sage: London.

Ewald, F. (1993), Two Infinities of Risk, in B. Massumi (ed.), *The Politics of Everyday Fear*, University of Minnesota Press: Minneapolis, MN.

Foucault, M. (1991), *Discipline and Punish*, Tavistock: London.

Giddens, A. (1991), *Modernity and Self-Identity: Self and Society in the Late-Modern Age*, Polity: Cambridge, UK.

Giddens,A. (1998), *The Third Way; The Renewal of Social Democracy*, Polity: Cambridge, UK.

Gilleard, C. and Higgs, P. (2000), *Cultures of Ageing: Self, Citizen and the Body*, Prentice-Hall: London.

Habermas, J. (1986), *Knowledge and Human Interests*, Polity: Cambridge, UK.

Krohn, W. and Krücken, G. (1993), *Riskante Technologien: Reflexion und Regulation*, Suhrkamp, Frankfurt a.M., Germany.

Latour, B. and Woolgar, S. (1986), *Laboratory Life: The Construction of Scientific Facts*, Princeton University Press: Princeton, NJ.

Loewenstein, G.; Weber, E.; Hsee, C., and Welch N. (2001), Risks as Feelings, *Psychological Bulletin*, Vol. 127, No. 2, pp. 267-86.

Luhmann, N. (1993), *Risk: A Sociological Theory*, De Gruyter: New York.

Lupton, D. (1999), *Risk*, Routledge: London.

Macnicol, J. (1998), *The Politics of Retirement in Britain, 1878-1948*, Cambridge University Press: Cambridge, UK.

Mölling, G. (2001), The Nature of Trust: From George Simmel to a Theory of Expectation, Interpretation and Suspension, *Sociology*, Vol. 35, No. 2, pp. 403-20.

Phillipson, C. (1998), The Social Construction of Retirement: Perspectives from Critical Theory and Political Economy, in M. Minkler and C. Estes (eds.), *Critical Gerontology: Perspectives from Political and Moral Economy*, Baywood: New York.

Phillipson, C. and Powell, J.L. (2004), Risk, Social Welfare and Old Age, in E. Tulle (ed.), *Old Age and Human Agency*, Nova Science: New York.

Powell, J.L (2005), *Social Theory and Aging*, Rowman and Littlefield: New York

Powell, J.L. and Wahidin, A. (2004), Corporate Crime, Aging and Pensions in Great Britain, *Journal of Societal and Social Policy*, Vol. 3, No. 1, pp. 37-55

Reddy, S. (1996), Claims to Expert Knowledge and the Subversion of Democracy: The Triumph of Risk Over Uncertainty, *Economy and Society*, Vol. 25, No. 2, pp. 222-54.

Slovic, P. (1999), Trust, Emotion, Sex, Politics, and Science: Surveying the Risk-Assessment Battlefield, *Risk Analysis*, Vol. 19, No. 4, pp. 689-701.

Slovic, P.; Finucane, M.; Peters, E.; MacGregor, D. (2002), Risk as Analysis and Risk as Feelings: Some Thoughts About Affect, Reason, Risk, and Rationality, paper given at the *Annual Meeting of the Society for Risk Analysis*, New Orleans, Louisiana, December 10.

Stearns, P. (1977), *Old Age in European Society: The Cast of France*, Croom Helm: London.

Thane, P. (2000), *Old Age in English History: Past Experiences, Present Issues*, Oxford University Press: Oxford, UK.

Townsend, P. (1981), The Structured Dependency of the Elderly: The Creation of Social Policy in the 20th Century, *Ageing and Society*, Vol. 1, No. 1, pp. 5-28.

Townsend, P. and Wedderburn, D. (1965), *The Aged in the Welfare State*, Bell: London.

Tulloch, J. and Lupton, D. (2003), *Risk and Everyday Life*, Sage: London.

Vincent, J. (1995), *Inequality of Old Age*, UCL Press: London.

Vincent, J. (1999), *Politics, Power and Old Age*, Open University Press: Buckingham, UK.

Walker, A. and Aspalter, C. (eds.) (2008), *Securing the Future for Old Age in Europe*, Casa Verde: Hong Kong.

Walker, A. and Naegele, G. (1999), *The Politics of Old Age in Europe*, OUP: Milton Keynes, UK.

Wynne, B. (1987), *Risk Management and Hazardous Waste*, Springer: Berlin.

Zinn, J.O. (2004), Health, Risk and Uncertainty in the Life Course: A Typology of Biographical Certainty Constructions, *Social Theory & Health*, Vol. 2, pp. 199-221.

Zinn, J.O. (2005), The Biographical Approach: A Better Way to Understand Behaviour in Health and Illness?, *Health, Risk & Society*, Vol. 7, No. 1, pp. 1-9.

Zinn, J.O. and Taylor-Gooby, P. (2006), The Challenge of (Managing) New Risks and Uncertainties, in P. Taylor-Gooby and J.O. Zinn (eds.), *Risk in Social Science*, Oxford University Press: Oxford, UK.

6

European Welfare States in Transition: The United Kingdom, France, Germany, Italy, and Sweden

CHRISTIAN ASPALTER

This chapter examines the fundamental changes of the welfare state in Europe over the last one to two decades, taking the examples of four leading welfare state systems—the United Kingdom, France, Germany, Italy, and Sweden. Each country case study is first examined with regard to their special features and policy designs before going into greater detail in terms contemporary (recent and current) changes with regard to welfare state reform.

The chapter concludes that, besides parametric changes, three kinds of systematic changes are well under way in these model countries—a trend that is supported by global developments. The first is the ongoing theme of privatization, often also partly identified as pluralization, in welfare state reform. The second is a process of "individualization," that is the introduction of individual accounts, notional individual accounts in social security systems, or a virtual shift from defined benefit (DB) system to de-facto defined-contribution (DC) system—e.g., a DB formula that takes into account "lifetime" contributions). The third development is a complete systematic change of the welfare state; here a common international trend has not been identified yet.

This chapter puts forward the idea that welfare states systems in the long run are capable of being very adaptive, though sometimes it takes a longer time period, up to two decades, to realize major parametric or systematic changes. Seen from a historical perspective, welfare state systems in historical perspective may be more flexible than commonly thought and expected—especially in the light of the coming of the super-aged society and the ongoing implications of economic globalization. While there is a strong showing of the importance of path dependence (Pierson, 1994, 2001a,b) in the developmental trajectory of modern welfare state systems, there is also plenty room for strong parametric and systematic changes over longer, and yet sometimes rather short periods of time (cf Palier, 2000, 2006; Fink and Talos, 2004; Palier and Martin, 2008).

The UK Welfare State in Transition

The Real-Typical Welfare State Model

The United Kingdom has its own variant of welfare state capitalism that has been founded along Beveridge-style universal social security programs. In the late 1940s and the 1950s, the British welfare state did not differ considerably from its Swedish counterpart. The main difference between Swedish and British welfare capitalism, ever since, is the quantity of welfare benefits. Whereas the Swedish welfare state has installed a social security system with highest levels of income maintenance, the British welfare state retained its characteristic feature of flat-rate social security benefits.

Nonetheless, the welfare state in Britain has experienced an expansion of welfare through to the mid-1970s owing to changing patterns of need, changing state priorities, and changing costs of social services. The greater share of the elderly in the population contributed to the increase in welfare needs, especially the share of those over age 75. As a result, social security, education, and housing expenditure continued to grow significantly (cf e.g. Clarke and Langan, 1989: 33-35). In the field of social insurance, there has been a sharp rise in the number of persons receiving pensions between 1950 and 1980, with 4.1 and 8.9 million persons respectively. Due to the change of the family allowance system in 1977, also those families with less than three children could receive family allowances. Whereas in 1950 there were 4.7 million children who attracted family allowances, 30 years later, 13.3 million children were covered by the family allowance system. The number of persons receiving unemployment benefits also increased significantly from 226 to 709 thousand persons during the same period.

From 1945 to 1948, the British installed the first modern welfare state in Europe. The Beveridge Plan promoted the inclusion of the entire population into social insurance schemes. The aim of doing so was to cure the great social problems of the common people, i.e. mainly the problem of income maintenance during old age, times of sickness, injury and unemployment, by compulsory, universal social insurance programs without sacrificing the individuals right of self-determination. Beveridge, a social-liberal politician, sought to manage a balancing act between collectivism and individualism with universal social insurance programs (cf Baldwin, 1992: 57). In 1946, a universal provision of health care was also set up by the National Health Service Act that was based on the Beveridge Report. However, the *shiny years* of the British welfare state should only last five years (cf Gregg, 1967) as the Labour Government was voted out of office on October 26, 1951. The next 13 years of Conservative hegemony in British politics brought a harsh wind of anti-welfare politics and led to a virtual standstill of welfare state development (cf Glennester, 1998). Only in the Labour dominated era between October 1964 and May 1979 (with the notable exception of the Conservative government of PM Heath from June 1970 to March 1974; cf Woldendorp *et al.*, 1998), a significant extension of the British welfare state what concerns social security expenditures occurred.

The verbal onslaught on the British welfare state under the Thatcher Government did not materialize in welfare state retrenchment until Margaret Thatcher began her third term in office as prime minister (cf

Castles and Pierson, 1996; Clarke and Langan, 1995; Gould, 1993) due to widespread middle-class support of popular social insurance systems.

The political debate, ever since, changed in favor of a new welfare strategy, which can be described, as follows "to achieve security by redistributing opportunity rather than just redistributing income" (Commission on Social Justice, 1994, quoted in Taylor-Gooby, 1997: 177). In the 1980s, the government kept relying on means tests for determining the eligibility for insurance-based and universal social security benefits, it "wanted to reduce the value of means-tested benefits and discourage too great a reliance on them" (Gould, 1993: 119).

In the 1990s, not extensive, general redistribution, but increased work incentives (as put forward by "workfare programs") and less welfare dependency have become core objectives in social policy under New Labour. Even though, the main logic of welfare state provision in the United Kingdom is built on the *principle of poverty reduction*, the British welfare state did not succeed in abolishing poverty, as well as major income and wealth inequalities, since there had been a significant slowdown in the extension of welfare programs since the 1960s (cf George, 1980: 56; Glennester, 1998; Lavalette and Penketh, 2003). British welfare capitalism, therefore, has not changed much in its overall appearance when compared to the late 1940s; i.e. some programs had been extended while others had been downgraded (e.g. the replacement of unemployment benefits with job-seeker allowances). The United Kingdom, over time, developed a unique form of welfare state capitalism that is mainly based on flat-rate universal social security programs and means-tested/workfare-based social assistance.

Contemporary Welfare State Reform in the United Kingdom

The story of welfare state reform in the United Kingdom is somewhat different from that of the rest of Europe. There was no immediate pension crisis, with regard to financing of the system, which was rather low in comparative European terms, and the demographic development. Yet pension reform took off much earlier than in the rest of Europe, preceding it by a decade (Walker, 2003).

The pension system was being reformed in the years 1980, 1986, 1988, 1995, and 1997, which resulted in cutting the share of GDP committed to public pension spending (Swank, 2002; Ward, 2003). The main features of these reforms were retrenchment and privatization of the pension system. Welfare state restructuring in the case of the United Kingdom, as in the Untied States and New Zealand, has undermined the welfare state, and was carried out for ideological reasons (Walker and Deacon, 2003). This is to be explained by the fact that in the United Kingdom the average middle-class taxpayer is bearing the brunt of welfare finance, while he or she is not benefiting a great deal from those benefits. The tax-heavy finance structure of the UK welfare state impedes any incentive for the middle and upper classes to support social solidarity what regards redistribution to the lower-income strata of society. The redistribution-biased institutional set up of the UK welfare state, which spends a great deal of resources to non-working and working poor, in combination with the exclusion of the middle classes from major welfare state benefits, is then also responsible for the mas-sive onslaught by both first the Conservative Party and then the Labour Party (cf Scharpf, 2002; Aspalter, 2002).

The National Health Services and Community Care Act of 1990 set out to "promote care in the community." As a result of this piece of legislation many long-term care hospitals for the elderly and those with severe disabilities, and institutional facilities for the mentally ill have been closed (Lavalette and Penketh, 2003). It also led to an increasing role for the private, voluntary, and the informal sector (i.e., mainly unpaid female relatives, which has negative effects on gender equality, cf Daly and Rake, 2003). New developments in the National Health Service are rather promising under the Blair Government, with extended budgets to address the chronic problem of under-capacity, especially with regard to doctors and nurses (cf e.g. Wanless, 2002).

State basic pensions in the United Kingdom are very low, and would be lower still were it not for a pensioner revolt in the autumn of 2000. Benefits under this scheme amount EURO 115 for single persons per week, and EURO 69 for a dependent spouse. The UK government plans the implementation of a second flat-rate pension system, which will gradually, over the next few years, replace the state-earnings-related pension system (SERPS) that has existed since 1978. SERPS now provides fairly small additional pension benefits after being cut back twice, in 1988 and 1997. Furthermore, the government plans to increase the role of means-tested social assistance for the elderly; it also plans to introduce a Pension Credit that will be delivered in due course through the tax system. The level of state spending, over the next 50 to 60 years, as a proportion of GDP, despite a 50 percent growth in the number of pensioners, is expected to stay more or less constant. The UK pension system is not steering towards a *"demographic time-bomb,"* but instead towards a *"poverty time-bomb,"* so Ward (2003: 276).

A great number of people in the United Kingdom remain in desperate poverty (cf Jones and Novak, 1999). There is still strong middle-class support for the government to run public services, and many people (even voters of the Conservative Party) feel strongly that "those who work for public services are under-paid and undervalued, and totally reject the Thatcherite idea of wholesale privatization" (*The Guardian*, 2001, March 20: cited in Lavalette and Penketh, 2003).

The new Labour Government under Tony Blair set out to reform social policy and do away with its past policies of large-scale redistribution. However, in essence, the content of major reforms introduced by New Labour does not disagree with, or distinguish itself a great deal from, that of a wide range of conservative and neoliberal reformers around the globe. In 1992, Frank Field, one of New Labour's social reformers, said that "the aim must be to illustrate the potential for redistribution in our society and how the main forms of redistribution to be enacted by a future Labour government not to involve more taxes" (quoted in Lavalette and Penketh, 2003: 82).

Further, in 1997 Tony Blair stressed the aim of fashioning "a modern welfare state, where we maintain high levels of social inclusion based on values of community and social justice, but where the role of government changes so it is not necessary to provide all social provision, and fund all social provision but to organize and regulate it most efficiently and fairly" (quoted in Lavalette and Penketh, 2003: 83; cf also Schmidt, 2002). Words of "social justice," "redistribution," and "social inclusion" appear in speeches that in essence propose *the end of social welfare as we know it*, without, essentially, proposing a new type of "social" welfare.

With the new emphasis on market- and private-based forms of social welfare provision, it seems that a true commitment of the State drifts farther away into the distant future. With the new, ideologically tainted emphasis on the market and market principles in the realm of social welfare provision and policies, social problems may worsen, rather than being reduced:

> "the UK experience provides warning signs against the dangers of an unbalanced approach to [for example] pension provision. Private funded schemes have a role to play in pension systems, but the dangers that arise when they are given a central role where they can act as an engine of social exclusion" (Walker, 2003: 22).

The French Welfare State in Transition

The Real-Typical Welfare State Model

During World War II, President Charles De Gaulle studied intensively the Beveridge model and the National Health Service of the United Kingdom. For this reason, the universal principles have penetrated deeply into the French social security system that is otherwise modelled after the Bismarckian system—where social security schemes are divided along occupational and geographical lines. Thus, there is redistribution in between each segment of the population, but not between different segments themselves.

France has developed a two-tier pension system for the private sector employees, with a basic pension to cover the risks of poverty and a mandatory supplementary pension system to cover income maintenance needs. The public sector employees and employees in public sector companies have separate pension schemes (such as e.g. railway employees, miners, as well as electricity and gas workers). The public sector employees' pension scheme is directly paid by the State. The French pension system is designed along Bismarckian (pay-as-you-go) principles—that is, pension benefits are based on, for the most part, intergenerational solidarity within each societal/occupational group. The mounting imbalance of incoming and outgoing payments, due to population aging and drastic decline in births, has been counteracted with the set up of a national reserve fund, "which is a collective pension fund in all but name" (Revauger, 2003: 151). This State-run fund has accumulated and invested funds provided by privatization of national industries.

The French health care system has been dubbed the best health care system in the world by the World Health Report 2000 (cf Landers, 2000; Navarro, 2000; Aspalter, 2005). The WHO ranking has been based on three types of indicators. First, the effectiveness of the health care system—mainly medical care and traditional public health services—in reducing mortality and morbidity. Second, the responsiveness of the system to the user, where responsiveness is understood as user-friendliness, a free choice of service providers, the ability to protect the user's dignity, confidentiality and autonomy, prompt delivery of care services, the supply of high-quality services, and access to social support. And, third, the degree of progressiveness in the funding of the public health care system.

At a closer look it becomes obvious that there is a high degree of inequality not only with regard to health care provision across different geographical regions, where especially the northern regions from the Bretagne in the West to Alsace in the East (apart from metropolitan Paris) are adversely affected by high premature mortality rates, i.e. low life expectancy, and lack of medical provision, especially with regard to the low density of health care professionals, especially general practitioners and specialists (which cluster in Paris and the sunshine coast of France, the Provence), and the relative lack of hospital facilities.

Also there is still a high incidence of premature male mortality owing to alcohol, smoking and accidents (especially traffic accidents). The consumption of alcohol and tobacco is concentrated in poorer regions, and intensified by high rates of unemployment (especially in the North, e.g. Bretagne and Normandy, but also right in the mountainous regions of Central France, in the Auvergne).

The French health care system is well-known for its high standards of care provision, in both quantitative and qualitative terms. Among the big industrial nations, France has the highest level of development in inpatient care, where France ranks well above average with regard to the number of hospital beds per population (9.3) and the inpatient admission rate per capita per year (21).

The public health care insurance system come up for about three quarters of the overall health care expenditure, the rest is almost evenly financed by patients' co-payments and complementary Voluntary Health Insurance (VHI) schemes. VHI schemes are provided by private for-profit companies, mutual insurance associations, as well as provident funds.

VHIs are on the increase, due to a general lowering of public reimbursement rates for health care services and devices. 43 percent of voluntary coverage is due to special agreements between employers and private insurance carriers, covering the employees at the time of employment (most pensioners and the employed workforce, especially the managerial staff is covered by this voluntary schemes). 59 percent of VHIs are run by mutual insurance associations, 21 percent by private companies, and 16 percent by provident funds—each accounting for 7.5, 2.8 and 2.1 percent of overall health care expenditure (Green and Irvine, 2001; Hardouin, 2001; HCPH, 2002; Rodwin, 2004; Rodwin and Sandier, 2005)

Contemporary Welfare State Reform in France

In the history of the French welfare state, the social security institutions have been first administered autonomously by the labor unions, from 1945 to 1967. The connection between the social security system, the system of industrial relations and employment, remained the cornerstone of the French welfare state system up to date. In the late 1960s, the state stepped in and took over a leading role in social security. Also, from 1967 onwards, the employers' associations were integrated in the management of the social security system to share power on an equal basis, which changed the logic of social security and welfare state politics, as a third party was added to sharply divided labor unions on the political left and the center. From then on the moderate unions could take over lead in social security and welfare policy by merging alliances with the employers' side (Ambler, 1991; Revauger, 2003).

The French pension system also underwent major changes. After the 1970s and 1980s, which have been dubbed the "Golden Age of Pension", the first major reform was the Balladur Reform in 1993 (Revauger, 2003; Hervier and Palier, 2008). As a result the pension formula was revised to avert the looming pension crisis in an increasingly aged society, due to longer life expectancy of people (especially women in France) and very low birth-rates. The 2003 Fillon Reform which undertook a major equalization of benefits for different pension clienteles. The pensions of public sector employees have been changed to match, to a greater degree, those of private sector employees. In addition a two-fold bonus/sanction system has been put in place to induce later actual pension ages—that is, to reduce and delay the practice early retirement. Those retiring beyond the number of years set to gain a 100 percent pension, will get an extra bonus ("surcote"), while those pensioners who retire earlier than that will get an additional deduction ("décote"). On top, the government set up two new types of individual and collective voluntary savings accounts, that are devised to make up the losses incurred by the downward adjustment of benefits in the Bismarckian pay-as-you-go pension system. In 2007, the process of further universalisation of the occupationally divided public pension system continued with the equalization of the benefit formula for employees working in public enterprises, who formerly were covered by rather generous schemes (Hervier and Palier, 2008; Palier, 2006).

As to health care, the continuous extension of the coverage of the statutory health insurance system has marked a half-a-century long transition from the Bismarckian system of national health insurance schemes to a "modified universal" insurance system. The transition proceeded in stages and was realized in the year 2000, after the passing of the 1999 Universal Health Insurance Coverage Act (the CMU). The public health care system, in actual fact, provides high levels of equality in health care provision across different social segments, occupational groups, as well as social and income classes.

Today the universal character of the French health care system has been both weakened and strengthened at the same time. With regard to coverage the 1999 Universal Health Insurance Coverage Act extended and quasi-universalized health insurance coverage, while a strong fragment of Bismarckian, occupational, division of beneficiaries is still in place. On the other hand, the private economy has been subsequently integrated and a variety of supplementary health insurance schemes that form today the *second column of the public health care system*, the VHI schemes, which are operated by private companies, mutual insurance associations, as well as provident fund schemes (Aspalter, 2005).

In a nutshell, the last two decades of welfare state reform in France saw a strengthening of *formal universality* (while at the moment complete universality is far from being accomplished), while the *universality with regard to substance* (i.e., benefits) has been rather weakened. This development has been observed in both the French public pension and health care system.

The German Welfare State in Transition

The Real-Typical Welfare State Model

Though a Conservative, Otto von Bismarck, set up the first statutory social-insurance programs for the better-off workers in Germany in the 1880s, it were the Christian Democrats who determined the course of the welfare state development after World War II. The Christian Democrats created, under the leadership of economic minister Ludwig Erhard, the concept of "social market economy," which led the way in economic and social politics since the beginning of the 1950s. Social market economy combined, in essence, liberal economic thought with Germany's long-term experience of state planning in economic affairs. Moreover, social policy making was based on Christian social teachings that had been directly derived from the teaching of Bishop Ketteler and the papal encyclicals *Rerum Novarum* and *Quadragesimo Anno*.

The Christian Social teachings embraced the principle of subsidiarity (the duty of self-help according to ones capabilities and the duty of State's help in case of need) and the principle of solidarity at the same time. Both, the concept of social market economy and Christian social teachings were promoted intensively by the Christian social wing of Germany's two large Christian Democratic parties, the Christian Democratic Union (CDU) and the Christian Social Union (CSU). It is for these reasons that we cannot refer to Germany as representing the outcome of conservative politics, but instead, must recognize the vital role of Christian Democrats and their labor unions in German social policy making (cf Klausen, 1998: 168-69; Lawson, 1996: 32; Aspalter, 2001; cf also Kersbergen, 1994, 1995; Huber and Stephens, 2001).

In Germany, until now, there have three major columns of welfare state programs: social insurance, social assistance, and social welfare services. Social insurance programs are occupationally divided, benefits are based on contributions, and the insurance system is run by semi-governmental insurance institutions controlled by the State, labor unions and employers' associations. The various programs of the German social insurance system cover all major risks, i.e. health, pensions, unemployment, and even long-term care needs (introduced in 1995). Social assistance—though largely directed by the State—was conducted by the municipalities and the *Länder* governments. The local governments provided most of the financial means needed (i.e., up to 80 percent). Social assistance was means tested and it took the responsibility of the family into account when determining the eligibility of those seeking social assistance. As of January 1, 2005, a new benefit system combines unemployment benefits with social assistance benefits (effectively transforming social assistance into workfare programs). In addition, social welfare services are operated by local authorities as well as welfare NGOs (cf Toft, 1997: 152).

The minimum-security function of the German welfare state system is exercised by social assistance and/or workfare programs, and not national social insurance programs (as it used to be the case in Sweden, and still is the United Kingdom). Germany's social insurance schemes provide, on the other hand, living standard security for the insured and their dependents (cf Döring, 1997: 46). Welfare capitalism in Germany is characterized by the existence of comprehensive social insurance schemes for occupational groups, which emphasize group solidarity with regard to risk pooling and income redistribution. The collective responsibility for the societal well-being—as promoted by Christian democrats and social democrats—has been modified according to the principle of subsidiarity which lays down the right level of responsibility (e.g., State, *Länder*, municipalities, NGOs, family, individual) case by case.

Though also providing high levels of social security, Germany after World War II, set up a dual social security system, where social assistance schemes guaranteed minimum security, and social insurance schemes were designed to the needs of the better-off societal groups.

With recent welfare reforms being implemented, the German welfare state system, in fact, represents more than ever before a prototype of a social-insurance-based welfare state model, with the principles of *equivalence* (focusing on contributions/work-records) and *compensation* (eliminating the employment-related risks to income) forming the core of the system. Principles of prevention and redistribution (from rich to poor) are not emphasized as key elements in system design (cf Daly and Rake, 2003).

Contemporary Welfare State Reform in Germany

With the formal unification of Germany in 1990, the German welfare state entered a period of dramatic challenges. With the privatization of state-owned enterprises, about 40 percent of employment was lost in former East Germany. The financial burden of this unemployment, the direct privatization costs, the costs infrastructural modernization, and the transfer of the social insurance pillars to the East were substantial—with the average annual cost of unification amounting to 4 to 6 percent of West German GDP (Swank, 2002).

In 1992, pensions were linked to net instead of gross earnings, which effectively reduced pension benefits from this time onwards. In 1993, the government introduced the Solidarity Pact, the Federal Assistance Act, which reduced the level of social assistance benefits, and another health care reform (that followed one conducted earlier in 1989) of the same year started out to cut social expenditures of the government. This was followed by the 1994 Saving, Consolidation, and Growth Pact, which reduced replacement rates for unemployment benefits, child benefits, housing allowances, and student grants. In 1995, the maximum duration for unemployment benefits was cut from 36 to 24 months. The year 1995 also saw the introduction of a new column of the German welfare state system, the long-term care insurance (the *"Pflegever-sicherung"*).

In 1996, pension insurance contributions were raised from 18.6 to 19.2 percent of earnings, possibilities for early retirement were curbed, and work requirements for unemployment benefits were tightened. However, a number of other attempts of the Kohl Government were withdrawn or defeated. In 1995, a measure that aimed to reduce further social assistance benefits was rejected by the Upper House of the Parliament, the *Bundesrat*, that has been controlled by the Social Democrats. In 1996, the Program for Growth and Employment proposed a reduction in the employer-paid first six weeks of sick pay from 100 to 80 percent of current earnings. Labor unions, left parties, and the population at large (350,000 people demonstrated in Bonn) rejected the reform, successfully. In 1997, the Christian Democratic Government enacted a pension reform act, which was then rescinded by the new Social Democratic Government one year later (Swank, 2002; Bode, 2003).

The German welfare state model does not provide full employment security as it is the case in Sweden. In the past, it systematically worked to reduce overall employment levels—by way of early retirement schemes, easy access to invalidity pensions, exclusion/non-integration of women into the labor market, and high wage costs (due to high contribution rates of a social insurance system with low capital productivity, cf Börsch-Supan, 2001; Schmid, 1998, 2002; Esping-Andersen, 2002).

In Germany, the public, in addition to the labor unions (i.e., both Christian and Social Democratic Labor Unions), and a sizeable part of politicians (from both camps), still supports a positive role of the state in social policy and welfare provision. Welfare state reform in Germany was not comprehensive (as it was the case in Italy) in the 1990s, due to the political and public opposition to welfare cuts (which is similar to the case of Sweden, cf below). A daunting demographic development has not yet altered the course of the welfare state, nor the fiscal constraints that sprang up from German Unification, or the implementation of the Euro Zone. On top of the perturbing developments caused by demographic changes and the in-built financial instability of the pay-as-you-go social insurance system, there is also an increasing need to cater to people who do not have "normal" biographies, such as the long-term unemployed, persons who are frequently out of work (especially women and sporadically employed youngsters), people in early retirement, and the poor.

The history of German welfare state reform in the last quarter of the 20th century was marked by frequent and incremental changes—the cumulative effect of which, however, has already reduced the redistributive element of the German welfare state. Hitherto, welfare state reforms left the institutional structure largely intact (cf Lawson, 1996; Pfaller, 1997; Hemerijk, 2000; Alber, 2000; Clasen and Oorschot, 2003).

The Italian Welfare State in Transition

The Real-Typical Welfare State Model

The Italian welfare state leads the group of "Latin Rim" welfare states. This league of welfare state systems includes Italy, Spain, Portugal, and Greece, and to some extent France and Ireland (Leibfried, 1992; Palier and Bonoli, 1995; Ferrera, 1996; Martin, 1997). Welfare capitalism in Southern Europe is characterized, in essence by a mix of Bismarckian and Beveridgean social insurance systems, i.e. contributionary non-universal and non-contributionary, universal social security systems respectively.

In Italy, first social security system had been set up in the Liberal political era between 1880 and 1920. On the contrary to other Continental European welfare states in the North, Italy did not correspond as quickly to the labor question of the time and, thus, found itself in a "*tabula-rasa*" situation, which enabled the introduction of universal social security schemes later on. Between 1990 and 1920, social legislation progressed more rapidly. In 1907 and 1909, working standards for women and the youth had been regulated. The coverage of the accident (*anti-infortunista*) insurance had been extended to the tobacco industry, salt-works, and the agricultural sector. Moreover, pension and invalidity insurance schemes and an obligatory maternity insurance scheme for female workers had been set up. There were a series of proposals for making pension insurance obligatory for workers, and for introducing sickness and unemployment benefits (Ferrera, 1993).

Today, the Italian welfare state represents a mix of occupationally fragmented social security systems (i.e., the German or Bismarkian system), especially with regard to pensions, and social security systems that are based on universal coverage (i.e., the British or Beveridgean system) as in the field of health care provision. Italy, hence, represents a mixed model of societal and occupational solidarity.

The national health services, the "Servizio Sanitario Nazionale" (SSN), introduced in 1978, is a universal health insurance scheme. The SSN introduced a new era of social politics that was in favor of universal welfare provision. The high share of self-employed in the Italian labor force pushed coalition governments, which were dominated by the Christian Democratic Party, to implement universal rather than occupational social security programs. Another factor behind universal social politics was the Article 32 of the Italian Constitution, which emphasized the importance of the inclusion of social groups in the social security system and the unity of social insurance schemes. The Article 32 stressed the fundamental right of the individual and the interest of the collective for such welfare arrangements.

From 1950 to 1966, social legislation was characterized by a massive extension of the welfare state that aimed at political clienteles, and not the collective, the society as a whole. Due to greater inclusion of left-wing political forces into government since 1963, i.e. especially the Socialist Party and the Social Democratic Party, the dominant political ideology shifted in favor of universal welfare programs. The Law 833 of the year 1978 introduced a completely universal social insurance scheme, the SSN. The new scheme guaranteed the right for free medical treatment and drugs. The Italian health care and social service sectors are, moreover, highly relying on the support of the Third Sector (France, 1996; Woldendorp *et al.*, 1998; Ferrera, 1993; Maino, 2003).

Italian-style welfare capitalism represents, in essence, a mix of German-style Christian Democratic social policy with a focus on occupational insurance schemes and means-tested social assistance, and British-style liberal (i.e., Beveridgean) social policy based on universal social insurance schemes. Another characteristic of the Italian welfare state is its fragmentation (that resulted from historical regionalism and dispersion of power) and inherent dualism of overprovision (public sector workers) and under-provision (the mass of the people), as well as a huge divide in the geographical distribution of social welfare provision—with good support systems in the rich North, and a lack of social welfare provision in the poor South (cf Daly and Rake; 2003; Maino, 2003).

Contemporary Welfare State Reform in Italy

The major factor for reforming the pension system in Italy is the demographic transition from a balanced society to an aged society. Rapid aging of society, in combination with a high-benefit pension insurance scheme that was based on the defined-benefit principle, made a systematic reform in the public pension system indispensable. In 2021, there will be 16 million people over 60 years of age, compared to only 8 million people who will be younger than 20. Another aspect of an aging society is the rising share of dependent elderly people in the so-called "fourth" age (more than 75 years of age), who are especially exposed to health problems, up to a degree of total dependence (Maino, 2003). In addition, there is the problem of rising number of years in retirement—which in Europe have, on an average, doubled—and the falling number of contribution years—which in all of Europe has dropped by around 25 percent (Walker, 2003).

In the 1990s, there have been three major pension reforms, in 1992, 1995, and 1997. The 1992 Amato Pension Reform introduced a gradual elevation from 15 to 20 years of the minimum contribution requirement for old-age benefits; an elevation of the retirement age from 55 to 60 for women and 60 to 65 for men, with a gradual phasing in by 2002; a gradual increase of the contribution requirement for early retirement to 36 years for all workers (including a gradual phase-in for civil servants, who previously enjoyed the privilege of a much lower 20-year requirement); a new increase in contribution rates; a replacement of wage indexation for benefits with a cost-of-living indexation; and, last but not least, a gradual extension of the reference period for pensionable earnings from the last 5 years to the last 10 years—while pension benefits for new entrants to the labor market will be calculated on the basis of their lifelong earnings.

The 1995 Dini Reform brought the following new changes: a shift from an earnings-related formula to a contribution-related formula, to be phased in by 2013; the introduction of a flexible retirement age (57 to 65), the introduction of an age-threshold for early retirement for all workers, to be phased in by 2008; the gradual standardization of rules for public and private employees; a graduation of survivor benefits according to income; stricter eligibility rules; an increase of contribution rates; plus mandatory coverage for self-employed workers.

The 1997 Pension Reform included the following measures: more severe contributory, i.e. age, requirements for early retirement; further standardization of rules for public and private employees; a one year freeze, for 1998, on all pensions above approximately EURO 1.700 per month (net); and less favorable indexation rules for such pensions for the years 1999 to 2001; an increase of contribution rates; an increase in minimum and social pensions; as well as higher tax deduction for pensioners with lower incomes (Ferrera and Gualmini, 1999; Maino, 2003). In 2004, the Berlusconi Government abolished the so-called seniority pensions, which currently allow Italians to retire at age 57 if they have worked 35 years. Beginning in 2008, Italians will be allowed to retire only if they had worked for 40 years or had reached age 60 for women and 65 for men.

Italy's health-care system, the *Servizio Sanitario Nazionale*, started to undergo major reform in the early 1990s. On the funding side, the Regional Governments got greater control on the expenditure side, while the national contribution has been fixed, with the implementation of a per-capita quota (the *Quota Capitaria*). Any share not covered by the per-capita quota hence needs to be financed by the Regional Governments. To stimulate greater efficiency and more attention to quality of service, measures were taken to separate purchasers and providers and to encourage an element of competition. To reduce bureaucracy and improve management, the existing 659 Local Health Units ("*Unità Sanitarie Locali*") were transformed into 197 Local Health Enterprises ("*Aziende Sanitarie Locali*"), with more operating autonomy, comercial accounting procedures and performance auditing, and administered by senior managers appointed by the regional government for five years with performance-related wages. In the early 1990s, the *Servizio Sanitario Nazionale* has also taken steps towards "*targeting out,*" i.e. excluding benefits or higher co-payments for the more well-to-do classes (Maino, 2001, 2003; Ferrera, 1998a).

In the late 1990s, the center-left Prodi Government reformed social assistance schemes, by mainly standardizing the criteria used for targeting, which varied greatly over time, across levels of government, and territorial areas. However, due to the increasing political polarization of the Italian political landscape, with the formation of a strong political party, the Lega Nord, a new North-South divide seems to emerge, not only in politics, but also in national social welfare provision—that is, by way of new *tax and welfare federalism*. With supporters only in the North of the country, the *Lega Nord* opposes inter-regional financial transfers from the rich North to the poor South. The Chairman of the *Lega Nord*, Umberto Bossi, in essence declared the independence of Northern Italy—under the name of *"Padania"*—as an ultimate goal of the party (Ferrera, 1998b, 2000). Thus, not only the demographic situation, and the in-built fiscal constraints of the social security system, but also politics plays an important factor in shaping the present-day and future configuration of Italian welfare state.

The Swedish Welfare State in Transition

The Real-Typical Welfare State Model

The Swedish welfare state represents a distinct form of welfare capitalism that guarantees highest levels of equality and incorporates the majority of the population into welfare state arrangements. The Swedish welfare state represents an institutional welfare state that, in addition, emphasizes the social right to public social welfare and tries also to prevent rather than just meet welfare needs. In Sweden, welfare state programs are, for the most part, financed out of taxes. Social policies are guided by the principle of equality rather than a needs-based ideology (cf Olsson Hort, 1993a,b).

The Swedish welfare state is based on the conviction that the welfare of the individual is the responsibility of the social collective (Esping-Andersen and Korpi, 1987: 40). The Swedish welfare state is widely attributed to the achievements of Swedish social democracy. However, the birth of the Swedish welfare state preceded the establishment of the Social Democratic labor movement (cf Esping-Andersen, 1992b: 35), as the governing Liberal party set up a Royal Commission to prepare proposals for workers' insurance in 1884. In 1913, the Swedish parliament passed a universal pension and invalidity system. The year 1932 marked a watershed in Swedish social politics because, from then on, there was a long-term collaboration between the "reds" (i.e., the Social Democrats) and "the greens" (i.e., the farmers' party, the Agrarians, or Social Liberals). This grand collaboration lasted until the late 1950s. Both the social democrats and the social liberals introduced a series of welfare reforms that had lasting effects on the Swedish welfare state system (cf Olsson Hort, 1993b).

Until the year 1948, pensions were subject to means tests. The 1948 pension law introduced a universal, unconditional flat-rate pension system with additional means-tested supplements to ensure the level of subsistence of the very needy (Baldwin, 1990). In 1954, a universal compulsory accident insurance replaced the formerly voluntary accident insurance (implemented in 1901). One year later, the government introduced a universal, compulsory state financed sickness insurance system with wage and earnings-related benefits, which replaced the voluntary sickness insurance system (implemented in 1891).

The superannuation (supplementary pension) issue of the late 1950s lead to the breakup of the long-standing red-green coalition that was replaced by Social Democratic hegemony in Swedish politics. A universal, earnings-related second-tier pension (superannuation) system had been introduced in 1959—the ATP pension, an earnings-related pension system. The new pension system varied pensions by supplementing basic pensions. It was compulsory for employees, and voluntarily for the self-employed and non-employed.

The introduction of the income-related health insurance, unemployment benefit and ATP pension systems marked a shift in Social Democratic social politics, i.e. the replacement of working class politics by middle-class politics (cf e.g. Bergström, 1991; Esping-Andersen and Korpi, 1987).

The Swedish type of welfare capitalism was born only in the 1960s, since before it had not yet developed features of its own kind. High income-replacement schemes for all citizens mark the widely praised

Swedish welfare state that is highly associated with Swedish social democracy. However, the first five decades of welfare capitalism in Sweden had been shaped much more by the social liberals than the social democrats. The principle of universalism was introduced by the social liberal party (an agrarian-based, social liberal party)—and this, at a time even before the social democratic labor party has been established. The social democrats took the shape of the welfare system that they inherited from the social liberals, and heaved the level of welfare provision to new heights. With the notable exception of the public pension system—which is separated into basic pensions and second-tier/ATP pensions—these universal insurance schemes provide not minimum, but living standard security—that is, high income-replacement rates that ensure comfortable living standards (Baldwin, 1990; Esping-Andersen, 1992a; Aspalter, 2001).

Today, the Swedish welfare state represents itself in a very positive light what regards social rights, the high quantity and quality of social services provided by the state, and the favorable effects of large-scale public employment (especially for women), and general high levels of employment (again, especially for women) (cf Ahn and Olsson-Hort, 2003; Benner and Bundgaard Vad, 2000; Mishra, 1999). The Swedish welfare state is still regarded as the prototype of a social-citizenship-oriented model, even though benefits and services are more and more subject to cuts and privatization, but the main body of welfare state provision stands very solid, and has not been altered significantly in recent years. The defined-benefit principle in social security provision has been more and more replaced by the contribution-based principle (a longer period of contribution is required for the full public pension and benefits are now more closely related to contributions). The number of people living on social assistance, however, increased a great deal due to high unemployment (Abrahamson, 2003; Mishra, 1999).

Contemporary Welfare State Reform in Sweden

Though it is a commonplace to believe that Sweden has created some sort of "paradise," successfully integrating both the best features of *free-market* capitalism and that of *interventionist* socialism (Gould, 1993), without suffering severely from the consequences of market failures and government failures, one must admit that the truth is still far away from this. There is also poverty in Sweden, and there is gender injustice and discrimination (cf Olsson-Hort, 2000; Sainsbury, 1996, 1999). Sweden was hailed to be socialist, or strongly social democratic, completely different from the rest of the world or that of Europe. But Sweden has gone a long way in the meanwhile, as it transformed its welfare state system a great deal in the 1990s. This fact is only gradually acknowledged in the international arena. And yet again Sweden serves as a model, but this time, for fundamental (radical) welfare state reform—in the absence of major strikes, public discontent, and political infighting (e.g., Gough *et al.*, 1997; Kuhnle, 2000).

Sweden was once seen as a prototype of modern society, where the mass of people enjoy a standard of living, a quality of life, and a degree of social security that were the envy of many other countries (Gould, 1993). The Swedish welfare state model today is much less unique as it used to—even though a number of key features of the Swedish welfare state model are intact and hence continue to be admired by Swedes and people around the world.

In the 1990s, a new trend of *Europeanization* of the Swedish welfare state model emerged. Elements of individualization, decentralization, more reliance on family and kin, and market solutions are pushing Sweden—and Scandinavia as a whole—closer to principles that are governing the other European welfare state systems. With regard to the overall financing the welfare state, the share of taxes is decreasing (Abrahamson, 2003; Ahn and Olsson-Hort, 2003).

Economic conditions in Sweden deteriorated in the 1989-1991 period, with 0.5 percent (1990) and –1.7 percent (1991) of GDP growth; inflation jumped to 6.4 (1989) and 10.5 (1990) percent; unemployment rose from 1.6 percent in 1990 to 9.5 percent in 1993, then to 10.3 percent in 1997; the budget deficit amount to 14 percent of gross national product in 1994. In the light of this, the Swedish government embarked on a neoliberal mission to cut benefits and redirect welfare state development towards reduction of welfare costs and welfare spending. There had been a series of public sector and health care efficiency reforms, as well as new social policies that aimed at cost-control measures in social insurance. In the year 1992, things even got worse; with a negative GDP growth rate of –2.1 percent (Swank, 2002; Merrien, 2002).

The new Conservative Government (1991 to 1994) set out to slash welfare state spending even further. But, what happened was not what we may have expected at this point in time. The effects of the major reform push of the government had been only minor, due to public resistance. Social movements and pressure groups were key in preventing a major turnaround in Swedish welfare state politics—"when the attack on the welfare state reached its height in the first half of the 1990s the new feminist movement came to its rescue" (Ahn and Olsson-Hort, 2003: 108). Pressure groups ferociously attacked cutbacks in welfare services and lay-offs in the public sector whereby it managed to get popular support as well as institutional support from the labor unions. "Half a year before the election of 1994 this rather small but media-strong platform of pressure groups challenged the traditional party system to such an extent that politicians in most political parties took them seriously and in many cases even extensively flirted with them and their potential voting group" (ibid.).

Reforms have continued until today. The most outstanding reform that changed the logic of the welfare state quite a bit were the alterations of pension benefit formula—earnings-related pensions (ATP-pensions, the second public column of the pension system) are from now on based on lifetime contributions, and not 30 years of contributions for full pension with the "best 15 years" determining pension amounts, and new social insurance contributions were planned where employees would ultimately pay 9.25 percent of their salaries to the ATP fund. With regard to the first column, the flat-rate universal pension scheme, a new 40-year residence rule, and not (political) citizenship, was implemented to henceforward determine eligibility (Swank, 2002).

Another significant characteristic of the new public pension system is that a minor part of contribution will be set aside for individual risk investment. This particular system of notional defined-contribution accounts follows strictly the logic of provident fund systems applied elsewhere. Insured persons will have now a choice of how to save a certain part of their contributions to the pension system. No risk sharing (no redistribution) is built into this part of the pension system. Private insurance companies (including those owned by labor unions) will join the competitive race in providing high returns on investment of funds. The competitive race between the 500 recognized funds started well in advance of the possibility to choose those funds (Ahn and Olsson-Hort, 2003). If the accumulated pension falls below a minimum level, the pensioner is entitled to a tax-financed guarantee pension. Unlike the national pension, the guarantee pension will be paid only to those with no, or a very low, earnings-related pension. This amounts to eliminating the universal element in the Swedish pension system (Timonen, 2003).

The Swedish ATP pension system continues to be a pay-as-you-go system, but it now applies a contribution-based formula within a benefit-defined scheme, signaling a transition from the benefit-defined to a contribution-defined pension system—the systematic change will take effect in the next 20 years. That is to say, pension benefits, instead of being predetermined as a percentage of wages earned during the highest earning years, are based hence on contributions throughout a person's working life (cf Abrahamson, 2003; Timonen, 2003; Merrien, 2002).

In 1993, unemployment insurance was made compulsory, with contribution rate of 1.5 percent of employees' salaries. In 1994, the new social democratic government abolished the system again, but now tightening eligibility rules for unemployment benefits—taking part in employment programs no longer restored a person's right to such benefits. In the 1990s, over 50,000 jobs disappeared from the Swedish public sector, as both conservative and social democratic governments continued to cut overall public spending, which resulted in a significant decline of public spending since 1993 (Timonen, 2003). Social security benefits have been cut, such as benefits for unemployment, sickness, and parental leave, from 90 to 80 percent of income (after having been cut to 75 percent in 1994 these benefits have been raised again to the 80 percent level, after heavy criticism from the labor unions). Waiting days have been introduced for unemployment and sickness insurance benefits. Employers have been made responsible for the first 14 days of sickness insurance benefits in order to give them more control over "abuse" of benefits.

In the social service sector, new regulations helped to implement market mechanisms and to foster private welfare service provision (health and services for children and the elderly); additional user fees have also been implemented. The strategy of the social democratic governments was to cut welfare expenditure across the board rather than making radical reductions in specific programs like social insurance (Mishra, 1999; Benner and Bundgaard Vad, 2000; Swank, 2002; Merrien, 2002).

In future, the main objectives of the welfare state will include a lesser degree of redistribution—plus a greater emphasis on participation in employment (with active support of the government) and the social insurance system, while a strong publicly-financed social service net may be expected to stay unchanged in the near future. The groundwork for more substantial welfare state reform has been laid, and now it depends on the demographic development, the political and economic development alike how far this transition will go from here.

European Welfare States in Comparative Perspective: By Way of Conclusion

When looking at the international comparison of social benefits paid by the state, we see the effects of major welfare state reforms that have been implemented in European countries since the 1990s (Table 6.1). Whereas the basic design of welfare state systems, especially the distinction between Beveridgean and Bismarckian welfare state systems is still in place, the reform of financing of social insurance systems, and the tightened eligibility rules, in combination with modest reduction in benefits have, especially in the Nordic countries—and less so but still significantly in other Continental European countries—contributed to an absolute and relative decline in social benefits paid. Here, we make out some major exceptions, which again demonstrate the importance of the numerous welfare state reforms in the last two decades in shaping the landscape of European welfare state provision. Countries with high performance in social benefits and publicly mandated social expenditures are Belgium, Finland, France, Germany, Italy, Switzerland, and Sweden (Table 6.1).

Table 6.1: International Comparison of Social Benefits
(percent of GDP)

	1960	1969	1979	1989	1999	2003*
France	12.74	14.82	18.63	21.09	**23.55**	**29.8**
Belgium	11.35	13.70	20.85	20.62	**21.16**	**26.0**
Switzerland	5.94	8.54	12.93	13.36	**20.07**	n.a.
Italy	9.50	11.93	14.08	17.61	**19.70**	**25.3**
Finland	5.08	7.08	9.08	14.36	**19.54**	22.7
Netherlands	7.17	12.92	19.93	18.26	17.75	20.6
Denmark	6.17	8.68	14.96	17.81	16.92	23.8
Germany	12.83	13.53	16.95	16.19	16.70	**29.5**
Sweden	6.09	8.19	14.28	16.29	15.82	**29.2**
Austria	7.57	11.21	15.51	14.71	15.71	23.9
Norway	9.34	11.87	13.36	15.40	15.35	23.8
Japan	3.75	4.46	9.84	10.94	14.51	19.7
UK	6.06	8.35	10.55	10.47	13.12	22.8
Australia	4.92	5.06	9.23	9.62	12.55	20.6
US	5.72	7.23	10.72	11.33	13.75	18.9

Notes: based on OECD data on "social benefits paid" in Overbye (2003);
* "net publicly mandated social expenditure" OECD (2008).

The new trend of convergence in European spending on tax-financed social benefits—which holds especially for countries like Norway, Sweden, Denmark, Austria, Germany, the Netherlands—is the result of a shift under way in those countries to rely more on regulatory measures, in an age when increased fiscal strain can make it harder to finance tax-and-spend programs (MISSOC, 1999; Overbye, 2003). We also see a systematic shift from tax-financed to contribution-financed social security provision. This paradigm shift in the financing of welfare state regimes first occurred in the Continental European countries like the Netherlands, Germany, and Austria—starting already as early as in the 1980s. In Denmark, Sweden, and Norway (the Nordic reformers), the reforms took effect only in the 1990s (cf Table 6.1).

Table 6.2: Four Dimensions of Welfare State Reform

Reform in the Old/Existing System	**Individualization of the Old System**
cutting costs, cutting benefits, increasing contribution rates, increasing coverage, changing benefit formulas or indexation, introducing sustainability factors or new regulations regarding entitlements (e.g. bonuses and reductions), etc.	introducing virtual individual accounts (esp. in pension systems); integrating personal efforts/achievements/ work record/salary level/contributions made in the calculation of benefits; establishment of a fully-funded Provident Fund System; etc.
Privatization of the Old System	**New Design of the Welfare State System**
privatization of social insurance schemes and welfare provision (partially or fully); decentralization of schemes, conversion of social assistance to workfare programs, introduction and promotion of the idea of welfare pluralism, etc.	changing the logic of the welfare state as a whole: e.g. from tax-financed social insurance to tax-financed family planning and pro-natal welfare policies, from tax-financed social insurance to savings-financed social security; from direct to indirect redistribution; etc.

When looking at the global experience of welfare state reform around the world (cf e.g. Aspalter, 2003a,b; Mesa-Lago, 2003; Walker, 2003; Swank, 2002; Deacon, 1992, 1997), four major dimensions of welfare state reform become visible (Table 6.2).

First, most countries in Europe opted for both parametric and systematic changes in their existing social security and welfare systems. Systematic changes involve, by and large, two strategies: first, the privatization of welfare systems and schemes (e.g., pensions in the UK, health care in France, etc.), or, second, the individualization of social security and social welfare systems (e.g., the introduction of mandatory provident fund systems for pensions in Sweden and Italy, and the introduction of voluntary collective and individual savings accounts in France). A fourth strategy would be then to change the logic of the welfare state as a whole, which has been attempted in e.g. Germany in recent years with the introduction of a poll tax for health care insurance, or the introduction of (generous) carework salaries and a national minimum income for all citizens.

REFERENCES

Abrahamson, Peter (2003), The End of the Scandinavian Model? Welfare Reform in the Nordic Countries, *Journal of Societal and Social Policy*, Vol. 2, No. 2, pp. 19-36.

Ahn, Sang-Hoon and Olsson-Hort, Sven E. (2003), The Welfare State in Sweden, in C. Aspalter (ed.), *Welfare Capitalism Around the World*, Casa Verde: Hong Kong.

Alber, J. (2000), Der deutsche Sozialstaat in der Ära Kohl, in S. Leibfried and U. Wagschal (eds.), *Der deutsche Sozialstaat: Bilanzen, Reformen, Perspektiven*, Campus: Frankfurt a.M., Germany.

Ambler, John S. (1991), *The French Welfare State*, New York University Press: New York.

Aspalter, Christian (2001), *Importance of Christian and Social Democratic Movements in Welfare Politics: With Special Reference to Germany, Austria, and Sweden*, Nova Science: New York.

Aspalter, Christian (2002), Exploring Old and New Shores in Welfare State Theory, in C. Aspalter (ed.), *Discovering the Welfare State in East Asia*, Praeger: Westport, CT.

Aspalter, Christian (ed.) (2003a), *Welfare Capitalism Around the World*, Casa Verde: Hong Kong.

Aspalter, Christian (ed.) (2003b), *The Welfare State in Emerging-Market Economies: With Case Studies from Latin America, Eastern-Central Europe, and Asia*, Casa Verde: Hong Kong.

Aspalter, Christian (2005), *Health Care Reform: France and Italy*, Korean Institute of Health and Social Affairs: Seoul, Korea.

Baldwin, Peter (1990), *The Politics of Social Solidarity: The Class Bases of the European Welfare State*, Cambridge University Press: Cambridge, UK.

Baldwin, Peter (1992), Beveridge in the *Longue Durée, International Social Security Review*, Vol. 45, No. 1, pp. 61-83.

Benner, Mats and Bundgaard Vad, Torben (2000), Sweden and Denmark: Defending the Welfare State, in F.W. Scharpf and V.A. Schmidt (eds.), *Welfare and Work in the Open Economy*, volume ii, Oxford University Press: Oxford, UK.

Bergström, Hans (1991), Sweden's Politics and Party System at the Crossroads, in J.E. Lane (ed.), *Understanding the Swedish Model*, Frank Cass: London.

Bode, Ingo (2003), The Welfare State in Germany: Corporatism and the German Welfare Model, in C. Aspalter (ed.), *Welfare Capitalism Around the World*, Casa Verde: Hong Kong.

Börsch-Supan, Axel (2001), The German Retirement Insurance System, in A. Börsch-Supan and M. Miegel (eds.), *Pension Reform in Six Countries: What Can We Learn From Each Other?*, Springer Verlag: New York.

Castles, Francis G. and Pierson, Christopher (1996), A New Convergence? Recent Policy Developments in the United Kingdom, Australia and New Zealand, *Policy & Politics*, Vol. 24, No. 3, pp. 233-45.

Clarke, John and Langan, Mary (1995), The British Welfare State: Foundation and Modernization, in A. Cochrane and J. Clarke (eds.), *Comparing Welfare State: Britain in International Context*, Sage: London.

Clasen, Jochen and Oorschot, Wim van (2003), Classic Principles and Designs in European Social Security, in D. Pieters (ed.), *European Social Security and Global Politics*, Kluwer Law International: London.

Daly, Mary and Rake, Katherine (2003), *Gender and the Welfare State*, Polity: Cambridge, UK.

Deacon, Bob (1992), The Future of Social Policy in Eastern Europe, in B. Deacon *et al.* (eds.), *The New Eastern Europe: Social Policy Past, Present, and Future*, Sage: London.

Deacon, Bob (1997), *Global Social Policy*, Sage: London.

Döring, Diether (1997), Is the German Welfare State Sustainable?, in P. Koslowski and A. Follesdal (eds.), *Restructuring the Welfare State: Theory and Reform of Social Policy*, Springer: Berlin.

Esping-Andersen, Gøsta (1992a), The Three Political Economies of the Welfare State, in J.E. Kolberg (ed.), *The Study of Welfare State Regimes*, M.E. Sharpe: Armonk, NY.

Esping-Andersen, Gøsta (1992b), The Making of a Social Democratic Welfare State, in K. Misgeld, K. Molin, K. Amark (eds.), *Creating Social Democracy, A Century of the Social Democratic Labor Party in Sweden*, The Pennsylvania State University Press: Pennsylvania, PA.

Esping-Andersen, Gøsta (2002), *Why We Need a New Welfare State*, Oxford University Press: Oxford, UK.

Esping-Andersen, Gøsta and Korpi, Walter (1987), From Poor Relief to Institutional Welfare States: The Development of Scandinavian Social Policy, in R. Erikson *et al.* (eds.), *The Scandinavian Model*, M.E. Sharpe: Armonk, NY.

Ferrera, Maurizio (1993), *Modelli di Solidarietà, Politica e Riforme Sociali nelle Democrazie*, Il Mulino: Bologna, Italy.

Ferrera, Maurizio (1996), The Southern Model of Welfare in Social Europe, *Journal of European Social Policy*, Vol. 6, No. 1, pp. 17-37.

Ferrera, Maurizio (1998a), The Four Social Europes: Between Universalism and Selectivity, in M. Rhodes and Y. Meny (eds.), *The Future of European Welfare: A New Social Contract?*, Macmillan: London.

Ferrera, Maurizio (1998b), Welfare Reform in Southern Europe, in H. Cavanna (ed.), *Challenges to the Welfare State: Internal and External Dynamics for Change*, Edward Elgar: Cheltenham, UK.

Ferrera, Maurizio (2000), Targeting Welfare in a Soft State: Italy's Winding Road to Selectivity, in N. Gilbert (ed.), *Targeting Social Benefits: International Perspectives and Trends*, Transactions: New Brunswick, NJ.

Ferrera, Maurizio and Gualmini, Elisabetta (1999), *Salvati dall'Europa?*, Il Mulino: Bologna, Italy.

Fink, Marcel and Talos, Emmerich (2004), Welfare State Retrenchment in Austria: Ignoring the Logic of Blame Avoidance?, *Journal of Societal and Social Policy*, Vol. 3, No. 1, pp. 1-21.

France, George (1996), Governance of Two National Health Services: Italy and the United Kingdom Compared, in G. Pola *et al.* (eds.), *Developments in Local Government Finance*, Edward Elgar: Cheltenham, UK.

George, Vic (1980), Poverty and Inequality in the UK, in V. George and R. Lawson (eds.), *Poverty and Inequality in Common Market Countries*, Routledge and Kegan Paul: London.

Glennester, Howard (1998), New Beginnings and Old Continuities, in H. Glennester and J. Hills (eds.), *The State of Welfare*, Oxford University Press: Oxford, UK.

Gough, Ian *et al.* (1997), Social Assistance in OECD Countries, *European Journal of Social Policy*, Vol. 7, No. 1, pp. 17-44.

Gould, Arthur (1993), *Capitalist Welfare Systems: A Comparison of Japan, Britain and Sweden*, Longman: Harlow, UK.

Green, David G. and Irvine, Benedict (2001), *Health Care in France and Germany: Lessons for the UK*, Civitas: Institute for the Study of Civil Society: London.

Gregg, Pauline (1967), *The Welfare State*, Harrap: London.

Hardouin, Tanti N. (2001), *La Santé en France: Radiographie d'un Système*, Foucher: Paris.

HCPH, High Commission on Public Health, Government of France (2002), *La Santé en France*, Documentation Française: Paris.

Hemerijk, Anton (2000), Divergent Experience of Reform in Germany and the Netherlands, in S. Kuhnle (ed.), *Survival of the European Welfare State*, Routledge: London.

Hervier, Louise and Palier, Bruno (2008), Aging and the French Welfare State, in A. Walker and C. Aspalter (eds.), *Securing the Future for Old Age in Europe*, Casa Verde: Hong Kong.

Huber, Evelyne and Stephens, John D. (2001), *Development and Crisis of the Welfare State: Parties and Policies in Global Markets*, University of Chicago Press: Chicago, IL.

Jones, Chris and Novak, Tony (1999), *Poverty and the Disciplinary State*, Routledge: London.

Kersbergen, Kees van (1994), The Distinctiveness of Christian Democracy, in D. Hanley (ed.), *Christian Democracy in Europe*, Pinter: London.

Kersbergen, Kees van (1995), *Social Capitalism: A Study of Christian Democracy and the Welfare State*, Routledge: London.

Klausen, Jytte (1998), *War and Welfare: Europe and the United States*, St. Martins: New York.

Kuhnle, Stein (ed.) (2000), *Survival of the European Welfare State*, Routledge: London.

Landers, Susan (2000), The World's Health Care: How Do We Rank?, *www.ama-assn.org/amednews*.

Lavalette, Michael and Penketh, Laura (2003), The Welfare State in the United Kingdom, in C. Aspalter (ed.), *Welfare Capitalism Around the World*, Casa Verde: Hong Kong.

Lawson, Roger (1996), Germany: Maintaining the Middle Way, in V. George and P. Taylor-Gooby (eds.), *European Welfare Policy: Squaring the Welfare Triangle*, Macmillan: Houndmills, UK.

Leibfried, Stephan (1992), Towards a European Welfare State?, in Z. Ferge and J.E. Kolberg (eds.), *Social Policy in Changing Europe*, Campus: Frankfurt a.M., Germany.

Maino, Franca (2001), *La Politica Sanitaria*, Il Mulino: Bologna, Italy.

Maino, Franca (2003), The Welfare State in Italy, in C. Aspalter (ed.), *Welfare Capitalism Around the World*, Casa Verde: Hong Kong.

Martin, Claude (1997), Social Welfare and the Family in Southern Europe, in M. Rhodes (ed.), *Southern European Welfare States, Between Crisis and Reform*, Frank Cass: London.

Merrien, François-Xavier (2002), Globalization and Social Adjustment—The Case of Small Developed Countries: A Comparative View of New Zealand, Sweden, and Switzerland, in R. Sigg and C. Behrendt (eds.), *Social Security in the Global Village*, Transactions: New Brunswick, NJ.

Mesa-Lago, Carmelo (2003), The Welfare State in Eight Latin American Countries, in C. Aspalter (ed.), *Welfare Capitalism Around the World*, Casa Verde: Hong Kong.

Mishra, Ramesh (1999), *Globalization and the Welfare State*, Edward Elgar, Cheltenham, UK.

MISSOC (1999), *Evaluation of Social Protection in the Member States of the European Union*, Office for Official Publications of the European Communities: Luxembourg.

Navarro, Vicente (2000), Assessment of the World Health Report 2000, The *Lancet*, Vol. 356, November 4.

OECD (2008), website, *www.oecd.org*.

Olsson Hort, Sven E. (1993a), The Swedish Model, in J. Berghman and B. Cantillon (eds.), *The European Face of Social Security*, Avebury: Aldershot, UK.

Olsson Hort, Sven E. (1993b), *Social Policy and the Welfare State in Sweden*, Arkiv Förlag: Lund, Sweden.

Olsson Hort, Sven E. (2000), From a Generous to a Stingy Welfare State? Sweden's Approach to Targeting, in N. Gilbert (ed.), *Targeting in Social Welfare*, Transactions: New Brunswick, NJ.

Overbye, Einar (2003), Globalization and the Design of the Welfare State, in D. Pieters (ed.), *European Social Security and Global Politics*, Kluwer Law International: London.

Palier, Bruno (2000), "Defrosting" the French Welfare State, *West European Politics*, Vol. 23, No. 2, pp. 113-36.

Palier, Bruno (2006), Farewell to Bismarckianism? Welfare Reforms in France, paper presented at the conference: *A Long Good Bye to Bismarck? The Politics of Welfare Reforms in Continental Europe*, June 16-18, Center for European Studies, Harvard University, MA.

Palier, Bruno and Bonoli, Giuliano (1995), Entre Bismarck et Beveridge, Crises de la Sécurité Sociale and Politique(s), *Revue Française de Sciences Politiques*, Vol. 45, No. 4, pp. 668-98.

Palier, Bruno and Martin, Claude (2008), *Reforming the Bismarckian Welfare Systems*, Blackwell: Oxford, UK.

Pfaller, Alfred (1997), The German Welfare State After National Unification, *library.fes.de/fulltext/stabsabteilung/00073.htm*.

Pierson, Paul (1994), *Dismantling the Welfare State?*, Cambridge University Press: Cambridge, UK.

Pierson, Paul (2001a), Post-Industrial Pressures on the Mature Welfare State, in P. Pierson (ed.), *The New Politics of the Welfare State*, Oxford University Press: Oxford, UK.

Pierson, Paul (2001b), Coping With Permanent Austerity, in P. Pierson (ed.), *The New Politics of the Welfare State*, Oxford University Press: Oxford, UK.

Revauger, Jean-Paul (2003), The Welfare State in France, in C. Aspalter (ed.), *Welfare Capitalism Around the World*, Casa Verde: Hong Kong/Taipei.

Rodwin, Victor and Le Pen, Claude (2004), Health Care Reform in France: The Birth of State-Led Managed Care, *New England Journal of Medicine*, Vol. 351/22.

Rodwin, Victor and Sandier, Simone (2005), Health Care Under French National Health Insurance, *www.nyu.edu*.

Sainsbury, Diane (1996), *Gender, Equality and Welfare States*, Cambridge University Press: Cambridge, UK

Sainsbury, Diane (ed.) (1999), *Gender and Welfare State Regimes*, Oxford University Press: Oxford, UK.

Scharpf, Fritz (2002), Globalization and the Welfare State, in R. Sigg and C. Behrendt (eds.), *Social Security in the Global Village*, Transactions: New Brunswick, NJ.

Schmid, Josef (1998), Herkunft und Zukunft der Wohlfahrt: Entwicklungspfade zwischen ökonomischem Globalisierungsdruck, staatlich vermittelter Solidarität und gesellschaftlicher Leistung im Vergleich, *Occasional Paper*, No. 1, Institute of Political Science, University of Tübingen, Germany.

Schmid, Josef (2002), *Wohlfahrtsstaaten im Vergleich*, UTB: Stuttgart, Germany.

Schmidt, Vivien A. (2002), Values and Discourse in the Politics of Adjustment, in F.W. Scharpf and V.A. Schmidt (eds.), *Welfare and Work in the Open Economy*, volume i, Oxford University Press: Oxford, UK.

Swank, Duane (2002), *Global Capital, Political Institutions, and Policy Change in Developed Welfare States*, Cambridge University Press: Cambridge, UK.

Taylor-Gooby, Peter (1997), In Defence of Second-Best Theory: State, Class, and Capital in Social Policy, *Journal of Social Policy*, Vol. 26, No. 2, pp. 171-92.

Timonen, Virpi (2003), *Restructuring the Welfare State: Globalisation and Social Policy Reform in Finland and Sweden*, Edward Elgar: Cheltenham, UK.

Toft, Christian (1997), German Social Policy, in M. Mullard and S. Lee (eds.), *The Politics of Social Policy in Europe*, Edward Elgar: Cheltenham, UK.

Walker, Alan (2003), Securing the Future for Old Age in Europe, *Journal of Societal and Social Policy*, Vol. 2, No. 1, pp. 13-32.

Walker, Alan and Deacon, Bob (2003), Economic Globalization and Policies on Aging, *Journal of Societal and Social Policy*, Vol. 2, No. 2, pp. 1-18.

Wanless, Derek (2002), *Securing Our Future Health: Taking a Long-Term View*, The Stationary Office: London.

Ward, Sue (2003), The UK and Pensions: Maverick or the Only One in Step?, in D. Pieters (ed.), *European Social Security and Global Politics*, Kluwer Law International: London.

Woldendorp, Jaap *et al.* (1998), Party Government in 20 Democracies, *European Journal of Political Research*, Vol. 33, pp. 1-119.

7

European Welfare States in Transition: Poland, the Czech Republic, and Hungary

KIM JINSOO AND PARK SOJEUNG

The social security reforms of the East European countries can be described as shocking, compared to the changes that took place in the West European countries or other regions. The term "shocking" implies that the scope of the change is comprehensive, the extent of the change is great, and the resultant confusion is considerable. When we talk about the three countries' social security, the scope of changes involves the introduction of new systems, the degree of changes can primarily refer to the financing method, and the fact that there will be considerable confusion means that the new system will take considerably long to become firmly established due to the confusion resulting from the changes.

First, the new systems introduced as part of the social insurance reforms are the unemployment insurance system and cash benefits within the health insurance system. These changes suggest that unemployment has been recognized as an inevitable social risk caused by the transition from the planned economy of the past towards a market economy (cf Csaba, 2003; Rys, 2001). They also suggest that health insurance will now specifically cover the income loss, if not the expenses, resulting from diseases.

Second, although most social insurance systems are undergoing significant changes, the biggest change can be found in the pension system reform aimed at old-age security. The reason why the change in the pension system is the most shocking is because the pension system has such a big impact on the national economy that a partial improvement was not enough to maintain the state regime.[1] Of course, the three countries show considerable differences as to the nature of their pension system reforms. Nevertheless, the shock felt by all of them due to the reforms is equally tremendous and the reform itself cannot be considered complete as yet.

Third, there are considerable challenges for these changes in social insurance to become fully established. The challenges are manifold, from financial difficulty to administrative limitations to the lack of social consensus. These difficulties sometimes lead to concerns that the reforms may not be properly carried out, as well as to claims that the contents of the reform should be modified. In particular, such claims often conflict with each other. From the financial perspective, the policy directions tend to run against achieving social consensus. On the other hand, the new social insurance system sometimes loses touch with reality by not taking into account the time that the old economic system needs to embrace the market economy.

The changes in the social security system of Poland, the Czech Republic, and Hungary—among the many East European countries and those that became independent from the former Soviet Union—have important implications. The social security of these three nations is a preview of the future of the countries that are in third transition.[2] Of course, there are some East European countries whose social security systems exhibit greater stability than those of these three countries. Nevertheless, the reason why these three countries have been selected for analysis is because the changes in their social security systems are not only in line with the reforms taking place in the developed countries (i.e., mature welfare states), but at the same time show problems similar to those experienced by other developing countries. Such simultaneity can perhaps be considered an inevitable consequence of the transition from a planned economy to a market economy.

First, the three countries clearly reflect the situation faced by the advanced welfare states in that they are struggling with the problem of pension finance. Just as in other welfare states, the three countries exhibit financial problems from accumulated deficits which are caused by maintaining the public pay-as-you-go pension system, only that their situation is much worse than that of advanced welfare states. They also show why it is necessary to carry out radical pension reforms.

On the other hand, these three countries differ from the advanced nations in that, despite rapid changes in social security, their administrative systems are far too insufficient to support such changes. This problem is similar to the problem found in the management and operation system of underdeveloped countries. Prior to 1989, the social policies of the three countries were carried out under the centralized planned economy through strong regulation and redistribution, described as overinstitutionalized socialist paternalism. With the weakening and dissolution of the state apparatus, however, such a system became no longer viable (cf Deacon, 1992; Goetz, 2001; Simon, 2002).

Moreover, the economic conversion revealed difficulties in obtaining information essential for social insurance such as income levels, while the reliability and stability of the management and operation body differed completely from the old state system (cf Haynes and Husan, 2002; Keen and Mucha, 2004). Under these circumstances, the management of social insurance simply reached its limits.

The three countries show differences in their approach to solving these problems. It is difficult to assert, however, that each of them has made the appropriate judgment and choice appropriate for their situation. This is so because the three countries have been pressed for time in coming up with a solution, rather than taking enough time to discuss social insurance reforms including public pension scheme. Such urgency resulted from the absence of an information system necessary for the reforms (Ferge, 2001).

Amid such reform-induced confusion, and nearly 20 years after the introduction of reforms, the three countries now seem to be gradually consolidating their respective systems. They are also making efforts to minimize the consequences of past mistakes and make up for any inadequate regulation.

The analysis of these unusual cases—of rapid reforms and later correction of resulting mistakes—provides very important policy implications for both advanced welfare states and those of developing countries. This chapter will be dedicated to examining and evaluating the changes that have taken place in the social insurance system of the three countries.

Current Pension and Health Security System of Poland, the Czech Republic, and Hungary

Poland

Pension System. In Poland, the public pension system has been undergoing major structural changes in the past decade. As a result, it features today a notional defined contribution (NDC) social insurance system, and in addition to that mandatory individual savings accounts for old-age benefits, as well as a social insurance system for disability and survivor benefits.

The pension system covers all of the economically active population. For employees, contributions add up to 9.76 percent of gross earnings for old-age pensions (2.46 percent, first pillar; 7.3 percent, second pillar) and 6.5 percent of gross earnings for disability and survivor pensions. The self-employed however need to contribute 19.52 percent of insured income for old-age pensions (12.22 percent, first pillar; 7.3 percent, second pillar) and 13 percent of insured income for disability and survivor pensions. Polish employers have to pay 9.76 percent of payroll for old-age pensions (9.76 percent, first pillar; 0 percent, second pillar) and 6.5 percent of payroll for disability and survivor pensions.

The government comes up for the total cost of the guaranteed minimum pension; pays pension contributions on behalf of insured persons taking child-care leave or receiving maternity allowances, for persons receiving unemployment benefits, and for unemployed graduates.

Benefits under the old-age pensions system are based on the total value of contributions paid to the old-age insurance program (subject to adjustment) divided by average life expectancy at the age of retirement. Mandatory individual accounts provide an annuity that is purchased with the funds from the individual account. Conversely guaranteed minimum pension are being provided to persons if the total amount of the first- and second-pillar pensions (old-age pension and the annuity from the individual account) is less than the legal minimum old-age pension.

With regard to disability pensions, in case of full disability, the pension is calculated as 24 percent of national average earnings, plus 1.3 percent of the insured's earnings times the number of contribution years, plus 0.7 percent of the insured's earnings times the number of noncontributory years, and 0.7 percent of the insured's earnings times the number of projected years needed to give a maximum of 25 years of insurance coverage from the day of the claim up to age 60. The survivor's pension varies according to the number of survivors: one survivor receives 85 percent of the insured's old-age pension; two survivors, 90 percent; three or more survivors, 95 percent. If the deceased was not eligible for the old-age pension, the survivor pension is calculated on the basis of the disability pension.

The NDC pension insurance system is operated by the Polish Social Insurance Institute. The mandatory individual accounts are controlled by the Pension Fund Supervision Office (cf Müller, 2003; SSTW, 2006; OECD, 2007).

Health Care System. The public health insurance system covers all employees, and provides for cash and medical benefits. All employees are entitled to cash benefits, while medical benefits are granted to all employees, self-employed persons, artists, authors, pensioners, unemployment allowance beneficiaries, persons undergoing professional rehabilitation, students, and the insured's dependent family members.

Insured persons, be the employed or self-employed, have to contribute 2.45 percent of earnings for cash benefits, and 8.5 percent of earnings for medical benefits. Employers are exempted from contribution fees and the government provides subsidies for medical benefits.

Sickness benefits total 80 percent of average insured earnings (70 percent in the case of hospitalization) in the 6 months before the onset of the incapacity and is paid for 90 days; thereafter, 100 percent of earnings.

In addition also rehabilitation allowances, compensatory allowances, maternity benefits, and care allowances are being offered.

In Poland, the Ministry of Social Policy supervises cash benefits and the Social Insurance Institute administers them. On the other hand, the Ministry of Health supervises medical benefits, while the National Health Fund administers public health funds and contracts medical services (cf SSTW, 2006; OECD, 2008).

The Czech Republic

Pension System. The Czech Republic's pension system is based on the Bismarckian social insurance principle. It covers the employed and self-employed persons, including students; unemployed persons; persons caring for children; indigent persons; and military personnel. The contribution rate for employed persons is 6.5 percent of monthly earnings; the voluntarily insured contribute 28 percent of 9,100 CZK. There are no minimum and maximum of earnings for contribution purposes. The contribution rate for self-employed persons is 28 percent of monthly declared earnings. The employers' rate is 21.5 percent of payroll (again no minimum and maximum earnings for contributions). The government, as in most pay-as-you-go pension systems covers any deficit of the same.

As regards pension benefits, the Czech pension system follows the defined-benefit principle. The pension consists of a basic flat-rate monthly amount of 1,470 CZK and an earnings-related amount calculated on the basis of 1.5 percent of the personal assessment base per year of insurance. There is no maximum for the earnings-related amount. The personal assessment base is based on average gross earnings in the 10 years before retirement.

Pertaining to disability pensions, the monthly full disability pension consists of two elements: a basic flat-rate monthly amount of 1,470 CZK and an earnings-related amount based on 1.5 percent of the personal assessment base per year of insurance. Survivors' pension amounts to a monthly flat-rate basic amount (1,470 CZK) plus 50 percent of the earnings-related amount paid or payable to the deceased. Orphan's pensions, on the other hand, are entitled to a monthly flat-rate basic amount

(1,470 CZK) plus 40 percent of the earnings-related amount paid or payable to the deceased is paid to each dependent child.

The Ministry of Labor and Social Affairs manages the general supervision of the public pension system and is responsible for policy development for all areas of social security except health insurance. The Social Security Administration collects and administers contributions and delivers benefits through its central administration and 77 district administrations (cf Müller, 2003; SSTW, 2006; OECD, 2007).

Health Care System. The Czech health security system consists of a social insurance system that delivers cash benefits, and a universal medical benefit system. The former covers employees and insured self-employed persons (sickness insurance is voluntary for self-employed persons). All persons permanently residing in the Czech Republic, or employees whose employer resides in the country are entitled to universal medical benefits.

Employees pay 1.1 percent of monthly gross earnings (cash sickness and maternity benefits) and 4.5 percent of monthly gross earnings (medical benefits), with no maximum ceilings for contributions. The self-employed contribute 4.4 percent of monthly declared earnings (cash sickness and maternity benefits) and 13.5 percent of monthly declared earnings (medical benefits). Employers are mandated to add 3.3 percent of monthly payroll (cash sickness and maternity benefits) and 9 percent of monthly payroll (medical benefits) (with no maximum ceiling). As with pensions, the government also takes up the guarantor's position, and comes up for any deficits for cash sickness, maternity benefits, as well as medical benefits.

Sickness benefits for the first 3 days amount to 25 percent of the daily assessment base, thereafter 69 percent. The maternity benefit is equal to 69 percent of the daily assessment base and is payable for 28 weeks, and the maternity compensation benefit is equal to the difference between the earnings before and after job transfer.

The Ministry of Labor and Social Affairs is in charge of the general supervision for sickness insurance, however, regional and district offices administer cash benefits. The Czech Social Security Administration collects and administers contributions and delivers cash sickness benefits through its central administration, as well as its 77 district administrations (cf SSTW, 2006; OECD, 2008).

Hungary

Pension System. In Hungary the public pension system is based on two different systems: first, a Bismarckian social insurance system, and second, a personal savings (individual account) system. The public pension system covers employed persons, members of handicraft and agricultural cooperatives, as well as the self-employed. The contribution rate for employees that are covered by social insurance only is 8.5 percent of gross monthly earnings. Those employees who have both social insurance coverage and individual accounts pay 0.5 percent of gross monthly earnings for social insurance and 8 percent of gross monthly earnings for the individual account, plus a percentage of contributions and account balance for administrative fees. The self-employed with social insurance only contribute 26.5 percent of declared monthly earnings, while those who are covered by both systems pay 18.5 percent of declared monthly earnings for social insurance and 8 percent of declared monthly earnings for the individual account, plus a percentage of contributions and account balance for administrative fees. Employers on the other hand put in 18 percent of the monthly payroll for social insurance only.

The minimum earnings for contribution purposes are equal to the monthly minimum wage of 62,500 Forints. In case of deficit within the social insurance system, the government fills the gap with earnings from general tax income.

As regards old-age benefits from the social insurance system, pensions are equal to 33 percent of average earnings for the first 10 years of insurance coverage. The average earnings are based on average indexed monthly earnings since 1988. An insured person who has an individual account receives 75 percent of the social insurance pension. Pertaining to old-age pensions from individual accounts, pension benefits amount to the value of the insured's contributions plus accrued interest.

In the social insurance system, disability pensions for an insured person with less than 25 years of insurance coverage range from 37.5

percent to 63 percent of average earnings. As to the disability annuity, the recipient is entitled to 28,630 Forints per month. The monthly benefit for a temporary disability annuity is equal to 75 percent of the old-age pension payable to the insured at the normal retirement age. Conversely, a regular social annuity adds up to 20,390 Forints per month. Under the individual account system, no benefits are provided. For persons covered by the social insurance, survivor's pensions comprise the widow(er)'s temporary pension and the widow(er)'s permanent pension.

The Ministry of Social Affairs and Labor supervises the social insurance program. Central Administration of National Pension Insurance administers social insurance benefits through its local branches. The National Health Insurance Fund collects contributions through its local branches. Whereas, the Ministry of Finance is in charge of supervising the individual accounts. Only authorized private pension fund administrators are allowed to administer the individual accounts (cf Müller, 2003; SSTW, 2006; OECD, 2007).

Health Care System. The public health care system is organized in form of Bismarckian-type social insurance. Employed persons, members of cooperatives, apprentices in industrial training, artisans, self-employed persons, independent farmers, performing artists, lawyers, and recipients of unemployment benefits are entitled to receive in-cash sickness benefits. In addition, all pregnant employed or self-employed women who have worked for at least 180 days in the 2 years before childbirth may draw maternity benefits. Medical benefits are provide for all insured persons eligible for cash sickness benefits, pensioners, beneficiaries of unemployment benefits, beneficiaries of social assistance benefits and allowances, beneficiaries of pensions provided by Churches, full-time students who are Hungarian citizens residing in Hungary, and all dependent family members and children.

The contributions rates for employed persons stand at 4 percent of gross monthly earnings; voluntary contributors or persons in an exempted activity contribute a flat rate equal to 11 percent of the minimum monthly wage; whereas self-employed persons pay 15 percent of declared monthly earnings. The minimum declared earnings for contribution purposes are equal to 15 percent of the minimum monthly wage (62,500 Forints). The self-employed person's contributions also finance work injury benefits. Employers, on the contrary, have to pay 11 percent of monthly payroll and 1,950 Forints a month per employee to the National Health Insurance Fund. As usual in most Bismarckian social insurance systems nowadays across Europe, the government comes up for any deficits, and on top of that the government finances work injury benefits and reimburses the National Health Insurance Fund for cost incurred in providing health care for children.

Sickness benefits are equivalent to 70 percent of average daily gross earnings if the insured has more than 2 years of insurance coverage, and maternity allowance to 70 percent of daily average gross earnings before the expected date of delivery.

The health insurance system is controlled and monitored by the Ministry of Social Affairs and Labor, while the National Health Insurance Fund, with its County Health Insurance Funds, administers cash sickness and maternity benefits (cf SSTW, 2006; OECD, 2008).

Evaluation of Social Security

Common Features of Social Insurance Reforms

In the 1990s, East European countries all experienced similar levels of GDP reductions and high rates of inflation. It can be said that, in this situation, the fundamental basis of the social security policy is the neo-liberalism centered on economic reform. In the case of the Czech Republic, it implemented paramedic reforms in its public pension, resulting in a less serious situation than that of Hungary and Poland, but an analysis of the Czech social security system reveals that the difference is not that great.[3]

Moreover, the analysis indicates that government efforts to reform the system have had very limited results in real life. This was due to the fact that the government's rightist tendency has been met with a strong opposition and labor union and, consequently, the system has been reformed only to such an extent that it did not threaten the interests of a large section of the people.

Furthermore, the social security reforms have failed to narrow the greatly widened income gap. Although such tendency has become widespread around the world with the flood tide of neoliberalism, the problem in these three countries is that polarization has occurred while the national income is on the decline. Another feature is that the continuing social/economic confusion has created a situation where the level of security provided by the social safety net of the government is below the poverty line, leading to a greater likelihood for people, especially the vulnerable members of society, to fall into poverty.

The cause of this phenomenon can be attributed to the incapacity of the social security system to catch up with the rapid social/economic changes. Moreover, as the widening gap between rich and poor and the increase in absolute poverty are becoming widespread around the world, the warning that the social security system may become like the social structure of Latin America may become more convincing.

On the other hand, a common feature of the three countries is that, despite rapid transition towards a market economy, the old social security system controlled by communism had persisted to a large degree during the early days, and, although such security schemes may not be appropriate in a free market economy, they continue to exist with signs of gradual decrease. The relaxed regulation on child care in Poland, the level of unemployment benefits in the Czech Republic, and the disability and old-age benefit in Hungary and Poland can be cited as examples (cf e.g. Vanhuysse, 2004). These examples are all the more significant in that a similar environment is being created in all these countries.

In the case of Poland, there are various childbirth and childcare-related benefits. The survivor benefits are paid to all family members, with up to 95 percent of the pension amount being paid according to the number of family members, and maternity benefit, child benefit, and childcare benefit are also being offered. Moreover, as to the care allowance, it is paid in cash for 14 months until the healthy child reaches the age of 8, which is a result of the special interest that the previous communist regime had in childbirth and childcare.

The unemployment benefits in the Czech Republic are a typical policy designed to mitigate the shock that the people, long accustomed to full employment under the planned economy, would feel after losing their jobs as a result of the transition towards a market economy.[4]

Initially, the eligibility criteria for unemployment benefits in the Czech Republic were generous, but over time not only did they become stricter but also the level of benefits became gradually diminished. A similar trend has been observed in Poland and Hungary as well. The Czech Republic's unemployment benefits during the early days were subject to a much more relaxed regulation than today. In the initial phase of unemployment benefits—from its introduction to December of 1991—they were paid for 12 months. The unemployment benefits during the first six months were 90 percent of their previous wage amount and during the last six months, 60 percent. In 1992, the requirements for the unemployment benefits became stricter, with the benefits being reduced to 60 percent for the first three months and to 50 percent from the fourth month onwards. The benefits were reduced once more in 1999 to 50 percent for the first three months and to 40 percent for another three months, and the total amount of benefits could not exceed 1.5 times of the minimum cost of living. The unemployed people subject to requalification are eligible for 70 percent of their past income, which is 1.8 times the minimum cost of living. The payment of unemployment benefits is suspended after the sixth month, and the unemployed people seeking for a job receive unemployment assistance, the amount of which equals the minimum cost of living (cf SSTW, 2006).

The problem with the OADS (old-age, disability, and survivors pension) can be considered a common phenomenon in that the disability pension expenditure is high in all of the three countries (cf Figure 7.1). The actual retirement age in East European countries is generally low, which is due to the labor market policy whereby the government intentionally encourages older workers to retire through early retirement incentives.[5]

The disability pension system is a case in point. Strictly speaking, the disability pension is a system that provides pensions to older workers with diminished work ability, and not to the disabled ones, thus it is different from the disability defined by the workmen's accident compensation insurance. Hungary, Poland and the Czech Republic all had a relatively free medical assessment system, and state policy dictated that workers judged as disabled could receive the disability and old-age benefits instead of the unemployment benefits.

Figure 7.1: Pension Spending (% of GDP)

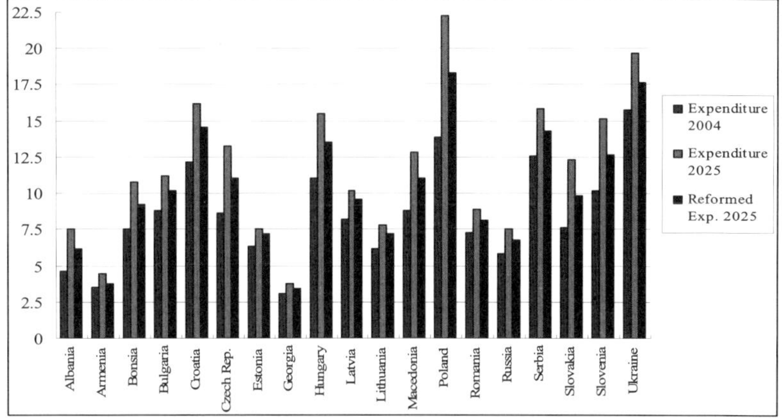

Source: World Bank (2007a).

Figure 7.2: Breakdown of Pension Expenditure (% of GDP, in 2004)

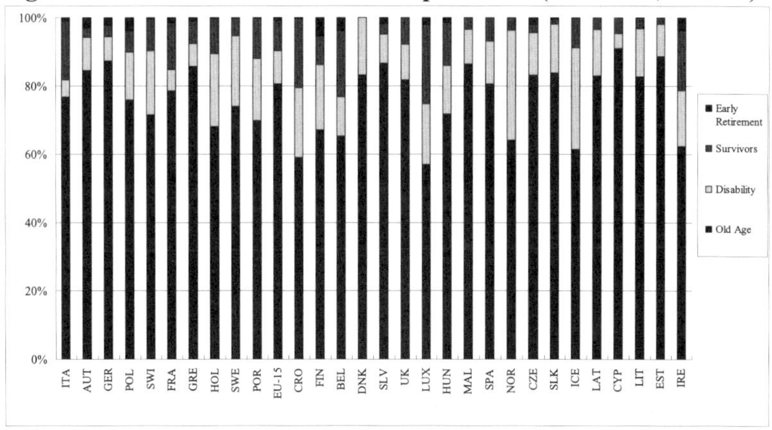

Source: Eurostat (2008).

This situation has provoked a the rapid increase in the number of disability pension beneficiaries, since workers who were in danger of becoming unemployed or had already lost their jobs could apply for the disability pension (cf Figure 7.2). In particular, the relaxed eligibility rules for the disability pension have led to the possibility of engaging in economic activities while receiving the disability pension. Moreover, pensioners could take advantage of the confusion created by the rapid economic and social changes to unofficially earn additional income. This kind of disability and old-age pension is expected to trigger a public pension crisis in the East European countries, just as it did in Western Europe.

Furthermore, the lower average retirement age and hence the lower employment rate of older workers in especially Poland and Hungary, as well as Slovakia, Slovenia, and Bulgaria, compared to that in Western Europe (EU-15) will further aggravate pension finances (cf Figure 7.3).

Figure 7.3: Employment Rate of Older Workers (age 55-64, in %)

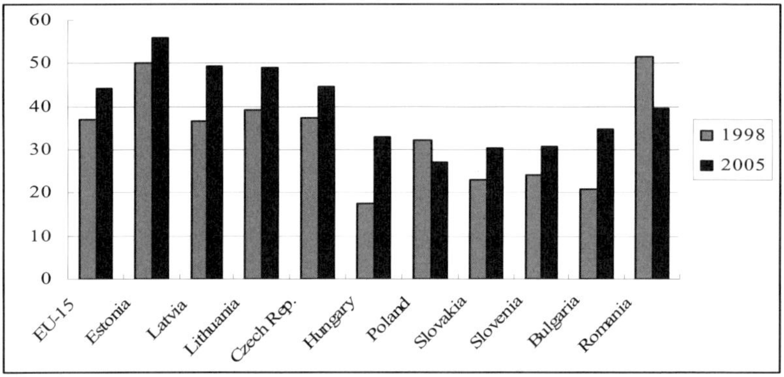

Source: Eurostat (2008).

According to the World Bank, the lower retirement age of East European countries suggests that the number of pension beneficiaries will be relatively higher and the duration of pension payments will be longer than those of West European countries. Women's low retirement age is particularly worrisome because the average life-span of women in Eastern Europe is similar to the European average, suggesting that the impact will be much greater (WB, 2007a).

Evaluation of the Social Security Reform

The evaluation of the social security reforms in these three countries may vary significantly according to the measures used for evaluation. The most important factor in assessing public pensions is the sustainability of the system, that is, its financial viability, while the health care system is evaluated based on the maximization of service quality in addition to financial stability. On the other hand, the evaluation of the management and operation system should take into account its ability to maximize cost efficiency and to protect subscribers' rights. In addition, in light of the characteristics of East European countries, another important consideration in assessing their social policies should be the capacity to minimize the shock resulting from the social security reforms. Each of these criteria for evaluation—sustainability, appropriateness, efficiency, and social integration—is mutually exclusive, interchangeable or independent rather than complementary. Thus, an objective evaluation of the social security reforms in each of the three countries may be impossible since it is likely to be based on subjective views.

First, Poland and Hungary have adopted the NDC model in their old-age security system including public pensions. This means that their pension benefits have been slashed considerably enough to expect a relative improvement of financial stability, but resulting in the neglect of their roles of achieving social integration or appropriateness. This may hinder social integration, because the social security system has been unable to absorb the shock caused by the reorganization of socialism and planned economy, leaving the groups alienated by the market economy exposed to risks. Moreover, the mandatory fully-funded DC approach-including the NDC approach of Poland implies that it should guarantee old-age security through a direct link with the minimum pension system, meaning that its role can be entirely changed according to the level of minimum pension benefits. In this sense, the mandatory fully funded DC model of Hungary and Poland can be differentiated from that of Sweden or Italy. By contrast, the Czech Republic has taken a more paramedic approach to reforming the system, which may render the system unsustainable over the long term. While the paramedic reform of the Czech Republic can be evaluated as limited in terms of ensuring the sustainability of the system, it has, at least, mitigated the shock created by the transition towards a market economy instead of transferring it to the people, which resulted in less fierce public resistance compared to Hungary or Poland (cf Table 7.1).

Table 7.1: Structure of Pension in Poland, the Czech Republic, and Hungary

	Main reform	Statutory schemes	
		PAYG	Funded
Poland	1998	NDC based	Mandatory fully funded DC (1999)
Czech Republic	1993-1995, 2003	DB, financed from social security contributions	None
Hungary	1998	DB, financed from social security contributions	Mandatory fully funded DC(1999)

Source: based on World Bank (2007a).

On the other hand, with respect to the administrative body, the transition towards a market economy may mean the participation of various private organizations in the management of social insurance. This is viewed as a positive aspect of the transition since it involves efforts to increase rationality and efficiency by introducing competition in the area of management and operation. Nevertheless, the participation of private organizations in the management of social insurance should take place after the state has at least removed or minimized any side effects that may occur as a result of the participation of the private sector so that these private players can be more effective than the public management body. If the management by private organizations is inefficient due to a lack of flexibility, expertise, or competitiveness, the resultant side effects will not only fail to achieve the goals of social security but will also cause only more serious problems, like public distrust (cf Simonovits, 2000; Müller, 2003).

It can be pointed out that the Czech Republic, which maintains a single management body for its public pensions, shows limitations in its ability to address the problems resulting from the loss of state control and to find any viable alternative. Hungary and Poland, on the other hand, are incapable of fully protecting subscribers' rights due to their lack of experience with the market economy and the appearance and disappearance of various management organizations. This shows that each country should take a different approach to complementing and improving their social insurance systems according to the kind of reforms they have undertaken.

As to health care insurance, the current major problem has its roots in the communist days of the past, when the state provided free health care for all people but the quality of whose benefits was poorer than that of Western Europe. After the transition, however, individual preferences began to be accepted while the public sector focused on maintaining financial stability (Lipsmeyer and Nordstrom, 2003; Novacek, 2000). As a result, we are witnessing a divided market where the public sector continues to provide the same low quality health care as that under the previous socialist regime, while the high quality health service that meets the needs of individuals is provided by the private sector. Moreover, it can be pointed out that in Hungary, which has introduced a cost-sharing system for in-kind benefits, the health security system has become worse than in the past.

Conclusion

There are two aspects to the challenges facing the social security reforms of these three East European countries. The first one is that they have to achieve sustainability by addressing financial instability, though efforts to reach this goal are still under way. A solution to this difficulty is, to a varying extent, more pressing and urgent for East European countries than for advanced welfare states. This is so because their efforts to reform a system plagued by accumulated financial deficits were much more belated than those of the advanced welfare states. Therefore, the attempts of the East European countries to stabilize their social security finances will entail a much more shocking and long-term difficulties for the people.

The other aspect of the challenges is the potential incapacity of social security to perform its functions, due to a lack of basic information infrastructure within the management and operation framework. The East European countries are in a transition period where the old political, economic, and social systems become collapsed and new ones are being created. Thus, they need to develop an effective management and administrative capacity to successfully perform the basic tasks associated with social insurance, such as the gathering of income information, taxation, collection, eligibility evaluation and payment. They also need to acquire expertise by raising funds and achieving a combination of profitability and stability from the management of such funds. As for private organizations, the key to their success is to win public confidence by developing the capability to perform public functions. This problem of management capacity is more related to welfare states in developing countries, rather than advanced welfare states.

Despite concerns in these respects, the social security system of the three East European countries is unlikely to experience the kind of problems and confusion that Latin America faced after its social security reforms. This is so because they have already gained membership to the European Union, which suggests that there will be considerable amounts of exchanges and controls, and that the East European countries must conform to the Maastricht Treaty regarding finances and national debt (cf EC, 2004, 2005). Moreover, the free movement of persons is the key focus of the EU integration and the principle of social security for all workers within the European Union is already being enforced (cf Wallace, 2002; Wagener, 2002). This suggests that all countries should act as part of EU's social security network rather than sticking to the systems unique to them. Thus, the EU will provide direct and indirect support to all of its members so that they can, over the long term, achieve similar levels of development. Nevertheless, considering that a stable settlement and development of the social security systems in East European countries depends on their economic/social development and stability, it still remains to be seen what the future may hold.

REFERENCES

1 Despite reform efforts, social expenditures around the world tend to increase along with per capita income, and pension expenditures as a percentage of GDP are still high with little change. The pension expenditures of Poland in 2004 were roughly 15 percent of GDP, the highest level among EU countries (WB, 2006).

2 The countries of Eastern Europe and the former Soviet Union are experiencing a third transition, a transition that overlaps with their recent political and economic transitions (WB, 2007b).

3 Potucek (2001) mentioned legislative efforts to limit the role of the state and its spending powers as a characteristic of the Czech social security policy, and expressed distrust in the mediating role of civil organizations in forming and implementing social policies. Such tendency was also evident in the process of identifying the priorities in the establishment of social policies. He pointed out efforts to strengthen the eligibility for social benefits, to provide social benefits based on universal income- and asset-tests, and to reduce general social expenditures.

4 Prior to the transition of 1989, Poland also maintained a fairly generous benefits eligibility and level. However, they became increasingly strict, particularly in the case of unemployment benefit, the qualifying conditions and benefit level became more stringent than those of Czech Republic. Noteworthy in such development is that the restriction imposed on unemployment benefits during mid-1990s resulted in benefit diversification but also increased number of people depending on social assistances.

5 The Czech Republic abolished early retirement privilege for certain professsions and social organizations, but other countries including Poland did not change the related existing system.

REFERENCES

Csaba, Laszlo (2003), Transition as Development, *Post-Communist Economies*, Vol. 15, No. 1, pp. 3-25.

Deacon, Bob (1992), East European Welfare, in B. Deacon *et al.* (eds.), *The New Eastern Europe: Social Policy*, Sage: London.

EC, European Commission (2004), *Social Protection in the Member States of the European Union*, European Commission: Luxembourg.

EC, European Commission (2005), Joint Report on Social Protection and Social Inclusion 2005, *europa.eu.int*.

Eurostat (2008), *ec.europa.eu/eurostat*.

Ferge, Zsuzsa (2001), Disquieting Quiet in Hungarian Social Policy, *International Social Security Review*, Vol. 54, pp. 107-27.

Goetz, Klaus (2001), Making Sense of Post-Communist Central Administration, *Journal of European Public Policy*, Vol. 8, No. 6, pp. 1032-51.

Haynes, Michael and Husan, Rumy (2002), Market Failure, State Failure, Institutions, and Historical Constraints in the East European Transition, *Journal of Contemporary European Studies*, Vol. 10, No. 1, pp. 105-29.

Keen, Mike and Mucha, Janusz (2004), Sociology in Central and Eastern Europe in the 1990s, *European Societies*, Vol. 6, No. 2, pp. 123-47.

Lipsmeyer, Christine and Nordstrom, Timothy (2003), East Versus West, *Journal of European Public Policy*, Vol. 10, No. 3, pp. 339-64.

Müller, Katharina (2003), Transformation of Pension Systems in Central and Eastern Europe, *European Social Policy*, Vol. 13, No. 2, pp. 201-21.

Novacek, Pavel (2000), A Sustainable Future for the Czech Republic: Transition and Human Values, *Foresight*, Vol. 2, No. 3, pp. 313-21.

OECD (2007), *Pension Panorama: Retirement-Income Systems in 53 Countries*, OECD: Paris.

OECD (2008), *www.oecd.org*.

Potucek, Martin (2001), Czech Social Reform After 1989, *International Social Security Review*, Vol. 54, pp. 81-106.

Rys, Vladimir (2001), Social Protection in Central and Eastern Europe Ten Years After, *International Social Security Review*, Vol. 54, pp. 3-8.

Simon, Rick (2002), Parties, State, and Democracy in Post-Communist Europe, *Contemporary Politics*, Vol. 8, No. 2, pp. 151-59.

Simonovits, András (2000), Partial Privatization of a Pension System: Lessons from Hungary, *Journal of International Development*, Vol. 12, No. 4, pp. 519-29.

SSTW, Social Security Throughout the World (2006), *socialsecurity.gov/policy*.

Vanhuysse, Pieter (2004), The Pensioner Booms in Post-Communist Hungary and Poland, *International Journal of Sociology & Social Policy*, Vol. 24, No. 1-2, pp. 86-102.

Wagener, Hans-Jürgen (2002), The Welfare State in Transition Economies and Accession to the EU, *West European Politics*, Vol. 25, No. 2, pp. 152-74.

Wallace, Claire (2002), Opening and Closing Borders: Migration and Mobility in East-Central Europe, *Journal of Ethnic and Migration Studies*, Vol. 28, No. 4, pp. 603-25.

WB, World Bank (2006), Pension Reform, *www.worldbank.org*.

WB, World Bank (2007a), World Bank EU8 Quarterly Economic Report, *www.worldbank.org*.

WB, World Bank (2007b), From Red to Grey, *www.worldbank.org*.

8

The Danish Welfare State: A Social Rights Perspective

PETER ABRAHAMSON

The beginning of the Danish experience of public welfare provision dates back a long time, but for the development of modern Denmark, the early beginnings were, like for most European countries in the latter part of the 19th century. Or though different states took different routes to the welfare state it is interesting to note, as Bo Rothstein (2000: 217) has reminded us recently that until the 1960s most advanced capitalist economies spend roughly the same amount on welfare provision measured as share of GDP. Since then, however, developments have diverged and Denmark along with the other Scandinavian countries has moved up among the big spenders. Judging the development during the last two and a half decades a process of maturation seems to have taken place, since expansion in relative terms have stopped. This chapter gains in details of description with time during developments of the 20th century. Hence, more space has been devoted to recent changes than earlier developments.

The welfare state is generally understood as a state form, which grants social rights to its citizens. The concept came to Denmark from

Britain where it had developed during wartime not the least by the publication of William Beveridge's *Social Insurance and Allied Services* in 1942. In this report Beveridge sketched out the institutional framework for the fight against what he understood as the five giant evils of modern society: want, disease, ignorance, squalor, and idleness. These evils could be fought by establishing the following institutions: basic income security in the case of inability to work (sickness, old age, child birth, invalidity, unemployment, accident, etc.), health care for all, housing, basic education, and full employment. Towards the end of the 1940s, Thomas Marshall defined social citizenship in a manner parallel to Beveridge. Marshall noted that citizenship is a status bestowed on those who are full members of a community. All who possess the status are equal with respect to the rights and duties with which the status is endowed. But in order to enjoy the privileges and duties of citizenship it is not enough to have civil and political rights. Social citizenship was seen as a precondition for exercising citizenship rights. Thomas Marshall, in particular, had in mind the whole range from the right to a modicum of economic welfare and security, to the right to share to the full in the social heritage and to live the life of a civilized being according to the standards prevailing in the society (Marshall, 1950, 1981).

A welfare state is hence a state that guarantees, or sees to guarantee, the welfare of its citizens. The development and current state of affair of social citizenship in Denmark is hence the content of this chapter. It starts out with a very brief description of the early beginnings of the Danish welfare society and identifies some major historical turning points: the 1890s, the 1930s, and the 1960s. But emphasis is on the maturation stage, ever since 1982.

Early Beginnings

The first social security net in Denmark was established in 1891, when the act on poverty and old-age support passed the Danish parliament. Before this act was passed, helping the poor was left to private charity and a very restricted help from the municipality in connection with sickness and old age. In 1891 the state established a real legislation and offered financial support to the poor and the old people. But there was made a clear distinction between the deserving and the not deserving poor. The not deserving poor were treated worse than the deserving poor. The help was means-tested by the municipalities, and the poor people could be placed in special "poorhouses," where they were forced to work. Furthermore, the not deserving poor lost some of their civic rights—for example, their franchise (Baldwin, 1990; Horneman Møller, 1992; Ingerslev and Ploug, 1996).

In the period from the 1890s to 1933, there was gradually established more and more social security provisions, especially for the workers. The purpose of these provisions was to secure the workers against the most common social risks—e.g., sickness, old age, unemployment, disablement, and work accidents. There was a change in the principles of social policy, from a pure principle of means-tested support to a principle of security, where the state offered financial support to the different insurance schemes; the help to self-help principle.

In 1933 came the first reform of the social protection system in Denmark. It was mainly a simplification of the social protection system, where all the different social acts were gathered into four main social acts. At the same time the legal principle was introduced as the bearing principle in the social legislation—that is, the social benefits were statutory rights in connection with certain events, for example, unemployment and sickness, on the contrary to means-tested benefits paid by the municipalities. But the means-tested benefits were still the main principle as regards the social assistance benefits. The not deserving poor were still exposed to strict control from the authorities and they still lost franchise. Along with the improvements in the social security system, still fewer were regarded as not deserving poor and subject to the humiliating social assistance scheme (Horneman Møller, 1994). In the period from 1933 to 1960 the existing provisions were gradually improved, but within the framework of the 1933-reform. But in the 1960s some important principles in the social policy were changed.

Before going into more detail about the development from the 1960s and onwards I shall briefly indicate some overall trends in Danish welfare development. One of the foundations of a Scandinavian type welfare state is the high rate of labor force participation. Figure 8.1

below illustrates what has happened to the activity rates of men and women from 1948 and till 2006:

Figure 8.1: Activity Rates for Men and Women in All of Denmark, 1948 to 2006

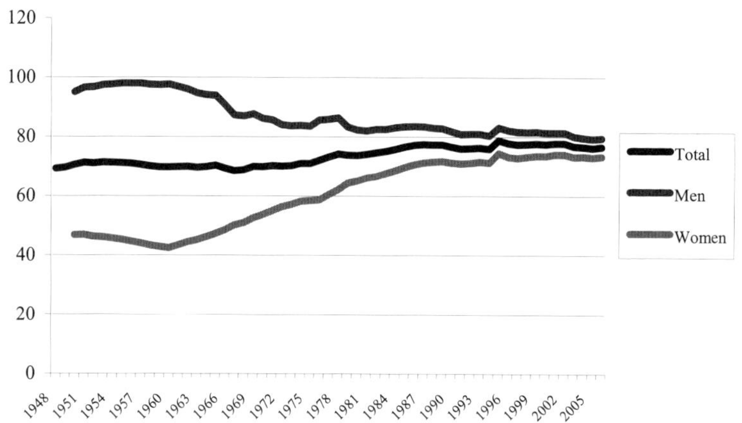

Source: Statistics Denmark (1995, 1999, 2007).

In 1950, 95 percent of men and 47 percent of women of working ages were affiliated with the labor market; in 1960 we found the biggest discrepancy between male and female participation: 98 percent of men and 43 percent of women were in the labor market then. Since 1960 the development has been so that men have decreased in participation down to 82 percent, which was reached in 1982 and has been rather stable at that level since, while women have increased their labor force participation to an all time high in 1995 of 75 percent. The overall effect has been a steady increase in the share of population being affiliated with the labor market in the post-World War II period and it is now around 78 percent, but movements since 1985 have been very small.

Unfortunately not everyone in the labor market has a job, so it is also important to look at the development in unemployment as shown in Figure 8.2.

Figure 8.2: Number of Unemployed Men and Women in Denmark (in thousands)

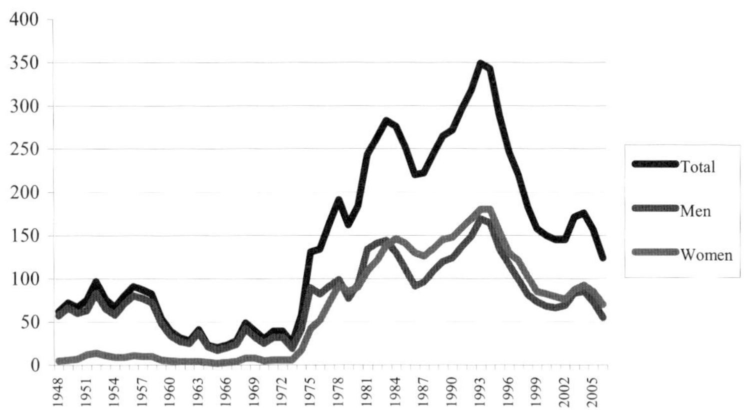

Source: Statistics Denmark (1995, 1999, 2007).

Remembering full employment to be one of the conditions of a welfare state we can conclude that such a situation prevailed in Denmark only from 1960 till 1974. Since the mid 1970s and till the all-time high in 1993 unemployment increased with a few minor improvements in 1980 and 1986. Since the mid-1980s more women than men have been unemployed. By the end of the 1999s the situation is as it was in 1980 with around 175,000 unemployed people, which is about 6 or 7 percent of the workforce; but by 2006 Denmark is experiencing the lowest un-employment since the 1960s, i.e. around 4.5 to 5 percent of the work-force (Statistics Denmark, 2000, 2007).

An indication of development of the Danish welfare state is the development of total social expenditure as share of the gross domestic product. These values show the degree of committing resources to collective welfare arrangements.

Figure 8.3: Total Social Expenditure as Share of GDP in Denmark (1945 to 2006)

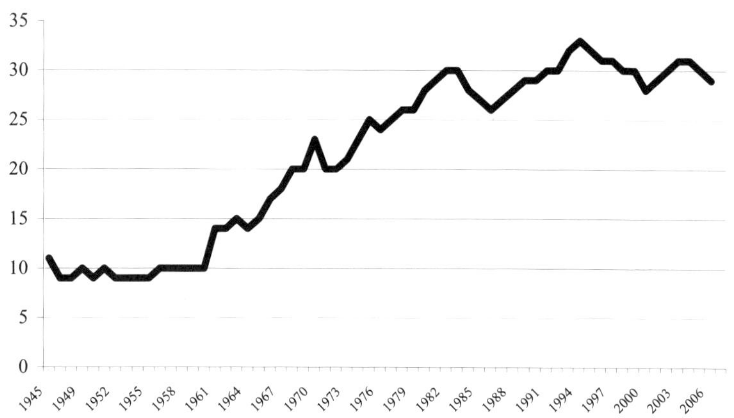

Source: Statistics Denmark (1995, 1999, 2007).

From the end of World War II to the year 1960 social expenditure took up about 10 percent of GDP (Figure 8.3). But since then it increased rapidly and steadily till it reached 30 percent in 1982. With some fluctuations this is also the share we found at the end of the century. It looks as if total social expenditure has stabilized itself around 30 percent of GDP in Denmark which is comparable to other European countries such as France, the Netherlands, Germany, and other, Scandinavian, countries (Statistics Denmark, 2007: 23).

If one development has been cause for worrying about the Danish welfare state it is the number of people of working ages that are permanently or for long periods of time totally dependent upon public support for there livelihood. Figure 8.4 shows the share of people on longtime public support from 1960 till 2004:

Figure 8.4: Share of Population Aged 18 to 66 on Long-Term Public Support, in percent

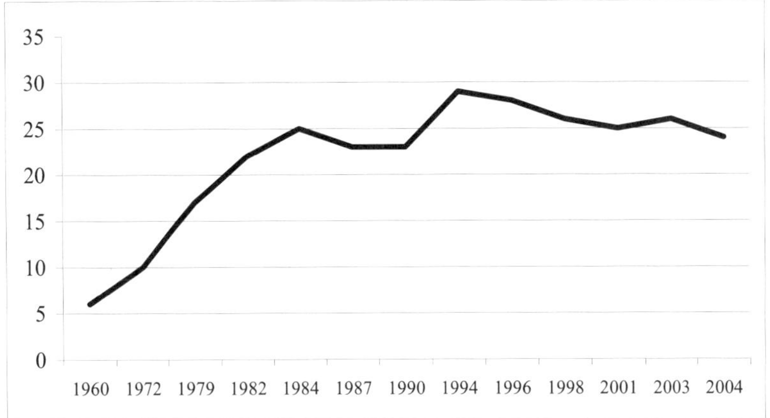

Source: Auken (1985), Hansen and Hansen (1999); Hansen (2006).

In 1960, only 6 percent of Danes 18 to 65 years of age were receiving public benefits, in 1973 it had increased to 10 percent and in 1984 it had reached 25 percent, and with fluctuations this is the level around which this figure seems to have stabilized itself. This brief statistical overview identifies 1960 and 1982 as watershed years in the development of the Danish welfare state.

The Golden Age of the Welfare State

In 1961 a new social assistance act was passed, which removed the remaining humiliating aspects of the division between the deserving and the not deserving poor. All civic rights were maintained, including the franchise. Now there were two categories of social assistance; common need and the need of special groups, e.g. single parents. The benefits for common need was fixed at the same level as the old-age pension, while the benefits for special groups were fixed at a somewhat higher level.

Another change in 1960 of great importance was the introduction of the rehabilitation principle, which was established in a special rehabilitation act. Until this time, social policy was concentrated on the creation of social security for the citizens, if they were exposed to social contingencies. Now social policy got a new task, namely to rehabilitate people, so that they were able to support themselves in the future. Another thing worth mentioning is, that an expanding number of social provisions and social services, was offered to the population, and a growing number of people received social benefits and social services during the 1960s. The social provisions were extended to cover the whole population, instead of being restricted to the vulnerable and poor.

In the late 1960s, Danish social policy was thoroughly reanalyzed in an expert-commission—the so-called *Social Reform Commission*. The time had come, where the framework of the 1933-reform with all its addings and expansions through the period should be re-examined. The 1960s was a time characterized by high economic growth, rising standard of living in the whole population, full employment and a minimum of social problems. The total social expenditure had grown from 7 percent of GDP in 1934/1935 to 17 percent in 1969/1970.

As stated by Peter Bogason, "Denmark completed, starting in the early 1970s, the most profound changes in the political-administrative system in the 20th century (Bogason, 1992: 95). The reform-complex bore the title "municipality reform" and covered four different, yet interrelated, laws:

1. The "division reform," which reduced the number of local authorities, municipalities, from 1388 to 277 (now 275), and changed the number of regional authorities, counties, from 25 to 14.
2. The "management reform," which streamlined the local administrations placing the financial committees centrally in the local bureaucracy.
3. The "burden distribution reform," transferring former central governmental responsibilities to regional and local levels (institutions for mentally handicapped were taken over by the counties in 1976 and 1980, and sick pay was transferred to the municipalities in 1973). Most importantly, the financial support from central to local

government was changed from a percentage reimbursement to block grants.
4. The "social reform," building upon the principles laid down by the Social Reform Commission:

The objectives of the new social policy reform can be illustrated by the following quotation from the chairman of the Social Reform Commission, Bent Rold Andersen:

"to reduce the occurrence of substantial social adaptation problems or problems of loss of income and to contribute actively to solve such problems, wherever they occur."

This quotation contains the main principles of the new social reform, which was carried out in the beginning of the 1970s.

1. *The prevention-principle.* The number of cases, where permanent or long lasting support is necessary, should be reduced by an early and sufficient effort. Preferably, when it is possible to foresee, that there is a risk that problems will develop to be greater and long lasting or even permanent.
2. *The principle of income-loss.* In case of temporary loss of income, a generous and means-tested financial compensation should be granted. This should prevent a social deroute because of temporary economic problems.
3. *The rehabilitation principle.* In case a person is unable to support himself or his family, he should be rehabilitated, e.g. by education, reeducation, or training.
4. *The principle of means-test.* Every single case should be examined, to give proper and sufficient help without regard to what has caused the problem.
5. *The totality principle.* When examining the need for help attention should be paid to the various aspects of the client's situation,

6. *The unity principle.* There should only be one place to apply for help
    and preferably only one social worker at the social security office to
    contact.

These principles were the basis of the new social reform in the 1970s
(Andersen *et al.*, 1970, 1971, 1972). The social reform consisted of the
following acts: the Social Administration Act, the Social Appeal Act,
the Health Insurance Act, the Maintenance Allowance Act, the Social
Assistance Act, and the decentralization of the care for disabled persons.

The last resort of the social protection system was stated in the
Social Assistance Act, the Maintenance Allowance. This benefit was
only granted, when all other forms of help from the social protection
system were not available, e.g. cash benefits or pensions. The Maintenance Allowance was granted to *"a person, who is prevented from
getting the means to support himself or his family, because of changes in
his situation."* The measuring of the Maintenance Allowance should pay
attention to the total situation of the client, and be means-tested by the
social worker at the social security office. The amount of the Maintenance Allowance was not fixed in the act, but several regulations were
issued to instruct the social workers.

The Social Assistance Act began to operate in 1976, but there have
been several changes in the legislation until it was finally replaced by a
set of acts in 1997. The overall consequence of this reform-complex was
decentralization—that is, municipalization—of the Danish welfare structure, hereby seeking a more effecttive and rational resource allocation.

This whole reform-complex was initiated on the background of the
prosperity of the 1960s and a situation of full employment. Therefore,
the central ideas behind social reform were those of rehabilitation and
prevention. Because of shortage of labor it was imperative for the
welfare policy to be able to contribute to a qualified and quick "repair of
injured labor," or, preferably, a prophylactic policy, avoiding social
casualties of all sorts.

The 1979-Reforms: The Crisis and Unemployment Were Here to Stay

Unfortunately, the reform-complex developed during the 1960s was not implemented until the 1970s, in a situation with profoundly changed societal conditions. From the first oil crisis and onwards—that is, from 1973/1974 onwards—Denmark has experienced high levels of unemployment and moderate growth rates. So, from the outset there has been a tension between the intentions of the reform-complex and the societal reality.

A moderate adjustment to the high unemployment situation could be identified towards the end of the 1970s. Until then the then social democratic lead governments had tried to promote the return of prosperity through Keynesian means of effective demand through public spending, e.g. by extending the possibility for long-term unemployed to collect benefits. In 1979, however, two laws were inaugurated which signal a change in welfare strategy, accepting that unemployment was not to be regarded as a temporary phenomenon easily dealt with by traditional fiscal policies. With the Job-Offer Scheme and the Early Voluntary Retirement Pensions Scheme (VERPS) welfare policy was seen as instrumental to the labor market situation (cf Abrahamson, 1991a; Andersen, 1997).

The Job-Offer-Scheme

With the introduction of the Job-Offer-Scheme in 1979 the first step was taken towards the effort of transforming the Danish welfare system from one of passive support to one of active involvement. Through this law all long-term unemployed members of an unemployment fund had the right to a suitable job of seven to nine months length. It was administrated by the local public employment offices and, to a large degree, financed by the central government.

The idea was to enhance employment through wage-subsidies granted by the authorities. Thus, it was expected that private sector would enlarge its employment with the encouragement of public support for nine months, and then, hopefully, the companies would be satisfied with the additional labor, and keep them on the work force. Unfortunately, businesses were not very attracted to this situation, and the end result was that the public sector, finally the municipalities, was given the responsibility of finding jobs within their own institutions for the long-term unemployed. In practice, all long-termed unemployed were laid-off after seven months of public employment; after just enough employment to make them eligible for another period of unemployment benefits.

The Conservative Schlüter Government taking over in 1982 have continued the Job-Offer-Scheme and enlarged it to include a so-called enterprise benefit, where-by one was enabled to try and start ones own business while receiving 50 percent of benefits for two years (1985). From this time the job offer could only be received twice; yet, the second time it could be replaced by a so-called education offer, granting training opportunities to the long-term unemployed while they continue collecting benefits.

Seen from the point of view of recipients the Job-Offer-Scheme must be regarded as highly successful, since it enabled long-term unemployed to stay within the benefit system for up to nine years. Viewed on the background of the intentions, however, the Job-Offer-Scheme was not able to create any additional employment in society. What was happening was a circulation of the unemployed in and out of "artificial employment" (cf Abrahamson, 1992; Andersen, 1997).

National Pension

The Danish old-age pension (or national pension as the official sources have it) is a non-contributory pension financed out of general taxation, which all residents are entitled to. In order to receive the full amount one has to have lived in the country for 40 years from the age of 15 to 67. A minimum of three years for nationals and 10 years for non-nationals are required. If one has lived in Denmark for say 20 years one is entitled to 20/40 of the full amount and so on. From 2004 onward, the retirement age will be reduced from the current 67 years of age to 65 (MISSOC, 2000). The basic principles have been unchanged since the pension was first introduced in 1956. In 1998 a single pensioner received an amount equivalent to 63 percent of an average production worker's net disposable income (APW), while a couple received 52 percent (of 100 percent APW plus 75 percent AWP) (NOSOSCO, 2000).

Voluntary Early Retirement Pension Scheme (VERPS)

Simultaneously with the introduction of the Job-Offer-Scheme in 1979, the VERPS was introduced. The law enables older workers (aged 60 to 66) who are members of an unemployment fund to withdraw from the labor market receiving a scaled-down proportion of unemployment benefits, before qualifying for the state old-age pension at 67 years of age. Again, the intension was both social policy and labor market policy. On the one hand the law grants older worn out workers the opportunity to withdraw from the labor market before official retirement age (67 then, now 65); and on the other hand it was expected that younger workers would replace the older ones, so that overall unemployment would be reduced substantially.

Of course, the introduction of the VERPS in 1979 had an impact on unemployment statistics since a large number of unemployed transferred to it. However, with regard to the jobs being vacant when older workers in employment started receiving VERPS, the replacement ratio was considerably less than 100 percent, making the overall employment effect rather modest. With some minor changes this law has been continued under the Conservative Schlüter Government, and is—together with activation—still an important part of current Danish welfare policy. It was, however, significantly changed in 1998 in order to discourage the 60 to 61 year-olds to seek early retirement. Now it is not very attractive to go on VERPS before 62. Furthermore, an obligatory contribution fees has been established moving the financing more in the direction of Continental European schemes (cf Abrahamson, 1991a; Christiansen and Petersen, 2001; Jensen, 2004).

The Structure of Social Citizenship in Contemporary Denmark

Around 1982 the welfare state as we know it today was already in place and we can sum it up generally as follows. If we accept a simple model of social citizenship we can follow Dahrendorf (1994) and say that social rights can be derived in two ways either as *entitlements* or as *provisions*. Entitlements are based on citizenship rights, and are as such *universal*; provisions are either granted with reference to *merit*, as in a contributory system (in accordance with the achievement-performance model of social policy), or with reference to *need*, as in a discretionary system based on means and/or needs test. We have, hence, a tripolar differentiation of social citizenship (Table 8.1).

Table 8.1: Three Ideal-Typical Models of Social Citizenship

	UNIVERSAL	PERFORMATIVE	CLIENTELISTIC
Rights based on	Citizenship (or residence)	corporate contract	needs-test, means-test (assets, income)
Obligations based on	parental status (parents' obligation to provide for their children)	familiar status (parents' obligation to provide for their children; adult children's obligation to provide for their old parents; spouses' mutual obligation to provide for each other) combined with employers' obligations towards employees	parental status (parents' obligation to provide for their children) and marital status (spouses' mutual obligation to provide for each other) combined with behavioral duties (man-in-the-house rules; workfare)
Social policy model (Titmuss)	institutional	achievement-performance	residual
Central welfare state activity (Marshall)	public social services	social insurance	social assistance

Table 8.2: Functional Distribution of Social Rights in Denmark 1998 with Reference to Main Categories of Risk (parentheses indicate commercial alternative)

		UNIVERSAL	PERFOR-MATIVE	CLIENTEL-ISTIC
Health	primary health care (general practitioners)	x		
	secondary health care (hospitals)	x	(x)	
	sick pay		x	x
Old age, handi-cap, invalidity	home help, meals on wheels, etc.	x		
	nursing homes	x	(x)	
	pensions	x	x	
Unemployment	education, vocational training		x	
	job guarantee, workfare		x	
	unemployment benefits		x	
Families (children)	day-care institutions	x		
	housing allowances	x		
	child benefits	x		
Social assistance	activation			x
	(therapeutic) institutions			x
	poor relief			x
Education	primary school	x	(x)	
	technical/ craft/ practical	x	x	
	higher education	x		

In any given state at any given time the social rights package will be a combination of the three basic models. In Table 8.2 the functional distribution of social rights in Denmark is given. If provisions are dependent upon user-fees resembling the market price or, at any rate, are substantial, I identify them as performative:

Health care services are universal, but can be supplemented or substituted by commercial provisions; while entitlement for sick pay is obtained either by labor market participation (i.e., performative) or by need (i.e., clientelistic).

Services for the elderly, invalids and handicapped citizens are universal, yet some are subject to a needs test, and there exists commercial alternatives to the public services; old-age pension is universal, but many groups in the labor market supplement with occupational pension; early retirement is based either on needs assessment or on labor market performance. There exists no obligation to provide for older relatives.

The unemployment benefit system is, in principle, a social insurance scheme, hence, entitlements to both transfers and services are tied to labor market performance; entitlements are also dependent upon obligations to participate in various job training and educational activities.

Entitlement to family benefits such as day care and family allowance are universal, while housing allowances are needs and means-tested. Parents have an obligation to provide for their children until these reach the age of 18.

Eligibility for social assistance, whether services or transfers, are per definition subject to means, needs, and work test; it is a discretionary—that is, a clientelistic system. Recipients are obliged to undertake activities, such as education, training, workfare, or the like.

Danish citizens/residents have a right to public primary education and an obligation to receive education but not to go to school; commercial alternatives exist. Further education is either a universal right as is the case with higher education and part of the practical educational system, while other parts of this system is based on labor market affiliation.

New Governments, New Policies? 1982 and Onwards

When the Conservative-lead government took over in 1982 it started introducing some principles for a "modernization of the public sector" (Ministry of Finance, 1983). Three dimensions were highlighted as guiding principles for future public sector organization: (1) privatization, (2) de-bureaucratization, and (3) decentralization.

Retrospectively seen, the implementation of theses new guiding principles have been modest and cautious. Privatization has been interpreted as placing more emphasis on user rates and fees; e.g. increasing workers contributions to the unemployment funds; smaller fees regarding enrollment to some higher education institutions; etc. De-bureaucratization has been interpreted as placing more emphasis on the voluntary and informal sector regarding the distribution of social services, through financial and political encouragement. Finally, the trend towards de-centralization of Danish welfare society has been continued during the 1980s, trying to further the development from central to local authorities to continue further into the local communities and neighborhoods.

Flexibilization Through Experimentation

Instead of a profound change in Danish welfare administration the 1980s and 1990s show a commitment towards flexibilization of services and transfers, e.g. by allowing some experimentation by the municipalities in the provision of social services *and at the same time* a commitment to reducing the increase in public expenditure, i.e. *increased "flexicurity"* (cf Kautto, 1999; Rassmussen, 2007).

The emphasis on flexibilization is reflected in the so-called Social Experimentation Fund, which was introduced in 1988, providing 350 million DKK (47 million EURO) to new ways of dealing with social problems and social services locally over the period of time from 1988 to 1991. This was just one of many experimental programs launched during the 1980s; others regarded schools and education (the so-called "ten points program," and the primary school development program) and the health sector (the so-called "health pool").

Lis Adamsen and Jesper Fisker judge that "in Denmark during the period 1980 to 1990 more than one thousand experiments and development projects have been carried out, and from private funds and public pools alone, more than one billion DKK have been granted" (Adamsen and Fisker, 1990: 4).

Family Policy

The Conservative-lead government introduced a general child allowance in 1984. Since then all children under 18 years of age have received a so-called "children's check." Currently, the amount differs according to the age of the child. Children aged zero to two receive DKK 12.100 yearly; children aged 3 to 6 receive DKK 11,000; and children between 7 and 17 years of age receive DKK 8,600 (Told and Skat, 2001). Expansion of child-care facilities continues and the child maintenance system is upheld.

Elderly Policy

During the 1960s and 1970s institutions for the elderly, especially, nursing homes had expanded in Denmark. But one of the central ideas coming out of the government's "Elderly Commission," which completed its work in the early 1980s was the elderly policy should be guided by the principle of "staying as long as possible in the own home." Such a policy calls for extensive home-help and around the clock home-care; and currently, most municipalities have established such new service structures.

In 1987 new legislation was passed concerning housing for the elderly, which entitles the municipalities to subsidies for the building of so-called *"elderly flats."* An *elderly flat* is a home (max. 55 m^2) with kitchen and bathroom, easy access with wheel chair, and suitable for care in the home services. The intention was to substitute the nursing homes with these more independent housing units, which again, should be serviced by the municipal home help and home care (cf Abrahamson, 1991b; Christiansen and Petersen, 2001).

New Policies Since 1990s: Activation and Inclusion

Gradually, during the 1990s the Social Assistance Act has been changed regarding support for the young. Through the introduction of the so-called "youth-allowance" the 18 years old and the 19 years old cannot any longer receive social assistance passively. They have to summit themselves to either a job or a training activity, offered by the municipality, in order to receive cash benefits. As of April 1992, the youth-allowance has been expanded to encompass all 18 to 24 years old applying for held according to the Social Assistance Act. Within two weeks, municipality is supposed to have found a suitable job, training, education, or other activity, for which the young person will be paid the equivalent of what they used to collect in assistance payments.

This legislative change is indicative for the current trends in Danish welfare policy emphasizing the change from passive support to active involvement introduced in 1979 with the Job-Offer-Scheme, and now expanded into other areas of the welfare system. In 1993, Denmark got a new government, for the first time in more than ten years lead by the Social Democrats. Yet, we saw a continuation of the policy taking shape during the 1980s as described briefly above.

The Work of the Social Commission

During the last 20 years there has been a gradual change in emphasis regarding social protection in Denmark. The development has been described as a move away from passive support towards active involvement. In this spirit, the former Schlüter Government in August 1991 appointed a so-called "Social Commission" with the task of analyzing and suggesting changes with regard to the Danish social transfer systems: "to suggest how human and financial resources can be strengthened maximally through the social policy system." The Commission shall analyze the composition of recipients of social transfers, and the development in dependency hereof. It shall then analyze "the level of transfers and judge the incentives of recipients with regard to leaving the system and join the labor market."

The appointment of the Social Commission was made with reference to a changing demand, which "the European integration and the anticipated changes in the composition of the population pose to a more active use of social resources." Based on its analyses the Commission is supposed to suggest changes regarding the social transfer systems which emphasize a better utilization of the recipients' own resources. The financing of transfers systems shall also be analyzed, including the use of the insurance principle. The overall task is to "create a future-safe, more coherent and simple transfer system, with an eye to use the means more actively" (Socialkommissionen, 1992: 8).

Because of the change of government the new government did not officially pay so much attention to the "old" government's Social Commission reporting in 1993 (cf Green-Pedersen, 2001). Nevertheless, the proposals suggested by the Social Commission was for a large part identical to the new acts proposed by the Social Democratic-led government, such as the Labor Market Reform of 1993 and the Act on Active Social Policy from 1997. Both laws were hammering the activation approach into welfare legislation.

The New Danish Welfare State System

Over the past two and a half decades, the share of social transfers, by and large, did not change in relation to the overall development in total social spending. Although, total social expenditure as a share of GDP has changed quite a bit since 1982. It oscillated between 26 to 30 percent with the lowest value of 26 percent in 1986 and the highest in 1994 with 33.1 percent (Statistics Denmark, 1998: 24).

Table 8.3: Total Social Expenditure as a Share of Total Public Expenditure 1979 to 2006, selected years, in percent

1982	1987	1991	1996	1999	2002	2003	2004	2005	2006
47.6	42.5	47.3	43.4	40.8	39.9	40.1	41.7	41.8	42.7

Source: Statistics Denmark (1998, 2001, 2007).

Another way of judging the development in social citizenship is to give the share of total public expenditure, which is devoted to social expenditure. The Table 8.3 shows that social expenditure has been decreasing its share relatively from 47.6 percent in 1982 to the low point of 2002 with 39.9 percent.

Turning to the share of financing the period of time since the late 1970s shows a considerable change: Relatively seen, the central government finances a smaller and smaller share; the municipalities increase their share a bit; but together the public sector reduces its overall share over the period from 87.3 percent in 1982 to 69.8 percent in 1999. The employers' contribution is stable at around 10 percent, so, obviously, the employees' share must have been increasing significantly. It has so, indeed, from 3 percent in 1982 to 20.3 percent in 1999. Thus, the employees' share has increased with a factor six, or more than 600 percent. The general tendency in financing social citizenship in Denmark is away from central government towards local government and especially toward people themselves via contributory systems—that is, a strengthening of the performative kind of citizenship.

Figure 8.5: Total Social Expenditure in Denmark in 2006, broken down according to different functions, in percent

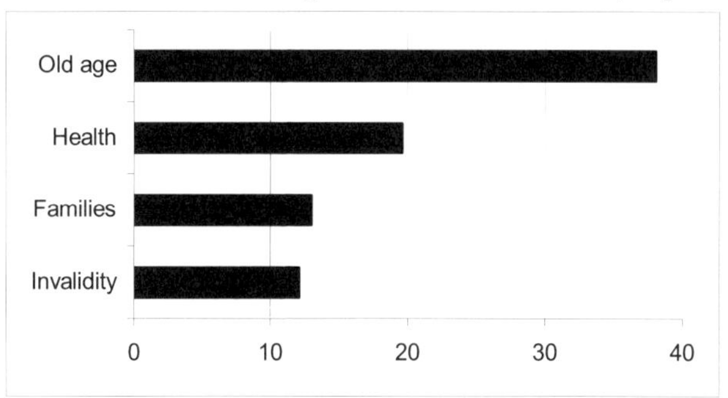

Source: Statistics Denmark (2007).

In order to give a more detailed picture, we will have to break down total social expenditure according to its different functions or categories of risk. Figure 8.5 shows the situation in 2006, and we can see that the biggest group is old age with nearly 40 percent of total social expenditure, followed by health with nearly 20 percent, and families and children as well as invalidity with 12 to 13 percent of total social expenditure.

To get some ideas about the changes over time the following table has been computed showing the development of the functional break down of expenditure set against GDP (Table 8.4).

Table 8.4: Relative Weight of Various Categories of Social Expenditure Set Against GDP in Denmark 1979 to 2006, selected years, in percent

	1979	1983	1987	1991	1996	1999	2001	2004	2006
Health	7.4	6.5	5.8	5.9	5.4	5.7	5.8	6.2	6.1
Invalidity & handicap	2.6	2.4	2.4	2.6	3.3	3.5	3.5	4.2	4.2
Old age	9.1	10.1	10.1	10.6	11.8	11.1	10.8	11.1	10.7
Families	2.8	2.9	3.2	3.6	3.8	3.8	3.8	3.9	3.7
Employment	3.3	5.3	3.5	4.9	4.2	3.2	2.8	2.8	2.0
Housing	0.4	0.5	0.5	0.7	0.7	0.7	0.7	0.7	0.7
Social assistance (and others)	0.8	1.1	1.1	1.4	1.2	1.1	1.0	1.0	0.8
Total	26.7	29.1	26.9	29.9	30.5	29.7	29.2	30.9	29.1

Note: Totals may not add up since we have omitted two small categories of work injuries and widowers pensions
Source: Statistics Denmark (1983, 1985, 1989, 1998, 2001, 2007).

The general picture is that of health giving way to old age over time, and to a minor extent also to the other categories. In relation to the national economy (GDP) the situation has been quite stable during the whole period of time, as Denmark devotes about 30 percent of the total economy to maintaining social citizenship of some sort. Measured per capita Denmark tends to spend more and more; but social expenditure has been a relatively declining part of total public spending since 1979. It is with respect to financing of social expenditure we find the most substantial changes for social citizenship—that is, a declining share is financed by central government, and more and more is being paid by the employees and the municipalities and counties. Apart from indicating a trend towards further decentralization of financial responsibilities it also indicates a turn towards a performative model of social citizenship.

Social citizenship is often equated with social rights (cf Andersen *et al.*, 2006); but in the Danish case we are reminded that citizenship entails both rights and *obligations*. The general trend is to emphasize and clarify the obligations that citizens have with regard to claiming social rights. This was coined the *something-for-something principle* by former Minister of Social Affairs, Aase Olesen, and is still valid (Ministry of Social Affairs, 1990, 1991). The principle has been institutionalized with the so-called *activation* approach to social policies in general. Participation in active labor market policy measures or workfare schemes has become mandatory if continued financial support is to be expected. Also, proof of active job-seeking behavior has been strengthened (cf Torfing, 1999).

Another tendency is one towards more choice. Free hospital choice in the public secondary health care system, and the possibility of choosing private/market solutions by the opening up of a commercial segment of hospitals and clinics; predating this trend free choice of GPs was introduced; free choice of primary school, except for immigrants! In some municipalities immigrants are subject to quota systems re-allocating their children geographically in order to obtain a more "even" spread across the municipal schools. The emphasis on free choice echoes elements of a neoliberal approach to social citizenship; but it has been implemented in a universal regime. A third tendency is a stronger emphasis on citizens' involvement in decision-making and administration of social services such as child-care institutions, primary schools, elderly care, etc. Everything else being equal, this indicates a strengthening of our political citizenship. A child-care guarantee was issued by the government; but the responsibility lies with the municipalities, and a considerable part of them have not (been able to) complied.

This is an example of the decentralization process being challenged by the central government, and has led some observers to talk about a process of re-centralization (Hegland, 1994). Various leave-schemes have been introduced and reduced because of their popularity! Yet, taken together their introduction indicates a strengthening of social citizenship rights. Pension rights move towards the performative model because of a strengthening of occupational pension schemes. Such arrangements are currently, albeit slowly, being extended to blue-collar workers.

We have experienced a continuation of the so-called experimentation strategy, which means a diversification of social services with more involvement of civil societal institutions and actors such as volunteers, self-help groups, charities and businesses. This means a *complication* of social rights. Finally, the campaign for the social responsibility of companies and the quest for more social clauses in the industrial relations' agreements point towards the performative model of social rights.

A new series of Social Democratic-led governments came into power since 1993. The major changes are as follows: (1) leave-schemes with the labor market reform of 1994 (child-care leave; education leave; sabbatical leave); (2) New Social Assistance Act of 1997 (being split into: the *Active Social Policy Act* and the *Social Service Act* plus the *Social Provision Administration and Legal Guarantee Act*); (3) stronger financial and ideological support to the voluntary sector; and (4) a new campaign for the social responsibility of companies.

With the labor market reform of 1994 a couple of experimental leave schemes were made permanent. The *education leave* is a scheme enabling insured workers 25 years of age and older to take time out, at least one week, at the most one year, to participate in some kind of recognized education receiving benefits equivalent to unemployment benefits. In 1994 80,000 people and in 1995 53,000 people used this opportunity. The *child-care leave* is a scheme allowing parents with children up to eight years of age to take time out to care for their children up to one year and at least for 13 weeks. The scheme is open to everyone affiliated with the labor market, whether insured or on social assistance. Because of its popularity the benefits have been reduced from 100 percent to first 70 and now to 60 percent of unemployment benefits. While on child-care leave children cannot occupy a space in a public child-care institution. In 1994 47,000 people and in 1995 80,000 people went on this leave. Finally, the *sabbatical leave* is a time limited experiment running till 1999, allowing employed insured people 25 and older to take up to one year, and at least 13 weeks, out from the labor market provided they can find a substitute for them, to fill their spot, during the period of time. Benefits have been reduced to 60 percent of unemployment benefits. In 1994 13,000 and in 1995 3,000 people went on sabbatical leave (Andersen *et al.*, 1996).

The schemes were meant to increase the circulation in the labor market between unemployment and employment; but as the schemes became increasingly popular the government feared that they might create bottlenecks by reducing unemployment too much and they were therefore made less attractive. The child-care leave must be viewed as a universal right, while the other two leave sachems are reserved for workers belonging to the social insurance system, and thus is a performative trend.

With the New Social Assistance Act of 1997 the active labor market/workfare strategy has been strengthened indicating a stronger emphasis on the obligation of the claimants to participate in some activity arranged or referred to by the municipality. A majority of the claimants view this positively in so far as they say that they were quite satisfied with the offer received; yet many also state that it is a means of social control. This development is a demonstration of the government's focusing in on marginalized and socially excluded people. This targeting is a clientelistic trait.

The government/Ministry of Social Affairs are currently encouraging the voluntary sector to be more engaged in fighting social problems at various levels and in various ways. The encouragement takes the form of financial support for voluntary organizations. This is a tendency strengthening the welfare mix approach to social policy with its emphasis on new partnerships between public and private sector. The same can be said for the campaign: The *social responsibility of companies* where the government is trying to involve business more in fighting the marginalization and social exclusion that the companies produce in the first place (Holt, 1998). This is clearly a performative trend in the development of social citizenship rights in Denmark.

With respect only to social transfers Hansen (1998) indicates recent changes concerning the unemployment benefit system (social insurance) and early retirement:

"The duration of benefit period was shortened from seven to five years in 1996. Active labor market measures will no longer prolong the benefit period. Substantial changes were implemented in 1996 for young persons under 25 years of age. Unemployed young persons with no or only little formal education will be offered education after six months of unemployment unless they have a solid work record, in this case they will be offered job training. The benefits for those participating in education are 50 percent of maximum unemployment benefits, those in job training will receive maximum unemployment benefits. From 1997 the working condition was 52 weeks within the last three years, up from 26 weeks, before benefits could be received. Unemployed who are over 50 years when their unemployment benefits rights expire can continue receiving benefits until the age of 60 years if they by continued membership of the unemployment benefit scheme at that time will qualify for the early retirement scheme (*"efterløn"*). For unemployed over 60 years the duration of the benefit period is only two and a half years as a maximum, and there are no active labour market measures for this group. The temporary schemes for early retirement from the labour market [concerning people between 50 and 60] were closed for new entrants from February 1996 (Hansen, 1998: 46, 53).

We witness here a tightening of eligibility rules for receiving unemployment benefits, which must be interpreted as a reduction of social rights simultaneous with a strengthening of the obligations that unemployed people have to actively change their situation. Finally, user-rates are quietly becoming a part, or though still a small part, of Danish welfare policy. From 1993 to 1997 they were increased by 20 percent to DKK 36 billion; within the area of education they increased by 50 percent to DKK 9.3 billion; and in health care they doubled to DKK 3 billion. Throughout this chapter user-rates are viewed as a performative element of social citizenship (Information, 1998).

Conclusion

Not surprisingly, overall trends of development are not one-dimensional. With regard to health care we see a strengthening of commercial alternatives, introduction of user-rates and more choice, which move citizenship in a performative direction, and in relative, quantitative terms, health care is diminishing in importance within the total welfare package. Small local hospitals are being closed down and patients are being allocated to fewer and larger regional hospitals. Intentionally, this should give a better treatment and care; yet it is experienced as a reduction in social citizenship rights! Health care is one of the areas where popular dissatisfaction is aired most strongly.

Pension rights are being expanded due to more emphasis on occupational pensions, and at the same time it is more difficult to obtain early retirement. Elderly people are granted more influence on the municipal elderly care through the formation of so-called "elderly councils." So, in this case we see trends both towards a performative regime, a strengthening of political citizenship and a reduction of some social rights. Regarding the unemployed their obligations to participate in active labor market measures have been strengthened, and benefit periods have been reduced, which indicates a reduction in social rights in this respect. Benefits for families and children have been increased with a universalization of child-care leave arrangements and child allowances. Hence, here we have an implementation and continuation of a universal citizenship principle.

The social assistance reform emphasized more rights *and* more obligations, thus strengthening a clientelistic trend in the development of social citizenship with its stronger focus on the marginalized and socially excluded as a *separate* category of citizens. More emphasis on targeting must be considered a move towards a clientelistic model of social citizenship. Finally, regarding education political rights have been strengthen and the introduction of education leave fits this trend, or though the quality has been reduced because of the popularity of the scheme. Furthermore, this is the area in which the use of user-rates have increased the most which point towards a performative element of social citizenship. Viewed in another perspective, trends in Denmark follow a general pattern of change in welfare ideology, where emphasis is on: (1) de- and re-centralization (regionalization *and* internationalization); (2) obligations to be active in various arrangements (workfare); (3) user influence/participation; (4) voluntary involvement; (5) flexibilization (divisions of labor and new partnerships), and (6) experimentation.

Taken together, we can identify a diversification of social rights and obligations, which can be summarized as "a *welfare-mix* approach to social citizenship"—that is, mixing elements from the three ideal-typical models discussed above. Such a move cannot in itself be judged simply as a reduction or strengthening of social citizenship; it depends on the concrete mixes (cf Nielsen and Kesting, 2003). Yet, as the actual changes during the last two and a half decades have been analyzed here most changes have been away from the universal regime and towards a performative and a clientelistic regime (cf Ploug, 2008). In so far the universal citizenship regime is the ideal, as it has been in Scandinavia for many years, current developments point to an overall weakening of "traditional" rights and "new" and more obligations.

REFERENCES

Abrahamson, P. (1991a), Administrating Poverty Risk, in T. Knudsen (ed.), *Welfare Administration in Denmark*, Ministry of Finance: Copenhagen.
Abrahamson, P. (1991b), Welfare for the Elderly in Denmark: From Institutionalization to Self-Reliance?, in A. Evers and I. Svetlik (eds.), *New Welfare Mixes in Care for the Elderly,* European Center: Vienna.
Abrahamson, P. (1992), 1990'ernes Socialpolitik: Fra Forsørgelse til Selvhjælp?, *Samfundsøkonomen*, Vol. 10, No. 8, pp. 44-53.
Adamsen, L. and Fisker, J. (1990), Hvilke Spor Sætter Forsøgs- og Udviklingsprojekter?, *Dansk Sociologi*, Vol. 1, No. 2, pp. 4-21.
Albæk, E. (1995), Reforming the Nordic Welfare Communes, *International Review of Administrative Sciences*, Vol. 61, No. 3, pp. 241-64.
Andersen, B.R. *et al.* (1972), *Socialreformundersøgelserne*, National Institute for Social Research: Copenhagen.
Andersen, D.; Appeldorn, A., and Weise, H. (1996), *Orlov: Evaluering af Orovsordningerne*, National Institute of Social Research: Copenhagen.

Andersen, J.G. (1997), The Scandinavian Welfare Model in Crisis? Achievements and Problems of the Danish Welfare State in an Age of Unemployment and Low Growth, *Scandinavian Political Studies*, Vol. 20, No. 1, pp. 1-32.

Andersen, J.G.; Guillemard, A.M.; P.H. Jensen and Pfau-Effinger, B. (eds.) (2006), *The Changing Face Of Welfare: Consequences and Outcomes from a Citizenship Perspective*, Policy: Bristol, UK.

Auken, G. (1985), *Døgnet Skal Have to Dage*, Rosinante: Copenhagen.

Baldwin, P. (1990), *The Politics of Social Solidarity*, Cambridge University Press: Cambridge, UK.

Beveridge, W. (1942), *Social Insurance and Allied Services*. London: HMSO.

Bogason, P. (1992), *Forvaltning og Stat*, Systime: Herning, Denmark.

Christiansen, N.F. and Petersen, K. (2001), The Dynamics of Social Solidarity: The Danish Welfare State, *Scandinavian Journal of History*, Vol. 26, No. 3, pp. 177-96.

Dahrendorf, R. (1994), The Changing Quality of Citizenship, in B. van Steenbergen (ed.), *The Condition of Citizenship*, Sage: London.

Green-Pedersen, C. (2001), Welfare-State Retrenchment in Denmark and the Netherlands, 1982-1998: The Role of Party Competition and Party Consensus, *Comparative Political Studies*, Vol. 34, No. 9, pp. 963-85.

Hansen, H. (1998), *Elements of Social Security*, National Institute of Social Research: Copenhagen.

Hansen, H. and Hansen, F.K. (1999), Social Årsrapport 1999, Copenhagen.

Hansen, H. (2006), Social Årsrapport 2006, Copenhagen.

Hegland, T.J. (1994), *Fra de Tusind Blomster til en Målrettet Udvikling*, Forlaget Aluff: Aalborg, Denmark.

Holt, H. (1998), *En Kortlægning af Danske Virksomheders Sociale Ansvar*, National Institute of Social Research: Copenhagen.

Horneman Møller, I. (1992), *Den Danske Velfærdsstats Tilblivelse*, Samfundsliteratur: Frederiksberg, Denmark.

Horneman Møller, I. (1994), *Velfærdsstatens Udbygning*, Samfundslitteratur: Frederiksberg, Denmark.

Information (1998), Brugerbetalingen Stiger Støt, Denmark, April 15, p. 2.

Ingerslev, O. and Ploug, N. (1996), Velfærdsstatens Udvikling, in E. Dalgaard *et al.* (eds.), *Velfærdsstatens Fremtid*, Handelshøjskolens Forlag: Frederiksberg, Denmark.

Jensen, P.H. (2004), Ageing and Work: From Early Exit to Late Exit in Denmark, in T. Maltby *et al.* (eds.), *Ageing and the Transition to Retirement*, Ashgate: Aldershot, UK.

Kautto, M. (1999), *Scandinavian Social Policy: Changes in the Welfare State in Denmark, Finland, Norway and Sweden*, Taylor and Francis: London.

Marshall, T.H. (1950), *Citizenship and Social Class*, Cambridge University Press: Cambridge, UK.

Marshall, T.H. (1981), Value Problems of Welfare Capitalism, in T.H. Marshall (ed.), *The Right to Welfare and Other Essays*, Heinemann: London.

Ministry of Finance (1983), *Redegørelse til Folketinget om Regeringens*, Ministry of Finance: Copenhagen.

Ministry of Social Affairs (1990a), *Der er Brug for Alle*, Socialministeriet, Copenhagen.

Ministry of Social Affairs (1990b), *Der er Brug for Alle II*, Socialministeriet, Copenhagen.

MISSOC (2000), *Social Protection in the EU Member States and the European Economic Area, Situation on January 2000*, European Commission: Brussels.

Nielsen, K. and Kesting, S. (2003), Small Is Resilient: The Impact of Globalization on Denmark, *Review of Social Economy*, Volume 61, Issue 3.

NOSOSCO (2000), Social Protection in the Nordic Countries 1998, *www. nomnos.dk*.

Ploug, N. (2008), The Scandinavian Welfare Model, *www.um.dk/publikationer/ UM/english/denmark/kap3/3-1.asp*

Rassmussen, P.N. (2007), The Danish Model of "Flexicurity," *www.aarpinter national.org/resourcelibrary*.

Socialkommissionen (1992), *Uden Arbejde: Overførselsindkomst til Midter-gruppen,* Socialkommissionens Secretariat: Copenhagen.

Socialpolitisk Forening and CASA, Statistics Denmark (1995), *50-Year Review*, Statistics Denmark: Copenhagen.

Statistics Denmark (1983, 1985, 1989, 1998, 2000, 2001, 2007), Udviklingen i Sociale Ydelser 1991-1996, *Social Sikring og Retsvæsen 1998*, and other articles covering earlier years, Statistics Denmark: Copenhagen.

Statistics Denmark (1999), *10-Year Review*, Statistics Denmark: Copenhagen.

Statistics Denmark (2001), Udgifter til Sociale Ydelser 1994-1999, *Sociale Forhold*, Statistics Denmark: Copenhagen.

Titmuss, R. (1974), *Social Policy*, George Allen and Unwin: London.

Told and Skat (2001), Nye Satser for Børnefamilieydelse, *www.albertslund.dk*.

Torfing, J. (1999), Workfare With Welfare: Recent Reforms of the Danish Welfare State, *Journal of European Social Policy*, Vol. 9, No. 1, pp. 5-28.

Weise, H. and Brogaard, S. (1997), *Aktivering af Kontanthjælpsmodtagere: En Evaluering af Lov om Kommunal Aktivering*, National Institute of Social Research: Copenhagen.

9

Drugs, Prostitution, and the Swedish Welfare State

ARTHUR GOULD

In the last 15 years Sweden has introduced policies in the fields of drugs and prostitution, which many Swedes claim are a model for other countries to follow. Since the same claim was often—and in my view, rightly—made for the Swedish welfare state, it is worthy of some critical attention. For many decades following World War II, Swedes were admired for creating a system of state welfare, which provided all its citizens with a high degree of social security, health and social services of a high quality, and high standards of public housing and education (Furniss and Tilton, 1974). Indeed, it is precisely because of my interest in and admiration for the Swedish welfare state, that I became interested in these "side issues" in the first place. It was Richard Titmuss who argued that the study of one small aspect of social policy (in his case blood donation) may throw light on the nature of a country's welfare system (Titmuss, 1970). The issues of, and debates around, drugs and prostitution in Swedish society tell us something of signi-ficance about the Swedish welfare state, the way in which many Swedes think of their country, the problems they face and their relationship with and perception of the outside world. In a broader sense, the findings presented here illustrate the need to examine social policies in the wider contest of a society's structure, culture, and historical development.

This study will begin with a discussion of the nature of and debates around contemporary drug and prostitution issues. It will continue with an outline of the way in which Swedish policies in these areas have developed. This will be followed by a comparison of the similarities between the two policies. The study will conclude with an explanation for Sweden's *restrictive line*[1] in areas where much of Europe is becoming more pragmatic and liberal (cf e.g. Kautto, 2001).

Drugs and Prostitution in a Globalized World

People in every society have taken drugs to alter their mental states. Throughout history, people have bought and sold sexual services. Reactions to both these social phenomena have varied over time between tolerance and repression. There has always been a concern that some people use drugs to excess. There has always been a concern about the acceptability of prostitution (cf Bucken-Knapp and Karlsson, 2007). What gives these issues contemporary significance is that in an increasingly globalized world, it is not only the trade in consumer goods and financial services, which has increased. The trade in illegal drugs and in sexual services has also grown. We even give it a different name. It is called "trafficking." Indeed, it is the very lack of international control over this trade that often makes it seem so threatening. Because in so many countries drugs and prostitution have become, in part or totally, prohibited by law, the international dimension to their control is fraught with problems. We still exist in national states with national systems of law and order. Organized crime, at the international level, is difficult to combat.

A globalized world is increasingly multicultural. Economic and political migration is on the increase. However this does not simply mean that we have greater access to each other's traditions of dance, music, art and literature. It does not simply mean that we become exposed to different people's beliefs and religions. People take their drug and sexual habits with them wherever they go. They also take their criminal tendencies. This is not to suggest that immigrants are drug addicts, prostitutes and criminals but rather that globalization has many facets—negative as well as positive, unacceptable as well as acceptable. How national governments react to these new problems and issues is what makes crossnational policy analysis interesting.

It is not possible in this article to do justice to the variety of responses of different governments to the issues of drugs and prostitution. What can be done is to indicate the range of possible options illustrated by contemporary debates. A common response to drugs and prostitution has been to make them illegal. Drugs have been prohibited by international conventions since the early part of the 20th century. The US in particular has played a dominant role in encouraging other countries to engage in a war against drugs. As a result, most countries have legislation, which makes the production, sale and possession of specific drugs a criminal offence (Hartnoll, 1989). In the last decade, there have been a number of attempts to raise the possibility of international control and regulation of prostitution[2] but as Nadelman said in 1990, "in the case of prostitution the existence of a near universal moral notion that [it] is wrong has not translated into the evolution of a global regime to prohibit it" (Nadelman, 1990: 516). Individual countries have not acted on prostitution to the same extent as on drugs, but nonetheless, there is a growing awareness of the international dimension of some of the problems associated with prostitution and the need for an international response. Certainly there are individual countries where prostitution is a clear criminal offence.

To many observers attempts to control drug use and people's sexual habits by law is counterproductive. Prohibition, it is argued, makes the problems worse. They are driven underground. Their very illegality encourages the involvement of criminal elements. Once organized crime has established a vested interest in these activities, it becomes difficult for the authorities to exert any influence over them. In some countries prohibition has led to considerable corruption in police forces, the judiciary and the political system.

One alternative to prohibition is to argue that the drug trade and prostitution should be legalized. It is suggested that in this way they would be purged of their criminal associations. To the extent that both activities are "victimless" (drug users and those who buy and sell sexual services only harm themselves), society has no right to interfere with them. Others have argued for a more pragmatic approach, arguing that it is important that we should be able to help people at risk and that prohibition makes this very difficult by driving the trade in drugs and sexual services underground (cf Bucken-Knapp and Karlsson, 2007). Moreover, by decriminalizing these activities, we prevent ordinary people from being made into criminals unnecessarily.

Recent Developments in Swedish Policy

It is interesting therefore that Sweden—a European country with a reputation for being liberal and pragmatic on a range of social issues should have chosen a prohibitive or "restrictive" approach to drugs and prostitution in the last 15 years.

In 1988 two laws were introduced to make drug policy more restrictive (Gould, 1989). The "use" of illegal substances was made a criminal offence by a social democratic government. While many countries prohibit the sale, production and possession of drugs is illegal, use for one's own purposes is not. The logic behind this is that the user is damaging only him- or herself. Against this it was argued that there was no difference between a person having drugs in their possession one minute and inside their bodies the next. Initially, this offence was punishable only by a fine. In 1993 however—under a Center-Right coalition—it was made an imprisonable offence (Gould, 1994a). Users could be sent to prison for up to six months. Also in 1988 a law, which made it possible to take adult alcoholics and drug addicts into care compulsorily, was amended to lengthen the maximum period from 2 to 6 months.

The following year a proposal by the National Board for Health and Welfare to encourage the adoption of syringe exchange schemes (SES) was rejected. SES had been widely adopted by other European countries in the fight against AIDS (Gould, 1994b). They were seen as a means to prevent the spread of HIV. HIV was seen as a more dangerous threat to public health than drug misuse. In Sweden, drug misuse was seen as just as threatening as HIV. SES were seen as likely to encourage the use of drugs.

The change in the law concerning prostitution came into being in 1998, which consequently went into force on January 1, 1999 (Gould, 2001a). Previously a government commission had investigated the prostitution problem and recommended that both the prostitute and the client should be punished. The new law, however, accepted the argument that prostitutes themselves were innocent victims and that only their male clients should be prosecuted.

Within a short space of time—10 years—Sweden had enacted a restrictive approach to both drugs and prostitution. Superficially, the two issues and the two sets of policies had little to do with each other. They did not seem to arise from the same circumstance or pressures. They did not involve the same advocates and opponents. However, a closer look suggests a wide range of similarities which themselves indicate a common explanation.

Folk Movement Pressure

Many social and penal policies have a complex origin. Problems and issues may be highlighted by the mass media; major institutions of the state—including the civil service—may play an important role. Political parties, business and trade unions may bring pressure to bear on parliament and government. In the changes to Swedish laws on drugs and prostitution it was interest groups that were particularly influential in agitating for change. In Sweden, interest groups with shared values are often referred to as "popular movements" (folkrörelser). Swedish social democracy has been very influenced by the *labor movement.* The *temperance movement*—itself closely allied to the labor movement— had a considerable impact upon alcohol policy in the 20th century. While there are some today that argue that the popular movement tradition is in decline, the issues of drugs and prostitution would suggest otherwise. The *anti-drugs movement* and the *women's movement* played a significant role in each respectively.

The two organizations that argued in favor of a restrictive line on drugs were *The National Association for a Drug-Free Society* (RNS) and *Parents Against Drugs* (FMN). Throughout the 1980s they kept up a relentless pressure on ministers and members of parliament. They also gained considerable attention by the mass media. Together with like-minded organizations, they constituted a contemporary version of the temperance movement referred to above. They believed that drug use, if unchecked, would spread through society like an epidemic. It was necessary to focus on drug users since without them there would be no market in drugs. The slogans of the anti-drugs movement provide a brief guide to its rationale: "all use is misuse," "there is no difference between cannabis and heroin." The aim of the movement was to achieve a drug-free society. Anything less implied "capitulation." At the height of their influence FMN and RNS had only to label a person or policy proposal as being "liberal" on drugs for them to be regarded as "traitorous" or "un-Swedish." No political party opposed them. Those individual politicians and academics who tried to, did so at their cost. Their campaigns had something of the evangelical about them.

In the debate about prostitution it was the women's movement that played a pivotal role. The source of the idea to criminalize those who bought the sexual services of prostitutes originally came from *The National Association for Battered Women's Shelters* (ROKS) but once the proposal became identified with the issue of domestic violence, a wide range of women's groups joined the campaign (cf Ekberg, 2004; Bucken-Knapp and Karlsson, 2007). Sweden was late to recognize the issue of domestic violence—believing that it was a problem experienced more in other countries and by the immigrant population that by native Swedish men. Given that gender equality is something that Swedes claim to lead the rest of the world in, it was important to introduce tough domestic legislation to deal with the problem. This was passed in 1998 together with the law on the purchase of sexual services (sexköpslagen).

Although the Liberal and Conservative parties were opposed to the new prostitution law, many of their female members sympathized with it. In the Swedish parliament there are regular cross-party meetings of women MPs in which matters of common interest are discussed. The consensus on prostitution was not as total as on drugs but it was widespread. It did become difficult to oppose the reform without appearing to condone violence towards women. Again the campaign had an evangelical air, which made pragmatic argument difficult to advance. Prostitution was incompatible with the aim of a gender equal society. In both campaigns there was a moral absolutism, which insisted that no compromise was possible.

Prostitutes and Drugs

There is of course a more direct link between prostitution and drugs. It is often said that prostitutes use drugs in order to cope with the risky business in which they are involved. It is also known to be the case that many women who become dependent on drugs choose to be prostitutes as a way of paying for their habit. These connections would obviously assume importance in a country like Sweden where the aim is to become a drug-free society. A social democratic member of the Riksdag (the Swedish Parliament) expressed the concern clearly when she said, "we know that half the prostitutes on the streets do it to finance their drug misuse. We know through in-depth interviews that many of them are at risk. It is our duty to intervene" (Dagens Nyheter, 1998).

In the Riksdag debate, a spokesperson for the Environment Party, challenged the argument that prostitutes had a right to choose what to do with their own bodies by asking whether someone had a right to destroy themselves with drugs. Since Sweden has a law which prohibits the consumption of drugs, the answer was obviously, no.

A social work journal drew another analogy between the two issues when it stated "experience shows that prostitution is a form of *misuse* with a similar negative *dependence* and the way back is often laborious with unavoidable *relapses*" (Martinelli, 1995: 9, emphasis of the author).

Foreign Links

There are many indirect parallels between the two phenomena and the language used in policy debates. A particular concern was with the foreignness of drugs and prostitutes. Both were often described in the press as *flooding* into the country, implying that Sweden was somehow being swamped and polluted. This was corroborated by the fact that the countries of origin, Poland, Russia, Estonia—"the East"—conjured up images of decay and corruption. Other countries had serious drug problems that were being exported to Sweden (Gould, 2002).

The cover of an RNS journal showed a cartoon of a Swedish cottage on an island surrounded by rats bearing syringes. An official report, on the restrictive line on drugs, with the title "We Will Never Surrender" was illustrated by a photograph of the Swedish coastline. One newspaper talked about "an invasion of foreign girls from the East [who] have no tradition of using protection. They are used to unprotected sex and bring this habit further into Sweden" (Expressen, 1998).

Månsson, one of the country's experts on prostitution, in his concern about the "increased flood of pimp-managed prostitutes from the Baltic countries, Poland and Russia" claimed that few Swedish men used prostitutes. However 80 percent of those that did so, he claimed, went abroad and half of them became infected with HIV (Svenska Dagbladet, 1999; cf Gould, 2002).

Liberal Ideas

It was not simply drugs and prostitutes themselves that presented a foreign threat. The liberal ideas coming from countries like the Netherlands and Britain were also dangerous. In the field of drugs, ideas such as *harm reduction* and *decriminalization* represented a drift towards legalization. They were a sign that these societies had *capitulated* to the problem. Policies to decriminalize or legalize prostitution were also seen as foreign to the Swedish tradition (Gould, 2002). The Dutch acceptance of prostitution was attributed by a Swedish female politician to their history of colonial exploitation.

Choice and Force

It was in connection with Dutch policies that a Conservative MP in Sweden said "we don't discuss whether or not people want to be prostitutes. What sort of freedom is it to choose to sell your body?" (Gould, 2001a: 445).

The basis for the liberal argument on prostitution is that many prostitutes choose to sell their bodies. As sex workers, they are entitled like other workers to reasonable working conditions and social security benefits. It is important therefore for those advocating a restrictive line that prostitutes are shown to be victims—people who are forced into what they do. It was argued that most prostitutes had been victims of violence (Martinelli, 1995: 7). Women, it was said, were forced into prostitution either by pimps and those dealing in the contemporary slave trade in women, or by poverty, or because they were powerless as in the case of minors and the mentally disturbed, or because of their dependence upon illegal drugs. How could one speak of choice when women were forced by circumstances to be prostitutes?

Similarly those who took illegal drugs did not do so out of choice. They were said to be dependent upon their drugs. They were compelled to take them. Once people became addicted, they had no control over their lives. The restrictive drugs discourse admits of no distinction between "soft drugs" and "hard drugs." Nor is there any recognition of recreational, occasional or non-problematic use. All use is misuse. In the two debates, both prostitutes and drug users were defined as vulnerable. They were at risk, in need of protection by the authorities.

The Focus on the "Consumer"

Although an earlier proposal on prostitution had suggested that both prostitutes and the client should be prosecuted, in the end it was the purchaser of sexual services who was deemed to be the guilty partner. The focus in Swedish drug policy was also on the consumer. It was argued that the trade in drugs was so lucrative that one supplier could be replaced by another. What drove the drug trade was the consumer's habit. If you could stop people consuming, there would be no market.

Sweden as a Model, Sweden as Unique

Throughout these policy debates, it was often suggested that Sweden's restrictive line was a model for other countries to follow. This is odd when you consider that most European countries are becoming more liberal on the issues of drugs and prostitution. Nonetheless, there can be little doubt that Swedish representatives on the European Union Commission and in the European Parliament are determined to prevent or influence any attempt to harmonize drug and prostitution policies across member states (Gould, 1999a).

It was claimed in the debates that Sweden was unique. In 1994, the then deputy prime minister, Mona Sahlin, discussing drugs policy said "we are unique and successful in so many areas" (Thorgren, 1994: 92). An academic expert claimed that Sweden's law on prostitution was seen by organizations throughout Europe as "overwhelmingly positive, re-volutionary, and radical" (Månsson, 1998). In the postwar decades, Sweden had indeed been seen as a model welfare state, as having a model economy and a model labor market policy. Whenever Swedes identify good practice—it often happens in local authorities for ex-ample—there is a tendency to want to learn from it and promote it. In the postmodern era, there has been little mention of the Swedish model (Gould, 2005). The attempt to claim the mantel for drug and prostitution policies does not carry the same conviction. It is interesting however, to examine what it is about a country that its inhabitants choose to describe as unique.

Moral Panic

The author intends to argue that the policies referred to above are an example of moral panic. To qualify as moral panic, it is necessary to demonstrate that social reaction to an issue is exaggerated, that oppo-nents are vilified and that there is a broad elite consensus behind the reaction, which is amplified by the mass media (Goode and Ben-Yehuda, 1994).

For the reaction in Sweden to be deemed reasonable, one would expect there to be evidence of widespread drug misuse and a large growth in prostitution. Official evidence, on the contrary, suggests that drug-taking in Sweden is much lower than other European countries and that there are few prostitutes. Annual self-report surveys of 16-year old school students and military conscripts in the 1980s and 1990s show that the percentages of those who have ever used an illegal drug were ranged from 3 to 8 percent (CAN, 1999).

In some European countries the percentages are much higher. The number of prostitutes estimated to be active in Sweden in the early 1990s—when the government Commission was carrying out its investigation—was a mere 2,500, only 650 of whom were on the streets (SOU, 1995: 15). The author argues that the principle reason for these low figures is that the basic security provided by the Swedish economy, the welfare state, and labor market measures prevents the very social exclusion that drives some to take drugs and others to resort to selling their bodies.

In previous studies a number of examples have already been cited to demonstrate that the Swedish press has amplified the amount of drug use and the numbers of prostitutes in Sweden. The consensus referred to above coupled with the ostracism shown to opponents further demonstrate that the reaction to these issues is an example of moral panic. The questions then become—why Sweden, why in the last 15 years, and why these particular issues?

An Explanation

There are a number of factors, which would help explain why Sweden has adopted restrictive policies in the fields of prostitution and drugs since 1988. The Swedish economy has faced serious problems, Swedish living standards have declined in comparison with other similar countries and unemployment rose considerably in the 1990. People can afford to be much more liberal when their economy is growing; social attitudes may become much more restrictive in bad times. Moreover, there can be little doubt that there has always been a paternalistic, almost authoritarian, aspect to Swedish welfare throughout the last century (Holgersson, 1977).[3] Indeed Tham (1998) has argued that the liberal tradition in Sweden is weak. While each of these lines of explanation is worth developing further, the author wants to concentrate upon the issues of national identity and culture—partly because the evidence lends itself to such an analysis and partly because issues of culture and identity have been neglected in social policy analysis in the past.

In describing the similarities in the debates surrounding drug and prostitution policy in Sweden above, there was a dominant theme of nationalism. Not the kind of nationalism academics discuss when referring to fascist parties and liberation campaigns but what Mick Billig calls "banal nationalism"—the constant flagging up of national sentiments in daily life (Billig, 1995). This occurs literally in Scandinavian countries with many people hoisting the national flag outside their homes but it also occurs metaphorically whenever one's nation is discussed in relationship to the outside world. In many of the examples cited above, it is clear that there were fears about drugs and prostitutes coming into the country with the further threat of the spread of HIV and other sexually transmitted diseases. The "contamination" was seen as coming largely from the poorer countries of Eastern Europe. Developed countries with a more liberal approach to drugs and prostitution were also seen as a threat and were accordingly disparaged. Individual Swedes who disagreed with the official line were regarded as traitors or somehow un-Swedish. The behavior of immigrants was also associated with un-Swedish values. Sweden was seen as a having the right approach to social problems. Sweden had been a model in the past and was creating model solutions in the present.

It would seem that the reaction of Sweden to some contemporary social problems, is in part a fear of Swedish society becoming an indistinct part of a globalized society. Many Swedes feel they are losing not only their national identity and culture but also their place in the world. It was a remarkable achievement for a country of a few million people in the postwar years to be seen as the exemplar of modernity (cf Gould, 2005). Sweden at one time was seen as the "prototype" of a modern society (Tomasson, 1970). Through rational organization and planning, it exploited the best features of capitalism and socialism to create what some thought a "paradise." The mass of Swedish people enjoyed a standard of living, a quality of life and a degree of social security that were the envy of other countries. Although many features of the Swedish welfare state continue to be admired, there can be little doubt that Sweden's preeminence is no longer. In a postmodern world, US free market capitalism has become the dominant ideological force. The degree of control that national governments can exert over their own countries' affairs has become more limited. National states have become less able to manipulate their economies, their taxation systems and their public expenditure budgets than before. Politically and economically we are part of a wider world order. Culturally we have to accept that well-defined national cultures and identities are giving ways to less distinct mixes of multiculturalism.

Sweden itself has allowed many immigrants and refugees to live there since the 1960s. Indeed, the authorities would claim that enormous efforts have been made to ensure that its ethnic minorities are treated no differently to indigenous Swedes. Ethnic equality and multiculturalism are certainly the principles upon which official policies are based. However, recent reports have claimed that there is widespread discrimination against non-European ethnic groups. One suggested that there is a real danger of the emergence of "class stratification along ethnic and cultural lines" (SIB, 2001). Far from there being integration, there is considerable segregation and a "concealed" policy of assimilation (Westin, 2000). The Swedish Integration Board—*Integrationsverket*—worried that perhaps Swedes found it difficult to live alongside people whose behavior and attitudes were markedly different from their own (SIB, 2001). While overt racism is frowned upon officially, there can be little doubt that Swedes have found it difficult to accept that their population has become heterogeneous.

In these circumstances it is not surprising that some social developments are seen as more threatening than others. Sobriety—in its narrow and broad sense—has been an important part of Swedish social and cultural development. The capitalist work ethic and the discipline of the labor movement both depended upon the sobriety of the workforce. In Sweden a powerful temperance movement allied with social democracy defended temperance values and promoted a restrictive alcohol policy. That tradition has been succeeded in our time by an anti-drugs movement endorsing the same values. It is not hard to see why a society based upon sobriety should take alarm at the prospect of widening drug use. In recent years the issue has been given added significance by the demand by the European Union that Sweden give up 4 of its 5 state alcohol monopolies (cf e.g. Ugland, 2001).

Similarly, it is not difficult to understand why the women's movement should feel threatened by the growth in prostitution and trafficking in migrant women. Sweden has prided itself on being the most gender-equal society in the world. But gender equality in Sweden is very much linked to the importance and size of the public sector. Again, entry into the EU and the wider effects of the globalized economy have both led to a reduction in social and public expenditure in Sweden with the consequent threat to women's job's, their status and the degree of equality they have achieved. In these circumstances, prostitution—the selling of sexual services—has become symbolic of women's subordination generally (cf Ekberg, 2004; PR, 2008; Savage and O'Mahony, 2008).

In many respects Sweden would like to embrace the difference and diversity celebrated by postmodernists (Gould, 2005). But postmodernity has also introduced a greater degree of instability into people's daily existence than was evident in the modernist era. An economy based upon the predominance of the market, social policies dominated by welfare pluralism, the increase in labor migration and the decline of the nation state are all developments that stand in great contrast to the condition of modernity in which the Swedish welfare state thrived. Swedish culture emphasized the Apollonian values of order, control, sobriety, and rationality. Our postmodern world thrives on the Dionysian values of disorder, spontaneity, excess, and irrationality.[4]

Conclusion

The Swedish welfare state has been under threat for the last two decades (cf Gould, 1999b; Olsson Hort, 2000; Behrendt, 2002; Timonen, 2003). The culture and values that sustain it are also felt to be under threat. Much of this threat is seen to emanate from developments in the outside world. Popular discontent has become focused upon moral issues, which are seen to symbolize the crisis faced by the exemplar of modernity in a postmodern age (Gould, 2005). The empirical evidence suggests that the rhetoric used in debates about drugs and prostitution has been decidedly nationalistic.

The reaction of Swedish social policy since the 1990s when it comes to the issues of drugs and prostitution can be described as a form of "moral panic." I hence concludes that Sweden needs to prevent the worst excesses of Dionysian postmodernity not by unrealistic moral expectations and goals, but on the contrary through its comprehensive and universalist social policies.

Notes

1. The term "restrictive line" is used officially in Sweden to distinguish Swedish policies on drugs and alcohol from those liberal approaches. It is a useful term, which I shall employ to describe the Swedish approach to prostitution as well.
2. The 1993 Vienna Human Rights conference, the 1995 Beijing Women's conference and, in 1998, a joint conference in Brussels held by End Child Prostitution, Pornography and Trafficking groups in Europe and Defense for Children International.
3. Holgersson identified a repressive and authoritarian tradition in the early stages of welfare development and argued that it had continued in social services into the 1970s. There is no reason to suppose that the tradition suddenly ceased at that point in time—on the contrary.
4. Cf Gould (2001b, 2005).

REFERENCES

Behrendt, C. (2002), *At the Margins of the Welfare State: Social Assistance and the Alleviation of Poverty in Germany, Sweden, and the United Kingdom*, Ashgate: Aldershot, UK.

Billig, M. (1995), *Banal Nationalism*, Sage: London.

Bucken-Knapp, G. and Karlsson, J. (2007), Prostitution Policy Reform and the Causal Role of Ideas: A Comparative Study of Policy-Making, *sww.pol. gu.se*.

CAN, Centralförbundet för Alkohol- och Narkotikaupplysningen (1999), *Drogutvecklingen i Sverige*, Centralförbundet för Alkohol- och Narkotikaupplysningen: Stockholm.

Dagens Nyheter (1998), Politiker Försvarar Kriminalisering, August 3.

Ekberg, G. (2004), The Swedish Law that Prohibits the Purchase of Sexual Services, *Violence Against Women*, Vol. 10. No. 10, pp. 1187-218.

Expressen (1998), Invasion av Prostituerade, April 2.

Furniss, N. and Tilton, T. (1977), *The Case for the Welfare State*, Indiana University Press: Bloomington, IN.

Goode, E. and Ben-Yehuda, N. (1994), *Moral Panics: The Social Construction of Deviance*, Blackwell: Oxford, UK.

Gould, A. (1989), Cleaning the People's Home: Recent Developments in Sweden's Addiction Policy, *British Journal of Addiction,* Vol. 84, No. 7, pp. 731-41.

Gould, A. (1994a), Pollution Rituals in Sweden: The Pursuit of a Drug-Free Society, *Scandinavian Journal of Social Welfare*, Vol. 3, No. 2, pp. 85-93.

Gould, A. (1994b), Sweden's Syringe Exchange Debate: Moral Panic in a Rational Society, *Journal of Social Policy,* Vol. 23, No. 2, pp. 195-217.

Gould, A. (1999a), A Drug-Free Europe? Sweden on the Offensive, *Druglink,* Vol. 14, No. 2, pp. 12-13.

Gould, A. (1999b), The Erosion of the Welfare State: Swedish Social Policy and the EU, *Journal of European Social Policy,* Vol. 9, No. 2, pp. 165-74.

Gould, A. (2001a), The Criminalisation of Buying Sex: The Politics of Prostitution in Sweden, *Journal of Social Policy*, Vol. 30, No. 3, pp. 437-56.

Gould, A. (2001b), *Developments in Swedish Social Policy: Resisting Dionysus*, Palgrave: Basingstoke, UK.

Gould, A. (2002), Sweden's Law on Prostitution: Feminism, Drugs and the Foreign Threat, in S. Thorbeck and B. Pattanaik (eds.). *Transnational Prostitution: Changing Global Patterns*, Zed: London.

Gould, A. (2005), Resisting Postmodernity: Swedish Social Policy in the 1990s, *Social Work and Society*, Vol. 3, No. 1.

Hartnoll, R. (1989), The International Context, in S. MacGregor (ed.), *Drugs and British Society*, Routledge: London.

Holgersson, L. (1977), *Socialvård*, Tidens Förlag: Stockholm.

Kautto, M. (2001), *Nordic Welfare States in the European Context*, Routledge: London.

Månsson, S.-A. (1998), Döm Inte ut Lagen mot Könshandeln, *Göteborgs-Posten*, August 20.

Martinelli, E. (1995), Viktigt Våga Undersöka Gränserna, *Socionomen*, No. 4, pp. 7-11.

Nadelman, E. (1990), Global Prohibition Regimes: The Evolution of Norms in International Society, *International Organisation*, Vol. 44, No. 4, pp. 479-526.

Olsson Hort, S.E. (2000), From a Generous to a Stingy Welfare State? Sweden's Approach to Targeting, in N. Gilbert (ed.), *Targeting in Social Welfare*, Transactions: New Brunswick, NJ.

PR (2008), *www.prostitutionresearch.com/swedish.html.*

Savage, J. and O'Mahony, P. (2008), Swedish Prostitution: Gone or Just Hidden?, *www.thelocal.se/9621/20080110*.

SIB, Swedish Integration Board (Integrationsverket) (2001), *Rapport Integration 2000*, Swedish Integration Board: Norrköping, Sweden.

SOU, Statens Offentliga Utredningar (1995), 15 *Könshandeln*, Statens Offentliga Utredningar: Stockholm.

Svenska Dagbladet (1999), Folkhälsoinstituets Insatser Inte Alltid Politiskt Korrekt, May 27.

Tham, H. (1998) Swedish Drugpolicy: A Successful Model?, *European Journal on Criminal Policy and Research*, No. 6 pp. 395-414.

Thorgren, G. (1994), Vi Ska Inte Ge Upp, *Pockettidningen*, Vol. 24, No. 2, pp. 89-95.

Timonen, V. (2003), *Restructuring the Welfare State: Globalization and Social Policy Reform in Finland and Sweden*, Edward Elgar: Cheltenham, UK.

Titmuss, R. (1970), *The Gift Relationship*, Allen and Unwin: London.

Tomasson, R. (1970), *Sweden: The Prototype of a Modern Society*, Random House: New York.

Ugland, T. (2001), *Policy Recategorization and Integration: Europeanization of Nordic Alcohol Control Policies*, University of Oslo Press: Oslo.

Westin, C. (2000), *Settlement and Immigration Policies Towards Immigrants and Their Descendants in Sweden*, International Labor Office: Geneva, Switzerland.

10

From Welfare Laggard to Welfare Leader: The Welfare State in Switzerland

DOMINIQUE WANG AND CHRISTIAN ASPALTER

The welfare state system of Switzerland relies on strong social security systems, while also being coupled with a decent system of social assistance. The Swiss welfare state system does not apply large systems of general universal benefits, or social savings accounts. Most of the welfare legislation is conducted on Federal level, while the Cantons also take over a large responsibility in the financing and administration of social security and welfare systems (cf Appendix 1) (Obinger *et al.*, 2005).

The Swiss pension systems is allegedly aligned along the three-pillar system (*"Dreisäulensystem"*), combining: (i) compulsory universal old-age and survivor's insurance (*"Alters- und Hinterlassenenversicherung"*, AHV or federal pensions); (ii) mandatory private occupational pensions (*"Berufsvorsorge"*, BV); and (iii) voluntary individual retirement/ savings accounts. In actual fact, however, there are only two main columns of the Swiss pension system, the AHV and BV.

At a closer look one can identify outstanding characteristic of particularly its basic pension system—namely, its highly redistributive nature, which guarantees a high degree of poverty reduction and prevention among the working poor and their families (Aspalter, 2006a).

The Swiss health care insurance system is rather unusual (Civitas, 2006), in the sense that public, subsidized private and fully private elements have been intertwined. Also, the decentralization of the health care system has been given rise to significant differences between cantons in terms of health care spending and provision (Crivelli and Filippini, 2005). Despite—and, in fact, because—all the institutional extravagancy, the Swiss health care system belongs to the most inefficient health care systems in the world today (only to be surpassed by the health care system of the United States in terms of inefficiency) (Aspalter, 2005b; Huber and Orosz, 2003).

This chapter sets out to investigate the structure of the current welfare state system in Switzerland, and then goes on to compare the overall development of the Swiss welfare state system with that of the rest of Europe. In the final part of the chapter it is concluded that Switzerland is one of the leaders of welfare state systems in Europe, having increased its levels of social spending dramatically since the early 1990s.

The Universal Minimum Pension System

Basic pension in Switzerland are provided by a contributory, pay-as-you-go basic pension system, the "Alters- und Hinterlassenenversicherung" (the Old Age and Survivors' Insurance), with mandatory coverage for all employees, all self-employed and non-employed persons over age 20. The central fund of universal public pensions is operated by the federal government, while some branch-related funds are operated also partly by the labor unions and employers' associations—the social partners.

The Old-Age and Survivors' Insurance—Alters- und Hinterlassenenversicherung, AHV, is a mimimum pension system. It is universal, contributory, and highly redistributive. It also includes a system of partial pensions.

A person must have contributed in all years from age 21 to age 65 (64 for women). If this requirement is not met, partial pensions are paid out—a minimum period of one year is sufficient to qualify for partial pensions.

The Basic Pension system is funded by mostly on contributions, but also to some extent tax funding. The contribution rates for are 4.2 percent of earnings for employees and 4.2 percent of payroll for employers; self-employed persons pay 7.8 percent of income. The most important feature of the Swiss basic pension system is that there is *no income ceiling* for contributions to be made.

Benefits amount to 1,030 Swiss Francs a month. If the annual income is less than or equal to Francs 37,080, a flat-rate amount of Francs 9,146 is payable plus a variable amount that is calculated by multiplying the annual income by 13/600; if the annual income is above Francs 37,080, a flat-rate amount of Francs 12,854 is payable plus a variable amount calculated by multiplying the annual income by 8/600. The maximum old-age pension is Francs 2,060 per month. A partial pension is paid according to the relationship between the insured's number of years of contributions and the number of years of contributions made by others of his or her age group. In addition, dependent supplements are payable for each child under age 18, or age 25 in case of a student.

The qualifying age is 65 for men and 64 for women. A full pension requires contributions made in all years from age 21 (this also applies to survivors' pensions). For those who earn up to 37,080 Swiss Francs per year, the flat-rate benefit amounts to 9,146 Francs per year, plus a variable amount calculated by multiplying annual income by 13/600. If the average annual income exceeds 37,080 Francs, the flat-rate amount is 12,854 Francs per year, plus a variable additional amount that is calculated by multiplying the average annual income by 8/600.

The minimum old-age basic pension is 1,030 Swiss Francs a month. The minimum monthly survivors' benefit is 824 Francs; the maximum is 1,648 Francs (amounting to 80 percent of the insured's pension). Basic pensions are indexed-linked to a combination of wages and prices, each contributing to half of the index.

Contributions on income above about Euro 50,000 function as a classical tax, as they do not generate pension entitlements—they function as a redistributive tax (from rich to poor) as the poorer segments of society benefit over-proportionally from the basic pension scheme.

The Social Insurance Office of the Central (Federal) Government supervises the implementation of the basic pension, while the Federal Department of Interior provides additional, general supervision. A decentralized network of cantonal, industrial and federal compensation funds are responsible for collecting and recording incoming contributions and outgoing benefits. A separate central compensation office maintains a register for all insured persons and pensioners (Aspalter, 2006a; GS, 2005; BSV, 2005; Brunner-Patthey and Wirtz, 2005; GLI, 2003).

The Mandatory Private Pension System

The *Berufsvorsorge* (BV) is a compulsory, but limited, supplemental-pension insurance, which mixes defined-benefit schemes and defined-contribution schemes. In 2004, over 75 percent of insured in this system were under a defined-contribution plan.

Before the implementation of this mandatory second pillar in 1985, the occupational provision primarily covered workers in key export-oriented firms and financial sectors, leaving smaller firms and the crafts-dominated domestic sectors undeveloped.

In 2004, over 80 percent of the Swiss workforce was affiliated to an occupational pension plan. In the same year, the BV contributions that represent 16 to 17 percent of the income amounted to 10 to 12 percent of the GDP.

In 2003, occupational pension assets represented almost 150 percent of Swiss GDP. Due to the merger of *Berufsvorsorge* (BV) plans over the past years, the power of financial actors has been reinforced. The high fragmentation of coverage results, in addition, in high management expenses, sometimes amount to more than 10 percent of BV contributions. The main purpose of the BV pension scheme is to maintain people's living standard (Scharpf, 1999; Leimgruber, 2004).

The Health Care System

Swiss health care insurance combines public, subsidized private and fully private health care. Compulsory health insurance can be purchased from a limited number of insurance companies, both public and private, which are registered with the Federal Office for Social Insurance. There were 93 registered insurance funds offering compulsory health insurance in 2002. These insurance companies are not allowed to make profits from their compulsory health insurance activities (EOHCS, 2000; Civitas, 2006).

Compulsory health insurance covers a broad range of services. The main additions to the basic package of care were unlimited stay in nursing homes, home care, unlimited stay in hospitals, accidents (if not covered by accident insurance), diagnostic and therapeutic equipment, transport, limited dental treatment, etc. The services not covered by compulsory health insurance can be made up by supplementary health insurance. About 25 percent of the people in Switzerland have one of the major supplementary health insurance provided by private or semi-private policies. However, since there are no tax incentives to purchase supplementary insurance and due to the expansion of the compulsory health insurance benefits package and the rising premiums charged, the supplementary insurance has become less attractive (EOHCS, 2000).

Also, the Swiss accident insurance covers ambulatory and in patient treatment costs. All Swiss residents are free to choose their insurance provider for compulsory health insurance. People are allowed to change their compulsory health insurance companies twice a year. Even though the insurance companies must offer the identical benefits packages throughout the federation; however, they can compete with each other within each canton based on the level of premium, which might vary by 50 percent from canton to canton. In addition, managed care and quality competition is allowed too under compulsory health insurance; nevertheless, it is still not as common as premium competition (Civitas, 2006).

The latest revision of the health insurance law took place in the mid-1990s. The new law, which was passed by the parliament in March 1994, was approved by referendum in December 1994 and came into force in January 1996. The main reason for this reform were dramatic increases in expenditure over time. The cost upsurge has been the concern since mid-1960s. The other reason was that solidarity was being damaged by the possibility that insurance companies could discriminate based on risk. The reform pursued two objectives: to strengthen solidarity and to contain costs. The 1994 health insurance law reform made the following changes:

1. Health insurance became a compulsory insurance.
2. There have been significant changes to the systems of subsidies.
3. Expansion of the benefits package to include in particular nursing care.
4. Premiums were changed from risk-rated to community-rated (that is, the same for each person taking out insurance with a particular company within a canton or sub-region of a canton regardless of individual risk rating).
5. The widespread practice of cream skimming was prevented by legislation, forcing insurance companies to accept all applicants for compulsory health insurance.

The health insurance law of 1994 has substituted the health insurance law of 1911, which had only been reformed once in 1964. The health care system in Switzerland is influenced by the political system, which is characterized by both liberalism and federalism. The liberal factor restricts the state actively to intervene in the health care system. It only gets involved when private scheme fails to produce satisfactory results. It acts only as a safety net or provider of last option. This is why actors outside the public sector play the relatively major role in Switzerland's health care system. The confederation can interfere only when the Constitution allows doing so. This includes only the guaranteeing of social insurance, the regulation of medical examinations and qualifications, and certain public health activities. The Constitution only signs over limited powers to the Confederation over the health care system (Wang and Aspalter, 2006).

Decentralization of the health care system is marked in the 23 cantons, three of which split into demi-cantons, acting autonomously in the organization of health care in their area. Cantons are charged with regulation, hospital certification and finance for disease prevention and health education. This results in 26 slightly different systems. However, the cantons operate within a federal framework. The Federal Office for Social Insurance is responsible for the policies of health insurance, accident insurance and disability insurance. Federal Office for Military Insurance is responsible for the military insurance.

In Switzerland, spouses and children must also separately purchase the compulsory health insurance, as coverage does not extend to dependent family members automatically. However, premiums for children, teenagers, and young adults in training/education are much lower.

In 1997, public expenditure on health care provision amounted to 59 percent of total health care expenditure. Nearly 25 percent of total health care expenditure is financed from Federal, cantonal and municipal subsidies via tax revenues. This tax revenue covers: (a) cantonal subsidies to both private and public hospitals; (b) cantonal and municipal subsidies to nursing homes and homecare providers; and (c) cantonal and federal subsidies for compulsory health insurance premiums. Also, 27.5 percent of total health care expenditure is financed by compulsory health insurance premiums. Occupational and non-occupational accident insurance, old-age and disability insurance financed 6.7 percent of health care expenditure. About 40 percent is financed via private household and supplementary insurance (EOHCS, 2000; Civitas, 2006).

The Accident Insurance System

The Swiss accident insurance system comprises three components: (1) occupational and non-occupational accident insurance; (2) old-age and disability insurance, and (3) military insurance. For occupational and non-occupational accident insurance, employers are required to insure their employees for compulsory accident insurance.

People not in employment, can also obtain the benefits by purchasing supplemental accident insurance. Accident insurance covers ambulatory and inpatient treatment costs and transportation costs incurred due to occupational and leisure accidents. People, who are incapable to work, are handicapped and to the survivors by reason of an accident have claims for the payment. The cantons, under the supervision of the federal government, are responsible for accident prevention. The Swiss National Fund for Accident Insurance is an independent public body, which is the most important provider of compulsory accident insurance. There are other insurance companies that are granted licenses to offer accident insurance.

Old-age and disability insurance are financed from employer and employee contributions in accordance with the social insurance model. These contributions fund pensions and health care costs of the elderly and payments for people handicapped since birth. Disability insurance law defines disability as damage to health resulting in permanent or long-term inability to work. It covers the cost of medical, nursing and rehabilitation services. Cantons and the central state finance half of the total expenditures on a cost-sharing basis.

Military insurance is paid by the Swiss Confederation via federal taxes. Swiss military insurance insured all soldiers that are currently serving in the Swiss army. It covers health care, accident and transportation costs (Mbitha-Schmid, 2004; EOHCS, 2000; Armingeon *et al.*, 2004).

The Unemployment Insurance System

The Swiss unemployment insurance system is a federal system. Though, the legislative authority for unemployment insurance is the Swiss confederation, the execution and the implementation of active labor market policies is chiefly the task of the 26 Cantons.

The system is financed by mandatory contributions from all employers and employees. The total contribution is shared between the employers and the employees. The contributions of the unemployment system are processed in tandem with that of the pension system. The minimum contribution period necessary to be entitled to unemployment benefits is 6 months out of the 24 precedent months, while benefits are paid for a maximum period of 24 months (Gast *et al.*, 2006).

The Social Assistance System

Social assistance serves as a safety net of last resort for those who lack support from their families, receive insufficient income or social security benefits or have exhausted their social insurance rights. Social assistance is regulated, administered and funded by 26 cantons and about 3,000 municipalities. Many cantons have delegated social assistance to municipalities.

There are major differences in between Cantons, of how the social assistance net is set up, in general benefits do not vary too largely, but particularly French- and Italian-speaking Cantons offer additional means-tested benefits to e.g. long-term unemployed who have exhausted their entitlement to federal unemployment insurance, to single parents, or to families with children.

Federal responsibilities of social assistance is outlined by the Federal Law of Legal Responsibility for Support of the Needy (*Bundesgesetz über die Zuständigkeit für die Unterstützung Bedürftiger*). This law defines neediness, entrusts the canton of residence with support responsibility and regulates cost sharing and reimbursement between the home canton and the canton of residence (Armingeon *et al.*, 2002).

From Welfare Laggard to Welfare Leader: On the Increase in Swiss Social Spending

Evading the attention of most social policy experts in Europe and worldwide, the Swiss welfare state system underwent tremendous changes since the early 1990s; but this without the introduction of great new policies or social reforms. The extension of the Swiss welfare state was rather silent, but nevertheless salient.

Of vital importance here is the relationship between increasing social expenditure in the Swiss welfare state system and the particular political institutions of Switzerland itself (cf Obinger, 1998). The influence of direct democracy is vital for the understanding of increasing expenditure in the long run. Drastic, hurtful social security reform in Switzerland were absent, due to the powerful possible, and very real, interferences of veto-players in Swiss politics (cf Bonoli, 2000). But equally important is the influence of system-inherent factors, particularly the lack of proper control and organizational principles in e.g. the Swiss health care system (cf Wang and Aspalter, 2006).

Figure 10.1: Comparison of Social Protection Expenditure in Europe (as % of GDP)

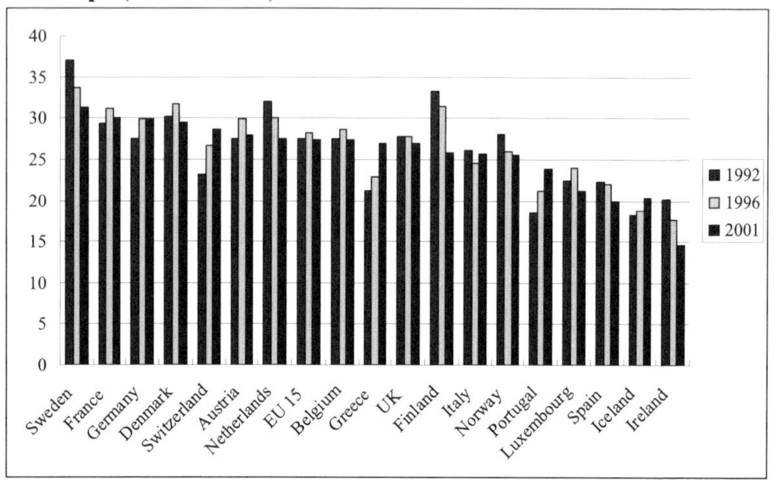

Source: Eurostat (2004).

According to the 1990 study of Esping-Andersen—which received widespread attention, especially after having become both a best-selling reference and textbook alike—the Swiss welfare state is a welfare laggard. It has been grouped by Esping-Andersen into the group of liberal (i.e., residual) welfare states—together with the United Kingdom, Australia and the United States. Giuliano Bonoli (2003) classified Switzerland as being half conservative (Christian Democratic) and half liberal—while describing the social security system to the Continental European welfare regime and the labor welfare system to the liberal/Ango-Saxon welfare regime.

But, today the Swiss welfare state is to be seen from a different perspective. It has indeed managed to climb to the top of welfare state systems, in terms of social security provided, redistribution achieved, and overall well-being of society secured. Since a couple of years (cf Figure 10.1), the Swiss welfare state ranks among the top nations with regard to the welfare state spending, in the accompany of only the most advanced welfare states on earth—i.e., Sweden, France, Germany, and Denmark.

In a nutshell the Swiss welfare state managed to change its overall performance, not by way of systematic changes and reforms, but rather by extending welfare benefits of existing social security schemes.

In today's world of ideal-typical welfare regimes, there is no doubt that *Switzerland constitute an integral part of the Continental/Christian Democratic welfare regime*, as identified by Aspalter (2005a, 2006b) and Huber and Stephens (1999), and theorized earlier on by Kersbergen (1994, 1995).

Internationally, a lot of attention has been paid in the last one and a half decades to the existence of welfare regimes—or families of nations that resemble each other in terms of welfare state systems and policies. So far, only four ideal-typical welfare regimes have been identified:

(1) the Scandinavian ("Social Democratic") welfare regime,
(2) the Continental ("Christian Democratic") welfare regime,
(3) the Anglo-Saxon ("Liberal") welfare regime, and
(4) the East Asian ("Conservative") welfare regime (Esping-Andersen, 1990, 1998; Aspalter, 2005a, 2006b).

The Social Democratic welfare state is build upon the assumption that both horizontal and vertical redistribution and public welfare provision (especially with regard to social services and public employment) form the heart of the welfare state. The Christian Democratic welfare state, on the other hand, is build on the premise that occupationally divided social insurance systems emphasize horizontal redistribution, while social assistance and taxation aim at vertical redistribution.

In stark contrast to that the Liberal welfare state is based on the conviction that redistribution needs to be highly limited or targeted. Redistribution, here, occurs mainly through targeted as well as means-tested social assistance schemes. Last but not least, the Conservative

(East Asian) welfare state systems put forward the idea that redistribution needs to concentrate also—and in fact primarily—on immaterial resources (mainly health and education)—that is, social investment, placing emphasis on productive, economy-friendly welfare programs.

Appendix 1: Responsibilities of the Cantons and the Federation in the Field of Social Security in 2000

Program	Type of Program	Legislation	Funding	Implementation
Old age and survivors' insurance	Universal insurance	Federation	Federation (Cantons)	Federation and cantons
Disability insurance	Universal insurance	Federation	Federation (Cantons)	Federation and cantons
Supplementary benefits	Universal insurance/ means-tested	Federation	Federation (Cantons)	Cantons
Unemployment insurance	Social insurance	Federation	Federation (Cantons)	Federation and cantons
Accident insurance	Social insurance	Federation	Federation (Cantons)	Federation
Health care insurance	Universal insurance	Federation	Federation and cantons	Federation and cantons
Family allowances	Social insurance	Cantons (Federation)	Cantons (Federation)	Cantons (Federation)
Unemployment assistance	Means-tested	Cantons	Cantons	Cantons
Social assistance	Means-tested	Cantons	Cantons	Cantons

Source: Obinger (1998).

REFERENCES

Armingeon, Klaus; Bertozzi, Fabio, and Bonoli, Giuliano (2002), Swiss World of Welfare, paper presented at the workshop *Federalism and the Welfare State—Comparative Perspectives on the Old and the New Politics of the Welfare State*, Hanse Institute for Advanced Study, Delmenhorst, Germany, May 24-27.

Armingeon, Klaus; Bertozzi, Fabio; Bonoli, Giuliano, and Obinger, Herbert (2004), *Switzerland: Social Policies and Politics in a Multi-Tiered Welfare State*, Institute of Political Science, University of Bern, Switzerland.

Aspalter, Christian (2001a), *Importance of Christian and Social Democratic Movements in Welfare Politics: With Special Reference to Germany, Austria and Sweden*, Nova Science: New York.

Aspalter, Christian (2001b), *Conservative Welfare State Systems in East Asia*, Praeger, Westport, CT.

Aspalter, Christian (2005a), East Asian Welfare Regime, in N.T. Tan (ed.), *The Challenge of Social Care in Asia*, Marshall Cavendish: New York.

Aspalter, Christian (2005b), *Health Care Reform in the France and Italy, Korean Institute of Health and Social Affairs*, KIHASA, Government of Korea, Seoul.

Aspalter, Christian (2006a), *Fighting Old-Age Poverty: Universal Pensions Schemes in the Netherlands, Switzerland, New Zealand, and Canada*, National Pension Institute, NPC, Government of Korea: Seoul.

Aspalter, Christian (2006b), The East Asian Welfare Model, *International Journal of Social Welfare*, Vol. 15, pp. 290-301.

Bonoli, Giuliano (2000), *The Politics of Pension Reform*, Cambridge University Press: Cambridge, UK.

Bonoli, Giuliano (2003), Switzerland: A Liberal-Conservative Welfare State, in Christian Aspalter (ed.), *Welfare Capitalism Around the World*, Casa Verde: Hong Kong.

Brunner-Patthey, Olivier and Wirz, Robert (2005), *Vergleich zwischen der AHV und der beruflichen Vorsorge (BV) aus wirtschaftlicher Sicht*, Report No. 5, Bundesamt für Sozialversicherung (BSV), The Government of Switzerland: Bern.

BSV, Bundesamt für Sozialversicherung, Government of Switzerland (2005), website, Bern, *www.bsu.admin.ch*.

Civitas (2006), The Swiss Healthcare System, The Institute for the Study of Civil Society, *www.civitas.org.uk*.

Crivelli, Luca and Filippini, Massimo (2005), *Regional Public Health Care Spending in Switzerland: An Empirical Analysis*, Faculty of Economics, University of Lugano: Lugano, Switzerland.

EC and WHO (1998), Highlights on Health in Austria, *www.who.dk*.

EOHCS, European Observatory on Health Care Systems (2000), *Health Care Systems in Transition-Switzerland*, EOHCS: Copenhagen.

Esping-Andersen, Gøsta (1990), *The Three Worlds of Welfare Capitalism*, Polity: Cambridge, UK.

Esping-Andersen, Gøsta (1998), The Three Political Economies of the Welfare State, in J. O'Connor and G.M. Olsen (eds.), *Power Resources Theory and the Welfare State: A Critical Approach*, University of Toronto Press: Toronto, Canada.

Eurostat (2004), Per Capita Social Protection Expenditure in the EU Rose by Almost 2% per Annum, *europa.eu.int/comm/eurostat*.

Gast, Jonathan; Lechner, Michael, and Steiger, Heidi (2006), *Swiss Unemployment Insurance Micro Data*, Swiss Institute of International Economics and Applied Economic Research, University of St. Gallen, Switzerland.

GLI, Gruppo di Lavoro Interdipartementale IDA ForAlt (2003), *Rapporto di Sintesi del Programma di Ricerca sul Futuro a Lungo Termine delle Previdenza per la Vecchiaia*, Report No. 13, Bundesamt für Sozialversicherung (BSV), The Government of Switzerland: Bern.

GS, Government of Switzerland, Alters- und Hinterlassenenversicherung (2005), website, *www.ahv.ch*.

Huber, Evelyne and Stephens, John D. (1999), Welfare State and Production Regimes in the Era of Retrenchment, *www.sss.ias.edu*.

Huber, Manfred and Orosz, Eva (2003), Health Expenditure Trends in OECD Countries, *Health Care Financing Review*, Vol. 25, No. 1, pp. 1-22.

Kersbergen, Kees v. (1994), The Distinctiveness of Christian Democracy, in D. Hanley (ed.), *Christian Democracy in Europe*, Pinter: London.

Kersbergen, Kees v. (1995), *Social Capitalism, A Study of Christian Democracy and the Welfare State*, Routledge: London.

Leimgruber, Matthieu (2004), A Closer Look at a World Bank Model: Unpacking the Swiss Three-Pillar Pension Model, paper presented at the conference *Pension Fund Capitalism and the Crisis of Old Age Security in the United States*, New School University, New York, September 10-11.

Mbitha-Schmid, Elisabeth (2004), Health Care System—Switzerland, *strategis. gc.c*a.

Obinger, Herbert (1998), *Politische Institutionen und Sozialpolitik in der Schweiz*, Lang: Frankfurt a.M., Germany.

Obinger, Herbert; Armingeon, Klaus; Bonoli, Giuliano, and Bertozzi, Fabio (2005), Switzerland: The Marriage of Direct Democracy and Federalism, in H. Obinger, S. Leibfried, and F.G. Castles (eds.), *Federalism and the Welfare State*, Cambridge University Press: Cambridge, UK.

Scharpf, Fritz W. (1999), The Viability of Advanced Welfare States in the International Economy: Vulnerabilities and Options, *MPIfG Working Paper*, No. 99/9, September.

Wang, Dominique and Aspalter, Christian (2006), The Austrian and the Swiss Welfare State System in International Comparison, *Journal of Societal and Social Policy*, Vol. 5, No. 2, pp. 25-49.

11

Feminization of Poverty:
Lessons from Albania

ENKELEIDA TAHIRAJ

This essay addresses the question of the feminization of poverty in Albania since the overthrow of communism and the transition to democracy in the 1990s. It opens with a brief foray into the scholarly and scientific study of poverty and the concept of feminization of poverty, the aim of which is to provide a context for understanding Albanian poverty. However, much of the examination thereafter is based on the gendered characteristics and experience of poverty in Albania during the transitional process. Many questions arise when considering the social and economic position of women in the world (Chen *et al.*, 2005).

Some of the questions that should be asked about women's status in post-communist Albania may well reflect some light on the status of women elsewhere. An inquiry into the roles of women in Albania certainly holds anthropological, economic and political as well as sociological interest, and invites comparison with the experiences of other post-communist countries.

Why should it have been that women's retreat from work was so much more rapid and disproportionately greater than men's, after the initial labor market reforms of the early 1990s? How pervasive has the reversion to type in gender roles during transition been—a reversion that has undone the gains that state socialism proclaimed to have achieved.

Does this indicate that those equalities, set in policy and implementted by a totalitarian regime, could not effect lasting, deeper social change over two generations and more? What hope then for modern liberal policies? If we grant that socialism did achieve great gains in equality, was there still a feminization of poverty in that system? Can we even talk of such a process, given the well-known problem of lack of workable data in Albania? Finally, what then in the way of lessons to be learned from the recent and more distant past, in order to impact policies that better promote women's issues and rights?

This study finds that there is circumstantial and documentary evidence to propose a feminization of poverty in Albania during transition. It concludes by suggesting that more comprehensive, systematic and scientific studies of poverty in Albania will allow for the recording and reporting of women's exposure to poverty. Further, that this may well be true for other groups in poverty or at risk of poverty. In this regard, the discrepancy between real, experiential poverty and its official determination needs consideration by the scholarly community.

Poverty and the Feminization of Poverty: The Need for Multi-Dimensionality in Poverty Thinking

We are now all accustomed to admitting a degree of relativism into our thinking. In poverty studies, we are well aware that attitudes to and perceptions of poverty have differed greatly over time, and that definitions of poverty are somewhat contingent to the political, social, economic and historical period—even as regards canonical poverty thinking. Abstracting awhile, and in disregard of mutual dependencies, poverty studies will be considered now in two strands—theories of poverty and their operationalization.

It has been well argued that we need to understand poverty as a multi-dimensional phenomenon, mostly because actual definitions fall short of completeness, and leave space for debates. The many theories of poverty, both descriptive and explanatory and as varied as attitudes to poverty, would seem to support the view that the concept defies attempts at a single essential definition, of the kind that fuels the natural sciences. This is not a result only of political difference or stubbornness though—there are indeed genuine philosophical reasons why this should be so which the reader is encouraged to pursue elsewhere (Tahiraj, 2007). Still, there is and has been, if not consensus, a certain canonicalism over the last hundred years of "scientific" poverty studies. On a more quotidian level, poverty doesn't escape capture by ostensive definition—although we don't quite agree in scholarly terms on what it is, most of us recognize poverty and can happily choose not to be confronted by it in our daily lives. In a similar way the question as to what, if anything, should be done about poverty is a question for another time (Spicker, 2007).

In the revolving door that is conceptual enquiry we find many other concepts being used in the effort to characterize or essentialize poverty—most notably deprivation (Sen, 1983), risk, vulnerability (Room, 1995; Abrams *et al.* 2008), exclusion (Townsend, 1979) and need (Bradshaw, 1999; Doyal and Gough, 1991).

We will discuss the latter briefly. The needs approach has long been at the core of poverty studies. Poverty could be understood as an absolute, where needs are defined in terms of a set of basic essentials assumed to be necessary for subsistence related to the need for health and nutrition. Yet need, if considered as anything beyond the (somehow seemingly inhuman) nutritional level required to maintain basal metabolic rate (BMR), is itself highly contingent upon time and place. Certainly any relative definitions lead us to consider that needs are socially determined, as has been long recognized:

"By necessaries I understand not only the commodities which are indispensably necessary for the support of life, but whatever the custom of the country renders it indecent for creditable people to be without" (Smith, 1776).

Various taxonomies of needs abound, to suit many purposes (Maslov, 1943; Bradshaw, 1999; Bradshaw *et al.*, 2000), hence various methods of needs assessment. What is important here is that we can agree that needs are continuously being adapted and augmented as both a product of and a force for change in society. Crucially it would seem *a priori* possible that increa-sing stratification in the social and economic spheres, as was witnessed to occur rapidly in transition countries, both creates and reconstitutes need (Townsend, 1970, 1979).

The issue of stratification leads us to touch on the causal relationship between exclusion and poverty (Millar, 2000; Atkinson, 1998). Whether in the context of an impersonal state regime, or an impersonal liberal market, it is argued that people become or remain poor because access to resources, positions of power and possibilities for betterment are closed to them in an impersonal way (cf Konopasek, 1991, 1992; Ray, 1996; Tomes, 1998).

This is something more than merely an unmeetable opportunity cost to wealth creation—it stems from the intertwined economic and power structures of modern societies. Implicit in this argument is that poverty is not simply about having a certain low level of assets or income (Rodgers and Van der Hoeven, 1995). Equally, the solution to poverty arises rather neatly, perhaps too neatly, from the analysis—the solution to the problem of poverty is to remove the barriers that cause exclusion, be they political, social or economic. Exactly how is a moot point, however. To use the exclusion argument to predicate the means of solution, whether to argue for a greater liberalist retrenchment of welfare or more punitive tax and redistribution for example, would amount to little more than special pleading either way.

Still, much primary research appears to validate the exclusion approach against the widely held supposition of the primacy of income measures of poverty (Chambers, 1983). Indeed, there are useful indexes of poverty as deviations from a standard of well-being, defined as "the capability to lead a long, healthy and creative life, to enjoy a decent standard of living, freedom, dignity, self-respect and the respect of others, as well as to participate freely in society" (UNPD, 1997: 63).

As regards gender issues, there is especial need to record the various "aspects of gender disadvantage, such as lack of power to control important decisions that affect one's life" (Razavi, 1999: 417), to explore the dynamics of poverty, the trade-offs that may lead into or out of it, and the many dimensions it is experienced across. focusing "not on incomes but on human outcomes" (Fukuda-Parr, 1999). This should be taken as an acknowledgment of the need to better the so-called scientific study of poverty, not as attempt to denigrate it. If we accept poverty as multi-dimensional, we must admit of a complexity of measures—especially the necessity of combining objective and subjective data obtained from a mix of participatory and statistical research methods, and analysis at micro as well as macro-levels.

Poverty is associated with the most pressing problems in our societies and appears as both cause and effect in many other domains. Ignoring poverty implies ignoring all the problems it correlates to—such as *inter alia* health, crime, education, gender, and age (Bradshaw, 1999). It is probably one of the best indicators we have of the failure of markets and the capacities of the welfare state. The study of poverty is an important component in helping us understand the nature of our social systems—it reveals much about our societies, in both values and mechanisms. It is important to be able to measure the effectiveness of interventions and welfare state efforts.

These efforts are more likely to be comprehensive when based on a diagnosis of the causes and dimensions of poverty—indeed, the effectiveness of remedial policies is directly related to the quality of knowledge of the root causes of poverty. This knowledge needs to be based on timely, consistent and reliable data that somehow reflects the varied needs we passed over before. Obtaining comprehensive and consistent knowledge of poverty should help in building effective preventive policies and understanding dynamic trends, so much needed in countries in transition. It is here where the distinction between reliable and non-reliable or non-existing scientific research and data enters into discussion. How reliable is the scientific research and data in post-communist countries? Subsequently, what affect does this have on the efficacy of policies based on these data?

The Feminization of Poverty

The initial analysis that led to the formulation of the feminization of poverty was rooted in a deconstruction of women's economic status across societies (Glendinning and Millar, 1987; Lewis, 1992a,b; cf Kingfisher, 1996, 2002). It has been a contentious issue for poverty researchers, as both concept and phenomenon, ever since. A central tenet is that more women experience poverty than men (poverty spread) and that poverty increasingly affects women more than men (poverty depth). While detractors have considered this as little more than a politicized restatement of the over-representation of women among the poor, for others it is a process, whereby women experience increasing rates of poverty, by means of an absolute increase in the number of poor women over time, or a relative increase in number of poor women against the number of poor men over time (Pearce, 1978). Of course, if this process is sustained long enough, it will lead to the former over-representation of women. Indeed, much contemporary research claims to be finding that globally both cases are true (cf UN, 1995, 1996). If we calculate poverty on indicators of well-being associated with human poverty, then unambiguously women are worse off than men in almost all contexts (Cagatay, 1998).

However, feminization of poverty as a process has implications beyond asking whether and why more women than men are poor. As a conceptual framework, the feminization approach bears many similarities to an exclusion approach. Overall though, its feminist foundation gives it a greater emphasis on activism than the latter. It is, for instance, a pivotal question as to whether and to what extent the feminization of poverty plays "a necessary part in the perpetuation and deepening of poverty" (Townsend, 1993: 108).

The fundamental lesson from this critique is that the cause of the phenomenon is among others structural, and that the causal explanation requires us to examine and act upon discrimination and power structures on many levels in society. Equally, feminization cuts across other non-material issues, such as culture, age and ethnicity and is difficult to disaggregate from these. As such, both feminist and non-feminist research has thrown up many possible, often interdependent explanatory causes, which actively operate to differentiate outcomes between genders.

These include, but are not limited to occupational segregation, wage inequities, non-participation in formal labor markets, legal discrimination, inequitable fiscal policy (Pressman, 2003), "laissez-faire" or neoliberal policies (Moghadam, 1998), structural adjustments during post-socialist transitions, intra-household inequalities, burden of familial responsibilities, welfare dependence and an increase in the number of singleton women heading households. Naturally, critiques of feminization have been used to support varied, even opposed interests—such as both pro- and contra-traditionalist virtues of marriage and well-paying jobs for men (Nuccio and Sands, 1992). Disputable as they are, many of these theories have influenced government policies and aid programs around the world. Indeed, the feminization of poverty is as much about the operationalization, as the concepts—about the way in which poverty methodologies explain the causes, the effects and challenges of poverty on women and the ways these policies need to respond in order to make women confident to stand for their rights.

Ultimately, and challengingly, the feminist critique argues for the breaking down of the conventional dichotomy between the public world of paid work and the private world of the home and family (Glendinning and Millar, 1987). Such a division, where the former as the domain of men and the latter the domain of women, has been a concern for feminist writers. Parsons and Bales (1956) write that the public world of paid work is the focus of public and economic policy. The private world, certainly according to functionalist sociological theory, is a heaven of expressive warmth and emotional support. Although "housework became distinct from other forms of work with the process of industrialization" (Deem, 1988: 53), it still "belongs to women" as a way of showing the different biological, cultural and social standards that distinguish man from women (cf Deem, 1988; Coltrane, 1996; Sentura, 1997).

Therefore this unpaid work that women do in the house must not remain invisible. The feminist critique also emphasizes the fact that men and women occupy unequal positions of power within the home as well as in the world outside—it is now commonly acknowledged that for the same position women are paid less than men (INSTAT, 2001a,b, 2005).

It has been strongly argued that this is true for "all types of society for which a reasonable range of information exists" (Townsend, 1993: 106). It is an open question as to what constitutes reasonable here, but this qualification shows how the feminization of poverty has proven difficult to substantiate. As recently as the last decade it could be said that "international comparisons of female poverty and the feminization of poverty are still rare, and the existing data are not usually comparable.

No thorough analysis of the subject exists" (Allen, 1992: 108). If the situation has improved for developed countries, certainly on the level of macro-studies such as the Luxembourg Income Study, research is still far from attaining anything like exactitude. What though can be said about countries where the "reasonable range of information" is either scarce, doesn't exist or is unreliable? What if the data can't support an argument about the issue? Much like the elusive "dark matter" of cosmology its existence or not has perhaps simply to be inferred from the observation of other attendant phenomena.

The Changing Role of Women in Albania: The Political and Institutional Setting

It possibly needs reminding that the Albanian transition to democracy was short, but more difficult than expected. The initial economic fall-out replicated the negative extremes seen elsewhere in Eastern Europe, with a collapse in GDP, the start of mass unemployment and high inflation. The Albanian experience during this time was one of "anomic poverty" (Tahiraj, 2007), with institutional collapse, lawlessness and other social unrest six years and more into transition. The country was, by any economic measure, poor under communism, and hence the poverty that was attendant to transition was far from a new phenomenon. However, the experience of poverty was different—and the novelty was in an evidently increasing inequality and deepening vulnerabilities of some in society. In this respect, many people in Albania certainly feel and are poor—a perception largely developed since the international isolation imposed by the communist regime eroded and amplified by an increased stratification in society.

While poverty did not officially exist under communism, poverty and its study have received not much more than reluctant political nods from democratic governments. As such, poverty studies have until quite recently often been little more hand-waving exercises than disciplined efforts in Albania. While poverty during transition manifests itself as cause and effect, its hidden correlates are perhaps still to be fully elaborated. It is evident that much of real poverty remains hidden in Albania, as indeed elsewhere, as objective measurements fail to capture the full picture. Hence, we may infer that this has contributed to the failure of contemporary policies to address the breadth of the phenomenon since, as regards poverty studies, the concepts we use to define poverty greatly determine the methods used to measure it, and predicate to some extent the subsequent policies and programs we employ to address it. Perhaps a broader consideration of the ways poverty can be measured might improve the way the issue is represented in the policy agenda.

Government reforms and programs can hardly be considered to have been very successful in responding to the dynamic needs of that part of the population who found themselves peripheral to nascent formal markets. While there are issues all around the policy-making cycle, efforts have all along been impeded on at least two crucial points. First, the absence of a structured, scientific method in social research, and poverty studies particularly, has limited the collection and availability of good quality, credible statistics—especially hampering comparative analysis (cf WB, 2003).

This was compounded by certain legacies of communism—little respect for data integrity, a weak understanding of the crucial role of data in policymaking, a lack of openness and an unwillingness to coordinate with other agencies. We might even say government has historically operated more on policy-based evidence than evidence-based policy. Secondly, low institutional capacities have stalled potential policy innovations.

There is administrative dependence on external technical aid for even basic analysis. Policies that were designed to respond to the immediate emergency situation post-1990 are still to be found in force as of 2008, albeit with some degree of modification. In truth, where either of these issues have been addressed, it has been due to external impetus and expertise rather than any native resolve, which in true Balkan style is politically rather than socially motivated.

This is a salient problem for post-communist societies, which are trying to reshape policies in an unfolding context of aggravated political instability and social problems—with poverty being just one, and perhaps not the most immediately insistent, of the costs of transformations.

Women and Poverty in Albania

The Official Picture of Poverty

Taking its lead from external actors such as the World Bank and IMF, Albania has defined poverty in terms of both absolute dollar-a-day and relative definitions. Income poverty in Albania is high for the region, with strong geographic variance between north and south, and rural and urban areas. The economy remains largely agrarian, informal and remittance based, with emigration proxying for social mobility. Contrarily, the unit of operationalization for Social Assistance, the only direct anti-poverty policy, is officially set to be at household level. This may go some way to explaining why it has been very weak at its intended aim of poverty alleviation, exhibiting patchy coverage of the poor, and doing little to close the poverty gap. Indeed, pensions have been found to alleviate poverty more and remittances constitute a major informal safety net for those excluded from benefits, as well as driving the economy (cf Tairaj, 2007).

Given the data problem discussed previously, the number of Social Assistance recipients has effectively acted as an unofficial proxy headline indicator for poverty—encouraging government efforts to reduce recipients by more stringent targeting. Aside from the issue of data-cycling, or breathing one's own exhaust, this raises issues for the disaggregation of data for gendered analysis. Indeed, as regards gender issues, the status, experiences and visibility of women in Albania has been inadequately researched, little acknowledged and poorly understood.

In relation to poverty, the female experience has been as through a glass darkly. There has been increasing interest in women's issues in the country, as in the South Eastern European region more widely (Fodor, 2006; La Cava and Nanetti, 2000), spurred on by the interventions of some active International NGOs. Perhaps one can sense a whiff of the donor's agenda—of actors creating issues rather than responding to them (Tahiraj, 2007)—if not a wholesale import of gender to the "issue market" and the adoption of gender issues *en masse.* Still, such possible distortions should not detract, especially when society's default is to neglect or ignore gender issues.

The literature has offered, let us say, an inconclusive array of treatments and results. A few years ago data simply were not reflecting gendered differenced in poverty (Tahiraj, 2003, 2004), while recently, there seem to be an array of articles trying to deconstruct gender indicators, focusing on differences in regard to health and education or access to employment (Tahiraj, 2007, 2008).

Some studies and reports have stressed that poverty and gender bear little correlation that gender differences in poverty in Albania are not significant or not found a gender-link to poverty. Such studies have often been based on data on households in receipt of Economic Aid, which obviously leads to intrinsic sample bias. At variance with this, it has been acknowledged that women are a vulnerable group at risk of poverty (Galliano, 2001) or that a large segment of them have already fallen into the poverty trap (GA, 2003, 2004, 2006). The issue regarding these "snapshot" sporadic studies is how comparable those indicators are to enable use to argue for or against feminization of poverty.

Meanwhile, some of the limitations of the Albanian Census, last conducted in 2001, create difficulty in obtaining a more comprehensive picture. The problem directly impacts our inquiry. What can meaningfully be said if the data just is not established or credible enough to support conclusions about over-representation of women in poverty, let alone the feminization of poverty?

The gulf between what data suggests and how reality is when it comes to issues such as the feminization of poverty should become a driver for research into non-income dimensions of poverty—in terms of access to basic services, exclusion and rights—and an exploration of the differences in gender perspectives of reported or subjective poverty.

Women and Family

From a policy perspective another concern in investigating this issue in the current Albanian context is how to measure women's poverty when anti-poverty policies target the family as the atomic unit, rather than individuals within it. We could consider family-focused welfare policies to be agnostic to the variety of household compositions, including the way power is distributed. Such policies, perhaps optimistically, implicitly assume household income pooling and either an equal or fair share of them among members. From a feminist perspective, and here we may say this is realistic or pessimistic, the idea of a unitary household simply will not wash. Such coarse-grained policy approaches may simply reinforce extant gender divisions and inequalities. It is a commonplace that men and women in marriage have different access to resources and a different economic position, most often resulting in women enjoying less financial autonomy within the household economy (Pascall and Manning, 2000; Pascall, 1986).

The reasoning for operationalizing poverty efforts at household and not individual level is officially given as due to the importance of the family unit in the Albanian culture and tradition. However, in terms of eligibility, it is the male head, or the eldest male adult in their absence, who is able to claim for the household, and as well, is paid the benefit. Aside from the obvious chauvinism, what this reasoning fails to capture are the dynamic changes in the culture and social networks in the last ten years in Albania, which has wrought a weakening of traditional extended family ties. The family as well as other social networks has undergone a process of transition, which means an ongoing process of shaping and reshaping roles and responsibilities, which by and large has shifted the focus from extended families to nuclear families, with the later still in transformation.

Recent demographic shifts include deferred entry into marriage and increasing number of singletons, adopting a more western lifestyle. Internal and external migration has also tilted the ratio of women to men towards the latter. Knowledge of these kinds of lifestyle diversifications needs to be researched and passed onto policy practitioners. The financial dependency of women within marriage is increasingly manifested by the fact that some women have little or no income—particularly women whose husbands have migrated while women tend to stay at home and take care of the household.

These families with the breadwinner abroad tend to be poorer. In the meanwhile, the irregular nature of much migration means equally that women who have left may not enjoy the same rights abroad as if they had migrated formally. In such scenarios women's poverty within families remains hidden and the question of women's independent access to resources is considered important.

Historically, the institution of marriage was supposed to afford some protection from poverty for both women and men, as two people living together are less at risk of falling into poverty. This reasoning however fails to take into account the cost of unpaid or domestic work, in the form of foregone earnings. In Albania, the idea that housework is no work (Maynard, 1985) prevails and has made women's position in the family more difficult. Definitely, increased household and family responsibilities have tended to change women's and children's but not men's allocation of time between home, market production and leisure (King and Evenson, 1983; Gerson, 1993; Gupta, 1999; Hartmann, 2006).

Not surprising then that marriage is perhaps not quite the institution it once was even in Albania. Major demographic changes have occurred in the form of increasing rates of marital breakdown in the last decade or so from 8.6 percent in 1995 to 14.2 in 2004 (INSTAT, 2005) with an increase in the number women asking for divorce, In which case women are often left, economically and legally, in the middle of nowhere.

Women In and Out of Work

As the socialist system is thought to have encouraged the masculinization of women (Culi, 2000) one can argue that perhaps women were not happy taking on men's roles and working night shifts in socialist factories. Can we perhaps speculate by thinking that women choose to withdraw home? Communism achieved emancipation, "women benefited from good cash and kind services, with work-based child-care" (Munday, 1998: 5). But, was that what women wanted?

Equally, is the "familialization" of women today what they want? (Pascall and Manning, 2000) Are these results of a tacit acceptance, a choice, or an imposition? It is equally of importance to discuss the role of the Albanian women in the family and in the labor market and how each of these has influenced the other. Further investigation is required to find out whether their new position was taken because they were glad to leave the workplace and have less responsibilities, it was (passively) accepted, or suffered due to market re-orientation. At this stage we can only hypothesize, since only further research may equip us with the answers.

The sociological definition of family, as described by Maynard (1985) consists of a unit within which people make economic decisions about paid and unpaid work in the household and outside it. There are reasons, however, to explore the origins of these decisions—with the suspicion that they do not come as a result of mutual agreement, rather than as a trade-off between bad choices, or the only-option.

The changes and disruptions of transition along with the strong patriarchal tradition may well have left women in Albania with no choice but to "to agree" to also to take on informal work, as well as more unpaid work. It seems to be a universal that "mothers and wives are likely to be affected first by any rise in unemployment" (Titmuss, 1976: 103) and women were by far the largest constituency of those that lost jobs with quite some immediacy (Tushi, 1998). Without a shred of doubt, the end of state support for services such has childcare was a driver for women to leave the workplace in the industrial or service sphere (Tahiraj, 2008).

In reality, this was due to a combination of many factors. First, families' shaken income security and the privatization of childcare meant that families were no longer able to afford child-care. The inaccessibility and dubious quality of such care meant that families did not trust these institutions, or whatever was left of them. Undoubtedly, this has led to the repositioning of Albanian women in society, and a reorienting of women towards the family.

In response to the limitations resulting from the welfare approach to poverty, it has been suggested elsewhere to widen attentions beyond paid work, to consider unpaid work and welfare, and examine how welfare policies relate to these structures in labor market and family (Lewis, 1992a,b; 1997; Sainsbury 1994, 1996, 1999, 2000; Pascall and Manning 2000). However, liberal policies have had reverse effect on the repositioning and assisting women, as families headed by women are 35 times more likely to be poor than the average household (WB, 2002). Furthermore, available data show that women are paid less then men for the same job (INSTAT, 2001b, 2005).

But is work a panacea for escaping poverty? It may seem that the informal economy present predominantly in transition economies may have helped people in the short run cope with poverty, but has it on the other hand created a potential poverty time-bomb. In the absence of efficient social policies people have taken steps to escape poverty in every possible way—to mention just a few, illegal migration and informal employment.

Yet, little has been done to raise an alarm about the risks of informality, and especially its impact on women. The risk is that in the near future we will see a category of poor pensioners by default, the new old poor, because amid efforts to escape poverty all their life they did not contribute for their old age.

Concluding Discussion

There is an observed disparity between reported poverty and what the data show about poverty—in terms of quality and experience, as well as in severity and effect. It remains an issue that our conceptions of poverty are limiting the data that should make the raw material for better evidence-based policies, reducing the potential positive impacts of official and other efforts. In Albania, this issue affects women in particular, among all groups at risk of poverty.

Returning to the opening part of this paper, we argued why we need to know about poverty and feminization of poverty—because poverty means a degree of failure of our welfare state and social policies. Changes in the society might show their impact on the family structure, which themselves have had an impact on the women's position within and out of the family.

Research needs to more fully explore and understands the dynamics of transition and reflects them on the policy intervention by flexible programs according to the needs and policies and programs need to be redesigned to address gender needs more effectively. If I would try to answer the question whether women are getting worse in Albania, based on personal feeling and research, I would say yes undoubtedly. They are getting worse, at a time when also the family is weakening.

But, as a researcher I would stress that there is need for data and research on this field, from research utilizing multidimensional perspectives that will provide a clearer understanding of this gap between the data and people's perceptions.

Concluding, I stress that the status, experiences, and visibility of women in relation to poverty is inadequately researched, little acknowledged, and poorly understood. There is a need for more systematic and scientific studies of poverty, which allow for the recording and reporting of women's exposure to poverty. The existing great disparity between felt poverty and official poverty needs consideration by the scientific community. It is in this "gap" that research should be focused. Only then, can we interpret and argue based on accurate data whether there is a feminization of poverty happening.

A common understanding of this phenomenon should be achieved by both the community and officials too. Growing out of poverty is not only about income; it is about having the power and confidence to exercise and be represented. A good social policy is one that not only deals with today's short-term solutions, but one that distinguishes and prevents the negative trends. Ignoring these facts means ignoring all the factors that relate to poverty and its feminization and leading as it has happened to policies that deal with coping and survival rather than wider politics (cf Pascall and Manning, 2000; Shaffer, 1998).

While Albanian socialism visibly addressed gendered poverty by offering services to help women, such a policy was also a state recognition of the existence of feminization of poverty. Thus, the feminization of poverty, considered from the multidimensional perspective, perhaps did exist in communism, and intervention in the form of an exchange of services was most likely considered necessary in order to promote equality and increase productive outputs.

Such an approach did much to improve the status of women in the country. The recent reverse of this highlights clear gender divisions in all aspects of experiences and perception of poverty. Still, one has to acknowledge at least a somewhat depressing lesson here, that even communism with its strong control did not achieve deep societal change. Perhaps even less so can actual welfare policies effect lasting positive change in the institution that is the Albanian family. Perhaps we can surmise that it is the family, then, that will hold the power of change, indeed even welfare starts there—and one cannot yet herald the decay of the Albanian family as yet.

REFERENCES

Abrams, D.; Christian, J., and Gordon, D. (eds.) (2008), *Multi-Disciplinary Handbook of Social Exclusion Research*, Wiley: New York.

Allen, T. (1992), Economic Development and the Feminisation of Poverty, in N. Folbre *et al.* (eds.), *Issues in Contemporary Economics: Women's Work in the World Economy*, volume iv, Macmillan: London.

Atkinson, A.B. (1998), *Poverty in Europe*, Blackwell: Oxford, UK.

Bradshaw, J. (1999), The Nature of Poverty, in John Ditch (ed.) *Introduction to Social Security—Policies, Benefits, and Poverty*, Routledge: London.

Bradshaw, J. *et al.* (2000), *Poverty and Social Exclusion in Britain*, Joseph Rowntree Foundation: York, UK.

Cagatay, N. (1998), *Gender and Poverty: Social Development and Poverty Elimination*, division working paper, UNDP: New York.

Chambers, R. (1983), *Rural Development*, Longman Scientific and Technical: Essex, UK.

Chen, M.; Vanek, J.; Lund, F.; James H.; Jhabvala, R., and Bonner C. (2005), *Progress of the World's Women 2005: Women, Work, and Poverty*, UNIFEM, New York.

Coltrane, S. (1996), *Fatherhood, Housework, and Gender Equity,* Oxford University Press: New York.

Culi, D. (2000), *Essays on Albanian Women*, QG: Tirane.

Deem, R. (1988), *Work, Unemployment, and Leisure*, Routledge: London.

Doyal, L. and Gough, I. (1991), *A Theory of Human Need*, Macmillan: London.

Fodor, E. (2006), A Different Type of Gender Gap: How Women and Men Experience Poverty, *East European Politics & Societies, Vol. 20, No. 1, pp. 14-39.*

Fukuda-Parr, S. (1999), What Does Feminization of Poverty Mean? It Isn't Just Lack of Income, *Feminist Economics, Vol. 5, No. 2, 1, pp. 99-103.*

GA, Government of Albania (2003), *Poverty Reduction Strategy Paper Annual Progress Report*, IMF Country Report N0.03/164, IMF: Washington D.C.

GA, Government of Albania (2004) *Poverty Reduction Strategy Paper Annual Progress Report*, IMF Country Report N0.04/204, IMF: Washington D.C.

GA, Government of Albania (2006) *Poverty Reduction Strategy Paper Annual Progress Report*, IMF Country Report N0.06/23, IMF: Washington D.C.

Galliano, E. (2001), *Vulnerability Needs and Institutional Capacity Assessment.* Washington DC: WB.

Gerson, K. (1993), *No Man's Land: Men's Changing Commitment to Family and Work*, Basic: New York.

Glendinning, C. and Millar, J. (eds.) (1987), *Women and Poverty in Britain*, Wheatsheaf: Brighton, UK.

Gupta, S. (1999), The Effects of Transitions in Marital Status on Men's Performance of Housework, *Journal of Marriage and the Family*, Vol. 61, No. 3, pp. 700-11.

Hartmann, H.I. (2006), *Women, Work, and Poverty: Women Centered Research for Policy Change*, Routledge: London.

INSTAT, Statistics Institute (2001a), *Men and Women in Albania*, INSTAT: Tirane.

INSTAT, Statistics Institute (2001b), *Results of Household Living Conditions Survey*, INSTAT: Tirane.

INSTAT, Statistics Institute (2005), *Results of Household Living Conditions Survey*, INSTAT: Tirane.

King, E. and Evenson, R.E. (1983), Time Allocation and Home Production in Philippine Rural Households, in M. Buvinic and S.W. Yudelman (eds.), *Women and Poverty in the Third World*, Johns Hopkins University Press: Baltimore, MD.

Kingfisher, C. (1996), *Women in the American Welfare Trap*, University of Pennsylvania Press: Philadelphia, PA.

Kingfisher, C. (ed.) (2002), *Western Welfare in Decline, Globalization and Women's Poverty*, University of Pennsylvania Press: Philadelphia, PA.

Konopasek, Z. (1991), *Poverty and Social Income*, Research Institute of Labor and Social Affairs: Prague.

Konopasek, Z. (1992), Escape from State Socialism: Which Way?, in B. Deacon (ed.), *Social Policy, Social Justice and Citizenship in Eastern Europe*, Avebury: Aldershot, UK.

La Cava, G. and Nanetti, R. (2000), Albania: Filling the Vulnerability Gap, *technical paper*, No. 480, World Bank: Washington D.C.

Lewis, J. (1992a), *Women in Britain Since 1945*: Blackwell: Oxford, UK.

Lewis, J. (1992b), Gender and the Development of Welfare State Regimes, *Journal of European Social Policy*, Vol. 3, pp 159-73.

Lewis, J. (1997), Gender and Welfare Regimes: Further Thoughts, *Social Politics*, Vol. 4, No. 2, pp. 160-77.

Maslov, A. (1943), A Theory of Human Motivation, *Psychological Review, Vol.* 50, pp. 370-96.

Maynard, M. (1985), Houseworkers and Their Work, in R. Deem and G. Salaman (eds.) *Work, Culture, and Society*, Open Society Press: Milton Keynes, UK.

Millar, J. (2000), Gender, Poverty, and Social Exclusion, in F. Bimbi and E. Ruspini (eds.), Poverta delle Donne e Transformazione dei Raporti di Genere, *Inchiesta*, No. 128, April-June, pp. 9-13.

Moghadam, V. (1998), The Feminisation of Poverty and Womens Human Rights, *Brown Journal of World Affairs*, Vol. 5, No. 1, pp. 225-48.

Munday, B. (1998), The Old and the New: Changes in Social Care in Central and Eastern Europe, in B. Munday and G. Lane (eds.), *The Old and the New: Changes in Social Care in Central and Eastern Europe*, European Institute of Social Services, University of Kent at Canterbury: Kent, UK.

Nuccio, K.E. and Sands, R.G. (1992), Using Postmodern Feminist Theory to Deconstruct "Phallacies" of Poverty, *Affilia*, Vol. 7, No. 4, 26-48.

Parsons, T. and Bales, R.F. (1955), *Family, Socialization, and Interaction Process*, Free Press: New York.

Pascall, G. (1986), *Social Policy: A Feminist Analysis*, Tavistock: London.

Pascall, G. and Manning, N. (2000), Gender and Social Policy: Comparing Welfare States in Central and Eastern Europe and the Former Soviet Union, *Journal of European Social Policy*, Vol. 10, No. 3, pp. 240-66.

Pearce, D. (1978), The Feminization of Poverty: Women, Work and Welfare, *Urban and Social Change Review*, Vol. 11, 28-36.

Pressman, S. (2003), Feminist Explanations for the Feminization of Poverty, *working paper*, No. 351, Luxembourg Income Study.

Ray, L.J. (1996), *Social Theory and the Crisis of the State Socialism*, Edward Elgar: Cheltenham, UK.

Razavi, S. (1999), Gendered Poverty and Well-Being: Introduction, *Development and Change*, Vol. 30, No. 3, pp. 409-33.

Rodgers, G. and Van Der Hoeven, R. (eds.) (1995), *The Poverty Agenda: Trends and Policy Options*, International Labor Office: Geneva.

Room, G. (1995), *Beyond the Threshold: The Measurement and Analysis of Social Exclusion*, The Policy Press: Bristol, UK.

Sainsbury, D. (ed.) (1994), *Gendering Welfare States*, Sage: London.

Sainsbury, D. (1996), *Gender Equality and Welfare States,* Cambridge University Press: Cambridge, UK.

Sainsbury, Diane (1999), Gender, Policy Regimes, and Politics, in D. Sainsbury (ed.), *Gender and Welfare State Regimes*, Sage: London.

Sainsbury, Diane (ed.), (2000), *Gender and Welfare State Regimes*, Oxford University Press, Oxford, UK.

Sen, A. (1983), Poor Relatively Speaking, *Oxford Economic Papers*, Vol. 35, pp. 153-69.

Sentura, K. (1997), A Woman's Work Is Never Done: Women's Work and Pregnancy Outcome in Albania, *Medical Anthropology Quarterly*, Vol. 11, No. 3, pp. 375-95.

Shaffer, P. (1998), *Poverty Reduction Strategies*, United Nations: New York.

Smith, A. (1776), *An Inquiry Into the Nature and Causes of the Wealth of Nations*, Home University Library: London.

Spicker, P. (2007), *The Idea of Poverty*, Policy: Bristol, UK.

Tahiraj, E. (2003), Feminization of Poverty: The Case of Albania, *Journal of Societal and Social Policy*, Vol. 2, No. 3, pp. 35-51.

Tahiraj, E. (2004), Poverty a 3D Perspective, in H. Rusu *et al.* (eds.), *Globalisation, European Integration and Social Development in European Post-Communist Societies*, Psihomedia: Sibiu, Albania.

Tahiraj, E. (2007), *Poverty and Anti-Poverty in Albania: Social Policy in Transition and Consolidation,* University of York: New York.

Tahiraj, E. (2008), May My Wife Live Long: The Politics of Gender, in E. Gjermeni (ed.), *Gender and Social Change in Albania's Transition*, GADC & Cordaid: Tirane.

Titmuss, R.M. (1976), *Essays on the "Welfare State"* Allen and Unwin: London.

Tomes, I. (1998), *Social Reform in Countries of Central and Eastern Europe on the Eve of the 21st Century*, paper presented in Max Planck seminar, Ringberg, Germany.

Townsend, P. (1970), *The Concept of Poverty*, Heinemann: London.

Townsend, P. (1979), *Poverty in the United Kingdom*, Penguin: Harmondsworth, UK.

Townsend, P. (1993), *The International Analysis of Poverty*, Harvester Wheatsheaf: New York.

Tushi, G. (1998), Varferia si problem social dhe kompleks, *Politikat Sociale, Vol. 4.*

UN, United Nations (1995), *World Summit for Social Development,* Copenhagen, March 6-12.

UN, United Nations (1996), *Food Security for All: Food Security for Rural Women*, International Steering Committee on the Economic Advancement of Rural Women: Geneva, Switzerland.

UNDP, United Nations Development Program (1997), *Human Development Report,* UNDP: New York.

WB, World Bank (2002), *Poverty in Albania*, World Bank: Washington D.C.

WB, World Bank (2003), LSMS documents,*www.worldbank.org/lsms/country/ albania/al96docs.html.*

12

Gendering the Welfare State: The Issue of Carework Salaries in Germany

MICHAEL OPIELKA

Just a view decades ago, financial transfers for the work of childcare and child-raising in the private family sphere to be paid in the form of a parental wage or more generally a *"carework salary"* would have seemed quite unthinkable. Of course in the feminist discussion of the 1970s the introduction of "wages for housework" was proposed, but this proposal never reached the general social policy debate, and was very controversial in feminist circles, too (cf Leipert and Opielka, 1998). However, in recent decades the options in the social policy arena have changed considerably. The superficial reasons for this are above all the demographic upheavals in practically all, and especially West European, OECD states, who on the one hand increasingly cannot guarantee care for older persons in the "natural" way within the family, and on the other hand have increasingly allowed children to become a scarce resource, which presents problems above all for financing old-age security and health insurance programs.

That the "natural" reproduction process in families is diminishing has other, socio-cultural causes, above all in connection with change in the gender self-image. While women still do feel primarily responsible for family tasks, their educational and occupational background is increasingly comparable to that of men, which, in a subsequent and successful integration into the work world, clearly causes a situation of multiple obligations. As a response, women withdraw from family carework to a societally significant extent, by avoiding living with (and in-home care of) parents (and/or in-laws), and by practicing anti-conception. From the point of view of payment for family-internal carework, the two problem-complexes mentioned here should be of course kept apart. The care for the elderly is dependent on other social-policy preconditions and consequences than is at-home care for children.

In this study we are concentrating on the latter—the discussion surrounding the introduction of payment for childcare within the family. Therefore when referring in the following to family carework, we necessarily mean childcare. Further, the study concentrates on Germany and the discussion, which is being carried on there. This discussion would seem however—in spite of the unusual historical factors, as will be seen—generally, and perhaps because of the historical specificity, even paradigmatically relevant.

Recently, changes in work in the family and the related socio-political issues have climbed up both international policy and research agendas, as a series of comparative studies of European family policy has shown (cf e.g. Pfau-Effinger, 1999; Opielka, 2001; Carling *et al.*, 2002).

The question of how to improve the status and increase the value of work in the family in relation to work in market-based employment is being currently raised anew, either on specific family policies (Leipert, 1999); in comparative studies on family policy and the welfare state in industrialized countries (Gauthier, 1996), as well as in a European context (Fahey, 2002); or the "male breadwinner" model (Lewis, 2001, 2002; Ostner and Lewis, 1995, 1998; Pfau-Effinger, 1999; Gottfried and O'Reilly, 2002). From the more general perspective, the issue of political importance of public childcare has been raised by Waldvogel (2001), and the socio-philosophical aspect of family policy has been invested further by Krebs (2002).

The old dichotomy between the private and the societal is in a practical and theoretical crisis. That dichotomy viewed work in the family not as economically productive, but as reproductive activity, one of the many non-monetary requirements of the money economy—like peace, natural resources, or economically friendly ethics. The practical crisis is apparent above all in sinking birthrates and their dramatic demographic consequences. The theoretical crisis can be recognized therein, that the feminist criticism of traditional disregard for important carework performed mainly by women is now reaching the core of contemporary democratic and economic theory, and that the old, market-capitalistic dichotomy is being challenged by newer theories stressing role of the social capital created in and by the family.

The most important societal bridge between the family and the work world by the end of the 20th century has been social policy. Social policy since its beginnings has had above all the tasks of organizing the process of establishing the wage-value of all work in society as a political compromise between Capital, Labor, and societal groups (e.g., Churches). At the beginning of the 21st century, nothing essential has changed in that respect. But social policy, with its expenditure system accounting in most European societies for about one-third of the population's income, constitutes today a distinct societal sector, the Welfare State. Of course the relationship between the family and employment spheres never has been really unproblematic. But only with the politicization of social policy, and with the increasing thematicization of value relations—such as of women's rights by the women's movement—did family policy appear on the public agenda. And if the basis of the relation between family and employment is put into question—that historical dichotomy of the private and the societal, of reproduction and production—then that must necessarily have an effect on family policy. Thus the relationship between family and the occupational sphere is practically, theoretically, and politically under discussion.

In the following we concentrate on the political aspects of this relationship. To get a better overview, we shall proceed in two steps. First, we look back along the three historical way-stations of German social policy, which were unique in the world in their culminating effect:

(1) the motherhood cult of National Socialism, (2) the socialistic work-religion of East German society and the idyllic conservative family ideal of postwar West Germany, and (3) the modernization family policy in united Germany. Second, we examine the German family-policy situation one decade after reunification—in the context of a new orientation for the welfare state.

This leads finally to a position that requires a new historical compromise for social policy. Work in the sphere of employment and in that of the family both are to be treated as qualitative goals. The fundamental relationship between the family and the state and/or the societal is drafted anew with a greater emphasis on the state and/or the societal sphere. It is now more than ever before the responsibility of the state to provide for: (1) care for children and other care-dependent persons—by way of professionalization of all care services, (2) adequate coverage of living costs—by financial transfers for children and carers, and (3) regulation of the time available for family and occupational duties—by appropriate labor policies. Through this reshuffle the Welfare State itself is changed. It adds a new principle to the workings of the welfare state—that is, that of being a "guarantor," to the three existing social policy principles, which are the principles of social insurance, social assistance, and social care (i.e., "*Versorgung*").

This position has important societal implications. For, if such a reorientation of social policy in Germany were to succeed, the social capital of our society should be guarded. The social capital of our society, to be sure, must be constantly renewed through investment. For the most part, this depends on the regulation of the relationship between family and occupational work.

Germany: A Family Laboratory

The compatibility of family and occupation is of course problematic not only in Germany, but there it is especially so. That is due not least to historical reasons—as the particular German path of social and family policy, beginning with the Nazi regime and its image of the woman, leading to the two separate systems of the German Democratic Republic (GDR, East Germany) and the Federal Republic of Germany (FRG,

West Germany), and finally to Germany as a united country seeking since 1989 its place in international developments.

The Nazi Mutterpflicht ("Duty of Motherhood")

One reads often that the housewife marriage model in Germany first became dominant with the policies of the Nazi regime. Of course the objection to this is—so Birgit Pfau-Effinger in her lucid study on the cultural bases of women's employment in Europe—that the housewife marriage model already significantly earlier appeared in the center of gender arrangement (Pfau-Effinger, 2000: 114). And in fact since the second half of the 19th century all societal groups (not only) in Germany were in favor of the family model of the male breadwinner marriage. This model, initially a development of the urban bourgeoisie, was successively adapted by the workers' movement and the social democrats—at first in contradiction to fact, for in the working class the gainful employment of women was still necessary and usual in the 20th century up to the 1950s (cf Hausen, 1993).

"The first, best and her proper place has the women in the family," exclaimed Joseph Goebbels in his opening speech on the occasion of the exposition "The Women" in March 1933 (cited after Mühlfeld and Schönweiss, 1989: 61). Nevertheless, the family policy path of the Nazis led actually less to the exclusion of women from the occupational sphere, for although many of their policy measures sought to promote the full-time housewife, typical was rather this paradox: women were to be reinforced in their identity of housewife and mother, but also available for work outside the home, and at the same time their traditional legal position in marriage and family was destabilized. The regime's racist objectives subjected women to marriage adeptness tests and forced sterilizations, but above all reduced men to their reproductive function and promoted social and sexual irresponsibility on the part of fathers (cf Czarnowski, 1991). Marriage was made a state function; the private bourgeois model was rejected. Motherhood became a national and racist-ideological duty.

The occupational participation of women was—after initial campaigns against so-called "double earners"—massively promoted with the transformation to war material production from 1936 onwards; starting from 1937 only employed women could be given loans for purposes of establishing a household (cf Kolinsky, 1989). The success of these measures—including even obligatory registration and work from 1943 on—remained however limited.

The level of women's employment from the beginning to the end of the war rose but little, from 14.5 to 14.9 million. "The essential cause lay in the fact that women whose husbands were away in the war received special financial support. Many women as a result discontinued their employment—an unintentional effect of the measure" (Pfau-Effinger, 2000: 115).

From the Nazi family policy there remains however, for our purposes, one problem—the housewife model of marriage, and more generally, the recognition of mothers' (work) contribution was seen in the postwar Germany—and above all for many critical intellectuals there after 1968—as a product of fascist motherhood-ideology. This was historically false, and theoretically serious. For now, motherhood began to be politically suspect.

The German Democratic Republic: The Right to and
Duty of Employment

In the Soviet occupation zone, women's policies, under the influence of the Soviet military administration, were consciously and radically delimited from those of the Nazi regime. With reference to the Marxist traditions of the German workers' movement, a new image of the women was propagated, which—with repeated modifications—was to remain valid until the end of the German Democratic Republic, the *DDR* (cf Bast and Ostner, 1992). The "woman's question" as a social problem was held to be resolvable only with the abolition of private property. Gender equality was to be reached only when the woman could be freed from enslavement in the family and her economic dependence on the man, and integrated as an independent economic party into societal production.

Therefore first of all establishing the formal equality of women in the workplace had priority. The family was—in contract to the situation in the Western occupation zones—for the moment no topic for politics. The extensive legal-political abstinence with regard to the family meant however, that the *status quo* of women's responsibility for the family was not touched; their equality was to be reached by way of occupational participation, without consideration of their familial duties (Schäfgen, 2000: 93). From the beginning of the 1960s the policy of women's integration into employment was extended with a qualifications-offensive, which was complimented by the first social policy measures aimed at reducing the double burden of occupation and family (such as the "*housekeeping day,*" etc.).

Looking back, the first phases of women's policy in the Soviet zone and the German Democratic Republic, until around 1964, could be considered as "the most progressive in the sense of creating gender equality" (Schäfgen, 2000: 102). But the success of these policies remained modest. With the introduction of a new family codex (1965), and the seventh SED party Congress in 1967, the family itself became now the object of political intervention. Both marriage partners became legally responsible for child-raising and housework. In reality little changed. Time-budget analyses from the GDR (for the period 1974 to 1985) show a constantly lower participation of men in family tasks—the men's share of household work did rise in this period from 26.4 to 30.1 percent; in childcare and time devoted to children their part rose from 24.1 to 25.8 percent, but these results are probably statistical artifacts, since the work commitment of the men in absolute terms did not rise; only the women's share diminished slightly in these time-budget categories (cf Manz and Winkler, 1998: 198). The family-policy transformation in GDR politics was accused of being "double-bottomed"—for in reality, according to Ute Gerhard, not concerned primarily with gender equality also within the family, as much as with, above all, the exploitative functionalization of the family as institution and socializing mechanism of the socialist state (cf Gerhard, 1994).

With the drastic birthrate decline since the mid-1960s, and after the eighth SED party congress (1972), family policy, and the then newly introduced concept of social policy, were subject to population policy objectives having the urgent priority of influencing the reproductive function of the family. The core of the package of measures (constantly broadened up until the final days of the GDR) was firstly the progressive increase in financial transfers linked to family establishment and the birth of children, and secondly the extension of pregnancy and childbirth leaves, and flanking that, the improvement of the service and care system, which should enable women after giving birth to return to the occupational system. The overriding objective of GDR social policy was securing full-time female employment in order to respond—considering the chronic shortage of labor—to the threat of increasing female part-time work.

From 1976 a *"baby-care year"* was introduced for those with a second child, and other benefits were improved, to bring about an increase in birthrates. Fathers at first could take neither the baby-care year (this only from 1986) nor the housekeeping day. "The special privileges of employed women (shorter work periods, longer occupational interruptions) meant a new reassignment of women's duties to mothers" (Schäfgen, 2000: 109). Women came to be risk factors for management and consequently, discriminated in their careers. This contradiction between postulated gender equality and actual discrimination was answered by women (also) in the GDR with reduced reproduction. From the beginning of the 1980s the model of the *three-child family* was propagated with new intensity, from 1986 the baby-care year could already be taken with the first child, and after the birth of the third child this was extended to 18 months.

The GDR birthrate fell in the 1980s despite these measures from 1.94 (1980) to 1.57 (1989) (Wendt, 1997: 119), approaching the consistently still lower rates of West Germany. Remarkable however is that fact that the number of childless women in the GDR also continuously fell, so that more women were giving birth to fewer children. Children and marriage in the GDR were part of normal existence; the family played a central role. Wendt speaks of the "standardized family" and "standardized motherhood" in so far as other family models, besides the double-earner marriage, were discriminated against socially and legally. Family forms besides the nuclear one, such as cohabitation or single parenting, increased however also in the GDR, at least in the 1980s (cf Wendt, 1997: 148-49).

In sum, the GDR policy of combining family and occupation has been aptly described by Hildegard Nickel as "combination-arrangement." Double employment of the marriage partners was combined with state childcare; but the concept of the full labor market integration of women was bound to woman's primary responsibility for the household and childcare. In the new (i.e., eastern) FRG *Länder* (federal states) women are today still trying to live after this model (cf Pfau-Effinger, 2000: 128).

The Federal Republic of Germany: The Adenauer Era:
From Complementarity to Partnership

The policies of the Federal Republic of Germany, differently from the case of East Germany, approved openly the bourgeois family model of the housewife marriage, which since the beginning of the 20th century had been culturally at the core of the gender arrangement.

Now, in the 1950s, it was actually practiced on a wide scale, in West Germany, as in the United States. Not being employed was seen generally as an indicator of a housewife's position of prosperity and privilege (cf Kolinsky, 1989: 24). Eva Kolinsky points to the fact that it was in no way only an alliance of men that sent women back to the household. In the immediate postwar era, it were essentially women who had organized physical survival, developing thereby practical competence often equal or superior to that of returning men, psychologically damaged from the repeated discouragements of war. These women wanted, so Kolinsky, to find in a time of chaos and destruction an alternative world of "normality," the "dream of normality, stability, and personal status in the family world" (cf Kolinsky, 1989: 37). Besides, it was above all working-class women who had been employed in the war economy; for middle-class women the occupational system offered, neither during nor after the war, qualified employment. "Women lost in this way a great historical chance," wrote Birgit Pfau-Effinger (Pfau-Effinger, 2000: 119), because never had the number of women in the population been so high: they made up 70 percent of the electorate. But women in West Germany were neither represented in leading political positions, nor had political parties there any particular intentions of bringing about gender-equality. "Exclusion strategies effected by male actors in the employment system, and the cultural orientation of a greater part of women apparently contributed to preventing any possible change in the gender arrangement" (Pfau-Effinger, 2000: 119).

Later the family policies of Adenauer's Germany were concentrated on assuring the housewife marriage model (by the so-called *Ehegattensplitting*, "spouse splitting," in the income-tax system, child allowances, and protection rights for mothers, among other schemes), which however also included "minimal" part-time work, so that women—though with an awareness of themselves as housewives enjoying the material protection of the male breadwinner—could obtain a low supplemental income of their own. A family-centered life-span among young women and among housewives, as well as an ambivalent attitude towards paid work, was predominant in the 1950s and 1960s. For with the democratization and liberalization of West-German society above all after 1968, and the appearance of a new women's movement, many women saw the possibility of their emancipation only in paid employment. But they were afraid of not being able to compete with men in that "outside world."

This has clearly changed as a consequence of the great expansion in educational opportunities since the beginning of the 1970s. For the daughters of the 1980s-and-1990s generation, employment history forms the core of their projected biographies. Pfau-Effinger (2000) explains this change in orientation of West German women *vis-à-vis* employment above all by the fact that on the cultural level there was a deepening of the contradiction between generally more civil liberty on the one hand, and traditional patterns of inequality in marriage on the other. Also, the values of foresight, sacrifice, and selflessness connected with the housewife role, lost more and more significance in times of individualization and hedonism. The decisive turning-point came in the 1970s, as those women who devoted themselves fully to their family were now—in a time when individuals were classified according to their position in the occupational hierarchy—disqualified as "non-working" (cf Pfau-Effinger, 2000: 21). Further reasons, for the value transformation for women in the relation family/work are to be found in the fragility of lifelong marriage agreements, in higher levels of prosperity and consumption standards and, because of educational expansion, in the new access of women to high-qualification occupation. Finally, of considerable importance was also the growth of the service sector in recent decades, by which employment opportunities for women in particular have increased.

Official family policy in the FRG—especially during the Social Democratic-Social Liberal coalition years (1969 to 1982)—reacted ambivalently to the new social and cultural change. On the one hand for example marriage laws were reformed with the objective of achieving partner equality, in the same manner that the Social Democratic Party (SPD) generally considered social reality to be formable by legislation.

Then again, women's employment was not only promoted (by occupational training, student allowances, etc.), but also problematized. The federal government declared in its second Report on the Family (1974) considerable "socialization disturbances" in the family, the causes of which were also claimed to have been found in the "regrettable increase in employment among married women." The SPD discussed (1979) the introduction of a financial allowance for child-raising, which was very controversial in the women's movement—while some saw in a "wage for housework" a codification of patriarchal dependency, others saw in the idea an overdue recognition of the societally essential work of mothers and housewives (cf Schäfgen, 2000: 80-81).

With the Christian Democratic-Social Liberal coalition from 1982 followed a rhetorical change of course, which, unlike in the former coalition, aimed less at promoting the division of family work among marriage-partners, as much as at emphasizing family values; and this new course was no longer directed at the objective of equal rights for partners (also to employment), but—beneath the slogan of a "new partnership between women and men" at the 33rd CDU National Party Congress (1985)—only at the equal valuation of housework and work outside the home. In 1986, federal legislation (at about the same time of similar regulations in the GDR) on child-raising leaves and allowances followed, whereby the initial payments were so low (and also not statistically adjusted to the rise of wages and living costs) that they were claimed almost only by women. It is worth noting that these reforms, as well as the introduction of the legal right to kindergarten care ten years later as part of a reform of youth-assistance laws, can also be interpreted as (family-)political compensation for simultaneous changes in the abortion law (Criminal Law, Art. 218).

In spite of the plausible feminist criticism of—relatively conservative European terms—FRG policies on the relation family/occupation, those policies do not seem to have been actually so far amiss of people's needs, at least in the longer term. Characteristic for West-German women was namely—and still in the 1990s—a dual-career arrangement based on reduced working-hours. In an opinion poll in 1996, 46 percent of women preferred being mothers and part-time employed, and 33 percent wanted to be exclusively housewife and mother; the latter were older-generation women. Only 8 percent of West-German women wanted to be full-time employed mothers, and only 9 percent states they would like to become or continue to be childless career-women (cf Pfau-Effinger, 2000: 126).

These attitudes are in no way unrealistic, as West-German men—similar to their East-German counterparts—have only to a very limited extent increased their attention to children and especially childcare. In the public debate, especially among the male leaders of all parties—in Germany, and if we may extend this observation, all around the world—the problem of compatibility of family and occupation is above all seen as problem of mothers, not for men.

It is certain that their partners' participation in housework and childcare is important to many women, and that this is often a source of conflict in households. At the same time, however, the male norm of full-time work, the role of the male "breadwinner" in the provider marriage, and the model of "one-and-a-half occupations" in the phase of active parenthood, are apparently also practically un-questioned by women of the youngest generation. "One could," writes Pfau-Effinger, "tendentiously call the basic idea 'gender equality in the difference' within the male-provider marriage: Many women want to be able to pursue female-specific objectives in their lifetimes, e.g. a family phase, with elements of private motherhood, without being societally disadvantaged vis-à-vis men for that reason" (Pfau-Effinger, 2000: 128; cf also Opielka and Ostner, 1987).

Following 1989: Joining the Modern Europe

At first, with German reunification, the gender-political difference between the East and the West collided. Even now the orientations of women in the "old" and "new" federal states (Länder) differ with regard to full-time employment, although they do show a certain convergence in the direction of Western models, after the principle of "equality with difference." As we have seen, this convergence can be based on the situation of necessity, which also in the GDR played a great role—even if this was ideologically resented.

One could describe the situation, simplified, as follows: in the main, women want children, and so do men. Since children cause work, the question arises, who is going to do it. In the western *Länder* much more than half of women do not see any solution in a professionalization and institutionalization of childcare for the first three years of life; in the East this percentage is notably lower.

But even with a high level of childcare professionalization, a lot of work, and the necessity of being present and ready, remains, especially with small children. Who is to make this investment of time, and when? Men do not want to change very much their occupational behavior, and women also support this. Thus, work in the family remains for the women to do.

Certainly, this is a simplified description, but it is supported by empirical findings—that is, in the vast majority of families the responsibility for the housework, by common consent, seems to lie with the women, while the participation of men in the household is interpreted as a helping role (Kaufmann, 1995: 127).

This is actually not only the case in reunified Germany, but also in other countries, and even in Scandinavia, which is seen to be more advanced in the issue of gender equality. Men there consider their participation in the household as "voluntary help," their "demonstration of love," whereby this is "highly dependent on the emotional stability of the partnership relation" (Kaufmann, 1995: 127).

Table 12.1: Typology of Family Models and Policies in Germany

Model	Wife	Husband	Family policy	Gender arrangement	Historical dominance in Germany
Natalism	mother	patriarchy	demographic orientation/ selectivity	difference	Nazi period (1933-1945)
Double breadwinner marriage	full-time employment + mother	full-time employment + father in free time	public childcare + promotion of women	equality	GDR (East Germany)
Male breadwinner	housewife + mother + low-level employment	family provider, moderately patriarchal	marriage- and provider-centered	moderate difference	FRG (West Germany, until 1990)
Partnership-based family	compatibility of family and occupation		public childcare + "childcare salary"	sharing participation	now

Furthermore, men show more verbal commitment to housework and child-raising than by their behavior. This indicates a certain inconsistency between con-sciousness and deed, but also surely some important objective obstacles. Namely, the longer the female partner has held the main paid position in the family—though the partners may be similarly qualified—the more the husband is apt to be motivated to do housework.

What makes the initial family-policy situation in the "new" Germany so interesting is the historical succession of the Nazi motherhood ideology, and then the postwar split into an "equality ideology" in the East and a "difference ideology" in the West, and at last united Germany that is joining modern Europe (cf Table 12.1). That is true at least for the cultural leitmotifs, but not necessarily for what concerns the family-policy instruments. For Germany in this regard is one of the rather unprogressive European countries, the attitude of its state (here with the 5th Report on the Family) and society towards the family can be described, in the words of Kaufmann, as one of "structural disregard for the family" (Kaufmann, 1995: 169-71).

Political Parties Between the Issues of Women's Employment and Childcare Allowances

Family policy, after a long time of leading a marginal existence, seems to have revitalized, which is the case not only in Germany. In other (Western) countries too the family has become a political problem (cf Gauthier, 1996; Ringen, 1997). In the United States, for example, it has been recognized that the situation of American children, and with them the future of the whole society, is endangered especially today (cf Kamerman, 1998), and that the United States in the past has spent much too little on childcare. Jane Waldvogel (2001) recapitulates a comparison of American and some European family policies by stating that the US should (1) introduce a paid general child-raising leave of at least 10 months; (2) more intensively support parents in financing childcare; and (3) improve the quality of childcare. In Germany, one would smile at such proposals as these. But if from Germany one takes a look at its European neighbors, the smile of superiority quickly fades. Other countries, most of all the Scandinavian countries and France, but also the Benelux states, offered significantly more support for young families in all or some areas (cf BMFSFJ, 1998). Therefore, it is not strange that the German political parties—certainly encouraged by a number of far-reaching decisions by the German Constitutional Court—have meanwhile launched a kind of contest for the best family policy.

The historical look back on the total German experience in the matter of family shows that even with wide acceptance of the middle-class family model since the beginning of the 20th century, the "gender system of work was considered generally extremely precarious and unstable" (Hausen, 2000: 350)—the topic of women's employment in continually new variations appeared on the political agenda, and time and again the attempt was made to orientate young women to the "natural" occupation of being a mother. The compatibility of family and occupation remained, wrote Karin Hausen, a "woman's dilemma. Since the 1980s, this dilemma has "appeared in newer packaging, as, in the face of the increasing occupational orientation of women, programs supporting the family were not imposed as family or men's, but rather women's, promotion programs" (Hausen, 2000; cf also Ostner and Lewis, 1998).

This appears to be changing since the beginning of the 21st century. In wide-ranging program papers the two large German parties, the Social Democratic Party (SPD) and the Christian Democratic Union (CDU), have made an effort to address the issue of the family. It is worthwhile to examine their positions more closely, because they define the actual dilemmas and in part come up with basically differing answers. The Green Party, which currently participates in a government coalition with the Social Democrats, above all did not, so far, develop a family policy concept that could be characterized as a sincere effort to overcome the historical and structural problems mentioned. It has, on the other hand, proposed that "family tasks should be shared equally between men and women," made possible by a "part-time work culture," and "free" kindergartens and other child-care facilities, and "comprehensive" all-day schools (cf Bündnis90/Die Grünen, 2001: 19).

The SPD: Compatibility Through Employment Integration

Much more intensive and professional has been the work on family policy by the two larger parties. Of them, the SPD had the greater remedial need in this area. In the past, no particular expertise was ascribed to this party in the area of family policy. For decades, it discussed the topic of family only under the heading of women's issues. It was thanks to the initiative of SPD alternate Chairholder Renate Schmidt that this situation changed. She initiated a party commission, which, immediately after the party's accession to power in 1998 and under the general watchwords "Future of the Family and Social Cohesion" and "Forum on the Family," was to formulate basic questions on a revaluation of the family, also by obtaining the opinions of party-bound academic specialists and representatives of organizations (cf SPD-Projektgruppe, 2000).

In a wide-ranging document presented at the SPD Party Congress in Nuremberg in 2001 a new orientation for family policy was proposed. In it, the departure from all feminist anti-family overtones is remarkable;

instead, there is the realistic formulation: Family, in the classical form of the nuclear family, i.e., an adult couple with biological children, has revealed itself more stable than suspected divorce and separation occur largely in childless couples. At the same time, the SPD complains the increasing division of society into family and non-family sectors (cf SPD-Parteivorstand, 2001: 4). The party concludes further that the desire for children and its realization often do not coincide, which is due to the unsolved incompatibility of family and occupation.

Above all two packages are suggested: (1) all-day supervision infrastructure for children of all age-groups, and (2) the further development of a recompensatory scheme for work in the family, in the direction of a change in the child-raising allowance, such that for one year it can function as a salary replacement (cf SPD-Parteivorstand, 2001: 13). The hope here is that fathers will become engaged more intensively in the care of small children, since fathers "today, because they earn more than mothers, and want to provide for their families' economic security, largely forego this opportunity" (SPD-Parteivorstand, 2001: 16). But, even with equal incomes, it has been found, that men and women tend to stick to the traditional gender arrangement, which speaks for deeply anchored cultural norms (cf Vaskovics and Rost, 1999).

It is noticeable that both instruments—all-day child supervision and parenting allowance as salary replacement—have been taken from the Scandinavian as well as the GDR family-policy models. Their main idea is "gender equality." But because men are not assuming female modes of life but very slowly, the solution to the problem is in the societalization of family tasks, while assuring the continuity of the occupational progress of women (even though modeled after that of men). In contrast to the GDR, the SPD (meanwhile) has approved part-time work solutions and flexible work-hours, thus joining ranks with Scandinavian countries already experienced in such family policies in the 1990s. This experience shows that male behavior patterns hardly change, or at best extremely slowly. Thus the "compatibility of family and occupation" in the SPD party program will also remain, for the moment anyway, a project for mothers, which nevertheless should expect signifycantly more societal support.

It needs to note that the Christian Democratic/Social Liberal coalition in the 1990s already undertook steps more decisively in the direction of an individualization of claims to family-policy benefits, and with that, a greater independence of mothers from male providers (by e.g. including child-raising leaves in public pension insurance, etc.). As a matter of fact, a transformation of the traditional, male-breadwinner "gender arrangement" has already taken place, and this not only in Germany, but also in other welfare states whose policies were based on the housewife model (cf Pfau-Effinger, 2001). The "Red/Green" coalition has, since 1998, in particular with the Parent-Leave Law (in application from the beginning of 2001) undertaken further steps towards a "cultural modernization of the male breadwinner model," such that: (1) parenting leaves and child-raising allowance claims can be delayed until the end of the child's eighth year; (2) fathers and mothers can take parenting leave simultaneously; but above all (3) a parent is conceded the legal right to switch to part-time work, at least in firms with more than 15 employees. Parenthood is taken thus a step further out of the exclusively private sphere and into the context of societal responsibility.

Taking up the terminology of Pfau-Effinger (2001), the SPD program can be defined as the "double breadwinner model with state childcare," for decades the dominant family and gender-policy model in Scandinavia and France. The SPD demand for the abolition of the German tax splitting model for spouses and an extension of all-day supervision facilities for children also fits in along this path of development. The increase of the child allowance to a level covering minimum needs has on the other hand has its political source in the wish to redistribute wealth in order to bring about social justice. Actually the SPD is attempting with this to achieve a kind of guaranteed basic income for children, which does not conflict with the party's central emphasis on employment, as would a guaranteed income for persons of working age. The SPD remains thus true to its historical roots: "*A citizen becomes a citizen by gainful employment, and that applies also to women.*" With regard to the obvious dilemma of women that employment and family tasks become a double burden, making the expectation of a full occupational career realistic only be renouncing on reproduction, the SPD tries to resolve by broadening public child supervision and fatherhood campaigns, in which fathers are encouraged to do voluntarily more work in the family.

The CDU: Compatibility Through Family Allowance

With the loss of its long-held governing position in 1998, there was created also in the CDU some "mental breathing space," in which it could examine its ideological assumptions anew for their basis in reality. In family policy this means above all recognizing the plurality of forms of family life, but also accepting this as a practically unalternable political fact. While the SPD program begins with the presumption of the "normality" of the nuclear family, the point of systematic revision for the CDU lies in the liberal realization of "non-normality."

The CDU also sees the compatibility of family and occupation as the "key question" in assessing the child-friendliness of a society. Their strategy for solving this question differs however significantly from that of the SPD. In order to understand the difference, it is worth looking at the CDU's own diagnosis: "The desired family-life model today is, for the majority, the simultaneous occupational activity of both parents. There are however still many women who wish to devote themselves exclusively to the family and child-raising. This must also in the future remain possible; the CDU stands for the principle of freedom of choice" (cf CDU Bundesvorstand, 2001: 39).

While the SPD demands an "all-day infrastructure" for the supervision of children, the analog CDU proposal of "need-based construction of all-day schools" (CDU Bundestagsfraktion, 2001: 7) sounds more restrained, though in essence, similar. The difference is to be found in the monetary transfer system for families ("Familienlastenausgleich"). While the SPD—with the argument of women's integration into employment and encouraging less occupational work by fathers—is betting on combination of employment and transfer system, the CDU wants to replace the existing "child allowance" and "child-raising allowance" with a "family allowance," which will be tax- and social contribution-free and—remarkably—unaffected by the extent of other employment and/or level of income. The amount quoted for this allowance is a sum of ca. 613 Euro per month for each child under three years, ca. 307 Euro for each child between 3 and 17, and ca. 154 Euro for older children while still attending school (CDU Bundestagsfraktion, 2001; CDU Bundesvorstand, 2001: 41-43). At the same time, as a broadening of the existence system, a "time account" for "family time" of three years with the first eight years of a child's life has been suggested, and it can be extended to 3 1/2 years as an incentive for fathers, if both partners share the family time.

The costs of such a measure are naturally considerable. The CDU parliamentary group has calculated that good 25 billion Euro extra will have to be spent yearly. The level of financing to be necessary is expected to be relatively low, due to employment and growth effects (cf Werding, 2001). In an accompanying strategy paper of the CDU parliamentary group, the family allowance ("Familiengeld") is discussed in the context of an employment-promoting policy (cf Koch, 2002). This leads to the emergence of an interesting logic, which permits the family allowance to be understood as something other than a usual "financial transfer." We can see here a new concept of a politically directed revaluation of societal work. That is to say, the family allowance should not be considered recompensation for lost wages (in line with the *social insurance principle*), nor as a welfare benefit linked to need (as it is the case with the *social assistance principle*). The social policy logic raised here follows the *principle of care* ("Versorgung") on the basis of special status. One could go so far as to see, in the idea of the family allowance, something like the nucleus of a "guaranteed basic income" for child-raising persons and, later, for children and youth in line with a new *guarantee principle* (Opielka, 2000a; Opielka, 2006; cf Vobruba, 2007).

The Family as Social Capital: Investment in the Future

Social policy is, more than most other policy areas, the art of compromise. The comparison of the family-policy programs of both popular parties reveals, in great part, similar and (while disregarding social- and cultural-related references) even identical ideas. Even the essence of the differences allows compromise to appear conceivable, also since the

SPD proposal of 2001 still needs to be incorporated into a new party program.

Our introductory considerations concerned the relation of the value of work in various societal spheres; here, of the work in the family vis-à-vis work in the market-centered occupational system. While for decades a positive revaluation of family work was ultimately only politically deflected, primarily by means of maintenance arrangements between the spouses, and negotiated as a women's problem, now a basic reassessment of family work seems at least to be on the horizon (cf Netzler and Opielka, 1998; Leipert, 2001; Krebs, 2002). This reassessment has become necessary, among other things, as a result of (1) the increased attention of society, and (2) the need for maintaining our "social capital"—which includes common bonds, values, norms, and institutions (cf Putnam, 2000), as discussed in the 5th Family Report of the FRG as "*human capital*" or "*human potential.*" The family plays an absolutely central role in the formation of social and human capital. Kaufmann (1995: 75) argues that it is realistic to assume that the total value of housework not calculated in studies on the social product makes up more than half of the social product. Since the recognition of the value of work done in the family is now empirically well founded, politics need to be asked at once to formulate suitable institutional structures.

A policy that aims at a real compatibility of family and occupational life, while respecting the legal equality of man and woman, will need to transpose more than ever before the transactional relationship between the private economic sphere, the state or public sphere, and the family; by (1) the supervision of small children and others needy of care by means of occupationalization or professionalization; (2) the financial assurance of living costs coverage by state-guaranteed transfers of money for children and carers; and (3) the surveillance of the compatibility of family and occupational duties by labor policy and labor laws. One can see that this process is already long underway. It has proved itself in the long run.

The fact that the present institutions of the gender arrangement and the compatibility of family and job are ineffective is being fortunately increasingly realized. At risk are, in fact, the foundations of modern society and its population, its people. The current acceleration of European integration and globalization of goods, labor, and social markets is destroying precisely social capital. It needs to be clear, the economic virtues of ability to confirm flexibility and mobility, on which our economic prosperity is based, are diametrically opposed to the virtues important to the founding of families and to the objectives of planning, security, and foresight in the personal biography, because they make difficult long-term bonds to people, and often completely exclude the usually life-long responsibility for one's life partner and children (Birg, 2001). What follows is a decline in births, the societal effects of which are indeed dramatic. Social security contributions will rise, and health and care costs will expand, which will necessarily increase wage costs per product and thus diminish the competitiveness of the national economy. The horror scenario of the consequences of climate change, so Birg (2001), is harmless in comparison to the threat of cultural and social desertification of our society owing to this drastic decline in birth-rates.

The solution to the population problem through immigration, propagated by many politicians and serious scientists, does not seem realistic. A certain influx of people from totally foreign culture groups of course enriches and revitalizes any society. But an immigration rate of 700,000 to 1 million people per year, which—assuming a constant birthrate of the native population—would be necessary to stabilize the German population (Kaufmann, 1997: 74), would mean the downfall of any government.

The rise of populist right-wing parties in the traditional welfare states of Scandinavia, which for long had been social democratic strongholds, shows a problem that cannot be reduced to a lack of liberality. The import of a labor force of social security payers can also, without a doubt, be interpreted as a particularly subtle form of neo-colonialism. Instead of taking care of the social capital already present, and investing in people, those proposing the import of people would parasitically exploit the social capital of other societies.

The fact that foreign citizens are more than twice as much unemployed, and more than three times as often receivers of social welfare benefits than the local population, indicates an existing, huge integration problem. And it should be first solved before further, politically conceived waves of immigration are induced, beyond the immigration of EU-citizens, East-European Jews, family members abroad, as well as civil war refugees and asylum-seekers that is already occurring, especially in Germany (cf Laer, 2001).

The compatibility of family and occupation shows itself therefore in socio-political perspective to be an issue that cannot be addressed by means of past solutions. It requires a fundamental broadening of the social policy program, a transformation of the employment-centered welfare state, and recognition of work in the family as societal work.

Carework Salary as Guaranteed Minimum Income?

In the preceding discussion of the introduction of a child-raising salary (or family allowance) there is almost no mention of the proposal of a guaranteed minimum income (cf Vobruba, 2007; Raventos, 2007; Opielka, 2006, Ackerman *et al.*, 2006; McKay, 2005; Fitzpatrick, 1999).

This has to do with the different spheres within which the discussion takes place. The family-policy debate has been—at least until now—carried on among experts, and only recently widened to include principal sociopolitical questions implicit in the considerable public echo in Germany following the OECD comparative educational study "PISA 2000," as well as in the undesirable demographic developments that are for the first time publicly associated with deficiencies in family policy (cf Opielka, 2000a,b).

The discussion over a guaranteed minimum income in Germany on the other hand has been stimulated especially by the labor market and tax policy considerations (negative income tax, combination wages for low-income earners), and is still highly controversial. Clearly a child-raising salary—depending on its actual form—has the same effect as a selective basic guaranteed income, limited to persons who raise children. The German welfare state is particularly wage-for-work-oriented. The introduction of *carework salaries* in the form of a *child-raising salary* or *family salary* would widen this orientation, establishing a new way of earning a living for persons raising children.

One can thoroughly see in this a step in the direction of a universal citizen-based family policy, the legitimacy of which will be the precondition to a general, freely available basic guaranteed income. To that extent, the new family-policy orientation in Germany (cf Opielka, 2000a, 2002; Leipert, 1999), together with similar developments in other European states such as e.g. France and Norway, may lead the way to the possible introduction of new guaranteed basic income models.

REFERENCES

Ackerman, B.; Alstott, A., and van Paris, P. (2006), *Redesigning Distribution: Basic Income and Stakeholder Grants as Cornerstones for an Egalitarian Capitalism*, Verso: London.

Bast, K. and Ostner, I. (1992), *Ehe und Familie in der Sozialpolitik der DDR und BRD—Ein Vergleich,* in W. Schmähl (ed.), *Sozialpolitik im Prozeß der deutschen Vereinigung*, Campus: Frankfurt a.M., Germany.

Birg, H. (2001), *Die demographische Zeitenwende: Der Bevölkerungsrückgang in Deutschland und Europa*, Beck: Munich, Germany.

BMFSFJ, Bundesministerium für Familie, Senioren, Frauen, und Jugend (ed.) (1998), *Übersicht über die gesetzlichen Maßnahmen in den EU-Ländern bei der Erziehung von Kleinkindern*, Kohlhammer: Stuttgart, Germany.

Bündnis90/Die Grünen (2001), *Diskussionspapiere für ein neues Grundsatzprogramm*, Bündnis90/Die Grünen: Berlin.

Carling, A.; Duncan, S., and Edwards, R. (2002), *Analysing Families, Morality, and Rationality in Policy and Practice*, Routledge: London.

Czarnowski, G. (1991), *Das kontrollierte Paar: Ehe und Sexualpolitik im Nationalsozialismus*, Beltz: Basel, Switzerland.

CDU/CSU Bundestagsfraktion (2001), *Faire Politik für Familien: Eckpunkte einer neuen Politik für Familien, Eltern und Kinder*, CDU: Berlin.

CDU Bundesvorstand (2001), *Freie Menschen, Starkes Land: Antrag des Bundesvorstands auf dem Dresdner Parteitag im Dezember 2001*, CDU: Berlin.

Fahey, T. (2002), The Family Economy in the Development of Welfare Regimes: A Case Study, *European Sociological Review*, Vol. 18, pp. 51-64.

Fitzpatrick, T. (1999), *Freedom and Security: An Introduction to the Basic Income Debate*, Palgrave Macmillan: London.

Gauthier, A.H. (1996), *The State and the Family: A Comparative Analysis of Family Policies in Industrialized Countries*, Clarendon Press: Oxford, UK.

Gerhard, U. (1994), *Die staatlich institutionalisierte "Lösung" der Frauenfrage: Zur Geschichte der Geschlechterverhältnisse in der DDR*, in H.

Kaelble *et al.* (eds.), *Sozialgeschichte der DDR*, Klett-Cotta: Stuttgart, Germany.

Gottfried, H. and O'Reilly, J. (2002), Regulating Breadwinner Models in Socially Conservative Welfare Systems: Comparing Germany and Japan, *Social Politics*, Vol. 9, No. 1, pp. 29-59.

Hausen, K. (ed.) (1993), *Geschlechterhierarchie und Arbeitsteilung: Zur Geschichte ungleicher Erwerbschancen von Männern und Frauen*, Vandenhoeck: Göttingen, Germany.

Hausen, K. (2000), *Arbeit und Geschlecht*, in J. Kocka and C. Offe (eds.), *Geschichte und Zukunft der Arbeit*, Campus: Frankfurt a.M., Germany.

Kamerman, S.B. (1998), *Does Global Retrenchment and Restructuring Doom the Children's Cause?*, lecture given at Columbia University, New York.

Kaufmann, F.-X. (1995), *Zukunft der Familie im vereinten Deutschland*, Beck: Munich, Germany.

Kaufmann, F.-X. (1997), *Herausforderungen des Sozialstaats*, Suhrkamp: Frankfurt a.M., Germany.

Koch, R. (2002), Familienförderung ist die beste Wirtschaftsförderung, *Soziale Ordnung*, Vol. 1, pp. 12-17.

Kolinsky, E. (1989), *Women in West Germany: Life, Work, and Politics*, Berg: Oxford, UK.

Krebs, A. (2002), *Arbeit und Liebe: Die philosophischen Grundlagen sozialer Gerechtigkeit*, Suhrkamp: Frankfurt a.M., Germany.

Laer, H.v. (2001), *Deutschland, Einwanderungsland: Das Denken in Quantitäten führt in die Irre, Frankfurter Allgemeine Zeitung*, No. 280.

Leipert, C. (ed.) (1999), *Aufwertung der Erziehungsarbeit: Europäische Perspektiven einer Strukturreform der Familien- und Gesellschaftspolitik*, Leske and Budrich: Opladen, Germany.

Leipert, C. (2001), *Familie als Beruf: Arbeitsfeld der Zukunft*, Leske and Budrich: Opladen, Germany.

Leipert, C. and Opielka, M. (1998), *Erziehungsgehalt 2000: Ein Weg zur Aufwertung der Erziehungsarbeit*, Institut für Sozialökologie: Bonn, Germany.

Lewis, J. (2001), The Decline of the Male Breadwinner Model: Implications for Work and Care, *Social Politics*, Vol. 8, No. 2, pp. 152-69.

Lewis, J. (2002), Individualisation, Assumptions About the Existence of an Adult Worker Model and the Shift Towards Contractualism, in A. Carling *et al.* (eds.), *Analysing Families, Morality, and Rationality in Policy and Practice*, Routledge: London.

Manz, G. and Winkler, G. (eds.) (1988), *Sozialpolitik*, Verlag die Wirtschaft: Berlin.

McKay, A. (2005), *The Future of Social Security Policy: Women, Work and a Citizens' Basic Income*, Routledge: London.

Mühlfeld, C. and Schönweiss, F. (1989), *Nationalsozialistische Familienpolitik*, Enke: Stuttgart, Germany.

Netzler, A. and Opielka, M. (eds.) (1998), *Neubewertung der Familienarbeit in der Sozialpolitik*, Leske and Budrich: Opladen, Germany.

Opielka, M. (2000a), Grundeinkommenspolitik, Pragmatische Schritte einer evolutionären Reform, *Zeitschrift für Gemeinwirtschaft*, Vol. 38, No. 3-4, pp. 43-59.

Opielka, M. (2000b), Das Konzept Erziehungsgeld 2000, *Aus Politik und Zeitgeschichte*, Vol. 3-4, pp. 13-20.

Opielka, M. (2001), Familie and Familienpolitik, in F.-M. Konrad (ed.), *Kindheit und Familie: Beiträge aus interdisziplinärer und kulturvergleichender Sicht*, Waxmann: Münster, Germany.

Opielka, M. (2002), Zur sozialpolitischen Theorie der Bürgergesellschaft, *Zeitschrift für Sozialreform*, Vol. 5, No. 48, pp. 563-85.

Opielka, M. (2006), *Gemeinschaft in Gesellschaft*, VS: Wiesbaden, Germany.

Opielka, M. and Ostner, I. (1987), Umbau des Sozialstaats?, in M. Opielka and I. Ostner (eds.), *Umbau des Sozialstaats*, Klartext: Essen, Germany.

Ostner, I. and Lewis, J. (1995), Gender and the Evolution of European Social Policies, in S. Leibfried and P. Pierson (eds.), *European Social Policy: Between Fragmentation and Integration*, Brookings Institution: Washington D.C.

Ostner, I. and Lewis, J. (1998), Geschlechterpolitik zwischen europäischer und nationalstaatlicher Regelung, in S. Leibfried and P. Pierson (eds.), *Standort Europa: Europäische Sozialpolitik*, Suhrkamp: Frankfurt a.M., Germany.

Pfau-Effinger, B. (1999), Change of Family Policies in the Socio-Cultural Context of European Communities, *Comparative Social Research*, Vol. 18, pp. 135-59.

Pfau-Effinger, B. (2000), *Kultur und Frauenerwerbstätigkeit in Europa: Theorie und Empirie des internationalen Vergleichs*, Leske and Budrich: Opladen, Germany.

Pfau-Effinger, B. (2001), Soziokulturelle Bedingungen staatlicher Geschlechterbedingungen, in B. Heinze (ed.), *Geschlechtersoziologie: Sonderband der KZfSS*, Westdeutscher Verlag: Opladen, Germany.

Putnam, R.D. (2000), *Bowling Alone: The Collapse and Revival of American Community*, Simon and Schuster: New York.

Raventos, D. (2007), *Basic Income: The Material Conditions of Freedom*, Pluto: London.

Ringen, S. (1997), *Citizens, Families, and Reform*, Clarendon: Oxford, UK.

Schäfgen, K. (2000), *Die Verdopplung der Ungleichheit: Sozialstruktur und Geschlechterverhältnisse in der Bundesrepublik und in der DDR*, Leske and Budrich: Opladen, Germany.

SPD-Parteivorstand (2001), *Kinder—Familie—Zukunft*, SPD-Bundesparteitag: Nuremberg, Germany.

SPD-Projektgruppe Zukunft der Familie und sozialer Zusammenhalt (2000), *Zukunft Familie*, SPD: Berlin.

Vaskovics, L.A. and Rost, H. (1999), *Väter und Erziehungsurlaub*, Kohlhammer: Stuttgart, Germany.

Vobruba, G. (2007), *Entkoppelung von Arbeit und Einkommen*, VS: Wiesbaden, Germany.

Waldfogel, J. (2001), International Policies Toward Parental Leave and Child-Care, *The Future of Children*, Vol. 11, No. 1, pp. 99-111.

Wendt, H. (1997), *The Former German Democratic Republic: The Standardized Family*, in F.-X. Kaufmann *et al.* (eds.), *Family Life and Family Policies in Europe*, Clarendon Press: Oxford, UK.

Werding, M. (2001), *Das "Familiengeld"-Konzept der CDU/CSU-Bundestagsfraktion: Ergebnisse einer IFO Studie zu Wirkungen der Reformpläne der Opposition*, CDU-Bundestagsfraktion: Berlin.

13

Children Leaving Care: "Corporate Parenting" and Social Exclusion in the United Kingdom

JIM GODDARD

"We have a special responsibility to young people who are in care or who have left care. As their corporate parent we owe them a special duty. I am determined that young people living in and leaving care will in the future get the same support, as far as possible, as other young people who are living at home and leaving home. This means a home to live in or return to, a shoulder to cry on, encouragement with work or school or college, someone to take you out for a meal or out for a drink, someone to help you with a bit of cash when you need it, somewhere to get the washing done" (DH, 1999: 5).

Thus did Frank Dobson, the first Minister for Health in the Labour government that was elected to govern the United Kingdom in 1997, encapsulate the essence of the concept of "corporate parenting." This concept was embodied in the measures that were introduced through the subsequent Children (Leaving Care) Act 2000, which became part of UK social welfare law in November 2000 and was implemented by local authorities with effect from October 1, 2001. The Act is part of a wider reform program for personal social services in the UK and sits alongside the Care Standards Act 2000 and the "Quality Protects" initiative for children in need—especially those in care (DH, 1998a)—as part of a multi-faceted attempt to improve the quality of state child care (cf Hayden *et al.*, 1999). It is, of course, difficult for the state to replicate the sort of flexibility that is described above. The ideal, however, is an important one and it is one of the animating ideas of recent policy with respect to children in care.[1]

As might be expected, leaving care policy and practice differs markedly between different countries and cultures (Goddard *et al.*, 2005). Relatively very little research has been conducted with regard to international comparison, but what data is available suggests that the problems experienced in the UK are not unique; they are similar to those experienced in some other countries, such as the USA, Canada and Australia (Pinkerton, 2002; Goddard *et al.*, 2005). Considering UK developments, therefore, is likely to provide insights that are relevant to other countries. This article therefore seeks to analyze the new policy approach to care leavers that has emerged in recent years. However, before outlining the origins of this approach, it is important to clarify the policy framework within which leaving care support is provided in the United Kingdom. Firstly, although we have identified our focus as the UK, the article centers primarily on policy in England and Wales. This is because although most social policy for the constituent parts of the United Kingdom stems from UK central government, Scotland and Northern Ireland have different practices and legislation in this field. Indeed, Wales is also increasingly deserving of separate attention as the new Welsh Assembly forges different approaches to social care. That said, there is a great deal of influence between the different systems and a significant number of issues and policy responses remain UK-wide.

In the UK, local government has had responsibility for personal social services for both adults and children for many decades. Within local authorities, it is personal social services departments that have overall responsibility for children in care and care leavers in their local area. However, local government in the UK is not very powerful and the central government department with overall responsibility in this field, the Department of Health, determines the overall direction of policy. That policy is passed down to local authority social services departments for implementation and interpretation, with some remaining but limited room for discretion. In recent years, central government has increasingly sought to exert control over policy delivery and standards of service. Such control is ensured through a number of means. As well as shaping the content of parliamentary legislation, central government also determines the details of implementation through the issuing of regulations and guidance and the use of inspection and monitoring tools such as the Social Services Inspectorate and the Commission for Care Standards. Such bodies oversee delivery and quality on the ground and report back to central government.

Children in Care, Leaving Care, and Social Exclusion

Since 1997, the Labour government's social policy has made a priority of tackling *social exclusion*. A focus on such exclusion differs both from traditional class politics and from new right conceptions of the "underclass." In contrast to the former, it is not concerned to radically alter general social structure but examines exclusionary processes at the meso or micro level, rather than the macro level. In contrast to the latter, it avoids focusing on individual behavior and instead focuses on structural issues and social processes. Its concern with the plight of specific marginalized groups in society is evident from Prime Minister Tony Blair's own definition of the concept:

> "There is a significant minority of people cut off, set apart from the mainstream of society. Their lives are often characterized by long-term unemployment, poverty or lack of educational opportunity, and at times family instability, drug abuse and crime. This problem has got worse, not better" (Blair, 1996; 141).

Discussions of social exclusion have often focused on people with disabilities, low paid workers, homeless people and the long-term unemployed. However, it is easy to see that significant groups of children can be attached to any of these categories as well as being an area of concern in their own right (cf Polakov, 2007). Following Labour's 1997 victory, the new government's "Social Exclusion Unit," based at the heart of government in Downing Street, focused considerable attention on children. Children in care and care leavers quickly became central to their reform agenda.

The congruence between the factors associated with exclusion—homelessness, joblessness, lack of educational qualifications, social isolation, poverty—and the leaving care experience for a significant number of young people is striking. One illustration of this linkage is that children in care are identified as an especially vulnerable group in each of the first three reports from the Social Exclusion Unit. The first of these reports pointed out that children in care are "ten times more likely" than average to be excluded from school (SEU, 1998a: 9). The second report, on rough sleeping, noted that "between a quarter and a third of rough sleepers have been looked after by local authorities as children" (SEU, 1998b: 5) and cited the early age of discharge and lack of support for care leavers as crucial factors. The third report, on teenage pregnancy, cited research suggesting that "a quarter of care leavers had a child by the age of sixteen, and nearly half were mothers within 18 to 24 months after leaving care" (SEU, 1999: 17).

Care leavers are a relatively small group of young people, currently about 8,000 each year (DH, 2000b: 57), who are disproportionately represented amongst figures for a range of social problems. Even before the Social Exclusion Unit reports, a ubiquitous set of statistics had began to be widely quoted in official sources—despite many of them being rather vague estimates.[2] Amongst the best known of these statistics were that between 50 percent and 75 percent of care leavers had no academic qualifications (compared to 6 percent in the general population), that 50-80 percent of care leavers were unemployed (at a time when it was below 15 percent in the general population of the same age), that 23 percent of adult prisoners and 38 percent of young prisoners have been in care, that 30 percent of the young single homeless had a care back-ground (Utting, 1997; SSI, 1997).

Such figures paint a bleak picture, even when one remembers that young people will have entered care in the first instance because they were already experiencing significant difficulties and disadvantages. As with disabled people and others with multiple disadvantages, these young people represent a "sticking point" on the road to an economi-cally and socially successful society. However, because they already live in the care of the state, they are particularly amenable to state action to improve their circumstances and outcomes.

A further reason for focusing policy attention on this group is that after falling from 62,000 in 1989 to 47,000 in 1994, the numbers of children in care (in England, at least) had risen to 59,700 by 2002 (DH, 2002). The rise is accounted for chiefly by an increase in the use of fos-ter care within families, while numbers in children's homes have conti-nued to decline. By March 2002, 66 percent of looked after children in England were fostered while only 10 percent were in children's homes. The rest were in a variety of other placements, such as residential schools (DH, 2002). That the overall figure still only represents 0.5 per-cent of the relevant age group (Sinclair and Gibbs, 2002) serves to indi-cate the depths of the problems that the above statistics represent.

One of the most significant ways in which government has long sought to tackle to problems of the state childcare system has been to promote the use of fostering and, increasingly in recent years, adoption. Fostering children within existing private families was seen as pre-ferable to the risks of "institutionalization" in children's homes, even in the relatively small children's homes (usually no more than a dozen children) that now predominate in the UK and elsewhere (cf Goddard *et al.*, 2005).

Past United Kingdom Policy on Leaving Care

In the UK, policy under the 1989 Children Act was for children to leave care for independence between the ages of 16 and 18. Having to become "independent" at such a young age has been the single biggest problem affecting the leaving care process. It is, of course, a problem that is not specific to the United Kingdom. In Australia, children also leave care between the ages of 16 and 18. This is associated with the same problems seen in the UK, such as poor educational achievement, homelessness and high teenage pregnancy rates (Maunders *et al.*, 1999). Under the 1989 Act, for care leavers between the ages of 16 and 21 local authorities had a duty to "advise and befriend" and a power to "assist." Such "assistance" could be in kind (such as emergency accommodation) or, in exceptional circumstances, in cash (for example, expenses associated with employment or with training courses). The "assistance" could stretch to the age of 24 for education or training begun before the age of 21.

However, this superficially promising legislative theory turned out to be very different from local authority practice. As well as much discretion lying with local authorities with respect to defining the "needs" of young care leavers (and hence the appropriate responses), significant problems also arose from its context. Firstly, the early 1990s were a time of economic recession and consequent financial pressures on local authorities. They were also a period of high youth unemployment. Secondly, other legislation during the 1980s and 1990s, in such areas as housing and social security, reduced the levels of state support available to young people generally. The overall approach of the Conservative governments that were in power in the UK during the 1980s and most of the 1990s, with respect to young people in transition to adult lives, was to seek to increase the role and responsibilities of families and to reduce the role of the state. These objectives came into conflict when the State was, in effect, the parent. Young care leavers fell through the cracks of this family-based model which, as a well-known writer on UK leaving care services puts it, "didn't seem to apply to the corporate parent (i.e., the state) of young people leaving care" (Broad, 1998: 43).

From this less than promising background, a number of factors explain the development of the new approach embodied in the Children (Leaving Care) Act 2000. The three most important of these factors are: firstly, the development of a highly critical body of research on past leaving care policy and practice; secondly, gradual official recognition of the wider failure of the state childcare system to produce good outcomes for children and young people; and, finally, as we have seen, the election in 1997 of a Labour government with a strong commitment to tackling "social exclusion."

Much of the research conducted on this subject in the 1980s and 1990s had suggested that leaving care problems resulted less from the level and quality of care provided while children were looked after by the state (although this did vary significantly and was particularly problematic with respect to education) and more from the specifically inadequate arrangements for leaving care. This comes across in studies which focus on the views of care leavers themselves. Stein and Carey's early (1986) study of leaving care, an in-depth, qualitative analysis of the lives of 45 care leavers in the north of England, painted a compelling picture of their experience of a range of problems—loneliness, isolation, family relationship difficulties, poverty, lack of preparation for independence, and lack of educational qualifications or employment. The most emphatic of their conclusions was a rejection of the then-prevailing consensus amongst policymakers that independence at the age of eighteen was either achievable or desirable. This sensible and somewhat obvious point was echoed in later studies (e.g., Biehal *et al.*, 1995) and buttressed by what we know about what is happening with the non-care population of young people. The UK government itself noted that 22 was now the average age of leaving home in the wider population (DH, 1998b: 24). Other estimates confirm that the early to mid-20s are now the typical age at which young people in the UK leave the family home (Coleman and Schofield, 2001: 11). Also, most of these young people will have the option of going home at various points in times of need. Helen Jones, in an important study of the process of leaving home in the UK, has argued that this option of going "home" for periods has become increasingly used and that "more recognition is needed that leaving home is a process and not necessarily a one-off event: returning home should be seen as part of the process" (Jones, 1995: 149). Such a gradual transition process was not possible for those leaving the care system; their bed or place would quickly be taken by another child. Moreover, we know that many young people leave home even later in other countries. In Spain, for example, one study calculated the mean age of leaving care as 24 for men and 23 for women, two years higher than the respective mean ages in the United Kingdom (Holdsworth, 2000: 206). Since Stein and Carey, the field of leaving care research in the UK has mushroomed and most of the research has served to reinforce the early findings (cf especially Stone, 1990; Biehal, *et al.*, 1995; Broad, 1998; Goddard *et al.*, 2005).

Partly as a result of such research, both elected and non-elected policymakers gradually became cognizant of widespread policy failure. The Department of Health began to recognize the growing consensus on the need for action and official investigations (Utting, 1997: 91-93; SSI, 1997) also found that: (1) post-care contact was often left to young people to initiate or maintain; (2) most young people were ill informed about available post-care support; (3) few young people had formal care plans; and (4) most local authorities found it difficult to keep track of 18-21 year olds. The outcome of such findings was a growing acceptance of the view that young people should be more effectively involved in the development of leaving care policy, that there should be one contact point or link person with social services that individual plans for young people should have realistic targets and that contact should be more systematically maintained.

The Children (Leaving Care) Act 2000

The reforming agenda of the new government built on this analysis to provide a strong momentum towards an improved policy approach for care leavers. This bore fruit three years later, with the passage of the Children (Leaving Care) Act. Whilst the Act did not go as far as some activists would have wished, it did ensure that local authorities would remain directly responsible for the welfare of their post-16 care leavers until at least the age of 18. They would no longer be able to shuffle off their caring and financial responsibilities before this age. It also ensured greater mandatory support between the ages of 18 and 21.

Although the Act applies overwhelmingly to England and Wales, an exception to this is the provisions with respect to exclusion from financial (social security) benefits between the ages of 16 and 18, which also apply to Scotland. This exception was designed to prevent young people from choosing or being encouraged by local authorities to cross the Scottish/English border in order to claim benefits from the state, thus evading the new local authority financial responsibility for young care leavers between the ages of 16 and 18. Broadly speaking, there are two groups of young people who are covered by the new legislation. Firstly, there are children aged 16 or 17 who either remain in care or who have already left. Secondly, there are those between the ages of 18 and 21 who were in care. Needless to say, the former group is entitled to much more help than the latter (cf Goddard, 2001). The help available to young people has been changed in a number of different ways. These are considered under three categories; benefits, assessment and planning; and the role of Personal Advisers.

State Welfare Benefits

One of the most significant developments was the removal of entitlement to central government financial benefits for children who leave care aged 16 or 17. This was designed to remove what was claimed to be a "perverse financial incentive" for local authorities to assist young people in leaving the care system as early as possible upon reaching 16. At this point, such young people became eligible to claim central government social security benefits and, if the left care, ceased to be a financial burden to the authority. This system was clearly problematic. While the government's own Children Act report had cautiously argued that "the increasing trend to discharge young people early from "voluntary care" may reflect cost saving measures by authorities" (DH, 2000b: 61), the figures alone were disturbing. For 16-18 year olds, the percentages leaving care aged 16 rose from 33 percent to 44 percent between 1993 and 1998 (DH, 1999: 12). The UK parliament's House of Commons Health Select Committee was convinced by the evidence of academics and young people of "young people being put under pressure to leave care and live independently before they are fully equipped with the skills and self-confidence to do so" and of "informal practices and formal policies," which lead to such pressure (HCHSC, 1998).

Under the new Act, financial support for such children remains the responsibility of the local authority during this time (with some exceptions, such as lone parents or young people with disabilities). These young people now only become eligible for mainstream social security benefits at the age of 18. Whilst local authorities are given some flexibility with respect to how they interpret this financial responsibility, the level of support is supposed to be "well above the level which would have been supplied through the benefits system" (DH, 2001: 63). In short, regardless of where or how these young people are living, the local authority from which the left care remains responsible for their living and accommodation expenses up to the age of 18.

Needs Assessments and Pathway Plans

The Act also introduced a new duty to assess the needs of future care leavers when they reach their 16th birthday. This assessment was designed to aid the leaving care planning process. It determines the form and levels of advice, assistance and support that young people require—both while they remain looked after and afterwards—and forms the basis of a "Pathway Plan" for the transition to independence. This assessment is based on input from the young person, their doctor, their school and various other interested parties. It is required to address such issues as the health and development of the young person, their education, training and employment needs, their existing available external support (such as from family members), their financial needs, their independence skills and their accommodation needs (DH, 2001: 31).

The subsequent Pathway Plan, which runs up until the age of 21 at least (beyond, if there are educational or training needs) identifies the local authority role in meeting needs up to that age. However, local authorities are only supposed to have a role where this is appropriate and necessary. It may be, for example, that family members of the young person will be able to provide support in various forms. The role of the local authority therefore becomes making sure that all the gaps in the care and support needs of these young people are filled. These plans need to deal with such matters as the young person's support network, their education, training and employment needs, their family and social relationships, the necessary levels of financial support and their health needs. It also needs to make some provision for contingencies.

The provision of support beyond the age of 21 for agreed education or training includes, up to the age of 24, the provision of (or support for) vacation accommodation for those who need it. Over time, this may become a very important provision. Separate initiatives to improve the education of looked after children (cf Goddard, 2000; Jackson *et al.*, 2003) will hopefully lead to increasing numbers of care leavers going on to university-level education in the UK. Accommodation and other support through that process—difficult enough for young people not from the care system—will be important for them to successfully complete such education.

Also, these plans have to be reviewed at least every six months. This allows for the effective rewriting of plans as the young person's needs develop (if, for example, they do well at further education and wish to go on to higher education). Importantly, such a mandatory review process also forces local authorities to make regular efforts to not only keep in touch with but also to meet with young people and discuss their ongoing needs. In the past, large numbers of care leavers have simply "disappeared" from social services sight within a few weeks or months of leaving care at 16, 17, or 18. Studies of care leavers (e.g., Stein and Carey, 1986; Lynes and Goddard, 1995) have shown that many care leavers felt an acute and personal sense of abandonment by local authorities at this transition stage in their lives and would have welcomed an ongoing relationship.

Personal Advisers

The introduction of "Personal Advisers" for all care leavers between the ages of 16 and 21 provides an identifiable contact point with social services departments and others who have looked after these young people. These new positions, generally expected to be occupied by people with a relevant and experienced background in social work, teaching or youth work, provide something of a personal "safety net" for young people. Such advisers have a primary role in keeping in touch care leavers and, if contact is lost, must take "reasonable steps" re-establish it. However, although these advisers are the principal point of contact on the Pathway Plan, their role is likely to vary considerably in light of the different circumstances and support networks of the young person concerned.

The role of these advisors overlaps, to some degree, with the Connexions service, which began to be phased in for all young people aged 13-19 in England from April 2001. Connexions Advisers are intended to provide support on careers and other transitional issues for young people and are part of the wider agenda for tackling social exclusion amongst young people more generally. Looked after children have access to these advisers on the same basis as other children from 13 onwards and their Connexions Adviser may even be the same person as their leaving care adviser from the age of 16 onwards.

Corporate Parenting

Prior to the 2000 Act, the concept of parenting that was used by local authorities was set out in the 1989 Children Act. This Act was a major piece of legislation which drew together most child welfare issues and continues to determine much child welfare policy in England and Wales, outside of those issues that are dealt with through family law (such as divorce), youth justice and the education system. With respect to "parental responsibility," the 1989 Act is necessarily vague.

The Act uses the phrase "parental responsibility" to sum up the collection of duties, rights and authority which a parent has in respect of his child. That choice of words emphasizes that the duty to care for the child and to raise him to moral, physical and emotional health is the fundamental task of parenthood and the only justification for the authority it confers (DH, 1989: 1).

Since that time, many policy activists and researchers in this field had been critical of the minimalist interpretation of this responsibility by local authorities that we have already noted. The complexities of the new policy approach are best understood if one keeps in mind the government's repeated reference to the central concept of "corporate parenting." The use of the concept in this context refers to the attempt to replicate the actions of "good parents." One can see this in the "Needs Assessment," for example. This assessment fulfils the same function as the discussions about the future that many parents engage in with their children prior them beginning post-compulsory education.

In the UK, such education begins at the age of 16, when approximately 68 percent of all children will move on to post-compulsory education within their existing school or at a local further education college. This figure contrasts with approximately 18 percent of looked after children making the same move (Jackson *et al.*, 2003: 8). The Needs Assessment and subsequent Pathway Plan are partly designed to bridge this gap by focusing extra attention on the long-term needs of these young people at this critical age. Similarly, the changes to the financial benefit system for 16-18 year olds are an attempt to preserve the parental purse strings in the way that they are maintained for most young people of that age. Other attempts to replicate supportive parenting patterns include the regular contact from the personal adviser up to the age of 21, the potential for support with training and the requirement to provide support with accommodation during university vacations.

This expansion of the state's direct parenting responsibilities has raised con-cerns that the individual rights of young people may be undermined by such paternalism (cf Polakov, 2007). There have been some misgivings, for example, about the removal of social security benefits for most care leavers between the ages of 16 and 18 (Calder, 2000: 11-13) and with the civil rights implications of the duty of local authorities to keep in touch with young people after the age of 18 (Hansard, 2000). However, most commentators have seen the needs of these young people for ongoing support as sufficiently strong to outweigh such concerns.

There certainly is potential conflict in this field between a rights-based approach to the relationship between the state and adolescents and the explicitly paternalistic model favored in the Act. However, in support of the latter one can argue that the reason for past failure on leaving care is that a rights-based approach is inappropriate for this group of young people. Indeed, just as important as the level of financial support available during the 16-18 age range is the element of compulsion involved. Just as we would commonly regard parents who cut off their ties to their offspring at such a young age—even if that is what the young person requests—as irresponsible, so we can justifiably view local authorities in the same way. Hence the new compulsion on local authorities and young people to maintain their relationship with each other until at least age 18 and on local authorities to go on doing this beyond 18.

Education and Leaving Care

Alongside the leaving care developments, there have been a range of other measures concerned with improving services and outcomes for children in care. Many of these have been promoted as part of what is called the "Quality Protects" initiative. This initiative provides extra money to local authorities to achieving performance improvements in specific areas. It incorporates a wide range of objectives, such as reducing disruption to the lives of children in care and ensuring that they get proper health care and educational support (cf Fawcett *et al.*, 2004). The most relevant feature of this initiative, with respect to leaving care, are the measures that have been introduced in relation to education.

By the late 1990s, there was a widespread acceptance that educational disaffection and low achievement levels were major problems within the care system (Goddard, 2000; HCEESC, 1998; HCHSC,). A consensus on the need to address this problem resulted in detailed official guidance on the subject (DHDEE, 2000). This guidance focused on both raising the priority of educational achievement for looked after children and on improving cooperation between social services departments and local schools.

It provided for the appointment of designated teachers within schools to ensure action for looked after children; for example, ensuring that each child would have a mandatory Personal Education Plan. It also prioritized educational continuity during placement moves by placing time limits on educational gaps that might occur around such moves. A significant number of children in care, especially those in foster care, experience frequent moves. Long periods of time between schooling have often accompanied such moves. These changes were designed to achieve, in the first instance, what some regarded as a woefully unambitious target on the part of the Department of Health. Local authorities were instructed to achieve the following: to improve the educational attainment of children looked after, by increasing to at least 50 percent by 2001 the proportion of children leaving care at 16 or later with a GCSE or GNVQ qualification; and to 75 percent by 2003[3] (DH, 2000a,b).

In response to the valid criticism from many quarters that one GCSE was virtually useless in the UK employment and education markets, a further target was introduced: to increase to 15 percent by 2003/2004 the proportion of care leavers aged over 16 with 5 GCSEs grades A-C (DH, 2003).

Even this target is low, since 50 percent of UK school children already leave with five or more GCSEs at this age (Jackson *et al.*, 2003). It is, however, indicative of the very low educational achievement base from which current policy proceeds.

The Impact of the Policy Reforms

It is too soon yet to assess the lasting impact of the Labour government's reforms with respect to leaving care, although there are ongoing research projects on various aspects of the reforms. However, there are some useful indicators of their initial impact. On the education front, progress has been slow. The low performance targets were not met by local authorities. The percentage of children leaving care with one GCSE or GNVQ rose through 2000 to 2002 from 31 to 41 percent. This meant that there was virtually no hope of reaching the 2003 target of 75 percent. The figures for children achieving 5 or more GCSEs at grades A-C fared even worse; the numbers merely rose from 4 percent in 2000 to 5 percent in 2002 (DH, 2003).

With no prospect at all of hitting the original targets, the government adopted the time-honored political strategy of changing the targets. The new targets are for 90 percent of care leavers to have sat (not necessarily passed) a GCSE exam by 2006 and for 15 percent to pass 5 or more GCSEs by 2006. The government also instituted an investigation into the subject by its own Social Exclusion Unit, which will feed into the future policy. This depressing downscaling of the government's ambitions in this area has significant implications, of course, for the numbers of care leavers who may go on to university in future years. No reliable figures are available on the present numbers at university, but all estimates suggest that it is still remains extremely low (Jackson *et al.*, 2003).

On leaving care support, there is more hopeful evidence. The government had also introduced performance measures in this area, such as keeping in touch with young people after they leave care and the percentages in training, employment or education. One target that they provided for local authorities concerned the level of employment, education or training of care leavers aged 19 in 2001/2002 who had been in care on their 17th birthday. This was supposed to reach at least 60 percent of the comparable level for young people in the local area, rising to 75 percent by 2003/2004. The first measures in this area found that 46 percent of care leavers met the criteria of being in education, employment or training in 2002. This compares to 86 percent of their non-care peers (DH, 2003). In short, local authorities are not meeting the target. However, they are much closer than in the case of educational qualifications. Also, the figure varies from authority to authority (depending on, for example, local employment rates) and 38 percent of authorities were actually meeting the 60 percent target. On the other hand, it is difficult to assess the meaning of this figure since it is the first time that such data has been available. It may, for example, reflect a realistically low initial target. It may also reflect the general good performance of the UK economy in recent years and the consequent significant fall in youth unemployment. Alongside this, measures were also introduced to assess how well local authorities were doing in keeping in touch with care leavers aged 19. In 2002, councils remained in touch with 75 percent of care leavers on or near their 19th birthday. This might seem a small achievement, but given what we know from past research about how quickly young people disappear from local authority sight, it represents significant progress.

Conclusions

After well over a decade of depressing research findings (Goddard, 2005) and increasing governmental acceptance of the seriousness of the problems in this field, there has been a distinct heightening of attention on care leavers in the UK. Recent initiatives have been widely welcomed by activists and social care professionals as a long-overdue attempt to tackle the manifest shortcomings of previous policy and practice. These developments were not, however, inevitable. Their introduction was prompted by the election of a Labour government in 1997 after 18 years of Conservative rule. This new government had a strong social reform agenda with respect to social exclusion and care leavers were quickly seen to occupy a central location in any attempt to tackle social exclusion amongst young people.

Whether the changes introduced will prove to be part of a successful long-term solution to some of the main problems of care leavers remains in some doubt at this point in time. The focus on education is bearing results, but slower than anticipated. The focus on maintaining contact and support is showing more apparent success, but the actual content of such support and contact will vary tremendously. One of the main successes in this area is that such data is being collected at all; at least now we have a realistic picture of care leaving in the UK. On the other hand, the central problem of leaving care for independence too early persists; though the worst features of young people leaving care for independence at 16 should be reduced. The age of 18 very extremely young to be leaving home, even for those with supportive families. Even if the new support systems work properly, most care leavers will continue to find their start to adult life much more difficult than their non-care peers.

The slow progress in the educational field may turn out to be indicative of wider problems of implementation by local authorities with respect to the government's ambitious objectives. This sort of problem has a long history in the difficult relationship between central and local government in the UK. It suggests that the legislation may not be implemented fully and consistently. This was a problem in relation to the 1989 Children Act and there is no reason to believe that local authorities have become more effective at responding to the enthusiasms of central government. It is precisely because of such problems that central government has resorted to setting explicit targets. Such targets are indicative of a general lack of trust between central and local government in the UK in recent years. Local authorities are under more pressure to perform in this field than they have been before, but such improved performance as we have seen looks likely to last only as long as central government keeps applying such pressure. To its credit, central government has done so thus far.

Notes

1. "Looked after children" is now the official, governmental term used to describe children in the United Kingdom who are cared for by local authorities and voluntary child welfare organizations under the approval of the state. Such children used to be most commonly referred to as "children in care" and that term is still widely used. It is also the term more commonly understood by international audiences (cf Goddard *et al.*, 2005). Hence my preference for using it throughout this article.
2. The lack of hard data about this group, in the UK and in other countries, is indicative of the low priority given to their welfare (Pinkerton, 2002; Goddard *et al.*, 2005).
3. For school children in England and Wales, the General Certificate of Secondary Education (GCSE) is the basic educational qualification at the end of compulsory schooling. It is given for individual subjects (such as history, mathematics or geography). Therefore, as well as through grades (A to E, with A being the highest), performance is also assessed on the basis of the number of GCSEs that a child has acquired. General National Vocational Qualifications (GNVQs) are more vocationally-oriented, rather than academically-oriented, qualifications.

REFERENCES

Biehal, N.; Clayden, J.; Stein, M., and Wade, J. (1995), *Moving On: Young People and Leaving Care Schemes*, The Stationery Office: London.
Blair, T. (1996), *New Britain: My Vision of a Young Country*, Fourth Estate: London.
Broad, B. (1998), *Young People Leaving Care: Life After the Children Act 1989*, Jessica Kingsley: London.
Calder, A. (2000), Financial Support for Care Leavers, *Poverty*, No. 106, pp. 11-13.
Coleman, P. and Schofield, A.J. (2001), *Key Data on Adolescence*, Trust for the Study of Adolescence: Brighton, UK.

DH, Department of Health (1989), *An Introduction to the Children Act 1989,* The Stationery Office: London.

DH, Department of Health (1998a), *Quality Protects: Objectives for Social Services for Children,* Social Care Group, Department of Health, London.

DH, Department of Health (1998b), *The Government's Response to the Children's Safeguards Review,* The Stationery Office: London.

DH, Department of Health (1999), *Me, Survive? Out There? New Arrangements for Young People Living in and Leaving Care,* Department of Health: London.

DH, Department of Health (2000a), *The Children Act Report, 1995-1999,* The Stationery Office: London.

DH, Department of Health (2000b), *Social Services Performance in 1999/2000,* Department of Health: London.

DH, Department of Health (2001), *Children (Leaving Care) Act 2000: Regulations and Guidance,* The Stationery Office: London.

DH, Department of Health (2002), *Children Looked After in England: 2001/ 2002,* National Statistics/Department of Health: London.

DH, Department of Health (2003), Care Leavers, *Department of Health Statistical Bulletin,* Department of Health: London, March 31.

DHDEE, Department of Health, Department for Education and Employment (2000), *Guidance on the Education of Children and Young People in Public Care,* Department of Health/Department for Education and Employment: London.

Fawcett, B.; Featherstone, B., and Goddard, J. (2004*), Contemporary Child-Care Policy and Practice,* Palgrave: Basingstoke, UK.

Goddard, J. (2000), Research Review: The Education of Looked After Children, *Child and Family Social Work,* Vol. 5, No. 1, pp. 79-86.

Goddard, J. (2001), Children (Leaving Care) Act 2000: A Commentary, *Welfare Benefits,* Vol. 8, No. 3, pp. 25-34

Goddard, J. (2005), Future Directions for the Study of Childhood, in J. Goddard, S. MacNamee, A. James, and A. James (eds.), *The Politics of Childhood: International Perspectives: Contemporary Developments,* Palgrave Macmillan: London.

Goddard, J.; McNamee, S.; James, A., and James A. (eds.) (2005), *The Politics of Childhood: International Perspectives: Contemporary Developments,* Palgrave Macmillan: London.

Hansard (2000), Children (Leaving Care) Bill, Second Reading, House of Commons, UK, June 21.

Hayden, C.; Goddard, J.; Gorin, S., and Van Der Spek, Niki (1999), *State Child Care: Looking After Children?,* Jessica Kingsley: London.

HCEESC, House of Commons Education and Employment Select Committee (1998), *Disaffected Children*, The Stationery Office: London.

HCHSC, House of Commons Health Select Committee (1998), *Children Looked After by Local Authorities*, The Stationery Office: London.

Holdsworth, C. (2000), Leaving Home in Britain and Spain, *European Sociological Review*, Vol. 16, No. 2, pp. 201-22.

Jackson, S.; Ajayi, S., and Quigley, M. (2003), *By Degrees: The First Year*, National Children's Bureau: London.

Jones, G. (1995), *Leaving Home*, Open University Press: Buckingham, UK.

Lynes, D. and Goddard, J. (1995), *The View From the Front: The User-View of Child-Care in Norfolk*, Norfolk County Council: Norwich, UK.

Maunders, D.; Liddell, M., and Green, S. (1999), *Young People Leaving Care and Protection: A Report to the National Youth Affairs Research Scheme*, ACYS/University of Tasmania: Hobart, Australia.

Pinkerton, J. (2002), Developing an International Perspective on Leaving Care, in A. Wheal (ed.), *The RHP Companion to Leaving Care*, Russell House: Lymme Regis, UK.

Polakov, V. (2007), *Who Cares for Our Children?*, Columbia University Press: New York.

SEU, Social Exclusion Unit (1998a), *Truancy and School Exclusion*, The Stationery Office: London.

SEU, Social Exclusion Unit (1998b), *Rough Sleeping*, The Stationery Office: London.

SEU, Social Exclusion Unit (1999), *Teenage Pregnancy*, The Stationery Office: London.

Sinclair, I. and Gibbs, I. (2002), Looked After Children, in J. Bradshaw (ed.), *The Well-Being of Children in the UK*, Save the Children: London.

SSI, Social Services Inspectorate (1997), *When Leaving Home Is Also Leaving Care, An Inspection of Services for Young People Leaving Care*, Department of Health: London.

Stein, M. and Carey, K. (1986), *Leaving Care*, Blackwell: Oxford, UK.

Stone, M. (1990), *Young People Leaving Care*, Royal Philanthropic Society: London.

Utting, W. (1997), *People Like Us: The Report of the Review of Safeguards for Children Living Away from Home*, Department of Health/Welsh Office, The Stationery Office: London.

14

Aging, Family Policy and Narrative: Lessons from the UK

JASON POWELL

There has been an increasing interest in aging and family, within sociological developments relating to aging and social policy since the late 1990s (Minkler, 1998). This is a trend that has cut across Canadian, American and European research (Walker and Naegele, 1999; Minkler, 1998; Bengtson *et al.*, 2000; Biggs and Powell, 2001; Cloke *et al.*, 2006; Carmel *et al.*, 2007). The reasons for such expansion are as much economic and political as they are academic. US and European governments recognize that the "family" is important for social and economic needs and this should be reflected in our understanding of aging, family processes and in social policy (Beck, 2005). This leads to the question: how can we theoretically contextualize this and what are lessons for family research in sociological theorizing?

"Narrativity" has become established in the social sciences, both as a method of undertaking and interpreting research (cf Kenyon *et al.*, 1999; Holstein and Gubrium, 2000; Biggs *et al.*, 2003) and as a technique for modifying the self (McAdams, 1993; Mcleod, 1997). Both Gubrium (1992) and Katz (1999) suggest that older people construct their own analytical models of personal identity based on lived experience and on narratives already existing in their everyday environments. By using a narrative approach, the meaning of family can be told through stories about the self, as well as stories "at large" in public discourse.

"Discourse" is a phrase more often used to denote a relatively fixed set of stories that individuals or groups have to conform to in order to take up a recognized and legitimate role. Such an understanding of discourse can be found in the earlier work of Michel Foucault (1977) and others (Powell and Biggs, 2001). Self-storying, draws attention to the ways in which family identities are both more open to negotiation and are more likely to be "taken in" in the sense of being owned and worked on by individuals themselves. Families, of course, are made up of interpersonal relationships within and between generations that are subject to both the formal rhetoric of public discourse, and the self-stories that bind them together in everyday life. The notion of family is, then, an amalgam of policy discourse and everyday negotiation and as such alerts us to the wider social implications of those relationships (cf Powell, 2005).

The rhetoric of social policy and the formal representations of adult aging and family life that one finds there, provide a source of raw material for the construction of identity and a series of spaces in which such identities can be legitimately performed. It is perhaps not over-stating the case to say that the "success" of a family policy can be judged from the degree to which people live within the stories or narratives of family created by it.

In fact, the relationship between families and older people has been consecutively re-written in the social policy literature. Each time a different story has been told and different aspects of the relationship have been thrown into high relief. It might even be argued that the family has become a key site upon which expected norms of inter-generational relations and late-life citizenship are being built. This chapter explores the significance of such narratives, using developments in the UK as a case example that may also shed light on wider contemporary issues associated with old age.

The structure of the chapter is fourfold. Firstly, we start by mapping out the emergence and consolidation of neoliberal family policy and its relationship to emphasis on family obligation, state surveillance and active citizenship. Secondly, we highlight both the ideological continuities and discontinuities of the subsequent social democratic turn and their effects on older people and the family. Thirdly, research studies are drawn on to highlight how "grandparenting" has been recognized by governments in recent years, as a particular way of "storying" the relationship between old age and family life. Finally, we explore ramifications for researching family policy and old age by pointing out that narratives of inclusion and exclusion often co-exist. It is suggested that in future, aging and family life will include the need to negotiate multiple policy narratives. At an interpersonal level, sophisticated narrative strategies would be required if a sense of familial continuity and solidarity is to be maintained.

Neoliberalism, Aging, and the Family

Political and social debate since the Reagan/Thatcher years, has been dominated by neoliberalism, which postulates the existence of autonomous, assertive, rational individuals who must be protected and liberated from "big government" and state interference (Gray, 1995). Indeed, Walker and Naegele (1999) claim a startling continuity across Europe is the way "the family" has been positioned by governments as these ideas have spread beyond their original "English speaking" base.

Neoliberal policies on the family, has almost always started from a position of *laissez-faire*, excepting when extreme behavior threatens its members or wider social relations (Beck, 2005). Using the UK as a case example, it can be seen that that neoliberal policy came to focus on two main issues. And, whilst both only represent the point at which a minimalist approach from the state touches family life, they come to mark the dominant narrative through which aging and family are made visible in the public domain (Cloke *et al.*, 2006).

On the one hand, increasing attention was paid to the role families took in the care of older people who were either mentally or physically infirm. A series of policy initiatives (UKG, 1981, 1989, 1990) recognized that families were a principal source of care and support.

"Informal" family care became a key building block of policy toward an aging population. It both increased the salience of traditional family values, independence from government and enabled a reduction in direct support form the state.

On the other hand, helping professionals, following US experience (Pillemer and Wolf, 1986), became increasingly aware of the abuse that older people might suffer and the need to protect vulnerable adults from a variety of forms of abuse and neglect (Biggs *et al.*, 1995; Brodgen and Nijhar, 2005). Policy guidance, *"No Longer Afraid: The safeguard of older people in domestic settings,"* was issued in 1993, shortly after the move to seeing informal care as the mainstay of the welfare of older people (UKG, 1993). As the title suggests, this was also directed primarily at the family.

It is perhaps a paradox that a policy based ostensibly on the premises of *laissez-faire*, combines two narrative streams that result in increased surveillance of the family. This paradox is based largely on these points being the only ones where policy "saw" aging in families, rather than ignoring it. This is not to say that real issues of abuse and neglect fail to exist, even though UK politicians have often responded to them as if they were some form of natural disaster unrelated to the wider policy environment. To understand the linking of these narratives, it is important to examine trends tacit in the debate on family and aging, but central to wider public policy.

Wider economic priorities, to "roll back the state" and thereby release resources for individualism and free enterprise, had become translated into a family discourse about caring obligations and the need to enforce them. If families ceased to care, then the state would have to pick up the bill. It was not that families were spoken of as being naturally abusive. Neither was the "discovery" of familial abuse linked to community care policy outside academic debate (Biggs, 1996).

Discourses on the rise of abuse and on informal care remained separate in the formal policy domain. However, a subtle change of narrative tone had taken place. Families, rather than being seen as "havens against a harsh world," were now easily perceived as potential sites of mistreatment, and the previously idealized role of the unpaid carer became that of a potential recalcitrant, attempting to avoid their family obligations. An attempt to protect a minority of abused elders thus took the shape of a tacit threat, hanging above the head of every aging family (Biggs and Powell, 2000). It is worth note that these policy developments took little account of research evidence indicating that family solidarity and a willingness to care had decreased in neither the UK (Wenger, 1994; Phillipson, 1998) nor the US (Bengtson and Achenbaum, 1993). Further, it appeared that familial caring was actually moving away from relationships based on obligation and toward ones based on negotiation (Finch and Mason, 1993).

Family commitment has, for example, to vary depending upon the characteristic care-giving patterns within particular families. Individualistic families provided less instrumental help and made use of welfare services, whereas a second, collectivist pattern offered greater personal support. Whilst this study focused primarily on upward generational support, Silverstein and Bengtson (1997) observed that "tight-knit" and "detached" family styles were often common across generations. Unfortunately, policy developments have rarely taken differences in care-giving styles into account, preferring a general narrative of often idealized role relationships. It is not unfair to say that during the neoliberal period, the dominant narrative of family became that of a site of care going wrong.

Social Democracy, Aging, and the Family

Social democratic policies toward the family arose from the premise that by the early 1990s, the free-market policies of the Thatcher/Reagan years had seriously damaged the social fabric of the nation state and that its citizens needed to be encouraged to identify again with the national project. A turn to an alternative, sometimes called "the third way," emerging under Clinton, Blair and Schröder administrations in the US and parts of Europe, attempted to find means of mending that social fabric, and as part of it, relations between older people and their families (Beck, 2005). The direction that the new policy narrative took is summarized in UK Prime Minister Blair's (1996) statement that "the most meaningful stake anyone can have in society is the ability to earn a living and support a family." Work, or failing that, work-like activities, plus an active contribution to family life began slowly to emerge, delineating new narratives within which to grow old (Hardill *et al.*, 2007).

Giddens (1998) in the UK and Beck (1998) in Germany, both proponents of social democratic politics, have claimed that citizens are faced with the task of piloting themselves and their families through a changing world in which globalization has transformed our relations with each other, now based on avoiding risk. According to Giddens (1998), a new partnership is needed between government and civil society. Government support to the renewal of community through local initiative, would gives an increasing role to "voluntary" organizations, encourages social entrepreneurship and significantly, supports the "democratic" family characterized by "equality, mutual respect, autonomy, decision-making through communication and freedom of violence." It is argued that social policy should be less concerned with "equality" and more with "inclusion," with community participation reducing the moral and financial hazard of dependence (cf Walker, 2002; Biggs *et al.*, 2003; Powell and Owen, 2007; Walker and Aspalter, 2008).

Through an increased awareness of the notion of ageism, the influence of European ideas about social inclusion and North American social communitarianism, families and older people found themselves transformed into active citizens who should be encouraged to participate in society, rather than be seen as a potential burden upon it (Biggs, 2001). A contemporary UK policy document, entitled *"Building a Better Britain for Older People"* (DSS, 1998) is typical of a new genre of western policy, re-storying the role of older adults:

> "The contribution of older people is vital, both to families, and to voluntary organisations and charities. We believe their roles as mentors—providing ongoing support and advice to families, young people and other older people—should be recognised. Older people already show a considerable commitment to volunteering. The Government is working with voluntary groups and those representing older people to see how we can increase the quality and quantity of opportunities for older people who want to volunteer."

What is perhaps striking about this piece is that it is one of the few places where families are mentioned in an overview on older people, with the exception of a single mention of carers, many of whom, it is pointed out, "are pensioners themselves." In both cases the identified role for older people constitutes a reversal of the narrative offered in preceding policy initiatives. The older person like other members of family structure is portrayed as an active member of the *social milieu*, offering care and support to others (Hardill *et al.*, 2007).

The dominant preoccupation of this policy initiative, is not however, concerned with families. Rather, there is a change of emphasis toward the notion of aging as an issue of lifestyle, and as such draws on contemporary gerontological observations of the "blurring" of age-based identities (Featherstone and Hepworth, 1995) and the growth of the grey consumer (Katz, 1999).

Whilst such a narrative is attractive to pressure groups, voluntary agencies and, indeed, social gerontologists; there is, just as with the policies of the neoliberals, an underlying economic motive which may or may not be to the long term advantage to older people and their families. Again, as policies develop, the force driving the story of elders as active citizens was to be found in policies of a fiscal nature. The most likely place to discover how the new story of aging, fits the bigger picture is in government-wide policy. In this case the document has been entitled *"Winning the Generation Game"* (UKG, 2000a). This begins well with "One of the most important tasks for 21st-century Britain is to unlock the talents and potential of all its citizens. Everyone has a valuable contribution to make, throughout their lives." However, the reasoning behind this statement becomes clearer when policy is explained in terms of a changing demographic profile: "With present employment rates" it is argued, "one million more over-50s would not be working by 2020 because of growth in the older population. There will be 2 million fewer working-age people under 50 and 2 million more over 50: a shift equivalent to nearly 10 percent of the total working population."

The solution, then, is to engage older people not only part of family life but also in work, volunteering or mentoring. Older workers become a reserve labor pool, filling the spaces left by falling numbers of younger workers. They thus contribute to the economy as producers as well as consumers and make fewer demands on pensions and other forms of support. Those older people who are not thereby socially included, can engage in the work-like activity of volunteering.

Most of these policy narratives only indirectly affect the aging family. Families only have a peripheral part to play in the story, and do not appear to be central to the lives of older people. However, it is possible to detect the same logic at work when attention shifts from the public to the private sphere. Here the narrative stream develops the notion of "grandparenting" as a means of social inclusion. This trend can be found in the UK, in France (Girard and Ogg, 1998), Germany (Scharf and Wenger, 1995), as well as in the USA (Minkler, 1999).

In the UK context the most detailed reference to grandparenting can be found in an otherwise rather peculiar place—namely from the Home Office—an arm of British Government primarily concerned with law and order. In a document entitled *"Supporting Families"* (2000b), "family life" we are told, "is the foundation on which our communities, our society and our country are built." "Business people, people from the community, students and grandparents" are encouraged to join a schools mentoring network. Further, "the interests of grandparents, and the contribution they make, can be marginalized by service providers who, quite naturally, concentrate on dealing with parents. We want to change all this and encourage grandparents—and other relatives—to play a positive role in their families." By which it is meant: "home, school links or as a source of social and cultural history" and support when "nuclear families are under stress." Even older people who are not themselves grandparents can join projects "in which volunteers act as "grandparents" to contribute their experience to a local family."

In the narratives of social democracy, the aging family is seen as a reservoir of potential social inclusion. Older people are portrayed as holding a key role in the stability of both the public sphere, through work and volunteering, and in the private sphere, primarily through grandparental support and advice (Cloke *et al.*, 2006). Grandparents, in particular, are storied as mentors and counselors across the public and private spheres.

Whilst the grandparental title has been used as a catch-all within the dominant policy narrative; bringing with it associations of security, stability and an in many ways an easier form of relationship than direct parenting; it exists as much in public as in private space. It is impossible to interpret this construction of grandparenthood without placing it in the broader project of social inclusion, itself a response to increased social fragmentation and economic competition. Indeed it may not be an exaggeration to refer this construal of grandparenting as neofamilial. In other words, the grandparent has out-grown the family as part of a policy search to include older adults in wider society. The grandparent becomes a mentor to both parental and grandparental generations as advice is not restricted to schools and support in times of stress, but also through participation in the planning of amenities and public services (BGOP, 2000).

This is a very different narrative of older people and their relationship to families, from that of the dependent and burdensome elder. In the land of policy conjuring, previously conceived problems of growing economic expense and social uselessness have been miraculously reversed. Older people are now positioned as the solution to problems of demographic change, rather than their cause. They are a source of guidance to ailing families, rather than their victims. Both narratives increase the social inclusion of a potentially marginal social group: formerly known as the elderly.

"Grandparenting" Policy

There is much to be welcomed in this story of the active citizen elder. Especially so if policy-inspired discourse and lived self-narratives are taken to be one and the same. There are also certain problems, however, if the two are unzipped, particularly when the former is viewed through the lens of what we know about families from other sources.

First, each of the roles identified in the policy domain, volunteering, mentorship and grandparenting, have a rather second–hand quality. By this is meant that each is supportive to another player who is central to the task at hand.

Rather like within Erikson's psycho-social model of the lifecycle, the role allocated to older people approximates grand-generativity and thereby contingent upon the earlier, but core life task of generativity itself (Kivnick, 1988). In other words it is contingent upon an earlier part of life and the narratives woven around it, and fails to distinguish an authentic element of the experience of aging.

When the roles are examined in this light, a tacit secondary status begins to emerge. Volunteering becomes unpaid work; mentoring, support to helping professionals in their eroded pastoral capacities; and grandparenting, in its familial guise, a sort of peripheral parent without the hassle. This peripherality may be in many ways desirable, so long as there is an alternative pole of authentic attraction that ties the older adult into the *social milieux*. Either that or the narrative should allow space for legitimized withdrawal from socially inclusive activities. Unfortunately the dominant policy narrative has little to say on either count.

Second, there is a shift of attention away from the most frail and oldest old, to a third age of active or positive aging, which, incidentally, may or may not take place in families. It is striking that a majority of policy documents of what might be called the "new aging," start counting from age 50, an observation that is true for formal government rhetoric and pressure from agencies and initiatives lead by elders (Biggs, 2001). This interpretation of the life-course has been justified in terms of its potential for forming intergenerational alliances (BGOP, 2000) and fits well with the economic priority of drawing on older people as a reserve labor force (UKG, 2000b).

Third, there is a striking absence of analysis of family relations at that age. Possibilities of intergenerational conflict as described in other literature (De Beauvoir, 1979), not least in research into three-generation family therapy (Hargrave and Anderson, 1992; Qualls, 1999), plus the everyday need for tact in negotiating childcare roles (Bornat *et al.*, 1999; Waldrop *et al.*, 1999), appear not to have been taken into account. This period in the aging life-course is often marked by midlife tension and multi-generational transitions, such as those experienced by late adolescent children and by an increasingly frail top generation (Ryff and Seltzer, 1996). Research has indicated that solidarity between family generations is not uniform, and will involve a variety of types and degrees of intimacy and reciprocity (Silverstein and Bengtson, 1997).

Finally, little consideration has been given to the potential conflict between the tacit hedonism of aging lifestyles based on consumption and those more socially inclusive roles of productive contribution, of which the "new grandparenting" has become an important part. Whilst there are few figures on grandparental activity it does, for example, appear that community volunteering amongst older people is embraced with much less enthusiasm than policymakers would wish (Boaz *et al.*, 1999). Chambre (1993) claims volunteering in the US diminishes in old age. Her findings indicate the highest rates of volunteering occur in mid-life, where nearly two thirds volunteer. This rate declines to 47 percent for persons aged between 65 and 74 and to 32 percent among persons 75 and over. A UK Guardian-ICM (2000) poll of older adults indicated that, amongst grandfathers, but not grandmothers, there was a degree of suspicion of child-care to support their own children's family arrangements. More than a quarter of men expressed this concern, compared with only 19 percent of women interviewed. The UK charity, Age Concern, stated: "One in ten grandparents are under the age of 56. They have 10 more years of work and are still leading full lives."

One might speculate, immersed in this narrative stream, that problematic family roles and relationships cease to exist for the work-returning, volunteering and community enhancing 50-plus "elder." Indeed, the major protagonists of social democracy seem blissfully unaware of several decades of research, particularly feminist research, demonstrating the mythical status of the "happy family" (cf e.g. Land, 1999).

What emerges from research literature on grandparenting as it is included in people's everyday experience and narratives of self, indicates two trends: (1) there appears to be a general acceptance of the positive value of relatively loose and undemanding exchange between first and third generations, and (2) that deep commitments become active largely in situations of extreme family stress or breakdown of the middle generation.

First, grandparents have potential to influence and develop children through the transmission of values. Subsequently, grandparents serve as arbiters of knowledge and transmit knowledge that is unique to their identity, life experience and history. In addition, grandparents can become mentors, performing the function of a generic life guide for younger children. This "transmission" role is confirmed by Mills' (1999) study of mixed gender relations and by Waldrop *et al.*'s (1999) report on grandfathering. According to Roberto (1990) early research on grandparenting in the USA has attempted to identify the roles played by grandparents within the family system and towards grandchildren. Indeed, much US work on grandparenting has focused on how older adults view and structure their relationships with younger people.

African American grandparents, for example, take a more active role, correcting the behavior of grandchildren and acting like "protectors" of the family. Accordingly, such behaviors are related to effects of divorce and under/unemployment. Research by Kennedy (1990) indicates, however, that there is a cultural void when it comes to grandparenting roles for many white families with few guidelines on how they should act as grandparents.

Girrard and Ogg (1998) report that grandparenting is a rising political issue in French family policy. They note that most grand-mothers welcome the new role they have in child care of their grand-children, but there is a threshold beyond which support interferes with their other commitments. Contact between older parents and their grandchildren is less frequent that with youngsters, with financial support becoming more prominent.

Two reports, explicitly commissioned to inform UK policy (Hayden *et al.*, 1999; Boaz *et al.*, 1999) classify grandparenting under the general rubric of intergenerational relationships. Research evidence is cited, that "when thinking about the future, older people looked forward to their role as grandparents" and that grandparents looked after their grandchildren and provided them with "love, support and a listening ear," providing childcare support to their busy children and were enthusiastic about these roles.

Hayden *et al.* (1999) used focus groups and qualitative interviewing and report that: "grandparenting included spending time with grandchildren both in active and sedentary hobbies and pursuits, with many participants commenting on the mental and physical stimulation they gained from sharing activities with the younger generation. Coupled with this, the Beth Johnson Foundation (1998) found that older people as mentors had increased levels of participation with more friends and engendered more social activity. With the exception of the last study, each has relied on exclusive self-report data, or views on what grand-parenting might be like at some future point.

In research from the tradition of examining social networks, and thus not overtly concerned with the centrality of grandparenting or grandparent-like roles as such, it is rarely identified as a key relationship and could not be called a strong theme. Studies on the UK, (Phillipson *et al.*, 2000), Japan (Izuhara, 2000), the US (Schreck, 2000; Minkler, 1999), Hispanic Americans (Freidenberg, 2000), and Germany, (Chamberlayne and King, 2000) provide little evidence that grandchildren, as distinct from adult children, are prominent members of older peoples reported social networks.

Grandparental responsibility becomes more visible if the middle generation is for some reason absent. Thompson, (1999) reports from the UK, that when parents part or die, it is often grandparents who take up supporting, caring and mediating roles on behalf of their grand-children. The degree of involvement was contingent however on the quality of emotional closeness and communication within the family group. Minkler, (1999) has indicated that in the US, one in ten grand-parents has primary responsibility for raising a grandchild at some point, with care often lasting for several years.

This trend varies between ethnic groups, with 4.1 percent White, 6.55 percent Hispanic and 13.55 African American children living with their grandparents or other relatives. It is argued that a 44 percent in-crease in such responsibilities is connected to the devastating effects of wider social issues, including AIDS/HIV, drug abuse, parental home-lessness and prison policy. Thomson and Minkler (2001) note that there is an increasing divergency in the meaning of grandparenting between different socio-economic groups, with extensive care-givers (7 percent of the sampled population) having increasingly fewer characteristics in common with the 14.9 percent who did not provide child-care. In the UK, a similar split has been identified with 1 percent of British grand-parents becoming extensive caregivers, against a background pattern of occasional or minimal direct care (Duckworth, 2001).

It would appear that grandparenting is not, then a uniform phenomenon, and extensive grandparenting or grandparent-like activities are rarely an integral part of social inclusion. Rather, whilst it is seen as providing some intergenerational benefit, it may be a phenomenon that requires an element of un-intrusiveness and negotiation in its non-extensive form. When extensively relied on it is more likely to be a response to severely eroded inclusive environments and the self-protective reactions of families living with them. Minkler's analysis draws attention to race as a feature of social exclusion that is poorly handled by policy narratives afforded to the family and old age. There is a failure to recognize structural forms of inequality, and action seeking to socially include older people as a category appears to draw heavily on the occasional helper and social volunteer as a dominant narrative.

Towards Diverse Narrative Streams?

Each phase of social policy, be it the Reagan/Thatcherite neoliberalism of the 1980s and early 1990s, the Clinton/Blairite interpretation of social democracy in the late 1990s, or the millennial Bush administration, leaves a legacy. Moreover, policy development is uneven and subject to local emphasis and elision, which means that it is quite possible for different, even conflicting narratives of family and later life to coexist in different parts of the policy system. Each period generates a discourse that can legitimate the lives of older people and family relations in particular ways, and as their influence accrues, create the potential of entering into multiple narrative streams.

A striking feature of recent policy history has been that not only have the formal policies been quite different in their tenor and tacit objectives, one from another, they have also addressed different areas of the lives of aging families. Where there is little narrative overlap there is the possibility of both policies existing, however opposed they may be ideologically or in terms of practical outcome. Different narratives may colonize different parts of policy, drawing on bureaucratic inertia, political inattention and convenience to maintain their influence. They have a living presence, not least when they impinge on personal aging.

Also, both policy discourses share a deep coherence, which may help to explain their co-existence. Each offers a partial view of aging and family life whilst downloading risk and responsibility onto aging families and aging identities. Neither recognizes aging which is not secondary to an independent policy objective. Both mask the possibility of authentic tasks of aging.

If the analysis outlined above is accepted, then it is possible to see contemporary social policy addressing diverse aspects of the family life of older people in differing and contradictory ways. Contradictory narratives for the aging family exist in a landscape that is a one and the same time increasingly blurred in terms of roles and relationships and split-off in terms of narrative coherence and consequences for identity. Indeed in a future of complex and multiple policy agendas, it would appear that a narrative of social inclusion through active aging can coexist with one emphasizing carer obligation and surveillance. Such a co-existence may occasionally become inconvenient at the level of public rhetoric. However, at an experiential and ontological level, that is to say at the level of the daily lives of older adults and their families, the implications may become particularly acute. Multiple co-existing policy narratives may become a significant source of risk to identity maintenance within the aging family.

One has to imagine a situation in which later lives are lived, skating on a surface of legitimizing discourse. For everyday intents and purposes this surface supplies the ground on which one can build an aging identity, relate to other family members and immediate community. However, there is always the possibility of slipping, of being subject to trauma or transition. Serious slippage will provoke being thrown onto a terrain that had previously been hidden, an alternative narrative of aging with entirely different premises, relationship expectations and possibilities for personal expression.

Policy narratives, however, are also continually breaking down and fail to achieve hegemony as they encounter lived experience. Indeed, it could be argued that a continuous process of re-constitution takes place via the play of competing narratives. When we are addressing the issue of older people's identity in later life we can usefully note Foucault's (1977) contention that there has been a growth in attempts to control national populations through discourses of normality, but at the same time this has entailed increasing possibilities for self-government.

Part of the attractiveness of thinking in terms of narrative, that policies tell us stories that we don't have necessarily to believe, is the opening of a critical distance between description and intention. Policy narratives describe certain, often idealized, states of affairs. Depicting them as stories, rather than realities, allows the interrogation of the space between that description and experience (cf Powell, 2005).

Conclusion

What does this examination of social policy discourse and everyday stories of family and aging selves tell us, and what are the lessons for future sociological research?

Firstly, we are alerted to the partial nature of the narratives supplied by social policy, which affects our perception of families as well as of older people. The simplifying role of policy discourse tends to highlight certain, politically valued, aspects of experience to the exclusion of other possibilities. These are also the discourses most likely to be reflected in policy-sponsored research.

Secondly, the inclusion of certain roles, activities and age bands in policy discourse has a legitimizing role. In other words, it not only sanctions the direction of resources and the action of helping professionals important though that is. It also contributes to the legitimated identities afforded to people in later life. This includes at least two factors key to aging identity: the creation of social spaces in which to perform aging roles and be recognized as such, and, the supply of material with which explicit yet personal narratives of self and family can be made.

Thirdly, a significant element in the "riskiness" of building aging and family identities under contemporary conditions may arise from the existence of multiple policy discourses that personal narratives, of family, self and relations between the two, have to negotiate. Research on the management of identity, should, then, be sensitized to the multiple grounds on which identity might be built and the potential sources of conflict and uncertainty may bring.

Fourthly, attention should be paid to the relationship between tacit and explicit influences on identity management in late-life families. The multiple sources for building stories "to live by" and the tension between legitimizing discourses and alternative narratives of self and family, would suggest that identities are managed at different levels, for different audiences and at different levels of awareness. There are implications here for both the conceptualization of familial and policy relations and for the practice of research. The story that the researcher hears and then records may be tapping a particular level of disclosure, depending in part upon how the research itself is perceived, and indeed, perceives itself.

REFERENCES

Beck, U. (1998), *Democracy Without Enemies*, Polity: Cambridge, UK.

Beck, U. (2005), *Power and Countervailing Power in the Global Age*, Polity: Cambridge, UK.

Bengtson, V.L. and Achenbaum, W. (1993), *The Changing Contract Across Generations*, Aldine De Gruyter: New York.

Bengtson, V.L.; Giarrusso, R.; Silverstein, M., and Wang, H. (2000), Families and Intergenerational Relationships in Aging Societies, *Hallym International Journal of Aging*, Vol. 2, No. 1, pp. 3-10.

BGOP, Better Government of Older People (2000), *Better Government for Older People*, BGOP: Wolverhampton, UK.

Biggs, S. (1996), A Family Concern: Elder Abuse in British Social Policy, *Critical Social Policy*, Vol. 16, No. 2, pp. 63-88.

Biggs, S. (2001), Toward Critical Narrativity: Stories of Aging in Contemporary Social Policy, *Journal of Aging Studies*, Vol. 15, pp. 1-14.

Biggs, S. and Powell, J. (2000), Surveillance and Elder Abuse: The Rationalities and Technologies of Community Care, *Journal of Contemporary Health*, Vol. 4, No. 1, pp. 43-49.

Biggs, S. and Powell, J. (2001), A Foucauldian Analysis of Old Age and the Power of Social Welfare, *Journal of Aging and Social Policy*, Vol. 12, No. 2, pp. 93-112.

Biggs, S.; Phillipson, C., and Kingston, P. (1995), *Elder Abuse in Perspective*, Open University Press: Buckingham, UK.

Biggs, S.; Estes, C., and Phillipson, C. (2003), *Social Theory, Social Policy and Ageing*, Open University Press: Buckingham, UK.

BJF, Beth Johnson Foundation (1999), *Intergenerational Programmes*, BJF: Stoke, UK.

Blair, T. (1996), *New Britain: My Vision of a Young Country*, Fourth Estate: London.

Boaz, A.; Hayden, C., and Bernard, M. (1999), Attitudes and Aspiriations of Older People. *DSS Research Report*, No. 101, CDS: London.

Bornat, J.; Dimmock, B.; Jones, D., and Peace, S. (1999), Stepfamilies and Older People, *Ageing and Society*, Vol. 19, No. 2, pp. 239-62.

Brodgen, M. and Nijhar, P (2005), Crime, Abuse and Social Harm: Towards an Integrated Approach, in in A. Wahidin and M.E. Cain (eds.), *Ageing, Crime and Society*, Willan: Devon, UK.

Carmel, S.; Morse, C.A., and Torres-Gil, F.M. (eds.) (2007), *Lessons on Aging from Three Nations*, Baywood: New York.

Chamberlayne, P. and King, A. (2000), *Cultures of Care*, Policy Press: London.

Chambre, S.M. (1993), Volunteerism by Elders: Past Traditions and Future Prospects, *The Gerontologist*, Vol. 33, pp. 221-28.

Cloke, P.; Johnsen, S., and May, J. (2006), Ethical Citizenship? Volunteers and the Ethics of Providing Services for Homeless People, *Geoforum*, Vol. 38, No. 6, pp. 1089-101.

De Beauvoir, S. (1979), *Old Age*, Penguin: London.

DSS, Department of Social Security (1998), *Building a Better Britain for Older People*, HMSO: London.

Duckworth, L. (2001), Grandparents Who Bring Up Children Need More Help, *Independent*, September 13.

Featherstone, M. and Hepworth, M. (1993), Images of Positive Ageing, in M. Featherstone and A. Wernick (eds.), *Images of Ageing*, Routledge: London.

Finch, J. and Mason, J. (1993), *Negotiating FamilyResponsibilities*,Routledge: London.

Foucault, M. (1977,) *Discipline and Punish*, Tavistock: London.

Freidenberg, J. (2000), *Growing Old in EL Barrio*, New York University Press: New York.

Giddens, A. (1998), *The Third Way*, Polity: Cambridge, UK.

Girrard, I. and Ogg, J. (1998), *Grandparenting in France and England*, paper presented to the British Society of Gerntology, Sheffield, UK.

Gray, J. (1995), *Enlightenment's Wake*, Routledge: London..

Guardian-ICM Poll (2001), *Grandparenting and Retirement Activities*, ICM: London.

Gubrium, J.F. (1992), *Out of Control: Family Therapy and Domestic Disorder*, Sage: Thousand Oaks, CA.

Hardill, I.; and Baines, S., and Six, P. (2007) Volunteering for All? Explaining Patterns of Volunteering and Identifying Strategies to Promote It, *Policy and Politics*, Vol. 35, No. 3, pp. 395-412.

Hargrave, T. and Anderson, W. (1992), *Finishing Well: Aging and Reparation in the Intergenerational Family*, Brunner and Mazel: New York.

Hayden, C.; Boaz, A., and Taylor, F. (1999), Attitudes and Aspirations of Older People: A Qualitative Study, *DSS Research Report*, No. 102, CDS, London.

Holstein, J. and Gubrium, J. (2000), *The Self We Live By*, Oxford University Press: Oxford, UK.

Izuhara, M. (2000), *Family Change and Housing in Postwar Japanese Society*, Ashgate: Aldershot, UK.

Katz, S. (1999), Busy Bodies: Activity, Aging, and the Management of Everyday Life, *Journal of Aging Studies*, Vol. 14, No. 2, pp. 135-52.

Kennedy, G. (1990), College Students Expectations of Grandparent and Grandchild Role Behaviours, *The Gerontologist*, Vol. 30, No. 1, pp. 43-48.

Kenyon, G.; Ruth, J., and Mader, W. (1999), Elements of a Narrative Gerontology, in V. Bengtson and K. Schaie (eds.), *Handbook of Theories of Ageing*, Springer: New York.

Kivnick, H. (1988), Grandparenthood, Life Review and Psychosocial Development, *Journal of Gerontological Social Work*, Vol. 12, No. 3, pp. 63-82.

Land, H. (1999), *The Changing Worlds of Work and Families*, Open University Press: Buckingham, UK.

McAdams, D. (1993), *The Stories We Live By*, Morrow: New York.

McLeod, J. (1997), *Narrative and Psychotherapy*, Sage: London.

Mills, T. (1999), When Grandchildren Grow Up, *Journal of Aging Studies*, Vol. 13, No. 2, pp. 219-39.

Minkler, M. (1999), Intergenerational Households Headed by Grandparents: Contexts, Realities and Implications for Policy, *Journal of Aging Studies*, Vol. 13, No. 2, pp. 199-218.

Phillipson, C. (1998), *Reconstructing Old Age*, Sage: London.

Phillipson, C.; Bernard, M.; Phillips, J., and Ogg, J. (2000), *The Family and Community Life of Older People*, Routledge: London.

Pillemer, K. and Wolf, R. (1986), *Elder Abuse: Conflict in the Family*, Auburn House: Westport, CT.

Powell, J. and Biggs, S. (2001), Rethinking Structure and Agency: Bio-Ethics, Aging and Technologies of the Self, *Sincronia*, Winter.

Powell, J. (2005), *Social Theory of Aging*, Rowman and Littlefield: New York.

Powell, J. and Owen, T. (2007), *Reconstructing Postmodernism: Critical Debates*, Nova Science: New York.

Qualls, S. (1999), Realising Power in Intergenerational Hierachies, in M. Duffy (ed.), *Handbook of Counselling and Psychotherapy with Older Adults*, Wiley: New York.

Roberto, K. (1990), Grandparent and Grandchild Relationships, in T.H. Brubaker (ed.), *Family Relationships in Later Life*, Sage: London.

Ryff, C. and Seltzer, M. (1996), *The Parental Experience in Midlife*, Chicago University Press: Chicago, IL.

Scharf, T. and Wenger, G. (1995), *International Perspectives on Community Care for Older People*, Avebury: Aldershot, UK.

Schreck, H. (2000), *Community and Caring*, UPA: New York.

Silverstein, M. and Bengtson, V.L. (1997), Intergenerational Solidarity and the Structure of Adult Child-Parent Relationships in American Families, *American Journal of Sociology*, Vol. 103, No. 2, pp. 429-60.

Thompson, P. (1999), The Role of Grandparents When Parents Part or Die: Some Reflections on the Mythical Decline of the Extended Family, *Ageing and Society*, Vol. 19, No. 4, pp. 471-503.

Thomson, E. and Minkler, M. (2001), American Grandparents Providing Extensive Childcare to Their Grandchildren: Prevalence and Profile, *The Gerontologist*, Vol. 41, No. 2, pp. 201-09.

UKG, UK Government (1981), Growing Older, HMSO: London.

UKG, UK Government (1989), *Community Care: An Agenda for Action*, HMSO: London.

UKG, UK Government (1990), *NHS and Community Care Act*, HMSO: London.

UKG, UK Government (1993), *No Longer Afraid: The Safeguard of Older People in Domestic Settings*, HMSO: London.

UKG, UK Government (2000a), *Winning the Generation Game*, www.cabinet-office.gov.uk.

UKG, UK Government (2000b), *Supporting Families*, HMSO: London.

Waldrop, D.; Weber, J.; Herald, S.; Pruett, J.; Cooper, K., and Jouzapavicius, K. (1999), Wisdom and Life Experience: How Grandfathers Mentor Their Grandchildren, *Journal of Aging and Identity*, Vol. 4, No. 1, pp. 33-46.

Walker, Alan (2002), A Strategy for Active Ageing, *International Social Security Review*, Vol. 55, No. 1, pp. 121-39.

Walker, A. and Naegele, G. (1999), *The Politics of Old Age in Europe*, Open University Press: Buckingham, UK.

Walker, A. and Aspalter, C. (eds.) (2008), *Securing the Future for Old Age in Europe*, Casa Verde: Hong Kong.

Wenger, C. (1984), *Support Networks for Older People*, CSPRD: Bangor, UK.

15

Corporate Crime, Aging, and Pensions in the UK

JASON POWELL AND AZRINI WAHIDIN

Corporate crime fails to feature in the vast majority of public responses about crime. Indeed, in mainstream mass media coverage in the UK, issues related to crime, law and order narratives covers "muggings," "robberies," "murders," and "street crimes" (cf Tombs and Slapper, 1999). The mass media give scantily attention to corporate crimes and their impact on the daily texture of day to day living of older people who are victims of such practices. By looking at the mis-selling of financial pension services this chapter seeks to demonstrate that corporate crime represents a significant crime problem for older people in the UK.

Similarly, the academic study of corporate crime in relation to older people is scarce (Phillipson, 1998; Wahidin and Cain, 2005; cf Michalowski and Kramer, 2006; Potell and Geis, 2006) and is as unreported as the actual corporate malpractices against older people. Indeed, it is pertinent to ask the question of what is "corporate crime"? It was in 1939 at the *American Sociological Association Annual Conference* that Edwin Sutherland (1940) introduced the idea of "white-collar" crime as "a crime committed by a person of respectability and high social status in the course of his occupation" (Sutherland, 1983: 7). This idea refuted the stereotypical view of the criminal as from the lower socio-economic groups. But it was not until the end of the 1960s that there was a renewed interest in this field that was also concerned with the social effects of corporate activity. For the purpose of this chapter and although there are limitations of this definition, Kramer's comments (1984: 18) on the concept of corporate crime is a useful starting point:

> "By the concept of 'corporate crime,' then, we wish to focus on criminal acts (of omission or commission) which are the result of deliberate decision making (or culpable negligence) of those who occupy structural positions within the organization as corporate executives or managers. These decisions are organizationally based— made in accordance with the normative goals."

It is has been over 25 years since the political formalization of private occupational pension schemes in the United Kingdom (Lansley, 2000). The practices of Corporations with regard to pension schemes have in the past decade received scantily uncritical sociological acclaim in the sub-disciplines of British Sociology despite some admirable research: in *Critical Gerontology* (Phillipson, 1998; Walker and Naegele, 1999; Estes *et al.*, 2003) and with even less coverage in *Criminology* (Clarke, 1996; Tombs and Slapper, 1999; Phillips, 2005). Yet, according to Walker and Naegele (1999) given the low incomes of the majority of older people in the UK, pensions are matter of great importance; though in disciplinary social science domains as Criminology and Gerontology such urgency have not been analyzed with as much coverage as it deserves—there is then, conversely, an urgency to reflect on and disseminate an understanding of relationship of corporate crime and old age (cf Powell and Wahidin, 2005).

Historically, pension policy has been based on liberal discourses of "choice" and "consumer freedom." Neville Chamberlain had been the first politician of importance to come out (April 1891) in favor of state organized old-age pensions. Lloyd George seemed to have sensed that, if Liberalism were to have a secure future, it would have to prove its legitimacy in the eyes of the working man and woman by showing entirely new kind of sensitivity to the problems thrown up by industrial society (Tombs and Slapper, 1999). This though was not the principal source of the social legislation, which characterized the 1908-1912 period. In rapid succession the Liberal Ministry carried old-age pensions (1908), and created the National insurance scheme covering sickness, invalidity, and unemployment. The tax system also changed, with the introduction of differentiation between earned and unearned income (1907).

In recent times, both state and private pensions were endorsed by many commentators as the political panacea for alleviating the alleged crises of an "aging time-bomb" (Jackson and Powell, 2001) confronting the public pension provision in the UK. In the British context, private pensions are ways in which the state continues to rely on "apocalyptic" projections ("demographic time bomb") about ageing populations in order to justify cuts in public expenditure (Powell, 2001). *The Guardian* newspaper (TG, 1989: 17) has echoed such fears of a moral panic of old age by stating:

"A demographic time bomb to tick into the next century—This year, Britain will be attempting to grapple with the implications of the time bomb—the decline of the British teenager, and the rise in the proportion of old people in the community."

This study constructs the hagiography surrounding private pensions in UK and provides a critical analysis of a number of corporate scandals that have impinged on old age. Before considering these criticisms, there will be a dissection of the failure of the government of both left and right persuasion to provide quality pension systems, which provides the sociological backdrop for the emergence of private pensions and correspondent lack of regulation and safety of such provision for older people in western world.

A critical examination of the emergence of private pension provision policy initiatives raises serious questions. Whose account was to count in the analysis leading up to its implementation under Reagan/ Thatcher in 1980s was based on a hierarchical vision of truth in which the definition of reality articulated by older people was secondary to reality defined by "experts"/state servants such as pension policy advisors and government ministers. This is not the place to explore both the epistemological and ontological debates concerning definitions of reality that have developed in social gerontology in recent years (Wahidin and Powell, 2001). However, it is important to note that pension policy fails to convey in any strong sense alternative definitions of truth or different visions of truth based on older people's subjective experiences of pensions in UK (Phillipson, 1998), Europe (Walker and Naegale, 1999) and USA (Longino and Murphy, 1995; Moody, 1999). Rather, the structural agism of private pension schemes directs its gaze downwards towards older people thus reinforcing:

> "an overall impression that [*older*] people who need to be researched, these are the ones who are out of step with 'social norms' or who are causing the problems (Smart, 1984: 150-51, *authors' emphasis*)."

Conversely, British pension policy rarely gazes upwards to look at "the locally powerful" (Smart, 1984) who in the case of older people are deregulated and democratically un-accountable financial organizations (Tombs and Slapper, 1999). The lack of any critical analysis of the role and practices of financial and corporate institutions constitutes a major policy weakness of government regulation impinging on safeguarding older people's finances (Powell, 2001).

The ongoing disputes between older people and central government before and after the introduction of private pension provision and the confusion and conflict between different state servants and older people during the 1980s to the present exemplifies pension politics (Jackson and Powell, 2001; Biggs and Powell, 2003). This provides clear illustrations of the fractured dislocation within government concerning pension policy and welfare policy in general for older people (Powell and Phillipson, 2004).

In the next part of this chapter we assess this contention through focusing on a number of major themes and issues contained on pension policy—the politico-ideological backdrop to its emergence: neoliberalism and ("Third Way") social democracy; and an evaluation of how

Corporations' practices on managing pensions have been detrimental to older people's financial safety in UK.

Neoliberalism and Pensions: A "Watershed" in Pensions

Political debate on pension provision since the Thatcher years, has been dominated by neoliberalism, which postulates the existence of autonomous, assertive, rational individuals who must be protected and liberated from "big government" and state interference (Gray, 1995; Biggs and Powell, 2003). Indeed, Walker and Naegele (1999) claim a startling continuity across Europe is the way pension politics based on marketization have been positioned by governments as these ideas have spread beyond their original western base from UK (Phillipson, 1998) to South Asia (Powell and Cook, 2000; Cook and Powell, 2003) and Australasia (Powell and Cook, 2001).

Although, the first state pension scheme in the UK was created in 1908, the present scheme has its origins from the Beveridge report of 1942 (Hill, 1998). This was supposed to be a universal benefit available to contributors to the National Insurance scheme and payable on a flat rate, subsistence basis (Alcock, 1999). Although, such provision were also "male" based, as Beveridge assumed that for the most part workers were male and that women would be covered by their husbands contributions (Hill, 1998). In the 1970s, the introduction of State Earnings Related Pensions Scheme was set up. This scheme sought to bring the benefits of pension provision to low paid workers and in particular women. It allowed members up to 20 years absence from the workforce for purposes of childcare gave full entitlement of pensions to widows and calculated the pension on the best 20 years earnings during membership of the scheme (Walker, 2000). The scheme never came into full effect and Thatcher cut the scheme in the 1980s and many pensioners were put in an impoverished position.

So, despite the "Beveridgean dream" on pensions being universal to the populace in UK, Neoliberal or Thatcherite policies on pensions have ideologically almost always started from a position of laissez-faire (Phillipson, 1998). It can be seen that that neoliberal policy came to focus on private provision whilst only represents the point at which a minimalist approach from the state touches pensions, they come to mark the dominant social discourse through which old age and pensions are made visible in the public domain to society at large.

Private pension provision became a key building block of policy toward an aging population in the UK. It increased the independence of individuals from government and enabled a reduction in direct support form the state. It is perhaps emblematic that a policy based ostensively on the premises of *laissez-faire* caused problems of pension provision for older people in 1980s. To understand this, it is important to examine trends tacit in the debate on pensions and aging that are central to wider public policy. Indeed, wider economic priorities, to "roll back the state" and thereby release resources for individualism and free enterprise, had become translated into a financial discourse about personal obligations and the need to enforce them. If older people did not have sufficient national insurance savings, then the state would have to pick up the bill. In summation, state discourses on pensions provided less help for older people running through Thatcherite 1980s and the John Major Government until 1997.

Social Democracy and Pensions: Citizens or Consumers?

Social democratic policies toward older people and pensions arose from the premise that by the early 1990s, the free-market policies of the Thatcher years had seriously damaged the social fabric of the nation state and that its citizens needed to be encouraged to identify again with the national project (Giddens, 1998). A turn to an alternative, sometimes called "the Third Way," emerging under Clinton, Blair and Schröder administrations in the US and parts of Europe, attempted to find means of mending that social fabric, and as part of it, relations between older people and the State.

Anthony Giddens (1998) in the UK and Ulrich Beck (1992) in Germany, both proponents of social democratic politics, have claimed that citizens, and in this case, older people, are faced with the task of piloting themselves through a changing world in which globalization has transformed our relations with each other, now based on avoiding risk.

According to Giddens (1998), a new partnership is needed between government and civil society. Government support to the renewal of community through local initiative, would gives an increasing role to voluntary organizations, encourages social entrepreneurship and significantly, supports the democratic individuality characterized by "equality, mutual respect, autonomy, decision-making through communication and freedom of violence." It is argued that social policy should be less concerned with equality and more with inclusion, with community participation reducing the moral and financial hazard of dependence.

Through an increased awareness of the notion of ageism, the influence of European ideas about social inclusion and North American social communitarianism, older people found themselves transformed into active citizens who should be encouraged to participate in society, rather than be seen as a potential burden upon it (Biggs, 2001).

In terms of setting up a pensions system consistent with its ideological outlook on social welfare, the New Labour government has set up proposals to create a scheme whereby the state will be responsible for those earning less that £9,000 a year with the basic pension topped up with a means-tested scheme, the minimum income guarantee which will be linked to earnings. The government has said that there will be a short-term state second pension for those in the income brand £9-18 thousand that will ensure that all contributors will have the benefits of an occupational pension.

As and when however the private pension sector brings about the "stakeholder" pensions of equal value the state model will be run down. In addition, all those earning over £18k will be expected to belong to a private or occupational scheme. Despite all this, the UK "public" pensioner earns £88 a week, the lowest income of a pensioner in Europe (Walker, 2000).

The dominant preoccupation of New Labour, is the assertion of citizenship but underpinned by people providing for their own pensions. There is a change of emphasis toward the notion of stakeholder pensions as an issue distinctive from neoliberalism, and as such draws on contemporary gerontological observations of the "blurring" of age-based identities (Featherstone and Hepworth, 1995) and the growth of the older consumer (Katz, 1999). However, in the field of pensions political parties of both neoliberal and social democratic persuasion have done little to intervene in order to facilitate active lifestyles in consumer spaces left void by malpractice and pension crimes. If this is an indictment on public pension provision in the UK then the next part of this study looks at private pensions and impingement on corporate crimes against older people (cf Wahidin and Cain, 2005).

"Pensions Mis-Selling"

Private occupational schemes became popular and for time had contributed to above average incomes for persons of pensionable age since 1979. In the 1998 Green Paper on pensions, the Government argued that the development of occupational pensions schemes might have peaked, particularly given the deadline in employments where the tradition of such schemes is strong, such as parts of the public sector. But as the pattern of employment changes with a growth in short term contracts, changing employment patters have affected the capacity to build up pension rights. SSAC concluded from its review of pension provision that:

> "while it is clear that private provision for retirement will have a continuing and increasingly important role for the future. For some people it can never provide more than part of the answer to ensuring a reasonable level of income. State provision will continue to be needed for people who have been unable to make their own provision, or adequate provision, for their retirement—for example, those whose opportunities to earn have been limited or disrupted by disability, unemployment or caring responsibilities" (SSAC: para 5.9).

A series of illegalities in pensions for older people is interesting not simply because of the scale of the economic consequences of the offences, but because of the way in which opportunity and motivation for these illegalities were created by deregulation, privatization and an ideology which combined a rolling back of state welfare and increased emphasis upon privatized welfare provision. Thus Clarke (1996) has documented how the gradual withdrawal of the Conservative Government from pension provision, coupled with deregulation of the retail financial services sector in the UK in the latter half of the 1980s (particularly with the Financial Services Act, 1986), contributed to the "biggest scandal of them all" in the sector.

Pensions providers launched into a hard sell, targeting many public sector workers in well developed pensions programs, wrongly advising many to cash in their contributions and transfer them to a new, private scheme about which they provided false and misleading information. Black refers to a survey conducted by the Securities and Investments Board, which found that only 9 percent of pensions companies had complied with legal requirements when originally advising on these pensions transfers (Black, 1997: 178). Moreover, once exposed:

> "the industry proved extremely reluctant to admit wrong doing, even by way of over-selling, still less mis-selling. Enquiries by the supervisory regulator, the Securities and Investments Board in the early 1980s, eventually produced an estimate that 1.4 million people may have been mis-sold personal pensions and had a right to have their cases reviewed and awarded compensation as appropriate; the costs of this were estimated at between £2 and £4 billion" (Clarke, 1996: 14).

Indeed, despite the establishment of a timetable for reviewing and if necessary compensating for cases, the pensions providers have consistently missed deadlines, ignored cajoling, and proven relatively resistant to government threats. While breaches had been first uncovered in 1990 (TG, 1997b), many of the offending companies—amongst whom were some of the UK's better-known and largest financial services retailers such as Abbey Life, Allied Dunbar, Co-op Insurance, Legal and General, Norwich Union, Royal Sun Alliance, Pearl Assurance, Prudential, and TSB Life—had resolved less than 10 percent of the cases under their respective review by 1997 (TG, 1997a).

Incredibly, a survey by KPMG Peat Marwick of pensions advice given during 1991-1993, a period after the mis-selling had been first exposed, revealed that in "four out of five cases" pensions companies were still giving advice which fell short of the legally required minima (cited in Black, 1997: 178, and footnote 143).

We have discussed above how the widespread mis-selling of personal pensions in the UK (from the mid-1980s onwards) typically involve what Bourdieu's terms an "objective complicity" between a wide variety of stakeholders—i.e., financial service providers and financial advisors (cf Bourdieu, 1993). What we have attempted to demonstrate is that these social fields are sites of struggles between different stakeholders. However, there is "an objective complicity" which underlies all these antagonisms, seen most clearly in the mis-selling of pensions, endowments, etc.

Personal finance and the life insurance industry is a promotional culture (Wernick, 1991), in which information and persuasion are inextricably linked. Firms, financial advisors compete and underlining their competition is an objective complicity of attracting investors into the field. These products are consumed in private.

By the end of 1997, the sum involved in this series of offences was consistently being referred to as £4 billion (FT, 1997b) and involving two million or more victims (TT, 1997). Not only did the regulatory bodies fail to prevent the mis-selling, but the great majority of victims still have not had their claims for compensation settled. In 1997 the number of *prima facia* victims who have been compensated (12,650 out of 570,000 priority cases—i.e., little over 2.2 percent) (FT, 1997a). Treasury Economic Secretary Liddell began resorting to consistent but apparently fruitless efforts to "name and shame" the (41) most recalcitrant offenders (TG, 1997c). Early in 1998, the new Regulatory Body, the Financial Services Authority, cited new research which estimated the final costs as "up to £11billion, almost three times the original estimate. The number of victims could be as high as 2.4 million" (TG, 1998: 11). As the cost of one particular series of crimes, this figure of £11 billion—even if ultimately an over-estimate, even though not an annual but a "once-and-for-all" cost—dwarfs the costs of almost all estimates of all forms of street crimes put together in the United Kindom.

Conclusion

Both governments of left and right political persuasion have spoken about the need for private pensions and constantly reinforced this point by talking about the effects of an ageing population will mean public finances could not fund a full pension (Phillipson, 1998; Walker, 2000; Walker and Aspalter, 2008). However, we have seen the effect of private pension schemes—a report by the Office of Fair Trading (1997) found that up to £11 billion had been lost by pensioners in private pension schemes which *The Times* claimed was "the greatest financial scandal of the century" (TT, 1998) Coupled with this, came the discovery after the death of Robert Maxwell that he had extracted by stealth £400 million from his companies' pensions schemes. Discussions of the mis-selling of pensions are replete with attributions of blame.

However, the victims here are those who no longer have the security they thought they bought with a private pension. The question that has to be addressed is why corporate crime is scarcely policed, rarely punished and how this failure contributes to facilitating this type of crime?

REFERENCES

Alcock, P. (1996), *Social Policy in Britain*, Heinemann: London.

Beck, U. (1992), *Risk Society*, Sage: London.

Biggs, S. (2001), Toward Critical Narrativity: Stories of Aging in Contemporary Social Policy, *Journal of Aging Studies*, Vol. 15, pp. 1-14.

Biggs, S. and Powell, J.L. (2003), Older People and Family Policy, in V. Bengston and A. Lowenstein (eds.), *Global Aging and Its Challenge to Families: The Life Course and Aging*, de Gruyter: New York.

Black, J. (1997), *Rules and Regulators*, Oxford University Press: Oxford, UK.

Bourdieu, P., (1993), Concluding Remarks: For a Sociogenetic Understanding of Intellectual Works, in C. Calhoun *et al.* (eds.), *Bourdieu: Critical Perspectives*, Polity: Cambridge, UK.

Clarke, M. (1996), *Citizens' Financial Futures: The Regulation of Retail Financial Investment in Britain*, Ashgate: Aldershot, UK.

Cook, I.G. and Powell, J.L. (2003), Active Aging in China, *Journal of Social Sciences and Humanities*, Vol. 26, No. 2, pp. 1-10

Estes, C.; Biggs, S., and Philipson, C. (2003), *Social Theory, Ageing, and Social Policy*, Open University Press: Milton Keynes, UK.

Featherstone, M. and Hepworth, M. (1995), Images of Positive Ageing, in M. Featherstone and A. Wernick (eds.), *Images of Ageing*, Routledge: London.
FT, Financial Times (1997a), Business News: Pensions, May 17, p. 15.
FT, Financial Times (1997b), Serious Business, September 19, p. 8.
Giddens, A. (1998), *The Third Way*, Polity: Cambridge, UK.
Gray, J. (1995), *Enlightenment's Wake*, Routledge: London.
Hill, M. (1998), *Understanding Social Policy*, Open University Press: London.
Jackson, S. and Powell, J.L. (2001), Understanding Social Policy in Europe, *Journal of Health Politics, Policy and Law*, Vol. 26, No. 6, pp. 181-89.
Katz, S. (1999), Lifecourse, Lifestyle, and Postmodern Culture: Corporate Representations of Later Life, paper presented at *Restructuring Work and the Life-Course: An International Symposium*, Institute of Human Development, University of Toronto, Canada.
Kramer, R.C. (1984), Corporate Criminality: The Development of an Idea, in E. Hochstedler (ed.), *Corporations as Criminals*, Sage: Beverley Hills, CA.
Lansley, J.W. (2000), Social Policy and Pensions, in A. Pratt and M. Lavallette (eds.), *Social Policy: A Methodological and Critical Introduction*, Sage: London.
Longino, C.F. and Murphy, J. (1995), *The Old-Age Challenge to the Bio-medical Model: Paradigm Strain and Health Policy*, Baywood: New York.
Michalowski, R.J. and Kramer, R.C. (eds.) (2006), *State-Corporate Crime: Wrongdoing at the Intersection of Business and Government*, Rutgers University Press: Chapel Hill, NC.
Moody, H.R. (1999), *Aging: Concepts and Controversies*, Sage: New York.
OFT, Office of Fair Trading (1997), *The Annual Report by the Office of Fair Trading 1997*, Office of Fair Trading, Government, UK.
Philipps, J. (2005), Crime and Older People the Research Agenda, in A. Wahidin and M.E. Cain (eds.), *Ageing, Crime and Society*, Willan: Devon, UK.
Phillipson, C. (1998), *Reconstructing Old Age*, Sage: London.
Pontell, H.N. and Geis, G.L. (eds.) (2006), *International Handbook of White-Collar and Corporate Crime*, Springer: New York.
Powell, J.L. (2001), Theorizing Gerontology: The Case of Old Age, Professional Power, and Social Policy in the United Kingdom, *Journal of Aging and Identity*, Vol. 6, No. 3, pp. 117-35.
Powell, J.L. and Cook, I.G. (2000), A Tiger Behind and Coming Up Fast: Governmentality and the Politics of Population Control in China, *Journal of Aging and Identity*, Vol. 5, No. 2, pp. 79-91.
Powell, J.L. and Cook, I.G. (2001), Understanding Foucauldian Philosophy: The Case of the Chinese State and the Surveillance of Older People,

International Journal of Language, Society and Culture, Vol. 8, No. 1, pp. 1-9.

Powell, J.L. and Phillipson, C. (2004), Risk, Social Welfare, and Old Age, in E. Tulle (ed.), *Old Age and Human Agency*, Nova Science: New York.

Powell, J.L. and Wahidin, A. (2005), Rethinking Criminology: The Case of Ageing Studies, in A. Wahidin and M.E. Cain (eds.), *Ageing, Crime and Society*, Willan: Devon, UK.

Smart, B. (1994), *Postmodernity*, Routledge: London.

SSAC (1994), State Benefits and Private Provision: The Review of Social Security, *Paper*, No. 2, Leeds Publishing Services: Leeds, UK.

Sutherland, E. (1940), White Collar Criminality, *American Sociological Review*, Vol. 5, pp. 1-12.

Sutherland, E. (1983), *White Collar Crime: The Uncut Version*, Yale University Press: New Haven, CT.

TG, The Guardian (1989), Corporate Business Problem, January 2, p. 17.

TG, The Guardian (1997a), Pensions in the UK, July 10, p. 5.

TG, The Guardian (1997b), Corporate News, October 9, p. 8.

TG, The Guardian (1997c), Corporate Problems and Pensions, November 19, p. 4.

TG, The Guardian (1998), The Hidden Costs of Pensions, March 13, p. 11.

Tombs, S. and Slapper, G. (1999), *Corporate Crime*, Longman: London.

TT, The Times (1997), A Pension Mess, September 10, p. 11.

TT, The Times (1998), Biggest Scandal of Pensions in UK, September 8, pp. 11-12.

Wahidin, A. and Cain, M.E. (2005), *Ageing, Crime and Society*, Willan: Devon, UK.

Wahidin, A. and Powell, J.L. (2001), The Loss of Aging Identity: Social Theory, Old Age, and the Power of Special Hospitals, *Journal of Aging and Identity*, Vol. 6, No. 1, pp. 31-49.

Walker, A. (ed.) (2000), *The Politics of Old Age in Europe*, McGraw Hill: London.

Walker, A. and Aspalter, C. (eds.) (2008), *Securing the Future for Old Age in Europe*, Casa Verde: Hong Kong.

Walker, A. and Naegele, G. (eds.) (1999), *The Politics of Old Age in Europe*, Open University Press: Buckingham, UK.

Wernick, A. (1991), *Promotional Culture: Advertising, Ideology, and Symbolic Expression*, Sage: London.

Index

About the Contributors

PETER ABRAHAMSON is Professor of Sociology, the Department of Sociology, University of Copenhagen, Denmark. Prof. Peter Abrahamson is one of the foremost leading scholars on pan-European Social Policy. His most recent publiccations include e.g. *Política Fiscal y Protección Social en Estados Pequeños: Comparando Escandinavia y Centroamérica* (El Instituto Centroamericano de Estudios Fiscales, 2007), *Welfare and Families in Europe* (with B. Greve and T. Boje, Ashgate, 2005), *Poverty in the European Union* (co-author, European Parliament, 1998), *Social Protection in Europe* (co-author, European Commission, 1993), and Free Trade and Social Citizenship: Prospects and Possibilities of the Central American Free Trade Agreement (*Global Social Policy*), Reconciliation of Work and Family Life in Europe: A Case Study of Denmark, France, Germany, and the United Kingdom (*Journal of Comparative Policy Analysis*), Family and/or Work in Europe (with C. Wehner, *Journal of Comparative Family Studies*), La nouvelle portée de l´espace et du lieu quant a la citoyenneté: Le cas de l`Union Européenne (*Lien Social et Politiques*), Coping With Urban Poverty: Changing Citizenship in Europe? (*International Journal of Urban and Regional Research*), Povery and Welfare in Denmark (*Scandinavian Journal of Social Welfare*), and Welfare and Poverty in the Europe of the 1990s (*International Journal of Health Services*).

CHRISTIAN ASPALTER is Professor of Social Policy, Social Work and Social Administration Program, Beijing Normal University-Hong Kong Baptist University United International College, Zhuhai, China. His most recent journal publications include The East Asian Welfare Model (*International Journal of Social Welfare*), New Developments in the Theory of Comparative Social Policy (*Journal of Comparative Social Welfare*), Freedom, Dehumanization and Welfare: An Asian Perspective (*Journal of Comparative Social Welfare*), Strategies of Welfare State Reform in Aging Societies (*Hallym International Journal of Aging*), *The American and the European Social Dream: The Competition of Welfare Regimes* (with J. Weidenholzer, *Journal of Comparative Social Welfare*), and The Asian Cure for Health Care (*Far Eastern Economic Review*). His latest book publications include *Debating Social Development: Strategies for Social Development, Vol. 1* (co-editor, with S. Singh, Casa Verde, 2008), *The State of Social Welfare in Asia* (co-editor, with A. Dashkina, A. Aldosary and S. Singh, Casa Verde, 2008), *Health Care Systems in Europe and Asia* (co-editor, with Y. Uchida and R. Gauld, Casa Verde, 2008), and *Securing the Future for Old Age in Europe* (co-editor, with Alan Walker, Casa Verde, 2008).

JIM GODDARD is Senior Lecturer of Social Policy at the University of Bradford, UK. His publications include *The Politics of Childhood: International Perspectives, Contemporary Developments* (co-editor, with S. MacNamee and A. James, Palgrave Macmillan, 2004), *Contemporary Childcare Policy and Practice* (with B. Fawcett and B. Featherstone, Palgrave Macmillan, 2004), *State Child Care: Looking After Children?* (with C. Hayden, S. Gorin and N. Van der Spek, Jessica Kingsley, 1999), as well as Street Children in Contemporary Greece (with P. Altanis, *Children and Society*), Youth Justice Policy in the United Kingdom (*Criminal Justice Studies*), New Labour, Children's Rights and the United Nations: Could do Better'' (*Journal of Social Welfare and Family Law*), The Education of Looked After Children (*Child and Family Social Work*), and Methodological Issues in Researching Criminal Justice Policy: Belief Systems and the Causes of Crime (*International Journal of the Sociology of Law*).

ARTHUR GOULD researched and taught before as a Senior Lecturer of Social Policy, at the Department of Social Sciences, University of Loughborough, UK. His publications include *Developments in Swedish Social Policy: Resisting Dionysus* (Palgrave Macmillan, 2001), *Capitalist Welfare Systems: A Comparison of Japan, Britain and Sweden* (Longman, 1994), and *Conflict and Control in Welfare Policy: The Swedish Experience* (Longman, 1989), as well as, The Criminalisation of Buying Sex: The Politics of Prostitution in Sweden (*Journal of Social Policy*), The Erosion of the Welfare State: Swedish Social Policy and the EU (*Journal of European Social Policy*), A Drug-Free Europe? (*Druglink*), Sweden's Syringe Exchange Debate (*Journal of Social Policy*), Pollution Ritual in Sweden: The Pursuit of a Drug-Free Society (*Scandinavian Journal of Social Welfare*), and Cleaning the People's Home: Recent Developments in Sweden's Addiction Policy (*British Journal of Addiction*).

KIM JINSOO is Professor at the Department of Social Welfare, Yonsei University, Seoul, Korea. His publications include *Industrial Welfare* (Nanam: 2001), *Income Security for the Elderly in the Western Industrialized Countries* (Korean Institute of Gerontology, 2001), *Annual Report of Social Welfare of Korea 2000* (Upung, 2001), *Income Distribution and Social Welfare* (Yegang, 2002), *Issues and Challenges in Social Welfare of Korea* (Upung, 2001), *Social Welfare Policy for the 21st Century* (Chungmok, 2002), *Social Welfare of Korea 2002-2003* (Upung: 2002), *The Third Way and Welfare Reform* (Gyeongsang University Press, 2003), *Social Security* (Chungmok, 2006), *Social Welfare of Korea 2004-2005* (Upung, 2004), *Social Welfare of Korea 2006-2007* (Upung, 2006), as well as *A Study on Ways to Fill Gap in the Coverage of Social Insurance* (Korea Institute for Health and Social Affairs), *A Study on National Strategy to Address Social Polarization* (The Presidential Commission on Policy Planning), *A Study on Institutional Improvement of Government Employees Pension* (Korea Development Institute), and *A Study on the Rationalization of Benefits Arrangement Overlapped Between the Industrial Accident Compensation Insurance and the National Pension Scheme* (Ministry of Labor of Korea).

MICHAEL OPIELKA is Professor of Social Policy, Social Work Program, Jena College, Germany. His book publications include, for example, *Gesellschaft für alle* (Murmann, 2008), *Werte im Wohlfahrtsstaat* (Vs, 2008), *Kultur versus Religion? Soziologische Analysen zu modernen Wertkonflikten* (Transcript, 2007), *Das Solidarische Bürgergeld* (with W. Strengmann-Kuhn und M. Borchard, Lucius und Lucius, 2007), *Bildungsreform als Sozialreform* (Vs, 2005), *Gemeinschaft in Gesellschaft: Soziologie nach Hegel und Parsons* (Vs, 2004), *Sozialpolitik: Grund-lagen und vergleichende Perspektiven* (Rohwolt, 2004), *Das garantierte Grundeinkommen* (co-editor, with G. Vobruba, Fisher TB, 1986), *Umbau des Sozialstaats: Das Standardwerk grün-alternativer Sozialpolitik* (with I. Ostner, Klartext, 1985), und *Die ökosoziale Frage* (Fischer TB, 1985).

PARK SOJEUNG is Researcher at the Department of Social Welfare, Yonsei University, Seoul, Korea. She is concentrating in her research on areas of comparative social security systems, particularly in Korea and Europe, as well as the study of family policy and social security, and farmers' social security protection.

GILLIAN PASCALL is Professor of Social Policy, School of Sociology and Social Policy, Nottingham University, UK. She has published mainly in the area of Gender and Social Policy, with a strong global perspective. Her publications include for example, Gender and New Labour: After the Male Breadwinner Model (*Social Policy Review*), Emerging Gender Regimes and Policies for Gender Equality in a Wider Europe (with J. Lewis, *Journal of Social Policy*), as well as *Gender Regimes in Transition in Central and Eastern Europe* (with A. Kwak, Policy, 2005),

Disability and Transition to Adulthood: Achieving Independent Living (with N. Hendey, Joseph Rowntree Foundation, 2001), *Women Returning to Higher Education* (with R. Cox, Open University Press, 1993), and *Social Policy: A New Feminist Analysis* (Routledge, 1996)

JASON L. POWELL is Senior Lecturer, School of Sociology and Social Policy, University of Liverpool, UK. His publications include e.g. Towards the Postmodernization of Aging: The Body and Social Theory (*Journal of Aging and Identity*), Ageing in the Risk Society (*International Journal of Sociology and Social Policy*), A Foucauldian Analysis of Old Age and Power of Social Welfare (with S. Biggs, *Journal of Aging and Social Policy*), Family, Caring and Ageing in the United Kingdom (with T. Gilbert, *Scandinavian Journal of Caring Sciences*), Corporate Crime, Aging, and Pensions in Britain (with A. Wahidin, *Journal of Societal and Social Policy*), Aging, Family Policy, and Narrative (*Journal of Societal and Social Policy*), China and Political Narratives of Aging (with I. Cook, *Asian Journal of Social Policy*), "Narrative, Citizenship and Aging" in *Advances in Sociology* (edited by J. Jaworski, Nova Science, 2006), "Risk, Social Welfare and Old Age" in *Old Age and Agency* (edited by E. Tulle, Nova Science, 2004), as well as *New Perspectives on China and Aging* (with I. Cook, Nova Science, 2007), *Reconstructing Postmodernism: Critical Debates* (co-editor, with T. Owen, Nova Science, 2007), *Foucault and Aging* (with A. Wahidin, Nova Science, 2006), *Rethinking Social Theory and Later Life* (Nova Science, 2006), and *Social Theory and Aging* (Rowman and Littlefield, 2005).

AZRINI WAHIDIN is Reader at the School of Sociology, Social Policy, and Social Work, Queens University of Belfast, Northern Ireland, UK. Her publications include *Prison Staff* (co-editor, with J. Bennett and B. Crewe, Willan, 2007), *Ageing, Crime and Society* (with M. Cain, Willan, 2006), *Foucault and Aging* (with J. Powell, Nova Science, 2006), *Criminology* (co-editor, with C. Hale, K. Hayward and E. Wincup, Oxford University Press, 2005), *Older Women and The Criminal Justice System: Running Out of Time* (Jessica Kingsley, 2004), as well as Understanding Old Age and Victimisation: A Critical Exploration (*International Journal of Sociology and Social Policy*), and Prison (Es)capes and Body Tropes: Older Women in the Prison Time Machine (*Journal of Body and Society*).

DOMINIQUE WANG is Assistant Professor at Beijing Normal University-Hong Kong Baptist University, United International College, Zhuhai, China. Her publiccations include, for example, The Austrian and the Swiss Welfare State System in International Comparison (with C. Aspalter, *Journal of Societal and Social Policy*), and The Swedish Health Care System in International Comparison (with C. Aspalter, *Journal of Societal and Social Policy*).

JOSEF WEIDENHOLZER is Professor of Social Policy and Dean, Institute of Social and Societal Policy, University of Linz, Austria. Prof. Weidenholzer is the President of People's Aid (*Volkshilfe*) in Austria and the President of SOLIDAR in Brussels. His publiccations include e.g. The European Dream of a Social Europe (*Journal of Societal and Social Policy*), The American and the European Social Dream: The Competition of Welfare Regimes (with C. Aspalter, *Journal of Comparative Social Welfare*), as well as *Partizipation und Gerechtigkeit* (co-editor, with C. Stelzer-Orthofer, Trauner, 2007), *Sozial- und wirtschaftspolitische Aspekte der sozialen Sicherheit* (with A. Radner, Berliner Wissenschaftsverlag, 2005), *Welfare State Development in East Asia* (co-editor, with C. Aspalter, Sozialwissenschaftliche Vereinigung, 2001), *Soziale Lösungen vor Ort* (co-editor, with W. Peterl *et al.*, Renner Institut, 1999), *Handlungsfelder kommunaler Sozialpolitik* (co-editor, with A. Podlaha *et al.*, Sozialwissenschaftliche Vereinigung, 1993), *Rekonstruktion der Sozialdemokratie* (editor, Sozialwissenschaftliche Vereinigung, 1987), *Zwischen Belegschaft und Unternehmensleitung* (co-editor, with C. Orthofer and P. Brandl, Sozialwissenschaftliche Vereinigung, 1985), *Der sorgende Staat* (Europaverlag, 1985), *Mündliche Geschichte und Arbeiterbewegung* (co-editor, with F. Karlhofer and G. Botz, Boehlau, 1984), and *Auf dem Weg zum Neuen Menschen* (Europaverlag, 1982).

CASA VERDE PUBLISHING

WELFARE CAPITALISM AROUND THE WORLD

Edited by Christian Aspalter, 2003
ISBN 986-80414-2-2
Hardcover, US$ 33,--
www.cv-pub.com

Contents

CASA VERDE PUBLISHING

THE WELFARE STATE IN EMERGING-MARKET ECONOMIES

WITH CASE STUDIES FROM LATIN AMERICA,
CENTRAL-EASTERN EUROPE, AND ASIA

Edited by Christian Aspalter, 2003
ISBN 986-80414-1-4
Hardcover, US$ 29,--
www.cv-pub.com

Contents

CASA VERDE PUBLISHING

NEO-LIBERALISM AND
THE AUSTRALIAN WELFARE STATE

Edited by Christian Aspalter, 2003
ISBN 986-80414-0-6
Hardcover, US$ 22,--
www.cv-pub.com

Contents

CASA VERDE PUBLISHING

THE STATE OF SOCIAL WELFARE IN ASIA

Edited by Christian Aspalter, Antonina Dashkina,
Adel S. Aldosary, and Surendra Singh, 2008
ISBN 978-986-83530-2-2
Hardcover, US$ 30,--
www.cv-pub.com

Contents

1. **The State of Social Welfare: An Introduction**, *Christian Aspalter and Surendra Singh*
2. **Alleviating Unemployment in Saudi Arabia,** *Adel S. Aldosary, Syed M. Rahman, and Mir Shahid*
3. **Affordable Housing in Saudi Arabia**, *Adel S. Aldosary, Syed M. Rahman, and Syed Munawer*
4. **The Development of Social Services in Russia**, *Antonina Dashkina*
5. **Poverty Alleviation Programs in Sri Lanka**, *Amarawansa Ranaweera*
6. **Territorial Justice in China**, *Christian Aspalter*
7. **The State of Social Welfare in Hong Kong**, *Ernest Chui*
8. **Social Welfare in Macau: A State of Transition**, *Samuel Y. Hui and Dicky Lai*
9. **Recent Social Change and Social Policy in Korea**, *Kim Jinsoo*
10. **Social Development Policy in Asia: Taking the Examples of India, China, Malaysia, and Japan**, *Surendra Singh*

CASA VERDE PUBLISHING

RESTORATIVE JUSTICE ACROSS THE EAST AND THE WEST

Edited by Katherine van Wormer, 2008
ISBN 978-986-80414-3-1
Hardcover, US$ 28,--
www.cv-pub.com

Contents

CASA VERDE PUBLISHING

DEBATING SOCIAL DEVELOPMENT
Vol. 1: STRATEGIES FOR SOCIAL DEVELOPMENT

Edited by Surendra Singh and Christian Aspalter, 2008
ISBN 978-986-83530-4-6
Hardcover, US$ 28,--
www.cv-pub.com

Contents

CASA VERDE PUBLISHING

SECURING THE FUTURE FOR OLD AGE IN EUROPE

Edited by Alan Walker and Christian Aspalter, 2008
ISBN 978-986-83530-1-5
Hardcover, US$ 28,--
www.cv-pub.com

Contents

CASA VERDE PUBLISHING

HEALTH CARE SYSTEMS IN EUROPE AND ASIA

Edited by Christian Aspalter, Yasuo Uchida, Robin Gauld, 2008
ISBN 978-986-83530-3-9
Hardcover, US\$ 33,--
www.cv-pub.com

Contents